Readers love *Eat What You Love*

More than 300 Recipes Low in Sugar, Fat and Calories!

Eat What You Love sits handily on the corner of my counter –always! In addition to the 52.5 pounds I have lost, I've rediscovered my passion for cooking and for great food, thanks to you. I always tell people, "her recipes may be healthy, but that woman is all about taste!" Great food has finally put my weight loss efforts over the top!
–Susan Jackson, Birmingham, Alabama

Thank-you for creating such awesome recipes!! At the age of 37, I was diagnosed with diabetes, high cholesterol and high blood pressure. I switched my diet to your recipes, and after 6 months was 50 pounds lighter, and off all medications! To date, I have lost an amazing 110 pounds, and have gone from a size 22/24 to a size 6/8. Your recipes make it easy to make eating well a part of my daily life, and my family absolutely LOVES everything I make!!
–Miriam Geraci Olson, New Britian, Conneticut

My friend bought *Eat What You Love*– then she made a *big* mistake ….she brought it to my house for me to see it. It has never left my home!!! I have literally shelves full of cookbooks. *Eat What You Love* is without exception my favorite cookbook. It has become my everyday go-to-cookbook. You have created the manual for putting delicious yet healthy food on the table for the whole family. Thank you!
–Amber Williams, Fort Lauderdale, Florida

I'm in LOVE! I bought your book to help me stick to the Weight Watcher's program, but had no idea your recipes would make it so easy—or that I would love the food so much! I have lost over 50 pounds and with your delicious easy recipes, know that this time, I will keep it off!!
– Vanessa Jones, Atlanta, Georgia

Eat What You Love is my bible!!! It has transformed my husband's and my life. He is no longer borderline diabetic, has lost 30 pounds and gotten off his high blood pressure medication, while I have lost over 50 pounds, dropped six pant sizes and am off my cholesterol medication. Thanks to your incredible recipes, I am healthy, fit, feel wonderful and am eating fabulous food!
–Becky Brewer, Olympia, Washington

© 2009 by Marlene Koch
Cover and interior photographs ©2009 by Steve Legato

Published by Running Press,
An Imprint of Perseus Books, LLC.,
A Subsidiary of Hachette Book Group, Inc.

Books published by Running Press are available at special discounts for bulk purchases in the United States by corporations, institutions, and other organizations. For more information, please contact the Special Markets Department at Perseus Books, 2300 Chestnut Street, Suite 200, Philadelphia, PA 19103, or call (800) 810-4145, ext. 5000, or email special.markets@perseusbooks.com.

All nutrition facts, including comparisons, have been verified in accordance with published data in the public domain at the time of publication.

The brand-names mentioned in this book are trademarks or registered trademarks of their respective companies.

Weight Watchers and SmartPoints are registered trademarks of Weight Watchers International, Inc. Weight Watcher point comparisons have been calculated based on published Weight Watchers International, Inc., information and do not imply sponsorship or endorsement of such comparison.

The publishers would like to express their gratitude to the following providers for their invaluable assistance in the production of this book: Manor Home, Philadelphia, PA; Open House, Philadelphia, PA; Scarlett Alley, Philadelphia, PA; Crate & Barrel, King of Prussia, PA; Polished Plate, Haddonfield, NJ; Foster's Urban Housewares, Philadelphia, PA; and Kitchen Kapers, King of Prussia, PA

9 8 7 6 5 4 3 2 1
Digit on the right indicates the number of this printing

Library of Congress Control Number: 2009934667
ISBN 978-0-7624-8988-6

Book design by Amanda Richmond
Edited by Jennifer Kasius
Typography: Avenir and Mrs. Eaves

Running Press Book Publishers
2300 Chestnut Street
Philadelphia, PA 19103-4371

Visit us on the web!
www.offthemenublog.com

Visit Marlene Koch on the web:
www.marlenekoch.com

EAT *what you* LOVE

More Than 300 INCREDIBLE RECIPES
Low in Sugar, Fat, and Calories

by MARLENE KOCH

Running Press
PHILADELPHIA

To my family, friends, kind readers,
and all of those who love to eat.
May you always eat what you love,
and love what you eat.

Table of Contents

New from Marlene

When I originally wrote this book, my main goal was to ensure that EVERYONE would be able to enjoy the foods they love! What I did not expect was the incredible number of people who would come to own and love this book. Since its publication I have heard from countless readers who have told me how my "easy", and most of all, "great-tasting" recipes have made this their go-to cookbook. As honored and delighted as I am by this praise, I feel even more privileged to have read their incredible success stories. From reports of weight loss and lower blood sugar, to stories of hungry husbands and kids who, for the very first time, look forward to eating healthy meals, I am thrilled to say *Eat What You Love* has more than met my expectations in delivering better health, with great taste.

As such, I am excited to offer even more features to help you enjoy all the foods you love—and maintain good health, too! First, as found in my newest book, Eat What You Love Quick & Easy, I'm happy to provide brand-new options for sweetening. With no- and lower calories selections (including all-natural alternatives), and details for using regular sugar, the choice is yours. If gluten is a concern you'll be pleased to find a guide with great tips and substitution ideas that make it easy to eat gluten-free while cooking and baking the foods you love (including dessert!). Also new in this edition are mouthwatering menus to help you create entire meals with everything from an Easy Fast Food Fix to tantalizing Asian take-out. Not only are these meals easy to make and incredibly delicious, the number of calories you can save is even greater than the calories you eat! Speaking of calories, if weight loss or keeping your blood sugar (or that of someone you love) in check is your goal, this edition excels. Not only will my weight-watching friends find comparisons to SmartPoints with every recipe, to help jump start weight loss I've included information on how to plan meals in a way that'll keep you energized, and give great results. The tips and recipes, along with two weeks of calorie/carb controlled sample menus, make this easier than you ever thought!

Last, but not least, if all you want are easy great-tasting recipes for the foods you and your family love, rest assured, you'll find them here. From luscious milkshakes and melty sandwiches, to crispy onion rings, cheesy chicken Parmesan, and Unbelievable Chocolate Cake, all the recipes are guaranteed to satisfy your every craving—and they're all guilt-free!

From my family to yours,

Eat What You Love... and Still Be Healthy

If you believe that eating for pleasure is different than eating for good health, you are not alone. When it comes to good health we all know the five recommended food groups: bread and whole grains, fruits, vegetables, dairy, and meats. These five groups comprise the foods we are supposed to eat everyday in order to stay healthy. But the reality is that many of us have our own favorite five food groups, perhaps best described as: salty, sugary, creamy, cheesy, and fried! These groups are comprised not of the foods we need, but of the foods we love—and for good reason. Research shows that we are naturally wired to enjoy foods high in sugar, fat, and sodium because they send signals to the reward center of the brain, which gives us pleasure. It's no wonder then that we love thick, creamy soups, melty cheesy sandwiches, crunchy coatings, and delectable sweets—it's only natural! My fabulous news is that eating for pleasure and eating for good health can be one in the same. I am thrilled to tell you that with this book you never again have to be deprived or sacrifice the foods you love for the sake of your health—yes, you really can have it all.

But before we get to the tantalizing recipes, in order to understand the healthy nutrition principles I have based them on, some nutrition basics are in order.

THE MIGHTY CALORIE

• • • • • • • • •

I'm starting off talking about calories for the same reason they're listed at the top of the food label and that's because calories are king when it comes to nutrition. A calorie is a measure of the energy we derive from the food we eat. Calories give us the energy we need to do everything in our daily life. If we didn't eat anything, we simply wouldn't have the fuel to survive. But just as the number of calories we eat has the ability to keep us in good health, eating too many calories makes us gain weight, which can lead to poor health. Unfortunately for our waistlines and our well being, eating more calories than we need is quite easy especially when you consider that the foods we eat today are richer, sweeter, and served in larger portions than ever before. When analyzing the nutritional content of the original restaurant dishes and traditional recipes that many of my healthier versions are based on, it became abundantly clear to me just how many calories we unknowingly consume. My assistants and I were stunned as time and time again we were confronted with the enormous number of calories (and sugar and fat and sodium for that matter) packed into many of our favorite foods. We found this information so compelling that you will find these comparisons shared in the Dare to Compare sidebars throughout the book. I am sure that you will be as astounded by the comparisons as we were, and yet delighted that you can have tasty and healthier versions of the same foods for just a fraction of the calories. (To put the Dare to Compare information into perspective, keep in mind that the USDA broadly estimates that the average American requires approximately 2,000 calories a day to maintain their weight. To calculate your daily calorie needs, go to www.marlenekoch.com and click on my Personal Calorie Calculator.)

FAT SENSE

• • • • • • • • •

When I began my career as a registered dietitian I worked in a hospital and counseled patients about their diets. At that time the message regarding fat was quite simple: fat was bad, but carbs were good. I vividly remember our education materials as they declared that butter and chocolate should be all but banned, but bagels and nonfat sugary foods (like nonfat frozen yogurt) were good for us. (It's no small wonder that bagel stores and yogurt shops proliferated!) Since that time, as new research has shed a better light on the good and bad health effects of fat, the message has not only evolved but has also become more complicated.

Nowadays we are bombarded with information on saturated fats versus unsaturated fats, monounsaturated fats versus polyunsaturated fats, and, let's not forget, the dangers of trans-fat. One day we are told we must lower the fat in our diets and then the next that it's the sugar, not the fat, that's making us fat. When making sense out of what's true (and what's not) here is what I've found:

Fat can make you fat. The truth is we all need some fat in our diets for good health, but it is very easy to eat too much. All fats (healthy and not) have nine calories per gram—more than twice the calories per gram of protein or carbohydrates. Consequently, foods high in fat tend to be high in calories, and foods that are high in calories are the ones that most easily pack on the pounds. Consuming a diet that's modest in overall fat (no more than 35 percent of your total calories) is not only good for your waistline, it's heart and diabetes smart, and just makes sense.

All fats are not created equal. Saturated fats, found in meats, butter, whole-fat dairy, egg yolks, and full-fat cheeses, are not good for your health. (The current recommendation is that no more than 7 percent of your total calories should come from saturated fats.) Since trans-fatty acids, found in some margarines, pastries, and packaged goods, may be even more harmful, they should be avoided when possible, or minimized in the diet. Monoun-saturated fats, or the "good fats," are found in olive oil, canola oil, nuts, and avocados. They are delicious and healthful additions to the diet but to control calories they too should be eaten in moderation (see #1).

Saturated fat raises cholesterol more than dietary cholesterol. It is prudent to keep an eye on cholesterol but even more important to moderate the total amount of fat, saturated fat, and trans fat in your diet. Thus, foods that are high in cholesterol but low in saurated fat, like shrimp and eggs, can be part of a healthy diet. Eating less than 300 milligrams of cholesterol a day is advised for those with diabetes.

Low-fat should never mean low flavor! Just as the science of fat has evolved, so has the science of healthy cooking and baking. For me taste is king, and the luscious recipes in this book are proof positive that you can have all of the satisfying taste of traditionally high-fat foods without worrying about unwanted fat and calories. I've made a point to explain how I created them, so that you can also deliciously reduce the fat in your own favorite recipes if you choose. In particular, I urge you to read my favorite tricks for creating deliciousand healthy luscious dressings on page 171. There are also charts to help you select the best dairy products to minimize fat on page 56 and on how to choose perfectly lean meats on page 294. Last, it's important to remember that it takes great ingredients to create great recipes, so check out "Eat What You Love... Essential Ingredients" on page 22 for more information.

EASY ON THE SALT

• • • • • • • •

Every chef knows that salt makes everything taste better. Salt not only suppresses bitter tastes, it brings out the sweet, and the sour, flavors in foods while adding its own distinct flavor. Unlike sugar, the taste for salt (also known as sodium chloride) is not innate, but acquired. Studies show that as we eat more salt, we taste it less—but we crave it more. It's estimated the average American consumes more than 3,500 milligrams of sodium a day or the equivalent of 15 pounds of salt a year! The trouble with salt is that, on average, as our sodium intake rises so does our blood pressure, and high blood pressure leads to serious health concerns. The current recommendation is that we should consume no more than 2,300 milligrams of sodium a day, which is less than one teaspoon of table salt. As I developed my recipes I made an effort to cut back on the salt by using reduced-sodium products whenever possible. These recipes contain ingredients such as reduced-sodium broth and light soy sauce, or instructions to drain and rinse canned beans. The result is that these balanced, flavor-packed recipes (even those that are a bit higher in sodium) contain far less sodium than those found in canned or frozen food, in the deli case, or at your local restaurant.

CARBOHYDRATES 101

• • • • • • • •

If you're like most people, when you think of foods that contain carbohydrates, the first thing that probably pops into your mind are foods full of starch, such as bread and pasta. But the reality is that there are several different types of carbohydrates (or carbs), and each has its own unique set of characteristics, both nutritionally, and when it comes to taste. The three main groups of carbohydrates are: complex carbohydrates (or starches), fiber, and simple carbohydrates (or sugar). (Note: On the food label the main heading "carbohydrates" shows the total amount of carbs. The fiber and sugar content are then separated out, like in my analysis, because of their healthy, or not so healthy, properties).

COMPLEX CARBOHYDRATES

This is the group of carbohydrates most people think of when they think of carbs, and it includes breads and grains, beans, lentils, and starchy vegetables, such as corn, peas, and potatoes. Complex carbohydrates, or starches, are composed of long chains of glucose hooked together that break apart upon digestion to provide us with energy. While complex carbohydrates are often called "good-for-you-carbs" because they are packed with vitamins and minerals (and they tend to raise blood sugar more slowly than more refined carbs), they are also a dense source of carbohydrates. And it's their density that can make the calories, and carbs, in starchy foods add up quickly. Specifically, a single serving of a starch in most meal plans consists of an average of 15 grams of carbohydrate (See Carbohydrate Counting). In food terms a serving equals half a cup of mashed potatoes, a third a cup of pasta or yams, or a quarter of a large bagel. When those portion sizes are compared to what most people eat, it's easy to see why eating starchy carbs in moderation can be challenging. In this book you will find that I used my kitchen magic to give you more bang-for-your-carbohydrate buck. First I used whole grains and fiber-rich carbohydrates wherever possible, and second, I used creative tricks to slash the starchy carbs, so everyone, even those on carb-controlled diets, can enjoy all the foods they love.

FABULOUS FIBER

When it comes to a good-for-you carbohydrate, it doesn't get any better than fiber. Fiber is composed of non-digestible carbohydrates, which add bulk to your diet without adding calories or raising your blood sugar. When added to an overall healthy diet, fiber has also been proven to promote weight loss and weight maintenance, as well as reduce the risk of type 2 diabetes and heart disease. The

recommendation when it comes to fiber is that we consume 20 to 35 grams a day by eating a variety of foods to ensure we reap the benefits of both types of fiber.

Soluble Fiber is able to dissolve in water and is known for its ability to slow the absorption of glucose, thereby lowering the glycemic index of foods and reducing cholesterol levels. Good sources of soluble fiber include whole grain oats, bran, beans, peas, brown rice, fruits, and vegetables.

Insoluble Fiber does not dissolve and provides the bulk that helps food pass more efficiently through the digestive tract. Significant sources of insoluble fiber include whole wheat breads and cereals, most other whole grains, nut seeds, and the skins of many fruits and vegetables.

This book includes a great number of whole- some recipes that make it easy, and delicious, to add fiber to your diet. For example, you'll find plenty of ingredients like whole grains, including white whole wheat flour and high- fiber tortillas, used along with fiber-rich oats and beans, instant brown rice, and a variety of great-tasting fruits and vegetables. Additionally, the bread chart on page 203 and the fruit chart on page 362 are designed to help you grocery shop with healthy fiber in mind.

SUGAR—
SIMPLE AND SWEET

Sugar, the simplest form of carbohydrates, may taste sweet, but it certainly gets a lot of not-so-sweet press. The truth is that we are born loving the taste of sugar, so you can blame your sweet tooth on Mother Nature. From the moment we first taste our mother's milk, our taste buds motivate us to seek out foods that are sweet, and with good reason: we need sugar to fuel our bodies (and our brains). Unfortunately, while the sugars found in whole grains, fruits, vegetables, and milk, may be what Mother Nature intended for us to eat, it is often the intense sweetness of "added sugars," such as granulated sugar, brown sugar, honey, and syrups, that we crave. The good news is that we all (including those with diabetes) can enjoy the sweet taste of added sugars in our diets—as long as we do so in moderation.

In reality, it's not the love of all things sweet that is the problem; it's the inability to limit the amount of sugar we eat that gets us into trouble. The consensus among most major health organizations, including the American Diabetes Association, is that an average person (with or without diabetes) can healthfully include 6 to 9 teaspoons of added sugars in their diet each day. This may sound like a lot, but sugars add up fast. So fast, that on the average we eat over 20 teaspoons of sugar per day (that's 170 pounds of sugar per year, per person). Unfortunately, consuming this amount of sugar does not come without health conse-

quences. There are many false myths about the dangers of sugar (such as the myth that people with diabetes must avoid sugar completely), but there are also many truths as to its detrimental effects. Here are a few of the not-so-sweet facts that inspire me to create lower sugar recipes:

Sugar offers no vitamins, minerals, or fiber, and is full of empty calories and carbohydrates. A single cup of sugar contains 768 calories and 192 grams of carbohydrate!

Sugar causes tooth decay and has been shown to significantly suppress the immune system. In fact, as few as eight tablespoons, the equivalent of the amount in a large smoothie, can suppress the immune system for up to five hours.

Excess sugar increases your risk of heart disease by raising triglycerides, and because sugar is both rich in carbohydrates and digests quickly, it can rapidly raise your blood sugar.

Excess calories from sugar can lead to weight gain and obesity, and excess weight increases your risk for many health concerns, including diabetes.

Like most Americans, I have a serious sweet tooth. I am also surrounded by people in my life who also love sweet treats, only they must watch their sugar intake more carefully because of diabetes. That's why I am *thrilled* to be able to share so many sweet new treats that we can all enjoy—without unwanted sugar orhealth consequences. If you are new to my recipes, you'll be pleased to discover that I offer several options for slashing added sugar, but not its sweet taste. By cutting the sugar I have significantly lowered the number of calories and carbs in the delicious hot and cold beverages and smoothies and shakes, but of course the savings are just as prominent in my extensive collection of incredible desserts. And while drinks and desserts may be obvious, you may be surprised to know that even seemingly healthful recipes, like glazed vegetables, salads with their sweet dressings, low-fat barbecue sauces, and Asian stir-fries, are often laced with hidden sugars. So you'll find I've eliminated the sugars in those recipes as well. You can learn more about sweeteners on page 382.

PROTEIN POWER

· · · · · · · · ·

The word *protein* comes from the ancient Greek word meaning "of greatest importance." Protein is a component of every part of your body, and of every function. In fact, when it comes to staying healthy, protein is vital. Protein serves as a major building block helping the body to maintain everything from strengthening bones and muscles to support-

ing skin and hair. Protein also helps to keep the immune system functioning and is a necessary element in creating vital enzymes and hormones, like insulin. But lately protein has gotten the most attention because of its ability to help control weight and blood sugar.

Recent studies support the fact that diets higher in protein and lower in carbohydrates may be more effective for losing weight, and for keeping it off. The reasons are not completely clear, but protein does help you feel full faster, and it keeps you feeling full longer. Eating more protein during weight loss also helps to preserve lean muscle mass. And lean muscle burns more calories than fat.

While exactly how much protein we need is a point of debate, what is agreed upon is that eating rich or fatty meats is not good for your waistline, or for your health. The trick to enjoying the power of protein is to use lean cuts of meat—in healthful preparations. On page 294 you will find a chart showing the lean meats and seafood I use to create tempting protein-packed entrées that only taste off limits. I'll also show you how to recreate leaner versions of some of your restaurant favorites at home so you can save money as well as calories. Yep, it's all here: mouth-watering burgers, juicy steak, crispy fried chicken, and sweet-and-sour shrimp. When it comes to satisfying protein, you can eat what you love.

Eat What You Love...
Diabetes

It wasn't all that long ago that while most people had heard of diabetes, few people actually knew someone who *had* diabetes. Today, that has all changed. If you or someone you love has diabetes, you are not alone. It seems everyone I meet knows someone, whether it be a family member, a friend, or a coworker, with diabetes—and that includes me. My stepdaughter has type 2 diabetes, and so did my father. Diabetes can be a frightening diagnosis as it is a serious condition, but for many people what is just as frightening is the fear of having to give up the foods they love. A recent poll reveals that *the* greatest fear for people recently diagnosed with diabetes is that they will have to change their diet—even more so than having to take meds or consider long-term consequences. With this book I hope to change all that for those with diabetes, and those who love them. Every recipe in this book fits easily into any diabetes meal plan. From sandwiches and pastas to starchy sides, cookies, cakes, and even milkshakes, eating what you love with diabetes has never been easier.

WHAT IS DIABETES?

Diabetes is a condition in which blood glucose (or blood sugar) is not regulated properly. When you have diabetes your body either does not produce enough insulin and/or the insulin you make is not effective. Insulin, a hormone produced in the pancreas, is necessary for moving glucose (which is made from the food you eat) from your blood into your cells where it is used for energy. When glucose cannot be moved into your cells it builds up in your blood. The diagnosis of diabetes is made when blood glucose (or sugar) rises above normal levels.

It is estimated that over 29 million people in the United States now have diabetes, and the number is rapidly growing. Perhaps more startling it is calculated that there are 86 million people with pre-diabetes, a condition in which the blood sugar is higher than normal but not yet elevated enough to require medication. When you add these two numbers together it reveals that *as many as one in three adults over the age of twenty-five already have diabetes or pre-diabetes*—yet most don't even know it.

THE WEIGHT CONNECTION

While there are many factors that can contribute to high blood sugar, such as a sedentary lifestyle, high blood pressure, ethnicity, and genetics, there is no single factor that contributes more to high blood sugar than being overweight.* The great news is that if you are overweight, losing as little as 5 to 7 percent of your body weight (that's as little as 10 pounds for a 200 pound person) can result in significant improvements in your blood sugar and in your overall health! If you have pre-diabetes the news is even better. If you start now and adopt a healthy lifestyle that includes exercise and losing a modest amount of weight along with eating a healthy diet, it has been clinically proven that you can substantially reduce the risk for, or even *prevent*, the onset of diabetes.

But it didn't take a study to prove this to me, as I've seen the results first-hand. For years I have been fortunate enough to have readers share their success stories of losing weight and maintaining their blood sugar by using my recipes. Many have been able to reduce the amount of medication they take, and some have even been able to eliminate their medications completely! The best part is that they tell me that they made these major health improvements not feeling deprived, but while enjoying delicious food–including dessert!

While I cannot say this will absolutelyhappen for you, I can absolutely say that the scrumptious recipes in this book are perfect for anyone who has or is concerned about reducing their risk for diabetes.

---

*This information refers to the most common type of diabetes— type 2. Type 1 diabetes is an autoimmune disease that attacks the pancreas. People with both types of diabetes can benefit from the healthy carbohydrate-conscious recipes in this book. Consult with your doctor before altering any medications.

Eat What You Love...
Meal Planning

Contrary to what you may have heard, there is no one universal "diabetic" diet (any more than there is one weight-loss diet). Every person on this planet can reap the benefits of a diet that's full of wholesome, good-for-you foods, including plenty of fruits and vegetables, whole grains, low-fat dairy, lean meats, and healthy fats.

That said, studies show that when it comes to achieving health goals having a discrete plan helps ensure success. A meal plan is a simple tool that can help you decide what, when, and/or how much to eat. Meal planning can help you curb mindlessly consuming excess calories, and for those with diabetes, meal planning is an important tool for keeping carbs in check. In this section you will find an array of information on meal planning, including the easiest way to balance a healthy plate. You will also find detailed information about how the nutritional information for each recipe was calculated, including portions, points, and optional ingredients. For two-weeks worth of mix and match weight loss/carb controlled menus featuring the recipes in this book, see page 446.

One plan I like, because it is the most effortless of all, is the plate method. You simply visualize how to construct a balanced healthy meal on your plate. Here's how it works: For lunch and dinner, using a 9-inch dinner plate, fill one-half of the plate with non-starchy vegetables and salad dishes, including any of those found in the "For the Love of Vegetables" or "Sensational Side" and "Entrée Salads" chapters (excluding the entrée or starchy salads). Next, fill one-quarter of the plate with one of my delicious Starchy Sides, and then fill the last quarter of the plate with any of the lean meat or seafood entrées in the book (that contain no more than 1/2 starch exchange). To finish your meal, add an 8-ounce glass of skim or low-fat milk or a whole grain roll plus one fruit serving (see page 362). The plate method also works great for controlling portion amounts when dining out. You can find more information about the plate method at *www.plate method.com*.

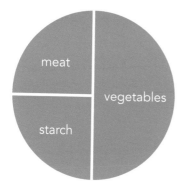

FOOD EXCHANGES

• • • • • • • • • •

Another tool that is helpful for meal planning is the exchange system. In the exchange system, similar foods, such as starches or fruit, are grouped together to form "exchange lists." The foods within each list contain a similar amount of calories, carbohydrates, protein, and fat. For example, in the starch group one starch exchange is a single slice of bread, one-half cup of cooked oatmeal, or a quarter of a large bagel. Thus, when following a meal plan based on the exchange system you can "exchange" a slice of toast for a half a cup of cooked oatmeal or a quarter of a bagel.

The food groups included in the exchange system as set forth by the American Dietetic and Diabetes Associations and used to determine the exchanges for the recipes in this book are as follows:

Starch (breads, pasta, rice, beans, potatoes and corn)

Vegetable (all non-starchy vegetables)

Fruit (all fruits and fruit juices)

Milk (nonfat and low-fat milk and yogurt)

Meat (lean and medium-fat meats, cheese, and eggs)

Fat (oil, margarine, nuts, and other added fats)

Carbohydrate (sugar and desserts)

The number of servings you are allowed to choose from each group at each meal or snack is determined by your individual needs for calories and for nutrients such as protein and carbohydrates. If you use the exchange system for meal planning, you will find I've taken care to make sure each recipe accurately lists the exchanges. To create a personal meal plan utilizing the exchange system, consult with your health care provider, a registered dietitian, or a certified diabetes educator.

CARBOHYDRATE COUNTING

· · · · · · · · ·

Of all the nutrients you eat, carbohydrates have the greatest impact on your blood glucose. Controlling the amount of carbohydrates consumed is vital not only for controlling blood sugar but for many weight loss diets. Carbohydrate counting is a meal planning tracking system that helps you monitor the total amount of carbohydrates eaten. Unlike the exchange system, carbohydrate counting lumps together all the foods that contribute carbohydrates in a meal or a snack (whether they come from the starch, vegetable, fruit, milk, or carbohydrate group) to form a carbohydrate total. (Current research shows the "total" amount of carbs is more important than where the carbs come from when it comes to blood sugar.) Carbohydrate Choices are then calculated by dividing the total grams of carbohydrate for a food, or a meal, by 15 (see Carbohydrate Choices). Because all carbohydrates are lumped together and your carbohydrate budget can be used for any carbs, carbohydrate counting is more flexible than the exchange system. To help you, I've included both the total number of carbohydrates and the number of carbohydrate choices for every recipe. Moreover, to calculate an estimated daily carbohydrate budget you may go to *www.marlenekoch.com* and click on my Carbohydrate Budget Calculator. One last note, while counting carbs may seem easy, keeping within a carbohydrate budget can be challenging. By reducing the sugar and watching all the carbohydrates in the recipes in this book the carbohydrate choices have been significantly reduced (making it easy to stretch your carbohydrate budget). If you need more information on carbohydrate counting or a personalized menu plan, a registered dietitian or certified diabetes educator can help you.

Carbohydrate Choices

This conversion chart shows how the carbohydrate choices were calculated in this book. As per the most current diabetes guidelines, when there are more than 5 grams of fiber per serving, one-half of the grams of fiber is subtracted from the total grams of carbohydrate before using this calculator.

CARBOHYDRATES	CARBOHYDRATES CHOICES
0–5	0
6–10	½
11–20	1
21–25	1½
26–35	2
36–40	2½
41–50	3
51–55	3½
56–65	4

NUTRITIONAL ANALYSIS

· · · · · · · · ·

A complete nutritional analysis complements every recipe so you may make smart and healthy choices based on your personal needs. The information was calculated using ESHA Nutrition Food Processor software in conjunction with manufacturers' food labels.

- **Food exchanges** have been provided for all recipes to assist in meal planning (see Food Exchanges on page 18) based on the American Diabetes Association Guidelines. Values have been rounded to the nearest one-half for ease of use.

- **Carbohydrate choices** have been added to this book to bring additional flexibility and convenience for those on the carbohydrate counting system. See Carbohydrate Counting and the Choices Conversion Chart on this page for more information.

- **Weight watcher point comparisons** are listed for all my weight watching friends. I have made the "comparisons" using the most up to date information available.

- **Realistic portion sizes are something** I pride myself on. As such, the portions in this book are similar to those you will find in any good cookbook. While not as large as today's over-sized restaurant portions, I guarantee you, you will not find the frustrating miniscule portions often found in other healthy cook-books and magazines.

  The serving sizes are not always consistent within a category (for example, soup servings range from 1 to 1½ cups) as I also factor in the richness of the food and whether it is expected to accompany a meal or be the main course. Remember to adjust the nutritional information if you eat more than one serving.

- **Garnishes**, as part of the recipe, that are normally eaten (sprinkled green onions or powdered sugar) are included in the nutritional analysis.

- **Optional ingredients** are not included in the nutritional analysis.

  Eat what you love, and love what you eat. Peek at the numbers, but most of all enjoy.

Eat What You Love...
Essential Ingredients

Creating foods that are simply low in sugar, fat, and calories is easy. Creating foods that are low in sugar, fat, and calories *and* taste terrific is far more challenging, and it all starts with the right ingredients. Each of the ingredients used in my recipes has been selected very carefully for the perfect blend of taste and texture. In this section you will find a pantry list along with information on the essential ingredients I depend on for my delicious better-for-you recipes.

Because I want you to enjoy the foods *you* love, I encourage you to feel free to adjust the seasonings, such as herbs and spices, to suit your taste, but keep in mind that ingredient substitutions may affect the nutritional content and/or quality. When it comes to baked goods, it is important to follow the recipes exactly as written for the best results. A well-stocked pantry takes the stress out of meal planning and makes it easy to create meals that are healthy—yet still delicious.

A well-stocked pantry takes the stress out of meal planning and makes it easy to create meals that are healthy—yet still delicious. Below is a list of the ingredients I like to keep on hand. With them you can simply "shop the pantry" and make most of the recipes with the addition of just a few fresh or added ingredients. Stock up by buying items when they are on sale, and be sure to replenish when you use them up. You'll find more detailed information about the ingredients marked with an * starting on page 24.

IN THE CUPBOARD

Baking Basics
- ❏ Applesauce, unsweetened (4-ounce cups)
- ❏ Baking Powder and Baking Soda
- ❏ *Baking Spray
- ❏ *Cocoa Powder (Dutch-processed and regular)
- ❏ Extracts (almond, coconut, lemon, vanilla)
- ❏ *Flour (all-purpose, cake, white whole wheat, Wondra instant)
- ❏ Molasses
- ❏ *Prune Puree (or baby food prunes)
- ❏ *Sugar (brown, granulated, powdered)
- ❏ Shortening
- ❏ *Sweeteners (No- and low-calorie granulated sweeteners)

Flavorful Condiments
- ❏ Barbeque sauce
- ❏ Hot Sauce (Tabasco)
- ❏ Liquid Smoke
- ❏ Mayonnaise, light
- ❏ Mustard (Dijon, yellow)
- ❏ Soy Sauce, reduced-sodium
- ❏ Worcestershire Sauce

Great Grains
- ❏ Bread Crumbs (plain, panko)
- ❏ Brown Rice, quick-cooking (Uncle Ben's)
- ❏ Cornmeal, yellow
- ❏ Couscous, plain

- ❏ *Oats (quick, old-fashioned)
- ❏ *Pasta (whole grain blends and white in a variety of shapes)

Miscellaneous
- ❏ Bacon Bits (real crumbled)
- ❏ Beans, canned, reduced sodium (black, garbanzo)
- ❏ *Bread (light white and/or wheat)
- ❏ Broth, reduced sodium (chicken, beef)
- ❏ *Cooking Spray
- ❏ Cornstarch
- ❏ Evaporated Milk, low fat
- ❏ Fresh Garlic
- ❏ Honey
- ❏ Jalapeno Peppers, jarred
- ❏ Jam, low-sugar (strawberry, orange marmalade)
- ❏ Maple-flavored syrup (light or sugar-free)
- ❏ Marinara, jarred
- ❏ *Oils (canola, extra-virgin olive oil, sesame)
- ❏ Peanut Butter
- ❏ Potatoes
- ❏ Pumpkin, 100% pure solid packed
- ❏ Salsa, jarred
- ❏ Spices, dried (variety)
- ❏ Tomatoes (crushed, diced, paste)
- ❏ Tunafish (canned albacore)
- ❏ Vinegar (apple cider, balsamic, rice wine)

Fridge

- ❑ Bacon, center cut
- ❑ *Butter
- ❑ Cheese, reduced-fat (cheddar, Mexican Blend, mozzarella)
- ❑ Chocolate Fudge Topping (sugar-free or light)
- ❑ *Cottage Cheese (low-fat)
- ❑ *Cream Cheese (light, nonfat)
- ❑ *Eggs, large (plus liquid egg substitute)
- ❑ Garlic, jarred, minced
- ❑ Ginger, jarred, minced
- ❑ *Margarine
- ❑ Milk, low fat (or alternative)
- ❑ *Nonfat Half-and-Half
- ❑ *Orange Juice (light)
- ❑ Parmesan Cheese
- ❑ Sour Cream, Light
- ❑ *Tortillas (high fiber flour, corn)
- ❑ *Yogurt, Greek and/or regular plain (low fat or nonfat)

Frozen

- ❑ *Beef, ground, 93% lean
- ❑ Chicken Breasts (skinless, boneless)
- ❑ Corn kernels, frozen
- ❑ Fruit, frozen (blueberries, strawberries)
- ❑ Ice Cream, vanilla (light or no-added sugar)
- ❑ Peas, frozen
- ❑ Shrimp, frozen
- ❑ Spinach, frozen
- ❑ Tilapia (or other white fish)
- ❑ *Whipped Topping, light

BREAD

All bread products are definitely not created equal as they vary substantially in calories and carbohydrates. See "For the Love of Bread" on page 203 for more information and a handy bread comparison chart.

BUTTERMILK

Buttermilk adds great flavor to recipes and tenderizes baked goods. To make your own, place 1 tablespoon of vinegar or lemon juice in a measuring cup; add enough 1 percent milk (or soy or almond "milk") to make 1 cup and let it sit for 5-10 minutes before using.

COCOA POWDER

I prefer Dutch process cocoa powder. Dutch processing reduces cocoa's natural acidity and bitterness, mellowing the cocoa and imparting a richer darker color. I use Hershey's Special Dark Cocoa powder, but any unsweetened cocoa powder may be substituted.

COOKING AND BAKING SPRAYS

Cooking sprays are a wonderful way to reduce fat. Use only flavorless vegetable or canola oil sprays and remember to keep the "trigger finger" light—two to three seconds is all it should take.

Baking sprays include both grease and flour to help release cakes and breads from their pans. If you only have a cooking spray, a light dusting of flour can be added to the pan separately.

COTTAGE CHEESE

Cottage cheese is an exceptional ingredient when it comes to cutting calories and fat and adding healthful protein to recipes—especially when it's creamed. The simple trick to creaming it, whether alone or with other ingredients, is to blend it (in a food processor preferably) until no curds are left. Low-fat or 2% cottage cheese is my preferred choice.

CREAM CHEESE

I like Philadelphia brand cream cheeses. You may select another brand—but be aware reduced-fat cream cheeses vary greatly in taste. Neufchatel cheese can be used in place of light tub-style cream cheese in any of the recipes. I also use nonfat cream cheese, but only in combination with low-fat—a technique that reduces fat while maintaining creaminess and flavor. I do not recommend substituting nonfat cream cheese when it is not specified.

DAIRY PRODUCTS

As a rule of thumb I prefer reduced- or low-fat dairy products over nonfat products. One percent milk is far richer than skim, low-fat yogurt is creamier than nonfat, reduced-fat cheeses have more flavor and melt better than nonfat, and light sour cream tastes richer than the fat- free kind. If you have nonfat brands you prefer, you may use them, but the texture may change. Non-dairy beverages, such as soy or almond "milk" can be substituted as desired. For more information on dairy ingre-dients, see "For the Love of Dairy" on page 56.

EGGS AND EGG SUBSTITUTES

To keep the total fat (and cholesterol) at a healthy level, and still maintain the taste and texture of whole eggs, I use a higher ratio of egg whites to yolk (or egg whites only when appropriate). I prefer this choice over using egg substitutes, especially for baking. There are some recipes, though, where egg substitutes work well, and I list them as options. If you choose to make additional substitutions, keep in mind:

1 large egg = 2 large egg whites
= ¼ cup liquid egg substitute

FLAVORINGS

Good-quality spices and flavorings make a big flavor difference in reduced-sugar and/or reduced-fat recipes. Vanilla extract should be "real," and dried spices should still be fragrant when you open the jars.

FLOURS

I use several types of flour and substitutions will change the finished product. All-purpose flour is the gold standard for traditional baking as it has the perfect amount of protein and offers a mild taste and light texture. Cake flour has less protein and is used specifically to create a lighter, more tender crumb. To make your own, use 2 tablespoons of cornstarch and enough all-purpose flour to yield 1 cup of cake flour. White whole wheat flour tastes and bakes similar to white flour, yet has the wholesome fiber of whole wheat. White whole wheat flour can be replaced with all-purpose flour or a 50/50 blend of white and whole wheat flours. Cup4Cup is a good gluten-free flour.

GROUND BEEF AND GROUND TURKEY

Lean ground beef and turkey make it possible to put many of our favorite foods back on a healthy table. It is important to note that 90% lean ground meat is 90% lean by weight, not by calories. In reality, 50% of the calories come from fat (see the chart on page 294). For the recipes in this book I used 93% lean ground beef and turkey. Meat any leaner is dry and mealy.

LIGHT WHIPPED TOPPING

Light whipped topping has only a fraction of the fat of real whipped cream and adds a great deal of flavor and creaminess to recipes. You can find it in tubs in the freezer section of your grocery store. Be sure to thaw it before using. I don't recommend the nonfat version, which is higher in sugar and not as creamy. Aerosol whipped cream cannot be used as a substitute except when garnishing.

MARGARINE OR BUTTER

 I specify margarine first in most recipes, because margarine has far less saturated fat. I use Smart Balance Original. Soft and tub margarines (unless over 65% fat by weight) cannot be substituted as their water content is too high for baking (which requires a more solid fat). For flavor, butter can't be beat. I reserve it for recipes where a small amount makes a notable taste difference. Use it where it suits you best.

NONFAT HALF-AND-HALF

Nonfat or fat-free half-and-half has the creamy richness of regular half-and-half but without the fat. The only quality substitute for nonfat half-and-half is real half-and-half, but this will add both fat and calories. Nonfat milk is not an appropriate substitute.

OATS

Old-fashioned oats, rolled oats, and the quick-cooking variety may be interchanged if necessary. My personal preference is the larger-cut, old-fashioned or rolled variety, especially for toppings. Don't substitute instant oatmeal for other oats.

OILS

All liquid oils contain the same amount of fat, so it's the flavor (or lack of) that primarily determines the type I use for each recipe. For a flavorless oil, I use canola, which is high in monounsaturated fat—but any flavorless vegetable oil will work in the recipes. When I specify extra-virgin olive oil, it is because the taste will clearly enhance the recipe and so it justifies the extra cost. For most recipes, regular olive oil is all that is required. Sesame oil (made from sesame seeds) has a strong nutty taste—and a big flavor impact. There is no equal substitute.

ORANGE JUICE

Although it is healthy, orange juice is a concentrated source of sugar. Light orange juice offers the taste of regular orange juice but with only one-half the sugar, carbs, and calories. I don't always specify to use light orange, though. In recipes where using light orange juice reduced the grams of carbohydrate less than one gram per serving, I opted for regular. Where the difference was more prominent I specify light orange juice. There are several brands of light orange juice on the market. Any of them will work.

PASTA

When it comes to types of pasta whole wheat is a wholesome choice, but it is not the only one. There are many good multigrain blend pastas that have the benefit of whole grains without sacrificing white pasta's taste. For better health, look for a pasta that offers at least 5 grams of fiber per serving. Ronzoni Smart Taste is one brand I like. For more information about pastas see "For the Love of Pasta" on page 225.

PURÉED PRUNES

Puréed prunes are great for low-fat baking. Where puréed prunes are specified you may use baby food prunes or "plums and apples." To make your own prune purée, combine 1¼ cups pitted prunes and 6 tablespoons very hot water in a food processor and blend until smooth. You can store it in a covered container

in the refrigerator for one to two months.

NO- AND LOW-CALORIE GRANULATED SWEETENERS

The choice is yours! Every recipe in this book was tested with both a generic no-calorie sucralose-based granulated sweetener and all natural stevia based Truvia for Baking. Both are found next to the sugar in most markets. No-calorie granulated sucralose measures 1:1 for sugar, and has the least carbs and calories (see chart on next page). Truvia for Baking (made with 25% real sugar) measures 1:2. Thus, when using Truvia for Baking *use one half as much—as it has twice the sweetening effect*, and expect slightly longer baking times (for more information see page 382).

REGULAR SUGAR SUBSTITUION

The conversion from no-calorie granulated sweetener to sugar is 1:1. For baked goods omit ¼ teaspoon of baking soda per cup of sweetener and expect to increase the baking time (see Granulated Sugar on page 382 for details). TIP: While the normal substitution for sugar is 1:1, you can cut one-fourth of the sugar called for in most baked goods with the only effect being slightly reduced sweetness.

TORTILLAS

Reduced-carbohydrate, high-fiber tortillas are amazing for creating healthier carb- and/or calorie-conscious recipes. They are widely available and found next to the regular tortillas. In addition to the traditional flour variety (which I prefer for my Chicken Caesar Wrap), you will also find many others to choose from. Mission Carb Balance and La Tortilla Factory Smart and Delicious Wraps are two brands I use. Look for tortillas that offer at least 8 grams of fiber and no more than 24 grams of total carbohydrate. 100% corn tortillas are gluten-free.

YOGURT

I specify plain Greek yogurt in many of the recipes, but you can use regular yogurt if you prefer. Thick and creamy Greek yogurt averages half the carbs and sugar and twice the protein of traditional American-style yogurt. Either non-fat or low-fat (2%) can be used.

TIP: To ensure the yogurt is truly "Greek," check the label to make sure the only ingredients are milk and active cultures and it has over 20 grams of protein per cup.

ZESTS

I can't say enough about the terrific difference citrus zest can make. Orange, lemon, and lime are interchangeable in most recipes. To zest a piece of fresh fruit, just wash it and simply grate off the brightly colored outer layer (rind) of the whole fruit (not going deeply into the bitter white pith). Zest is best when finely grated. If you do not have zester, use a box grater and then mince finely with a knife before adding it to the recipe.

	Granulated Sucralose (Any Brand)	Stevia/Sugar Baking Blend (Truvia Baking Blend)	Sugar
Equivalent Measure	1 cup	½ cup	1 cup
Calories	96	190	784
Carbohydrates	24	47 (usable)	190
Recipe Adjustments	None	May need a few more minutes baking time	See "Granulated Sugar" above

Eat What You Love...
Recipes

Hot and Cold Beverages

OLD-FASHIONED LEMONADE

STRAWBERRY LEMONADE

KEY LIME LIMEADE WITH FRESH MINT

EASY SONIC-STYLE CHERRY LIMEADE

FESTIVE FRUIT PUNCH

FRUIT JUICE SPRITZER

GINGERED CARROT SPRITZER

SOUTHERN SWEET TEA

AGAVE GREEN TEA

MARLENE'S MOCHA FREEZE

MARLENE'S FROSTY CHAI FREEZE

INSTANT COFFEEHOUSE CAFÉ MOCHA

COFFEEHOUSE CHAI LATTE

RICH AND CREAMY HOT CHOCOLATE

CINNAMON "SUGAR" STEAMER

STEAMING CRANBERRY-ORANGE SIPPER

HOT CARAMEL APPLE CIDER

MULLED TEATIME CIDER

HOLIDAY EGGNOG

Whether it's iced cold lemonade on a hot summer's day, a steamy mug of hot chocolate on a snowy afternoon, or the newest concoction at the local coffee shop, sweet beverages are a delicious part of every-day life.

And while we all know that water does a body good, it's sweet drinks that titillate our taste buds. In fact more than half of the beverages Americans drink are sweetened. Unfortunately, sweet drinks, while they taste great, tend to be low in nutrition and high in sugar and calories. Furthermore, studies confirm that the calories and sugar from bever-ages tend to be "extra," as we do not make up for them by eating less. Therefore, sweet beverages can be a major problem when it comes to extra pounds (and high blood sugar). To put it into real numbers a researcher at the Children's Hospital in Boston calculates that drinking just one 12-ounce sugar-sweetened beverage a day—averaging 140 calories—can lead to a one pound weight gain every three to four weeks (making that frosty concoction at the coffee shop or rich cup of hot chocolate not such a sweet treat after all)!

That's why I am thrilled that I can begin this book with a collection of hot and cold drinks that you can enjoy guilt-free, without any worry of added sugar, fat, or calories. From traditional refreshers, such as Old-Fashioned Lemonade and Festive Fruit Punch, to drive-thru favorites, such as Sonic®-Style Cherry Limeade and Southern Sweet Tea, I have you covered. If it's coffee creations you crave, look no further than the Mocha and Frosty Chai Freezes as well as the Coffeehouse Café Mocha and Chai Lattes (to the delight of your waistline—and your wallet). And for the holidays the Mulled Teatime Cider and Holiday Eggnog will ensure yours are only filled with joy.

Old-Fashioned Lemonade

Nothing quenches a thirst like a glass of iced-cold lemonade made from fresh-squeezed lemons. But as you already know, it takes a lot of sugar to sweeten up a lemon. In fact, most commercial lemonades contain more sugar than soda! Here's a simple way for the entire family to enjoy the great taste of sweet homemade lemonade without the added sugar.

MAKES 4 SERVINGS

¾ cup fresh-squeezed lemon juice (about 4 medium lemons)

½ cup granulated no-calorie sweetener)*

3¼ cups cold water

Zest of one lemon (optional)

Crushed ice

* See page 382 for sweetener options

1. Combine the lemon juice, sweetener, water, and lemon zest in a large pitcher and stir.

2. Serve over crushed ice or add 1 to 2 cups of crushed ice to the pitcher before serving.

Or try this: For *Sparkling Lemonade*, substitute sparkling water, either plain or lemon flavored (but not sweetened), for 2 cups of the water.

DARE TO COMPARE A medium lemonade at a fast-food restaurant like Hot Dog on a Stick contains 210 calories, 52 grams of carbohydrate, and the equivalent of 11 teaspoons of sugar.

*See page 382 for sweetener options.

NUTRITION INFORMATION PER SERVING (1 CUP)
Calories 25 | Carbohydrate 7g (Sugars 2g) | Total Fat 0g (Sat Fat 0g) | Protein 0g | Fiber 0g | Cholesterol 0mg | Sodium 0mg | Food Exchanges: ½ Fruit | Carbohydrate Choices: ½ | Weight Watcher Smart Point Comparison: 1

Strawberry Lemonade

One of my favorite ways to create pink lemonade is to add the luscious flavor and natural goodness of puréed strawberries. The result is a delicious, good-for-you, fruit-filled juice blend. However, if you prefer a clear, crisp, traditional lemonade, simply follow the directions in step three for a perfectly pretty pink-tinged lemonade.

MAKES 4 SERVINGS

1½ cups strawberries, halved (or if frozen, slightly thawed)

1 cup lemon juice (about 5 medium lemons)

⅔ cup granulated no-calorie sweetener*

3 cups cold water

2 teaspoons lemon zest

Crushed ice

1. Place the strawberries in a food processor or blender; process until smooth and pour into a large pitcher.

2. Add the lemon juice, sweetener, and water and stir well.

3. If desired, strain out the strawberry pulp by pouring the mixture through a strainer. Stir in the lemon zest.

4. Serve over crushed ice or add 1 to 2 cups of crushed ice to the pitcher before serving.

*See page 382 for sweetener options.

NUTRITION INFORMATION PER SERVING (1 CUP)
Calories 50 | Carbohydrate 12g (Sugars 9g) | Total Fat 0g (Sat Fat 0g) | Protein 0g | Fiber 2g | Cholesterol 0mg | Sodium 0mg | Food Exchanges: 1 Fruit | Carbohydrate Choices: 1 | Weight Watcher Smart Point Comparison: 2

Key Lime Limeade with Fresh Mint

Here's a great new twist on traditional sugar-filled limeade. This recipe uses Key limes, which are more fragrant than regular limes and prized for their wonderful tart flavor. Summer is the easiest time to find these juicy little gems, but don't fret if you can't find them. Bottled Key lime juice can be found next to the lemon juice in most supermarkets, making this a drink that can be enjoyed year round. Making just two simple changes—one to a sugar substitute and the second by adding light white grape juice—lowered this drink from 110 calories and 28 grams of sugar, to 30 calories and 5 grams of sugar per cup. Enjoy!

MAKES 8 SERVINGS

¾ cup Key lime juice (about two dozen Key limes)*

¾ cup granulated no-calorie sweetener

1 tablespoon sugar

2 cups light white grape juice

3 cups club soda

Crushed ice

Fresh mint and lime slices for garnish

* Regular limes (6 to 8) or lime juice may be substituted

1. Combine the lime juice, sweetener, and sugar in a large pitcher. Stir to dissolve the sweetener and sugar. Stir in the white grape juice.

2. Just prior to serving, add the club soda to the juice mixture. Add 1 to 2 cups of crushed ice to the pitcher or pour the limeade directly over crushed ice in tall glasses. Garnish each glass with fresh mint leaves and a slice of lime.

Or try this: For a festive holiday *Cranberry Limeade*— Substitute light cranberry juice for the light white grape juice and regular lime juice for the Key lime juice.

*See page 382 for sweetener options.

NUTRITION INFORMATION PER SERVING (¾ CUP)
Calories 30 | Carbohydrate 9g (Sugars 5g) | Total Fat 0g (Sat Fat 0g) | Protein 0g | Fiber 0g | Cholesterol 0mg
Sodium 0mg | Food Exchanges: ½ Fruit | Carbohydrate Choices: ½ | Weight Watcher Smart Point Comparison: 2

Easy Sonic®-Style Cherry Limeade

SONIC® drive-ins are famous for their beverages—and none more so than their terrific flavored limeades. This quick-and-easy pint-size clone satisfies my drive-in loving boys every time.

MAKES 1 SERVING

Crushed ice

¼ cup 100% cherry juice

1 lime, cut into 4 wedges, reserving one for garnish

Maraschino cherry (optional)

1 (12-ounce) can sugar-free lemon-lime soda

1. Place crushed ice in a large 16-ounce glass. Pour the cherry juice over the ice. Squeeze the juice of 3 of the lime wedges into the glass. Pour in the soda. Stir lightly.

2. Garnish with the remaining wedge of lime and a maraschino cherry, if desired.

DARE *TO* COMPARE ······························

Enjoy this instead of a medium regular cherry limeade at the drive-in and save 180 calories, 49 grams of carbohydrate, a whopping 12 teaspoons of sugar, (and 3 full carbohydrate choices).

NUTRITION INFORMATION PER SERVING ·····················

Calories 40 | Carbohydrate 10g (Sugars 8g) | Total Fat 0g (Sat Fat 0g) | Protein 0g | Fiber 0g | Cholesterol 0mg | Sodium 8mg | Food Exchanges: ½ Fruit | Carbohydrate Choices: ½ | Weight Watcher Smart Point Comparison: 2

Festive Fruit Punch

It's time for a party! Here is a terrific punch recipe everyone will love. Just a few simple changes from an old family favorite recipe were all it took to slash the sugar and calories—while leaving in all of the fun.

MAKES 12 SERVINGS

3 cups light cranberry juice, chilled

1 cup light orange juice, chilled

¼ cup lemon juice

⅓ cup granulated no-calorie sweetener*

1 (32-ounce) bottle sugar-free ginger ale, chilled

½ orange, cut into slices for garnish

¾ cup lime or orange sherbet (optional)*

* Addition of sherbet adds 4 grams of carbohydrate and 15 calories per serving,

1. In a very large pitcher or ½ gallon punch bowl combine the cranberry juice, orange juice, lemon juice, and sweetener and stir to combine. Keep chilled until ready to serve.

2. Just prior to serving pour in the ginger ale and stir lightly.

3. Add crushed or cubed ice to the pitcher or punch bowl and garnish with orange slices. Or, if you prefer, you can garnish with sherbet instead. Using a melon baller, scoop the sherbet into balls, if using. Add all of the sherbet balls to the punch mixture if serving in a punch bowl or one sherbet ball in each cup if serving in individual glasses.

Marlene Says: Because special occasions usually offer lots of tempting food choices, minimizing the sugar and calories found in your glass is one of the easiest ways to help keep your diet in check.

*See page 382 for sweetener options.

NUTRITION INFORMATION PER SERVING (¾ CUP) ⋯⋯⋯⋯⋯⋯⋯⋯⋯⋯⋯⋯
Calories 20 | Carbohydrate 5g (Sugar 4g) | Total Fat 0g (Sat Fat 0g) | Protein 0g | Fiber 0g | Cholesterol 0mg | Sodium 15mg | Food Exchanges: Free (½ Carbohydrate with Sherbet) | Carbohydrate Choices: 0 (½ with sherbet) | Weight Watcher Smart Point Comparison: 1

Fruit Juice Spritzer

Once an avid juice drinker, my stepdaughter, Colleen, quickly learned after her diagnosis of type 2 diabetes that large glasses of her favorite fruit juices—even those made with 100 percent fruit—would quickly eat up her carbohydrate budget and send her blood sugar soaring. This recipe is our refreshing solution to enjoying the great taste of your favorite juice without all of the unwanted sugar and calories. As you'll see, a mere quarter cup of juice is all that's needed for creating a perfect flavorful fruit spritzer.

MAKES 1 SERVING

Crushed ice

¼ cup 100% juice (pomegranate, strawberry, cherry, mango, etc.)*

¾ cup club soda

* Nutrition content based on juice that contains 130 calories and 32 grams of carbohydrate per 8 ounces.

1. Place the crushed ice in a tall 12-ounce glass or wine goblet.

2. Pour the juice over the ice and top with club soda. Stir lightly and serve.

Marlene Says: Similar to festive Italian sodas that combine fruit-flavored syrups and sparkling water, fruit spritzers are terrific party fare. To create *Fruit Coolers,* simply replace the club soda with sugar-free lemon-lime soda.

NUTRITION INFORMATION PER SERVING
Calories 32 | Carbohydrate 8g (Sugars 6g) | Total Fat 0g (Sat Fat 0g) | Protein 0g | Fiber 0g | Cholesterol 0mg | Sodium 15mg | Food Exchanges: ½ Fruit | Carbohydrate Choices: ½ | Weight Watcher Smart Point Comparison: 2

Gingered Carrot Spritzer

If you're looking to add more vegetables to your diet, here is a delicious way to do so. This pretty orange cocktail-like sipper makes a beautiful and unique addition to a Sunday breakfast or brunch.

MAKES 1 SERVING

Crushed ice

⅓ cup carrot juice

½ cup sugar-free ginger ale

2 orange wedges

1. Fill a large glass three-quarters full with ice. Pour the carrot juice over the ice.

2. Add the ginger ale and stir with a spoon.

3. Lightly squeeze the juice of one of the orange wedges into the glass and stir. Hook the other wedge onto the side of the glass as a garnish.

Marlene Says: This drink is a nutrition powerhouse, fulfilling 45 percent of your daily allowance for vitamin A and 20 percent for vitamin C.

NUTRITION INFORMATION PER SERVING
Calories 30 | Carbohydrate 7g (Sugars 2g) | Total Fat 0g (Sat Fat 0g) | Protein 1g | Fiber 0g | Cholesterol 0mg | Sodium 75g | Food Exchanges: 1 Vegetable | Carbohydrate Choices: ½ | Weight Watcher Smart Point Comparison: 1

Southern Sweet Tea

When it comes to Southern hospitality, Food Network star Paula Deen reigns supreme. Here I share one of her favorite beverages—her Southern-style sweet tea. This cool, refreshing, sugar-free version makes a full half gallon to serve to your own guests "Paula style" (or simply to enjoy all by yourself). I prefer the Luzianne brand for iced tea but your favorite will work, too.

MAKES 8 SERVINGS

2 cups water

2 family size (or 8 individual) tea bags

1 cup granulated no-calorie sweetener*

Fresh mint

Lemon slices for garnish

1. Bring the water to a boil in either the microwave or in a small pot on the stove.

2. Remove from the heat and add the tea bags. Add the sweetener, cover, and steep for 15 minutes.

3. Carefully place the entire mixture (including the tea bags) into a half-gallon container or pitcher. Add enough cold water to make ½ gallon (6 additional cups). Place tea in refrigerator until ready to serve.

4. To serve, fill tall glasses with crushed ice. Place a couple of sprigs of fresh mint into each glass and fill with tea. Garnish with lemon slices.

DARE TO COMPARE
On the road? Grab a bottle of Sweet Tea and your perk-up will cost you over 200 calories and 14 teaspoons of sugar. Go for a big 32-ouncer instead and you will be gulping down over 300 calories and more than a full day's worth of sugar!

*See page 382 for sweetener options.

NUTRITION INFORMATION PER SERVING (1 CUP)
Calories 10 | Carbohydrate 2g (Sugars 0g) | Total Fat 0g (Sat Fat 0g) | Protein 0g | Fiber 0g | Cholesterol 0mg | Sodium 0mg | Food Exchanges: Free Food | Carbohydrate Choices: 0 | Weight Watcher Smart Point Comparison: 0

Agave Green Tea

This all-natural, lightly sweetened tea combines two health-food favorites: green tea and agave nectar. Green tea is prized for its antioxidant properties and agave nectar, a sweet syrup made from the agave cactus plant, boasts a much lower glycemic index (the rate at which a food raises blood sugar) than either sugar or honey. Together they complement each other beautifully in this very tasty and inexpensive clone.

MAKES 8 SERVINGS

4 cups water

2 individual green tea bags

3 tablespoons amber agave nectar

1 long strip of orange peel

1 long strip of lime peel

1. Bring the water to a boil in either the microwave or in a small pot on the stove.

2. Remove from heat and add tea bags. Cover and steep for 15 minutes.

3. Carefully remove the tea bags and add the agave nectar and citrus peels to warm tea. Stir. Allow tea to cool at room temperature.

4. Serve tea over ice, or place in the refrigerator until ready to drink.

Marlene Says: An additional nutrition benefit of agave nectar is that it has approximately 1.4 times the sweetening power of table sugar, allowing you to use less.

NUTRITION INFORMATION PER SERVING (1 CUP)
Calories 60 | Carbohydrate 16g (Sugars 15g) | Total Fat 0g (Sat Fat 0g) | Protein 0g | Fiber 0g | Cholesterol 0mg Sodium 0mg | Food Exchanges: 1 | Carbohydrate Choices: 1 | Weight Watcher Smart Point Comparison:4

Marlene's Mocha Freeze

If imitation is the sincerest form of flattery, the creators of this popular drink should be *very* flattered. *There isn't a coffee shop that doesn't have its own version of this creamy, frosty, coffee-and-chocolate concoction. I'm proud to say I have my own signature version and it's quicker (no run to the coffee store), healthier, incredibly delicious (a touch ice cream does the trick), and a lot less expensive!*

MAKES 1 SERVING

2 teaspoons instant coffee (regular or decaffeinated)

⅓ cup lukewarm water

¼ cup nonfat half-and-half

3 tablespoons granulated no-calorie sweetener*

2 teaspoons cocoa powder

¾ cup crushed ice

¼ cup light, no-sugar-added ice cream (vanilla or chocolate)

1. Measure the coffee into a blender. Pour the water over coffee to dissolve.

2. Add the half-and-half, sweetener, cocoa powder, and half the ice. Blend to mix. Add the rest of the ice. Blend on high until thoroughly combined.

3. Drop in the ice cream and give a quick blend just until smooth. Pour into a tall glass and enjoy.

DARE TO COMPARE ·
Most creamy iced coffee drinks are loaded with sugar, fat, and calories. A medium (16-ounce) Mocha Blast at Au Bon Pain® has 440 calories, 17 grams of fat, and 80 grams of carbohydrate (including 74 grams of sugar), while a small (16-ounce) Toffee Coffee Cappuccino® made with frozen yogurt at TCBY® contains an eye-popping 791 calories, 31 grams of fat (with 20 of them saturated), and 114 grams of carbohydrate (including 105 grams, or two days', worth of added sugars!).

*See page 382 for sweetener options.

NUTRITION INFORMATION PER SERVING ·
Calories 115 | Carbohydrate 19g (Sugars 3g) | Total Fat 2g (Sat Fat 1g) | Protein 5g | Fiber 3g | Cholesterol 5mg | Sodium 90mg | Food Exchanges: 1 Carbohydrate | Carbohydrate Choices: 1 | Weight Watcher Smart Point Comparison: 4

Marlene's Frosty Chai Freeze

Another popular take on frozen drinks are those flavored with teas. Much like my Mocha Freeze, you will find my version to be a whole lot easier on your waistline—and your wallet! Be sure to look for a no-sugar-added ice cream that is also labeled "low-fat" or "light" to keep the fat in check.

MAKES 1 SERVING

⅓ cup water

1 individual chai tea bag

¼ cup nonfat half-and-half

2½ tablespoons granulated no-calorie sweetener*

½ cup crushed ice

¼ cup light, no-sugar-added vanilla ice cream

Dash of cinnamon

1. Place the water in a microwave-safe mug and heat until very hot (you may also do so in a small pot on the stove). Add the tea bag and let steep for 15 minutes. Remove the tea bag, draining the bag into the cup, and let tea cool (you can place it in the refrigerator to cool it more quickly).

2. Pour tea into a blender. Add the half-and-half, sweetener, and ¼ cup of the ice. Blend to mix. Add the rest of the ice and blend on high until thoroughly combined.

3. Drop in the ice cream and dash of cinnamon and give a quick blend just until smooth.

Or try this: For a *Frosty Green Tea Freeze*, substitute a green tea bag for chai.

*See page 382 for sweetener options.

NUTRITION INFORMATION PER SERVING ······················
Calories 100 | Carbohydrate 17g (Sugars 3g) | Total Fat 1.5g (Sat Fat.5g) | Protein 4g | Fiber 2g | Cholesterol 5mg | Sodium 85mg | Food Exchanges: 1 Carbohydrate | Carbohydrate Choices: 1 | Weight Watcher Smart Point Comparison: 3

Instant Coffeehouse Café Mocha

Who can resist the combination of steaming hot coffee and chocolate? Instant coffee makes it especially easy to "brew" a single cup, but you can also omit the instant coffee and water and pour your favorite hot coffee over the dry ingredients.

MAKES 1 SERVING

2 teaspoons instant coffee powder

1 tablespoon cocoa powder

1½ tablespoons powdered coffee creamer

2 tablespoons granulated no-calorie sweetener*

1 cup water

1. Mix together the first four ingredients in a microwave-safe mug.

2. Slowly add the water to the mug while stirring with a spoon (mixture will not be entirely smooth).

3. Place mug in microwave and heat on high for 1½ to 2 minutes until mocha is hot. Remove from the microwave and stir one more time.

*See page 382 for sweetener options.

NUTRITION INFORMATION PER SERVING
Calories 50 | Carbohydrate 16g (Sugars 1g) | Total Fat 1.5 g (Sat Fat 1.5g) | Protein 4g | Fiber 2g | Cholesterol 0mg | Sodium 15mg | Food Exchanges: 1 Carbohydrate | Carbohydrate Choices: 1 | Weight Watcher Smart Point Comparison: 2

Coffeehouse Chai Latte

I simply love this. Here the combination of creamy evaporated milk and just a touch of honey turns simple chai tea bags, with their luxurious blend of spices, into an incredibly delicious warm beverage. If you have ever enjoyed one of these at your local coffeehouse and wondered how to make one yourself, here's how. The recipe can be halved to serve one, but it's extra special when shared.

MAKES 2 SERVINGS

½ cup low-fat evaporated milk

1½ cups water

2 tablespoons granulated
   no-calorie sweetener*

2 individual chai tea bags

1 teaspoon honey

1. In a small pot whisk together the evaporated milk, water, and sweetener. Place over medium heat and bring to a low simmer.

2. Carefully add tea bags and continue to simmer on low for an additional 3 minutes.

3. Remove from heat and remove tea bags. Stir in honey.

4. Serve immediately. (You may also cool this and pour it over ice.)

DARE *TO* COMPARE................................
Enjoy this with your own homemade healthy Bran Muffin (page 77) and save as much as 450 calories, 60 grams of carbohydrate, and 24 grams of fat when compared to what is offered at your local coffeehouse.

*See page 382 for sweetener options.

⋮ **NUTRITION INFORMATION PER SERVING (1 CUP)** ··························
⋮ Calories 70 | Carbohydrate 10g (Sugars 6g) | Total Fat 1.5g (Sat Fat1.5g) | Protein 4g | Fiber 0g | Cholesterol
⋮ 5mg | Sodium 70mg | Food Exchanges: ½ Low Fat Milk | Carbohydrate Choices: ½ | Weight Watcher Smart
⋮ Point Comparison: 3

Rich and Creamy Hot Chocolate

This hot chocolate tastes downright decadent. When one of my kitchen assistants told me how much her mother enjoys the hot chocolate in Italy, because it's thicker than what she usually gets here, we rolled up our sleeves and recreated an Italian-style hot chocolate for her by adding a touch of cornstarch to a stovetop hot chocolate. To make it even easier to enjoy this luscious, silky drink I have adapted it for the microwave. Please follow the directions carefully to ensure it thickens without boiling over.

MAKES 1 SERVING

1 rounded tablespoon cocoa powder

2 tablespoons granulated no-calorie sweetener*

½ teaspoon cornstarch

¾ cup low-fat milk

¼ teaspoon vanilla (optional)

1. Combine the cocoa powder, sweetener, and cornstarch in a microwave-safe mug. (Use a standard 8-ounce mug or larger as drink needs to bubble up to thicken)

2. Add ¼ cup of the milk to the dry ingredients and mix with a whisk until smooth. Continue stirring while pouring in the remaining milk.

3. Place mug in microwave and heat on high for 1½ to 2 minutes, or until you see the hot chocolate bubble up to the rim of the cup. Immediately turn off microwave and stir hot chocolate, add vanilla if desired, and return to microwave for 15 seconds longer. Remove, stir, and enjoy.

Marlene Says: To make it feel extra special pour the hot chocolate into a lovely coffee cup with a saucer before sipping.

*See page 382 for sweetener options.

NUTRITION INFORMATION PER SERVING
Calories 110 | Carbohydrate 16g (Sugars 9g) | Total Fat 2.5g (Sat Fat 1.5g) | Protein 7g | Fiber 2g | Cholesterol 5mg | Sodium 95mg | Food Exchanges: 1 Low-Fat Milk | Carbohydrate Choices: 1 | Weight Watcher Smart Point Comparison: 4

Cinnamon "Sugar" Steamer

For my book Fantastic Food with Splenda *I created a Hot Vanilla Steamer made with milk that has become an all-time favorite for my son James. Hoping to create something new, but equally delicious, I turned to the great taste combination of cinnamon and sugar. I think you will agree that a couple of ingredients and a few minutes is all it takes to turn an ordinary cup of milk into something extraordinary. For a richer-tasting steamer, substitute 2 tablespoons of nonfat half-and-half for two tablespoons of the low-fat milk.*

MAKES 1 SERVING

1 cup low-fat milk

¾ teaspoon ground cinnamon

1 tablespoon granulated no-calorie sweetener*

1 cinnamon stick for garnish (optional)

1. Whisk together the milk, cinnamon, and sweetener in a microwave-safe mug.

2. Microwave on high for 1½ minutes or until warmed through (do not boil). If desired, place the cinnamon stick into the milk, stir, and serve warm.

Family Focus: Most American children, as well as adults, do not get their daily requirement of calcium. Milk is a great source of not only calcium, but magnesium, protein, and vitamin D. Milk also builds strong bones and can help lower high blood pressure and the risk of stroke. Adding creative flavors to low-fat or nonfat milk is a great way to encourage milk consumption.

*See page 382 for sweetener options.

NUTRITION INFORMATION PER SERVING ···
Calories 110 | Carbohydrate 15g (Sugars 12g) | Total Fat 2.5g (Sat Fat 1.5g) | Protein 8g | Fiber 1g | Cholesterol 10mg | Sodium 125mg | Food Exchanges: 1 Low-Fat Milk | Carbohydrate Choices: 1 | Weight Watcher Smart Point Comparison: 4

Steaming Cranberry-Orange Sipper

The flavors of cranberry and orange are natural complements in this soothing hot sipper. A mere teaspoon of honey adds the crowning touch.

MAKES 1 SERVING

¾ cup light cranberry juice

¼ cup water

1 large strip of orange peel

1 teaspoon honey

1. Measure all the ingredients into a microwave-safe mug. Heat on high for 1½ to 2 minutes or until the drink is hot.

2. Stir well before serving.

Marlene Says: Label warning: Just because the label says "no added sugar" doesn't mean your juice is not fortified with sugar. Many manufacturers add concentrated fruit juices that are packed with fruit sugars to sweeten up their beverages, allowing them to make "no added sugar" claims. Look for the grams of carbohydrate and sugar on the nutrition label to find the real amount of sugar in your juice.

NUTRITION INFORMATION PER SERVING
Calories 50 | Carbohydrate 13g (Sugars 6g) | Total Fat 0g (Sat Fat 0g) | Protein 0g | Fiber 0g | Cholesterol 0mg
Sodium 0mg | Food Exchanges: ½ Fruit, ½ Carbohydrate | Carbohydrate Choices: 1 | Weight Watcher
Smart Point Comparison: 2

Hot Caramel Apple Cider

There's no need to wait for fall to enjoy the winning combination of apple and caramel. This creamy warm cider sweetened with a hint of caramel can make any day of the year a cozy apple cider day. It's also a real kid pleaser!

MAKES 2 SERVINGS

1 cup water

1 individual cinnamon apple tea bag

¾ cup unsweetened apple cider

2 tablespoons sugar-free caramel topping or syrup

Cinnamon sticks (optional)

1. Measure the water into a small saucepan or large glass microwave-safe measuring cup (larger than 2 cups). Bring the water to a boil; turn off heat and add the tea bag and let steep for 3 to 5 minutes.

2. Remove the tea bag, and add the apple cider. Bring back to a simmer and stir in the caramel topping. Whisk until caramel completely melts into cider.

3. Pour into two 8-ounce mugs. If desired, add cinnamon stick to each mug and swirl.

Family Focus: Even juices without *added* sugar are quite high in natural sugars. The American Academy of Pediatrics recommends no more than 8 to 12 ounces of juice a day for kids 7 to 18 years of age, and even less for younger ones. Better bets for fit kids: whole fruit or diluted juice.

NUTRITION INFORMATION PER SERVING (1 CUP) ···
Calories 85 | Carbohydrate 16g (Sugars 10g) | Total Fat 0g (Sat Fat 0g) | Protein 0g | Fiber 0g | Cholesterol 0mg | Sodium 60mg | Food Exchanges: ½ Fruit, ½ Carbohydrate | Carbohydrate Choices: 1 | Weight Watcher Smart Point Comparison:4

Mulled Teatime Cider

Most mulled cider recipes call for lots of apple cider sweetened with spices and, often, additional sugar. Combining apple tea with apple cider is a great way to cut the calories of this holiday favorite in half without sacrificing great apple flavor. What's more, you can warm and serve it in a slow cooker, just as you would any mulled cider.

MAKES 8 SERVINGS

3½ cups water

3 individual cinnamon apple tea bags

3 cups unsweetened apple cider

3 cinnamon sticks

6 whole cloves

1 large piece orange peel

1. Bring the water to a boil in a small saucepot. Turn off the heat and add the tea bags. Allow to steep for 3 to 5 minutes. Remove the tea bags.

2. Add apple cider and remaining ingredients to apple tea. Cover and let simmer for 20 to 30 minutes.

NUTRITION INFORMATION PER SERVING (¾ CUP) ···
Calories 65 | Carbohydrate 17g (Sugars 15g) | Total Fat 0g (Sat Fat 0g) | Protein 0g | Fiber 0g | Cholesterol 0mg | Sodium 0mg | Food Exchanges: 1 Fruit | Carbohydrate Choices: 1 | Weight Watcher Smart Point Comparison: 4

Holiday Eggnog

The holidays are usually celebrated with foods that are rich and decadent. Eggnog is a perfect example. Because it's often made with cream and always sweetened with lots of sugar, it's hard to fit into any healthy diet. What's great about this version, besides being really easy to make, is that it only tastes decadent. It's hard to think of enjoying eggnog without a treat (or two). My Chocolate Almond Meringue Cookies (page 388) and Blueberry Cheesecake Bars (page 392) are two choices you can enjoy with a cup of this nog and still keep your calories (and carbs) safely under control. Happy holidays!

MAKES 8 SERVINGS

2½ cups low-fat milk

1½ cups nonfat half-and-half, divided

⅔ cup granulated no-calorie sweetener

½ cup liquid egg substitute

2 large egg yolks

2 teaspoons cornstarch

½ teaspoon nutmeg

2 teaspoons vanilla

1. In a medium pot, mix together the milk, ½ cup of the half-and-half (reserve 1 cup of the half-and-half in the refrigerator to keep cold), and the sweetener.

2. In a small bowl, whisk together the liquid egg substitute, egg yolks, cornstarch, and nutmeg. Add to the milk mixture and cook for 5 to 8 minutes over low heat, stirring constantly, until the mixture is thick enough to coat the back of a spoon.

3. Immediately turn off the heat and add the remaining cup of chilled half-and-half and the vanilla. Allow to cool slightly, then refrigerate until thoroughly chilled.

DARE *TO* COMPARE
The richest of homemade eggnogs are made out of equal parts heavy cream and whole milk, egg yolks, lots of sugar—and a pinch of nutmeg. Unfortunately, it all adds up to 300 calories in a mere half cup, with 16 grams of fat (9 of them saturated) and 37 grams of sugar.

NUTRITION INFORMATION PER SERVING (½ CUP)
Calories 90 | Carbohydrate 10g (Sugars 8g) | Total Fat 2g (Sat Fat 1g) | Protein 7g | Fiber 0g | Cholesterol 55mg | Sodium 115mg | Food Exchanges: ½ Low-Fat Milk, ½ Very Lean Meat | Carbohydrate Choices: ½
Weight Watcher Smart Point Comparison: 3

Super Smoothies and Shakes

Creamy, rich, and filling, smoothies and shakes are the ultimate treat in a glass. Unfortunately, these luscious beverages are in a class of their own when it comes to being loaded with sugar, fat, and calories. It's no surprise to any of us that drinking milkshakes can pack on the pounds, but you may be surprised to learn that most smoothies—though marketed as being good for you—can easily do the same. Common smoothie ingredients, such as frozen yogurt, sherbet, high-sugar juices, and frozen fruit, often skyrocket these delectable drinks off the charts both in terms of calories and sugar (natural or not). The lightest and smallest smoothies you can order may set you back only a few hundred calories, but even these are hefty in sugars. Richer style smoothies (again, for a small sized one) can ring in with up to 1,000 calories and 30 grams of fat and as much as one-half a cup of sugar. (That's 24 teaspoons of sugar in your cup!) If you love smoothies, however, there is no need to fret. The smoothies you'll find here are luscious, with all the taste of the smoothie shop but with only a fraction of the sugar and calories. Tall and filling, they offer a balance of fresh fruit, protein from yogurt or low-fat milk, and a minimum of added sugar. The slimmest entry, the Banana Breeze Smoothie, has only 75 calories, and the heavyweight, my Pumped Up Peanut Butter Smoothie, has just 320 calories (with enough protein to make it a fantastic mini-meal).

If it's milkshakes you prefer, look no further. While adding a medium chocolate shake to your meal at the golden arches will cost you a hefty 770 calories, 18 grams of fat, and over 100 grams of carbohydrate (with 84 of them from sugar)—and the one from the premium ice cream shop far more—I have found the tricks to make luscious milkshakes that are rich and creamy for under 200 calories! One sip of my Vanilla Cake Batter, Double Chocolate Pudding, or Banana Cream Pie Milkshake and you may decide your favorite shake shop is now a place called home.

For the Love of Dairy

Dairy products make shakes and smoothies (as well as dips, dressings, soups, pasta sauces, puddings, and custards) luscious and creamy. This handy reference chart compares the nutrition content of many of the dairy products that are used in this book with many you may have on hand. If you choose, use any non-dairy "milks" cup for cup. Plain unsweetened soy milk is the most similar to cow's milk for cooking and baking. Make up for less body in soups and sauces by stirring in ¼ to ½ teaspoon of cornstarch per cup of "milk".

DAIRY PRODUCT (PER 1 CUP)	CALORIES	FAT	SAT FAT	TOTAL FAT	CARBS	PROTEIN	SODIUM
Whole Milk	150	8g	5g	43%	12g	8g	120mg
Reduced Fat Milk (2%)	120	5g	3g	38%	12g	8g	120mg
Low-Fat Milk (1 %)	105	3g	2g	25%	12g	8g	120mg
Nonfat Milk (skim)	90	0g	0g	0%	13g	8g	125mg
Plain Soy Milk *	100	4g	0g	36%	8g	6g	120 mg
Unsweetened Soy Milk	80	4g	0g	45%	4g	7g	85mg
Vanilla Soy Milk	140	5g	0g	32%	16g	8g	100mg
Original Almond Milk	60	2.5g	0g	38%	8g	1g	150mg
Unsweetened Almond Milk**	40	3g	0g	68%	1g	1g	150mg
Low-Fat Plain Yogurt	145	3.5g	2g	22%	16g	13g	175mg
Nonfat Plain Yogurt	120	0g	0g	0%	17g	14g	190mg
Lowfat Greek Yogurt	150	5g	3g	30%	9g	19g	80mg
Nonfat Greek Yogurt	120	0g	0g	0%	9g	20g	80mg
Regular Vanilla Ice Cream	140	8g	4g	45%	16g	3g	40mg
Reduced-Fat Vanilla Ice Cream	110	4g	2g	33%	15g	3g	45mg
No-Sugar-Added Light Vanilla Ice Cream	80	3g	2g	34%	9g	3g	70mg

*Silk Brand, **Almond Breeze Brand

Breakfast in a Glass Smoothie

I first thought about calling this "Mock Orange Julius" because it tastes just like the popular frothy orange drink. I changed my mind, however, after I discovered that just one glass delivers as much muscle-building protein as two eggs, and over 20 percent of the daily requirement for vitamins A, C, and calcium. You couldn't ask for a better breakfast. A piece of whole grain toast is a nice complement.

MAKES 1 SERVING

⅓ cup light orange juice

⅓ cup nonfat Greek plain yogurt

3 tablespoons granulated no-calorie sweetener*

⅓ cup liquid egg substitute

Dash of vanilla

½ cup crushed ice

1. Place all the ingredients, except the ice, in a blender. Blend to mix.

2. Add crushed ice and blend on high until the ice is completely incorporated and drink is frothy.

Family Focus: Studies show everyone functions better when they start the day with a good breakfast. Healthy grab-'n'-go foods that can be eaten on the run include breakfast drinks or smoothies served in disposable cups, baggies filled with a favorite low-sugar cereal or homemade muffin, hard-boiled eggs or string cheese, and pieces of fresh fruit.

*See page 382 for sweetener options.

NUTRITION INFORMATION PER SERVING ···
Calories 125 | Carbohydrate 13g (Sugars 7g) | Total Fat 2g (Sat Fat.5g) | Protein 17g | Fiber 0g | Cholesterol 0mg | Sodium 170mg | Food Exchanges: 1 Lean Meat, ½ Nonfat Milk, ½ Fruit | Carbohydrate Choices: 1 Weight Watcher Smart Point Comparison: 3

Supreme Light Strawberry Banana Smoothie

When it comes to smoothies, nothing beats the great combination of strawberries and bananas. In fact, I found the single most-viewed recipe on a website devoted exclusively to smoothies was a recipe for a Supreme Strawberry Banana Smoothie. But after one look at the ingredients it was obvious that the smoothie was much too high in both sugar and calories. Here is my new "light" version of this thick and creamy, yet still supreme, smoothie.

MAKES 2 SERVINGS

1 cup light apple juice

½ cup low-fat milk

1 cup frozen strawberries

1 (6-ounce) container light strawberry yogurt

½ large banana, frozen

½ cup crushed ice

1. Place all the ingredients except the ice in a blender. Blend to mix.

2. Add crushed ice and blend on high until the smoothie is thick and smooth. Pour into two tall glasses and serve.

Marlene Says: Frozen chunks of peeled ripe banana are great to keep on hand for smoothies, but if you're in a hurry you can simply toss the entire banana in the freezer. When you are ready to use it, simply thaw slightly before removing the peel.

NUTRITION INFORMATION PER SERVING (1½ CUPS) ·······························
Calories 165 | Carbohydrate 32 (Sugars 28g) | Total Fat 1.5g (Sat Fat.5g) | Protein 6g | Fiber 3g | Cholesterol 0mg | Sodium 100mg | Food Exchanges: ½ Low-Fat Milk, 1½ Fruit | Carbohydrate Choices: 2 | Weight Watcher Smart Point Comparison: 8

Blue Wave Smoothie

The combination of Ocean Spray® grape juice and blueberries was the inspiration for the name of this lovely deep blue smoothie. The yogurt helps keep it nice and creamy while the blueberries contribute a powerful punch of healthy antioxidants. Enjoy this with a hard-boiled egg to balance the carbs and create a great breakfast to go.

MAKES 1 SERVING

½ cup blueberries, fresh or frozen

½ cup plain nonfat Greek yogurt

½ cup light white grape juice

1 tablespoon granulated no-calorie sweetener*

½ to ¾ cup crushed ice (use ½ cup with frozen blueberries)

1. Place all the ingredients, except the ice, in a blender. Blend to mix.

2. Add crushed ice and blend on high until the ice is completely incorporated.

*See page 382 for sweetener options.

NUTRITION INFORMATION PER SERVING
Calories 115 | Carbohydrate19g (Sugars 11g) | Total Fat 0g (Sat Fat 0g) | Protein 10g | Fiber 2g | Cholesterol 0mg | Sodium 100mg | Food Exchanges: 1 Fruit, ½ Low-fat Milk | Carbohydrate Choices: 1 |
Weight Watcher Smart Point Comparison: 4

Berry Berry Lime Smoothie

My son James's favorite smoothie combines the sweetness of berries with the tartness of lime. Unfortunately for those who need to watch the sugar in their diet, the combination of juice, fruit, and lime sherbet adds up quickly. Here I've recreated the same great taste while slashing the excess sugar and carbohydrates by using light juice with fresh lime and yogurt instead of sherbet. To control carbs and calories away from home, look for "light" versions and beware of smoothies made with "dessert ingredients" like frozen yogurt or sherbet.

MAKES 1 SERVING

¾ cup light cranberry juice

1 cup frozen strawberries

¼ cup nonfat plain Greek yogurt

1 teaspoon lime zest

Juice of one lime (about 2 tablespoons)

3 tablespoons granulated no-calorie sweetener*

¼ cup crushed ice

1. Place all the ingredients, except the ice, in a blender. Blend to mix.

2. Add crushed ice and blend on high until the ice is completely incorporated and smoothie is thick.

> **DARE TO COMPARE** ·······················
> Even "healthy" beverages can give you a lot more calories and carbs than you bargained for. A small all-fruit smoothie can easily contain 400 calories and over 90 grams of carbohydrate (the equivalent of 6 fruit servings).

*See page 382 for sweetener options.

NUTRITION INFORMATION PER SERVING ·····················
Calories 145 | Carbohydrate 30g (Sugars 21g) | Total Fat 0g (Sat Fat 0g) | Protein 8g | Fiber 6g | Cholesterol 0mg | Sodium 55mg | Food Exchanges: 1½ Fruit, ¼ Nonfat Milk | Carbohydrate Choices: 2 | Weight Watcher Smart Point Comparison: 6

Blushing Peach Smoothie

A smattering of frozen raspberries gives this creamy peach smoothie its blush. I use frozen peach slices so it's easy to keep the ingredients on hand year-round. However, fresh peaches in season are heavenly. To easily peel a fresh peach, plunge it into boiling water for thirty seconds, remove, and immediately plunge into ice water to stop the cooking process. The peel will slip right off with the help of a sharp paring knife.

MAKES 1 SERVING

½ cup low-fat milk

½ cup fresh or frozen peach slices

3 to 4 frozen raspberries

1½ tablespoons granulated no-calorie sweetener*

¼ teaspoon vanilla or almond extract (optional)

½ to ¾ cup crushed ice (use ¼ cup with frozen peaches)

1. Place all the ingredients, except the ice, in a blender. Blend to mix.

2. Add crushed ice and blend on high until the ice is completely incorporated and mixture is thick and creamy.

*See page 382 for sweetener options.

NUTRITION INFORMATION PER SERVING
Calories 120 | Carbohydrate 20g (Sugars 16g) | Total Fat 2g (Sat Fat 1g) | Protein 6g | Fiber 2g | Cholesterol 5mg | Sodium 60mg | Food Exchanges: 1 Fruit, ½ Low-Fat Milk | Carbohydrate Choices: 1½ | Weight Watcher Smart Point Comparison: 5

Banana Breeze Smoothie

Creamy, thick, and very filling, this super low-calorie smoothie takes delicious advantage of a nondairy beverage made from almonds. Almond milk is really not milk at all, but rather a creamy, slightly nutty, very low-calorie beverage made from pressed almonds and filtered water. Because it contains only 40 calories a cup (compared with 100 for low-fat milk) and 2 grams of carbohydrate (compared with 6 for low-fat milk), it's a great lower-calorie and lactose-free alternative to milk. Look for it next to other nonrefrigerated, nondairy beverages, such as soy and rice milks, in your local market.

MAKES 1 SERVING

½ cup unsweetened almond milk (like Almond Breeze)

½ medium banana

1 tablespoon granulated no-calorie sweetener*

Dash of vanilla

1 cup crushed ice

1. Place all the ingredients, except the ice, in a blender. Blend to mix.

2. Add crushed ice and blend on high until the ice is completely incorporated and mixture is thick and creamy.

Marlene Says: Almond milk can also be substituted for milk in coffee drinks, over cereal or oatmeal, and to create lower calorie and carbohydrate puddings. It is often fortified with both calcium and vitamin D to boost its nutritional content.

*See page 382 for sweetener options.

NUTRITION INFORMATION PER SERVING
Calories 75 | Carbohydrate 15g (Sugars 11g) | Total Fat 1.5g (Sat Fat 0g) | Protein 1g | Fiber 2g | Cholesterol 0mg | Sodium 95mg | Food Exchanges: 1 Fruit, ½ Fat | Carbohydrate Choices: 1 | Weight Watcher Smart Point Comparison: 4

Piña Colada Smoothie

This cold and creamy sipper is paradise in a glass. You can find coconut extract in the baking section of your local market. It will also come in handy when making Chicken Curry in a Hurry (page 299). To ensure you always have frozen bananas on hand for this recipe, make a habit of saving any extra-ripe bananas by peeling them, breaking them in half, and placing them in baggies to freeze.

MAKES 1 SERVING

⅓ cup nonfat plain Greek yogurt

¼ cup light orange juice

3 tablespoons crushed pineapple (packed in water)

2 tablespoons granulated no-calorie sweetener)*

½ teaspoon coconut extract

½ small banana, frozen

¾ cup crushed ice

1. Place all the ingredients, except the ice, in a blender. Blend to mix.

2. Add crushed ice and blend on high until the ice is completely incorporated.

DARE TO COMPARE..
Paradise not. Drop by Smoothie King® for a small Piña Colada Island® smoothie and you will consume 600 calories, 10 grams of fat, and 110 grams of carbohydrate (including the equivalent of ½ cup of sugar!).

*See page 382 for sweetener options.

NUTRITION INFORMATION PER SERVING ·······················
Calories 125 | Carbohydrate 25g (Sugars 17g) | Total Fat 0g (Sat Fat 0g) | Protein 8g | Fiber 3g | Cholesterol 0mg | Sodium 65mg | Food Exchanges: 1½ Fruit, ½ Nonfat Milk | Carbohydrate Choices: 2 | Weight Watcher Smart Point Comparison: 5

Soy Good for You Banana Smoothie

Yes, this soy-based smoothie is good for you, but that is not what I like most about it. Made with everyone's two favorite breakfast fruits, it's thick and creamy and tastes like an orange-tinged banana milkshake. (P.S.: If you prefer, you can substitute low-fat milk for the soy milk).

MAKES 1 SERVING

½ cup unsweetened soy milk

¼ cup light orange juice

½ medium banana, frozen

2 tablespoons granulated no-calorie sweetener*

¾ cup crushed ice

1. Place all the ingredients, except the ice, in a blender. Blend to mix.

2. Add crushed ice and blend on high until the ice is completely incorporated.

Marlene Says: While soy milk with its heart-healthy isoflavones *can* be a healthy choice, the nutrition content varies widely by brand and type. Flavored soy beverages, such as vanilla or chocolate, can have as much as 26 grams of carbohydrate and 140 calories per cup, while unsweetened varieties usually contain fewer calories and carbohydrates than even nonfat milk, averaging 80 calories and 4 grams of carbohydrate per cup. Compare labels; lite and unsweetened varieties are your best bets.

*See page 382 for sweetener options.

NUTRITION INFORMATION PER SERVING ·····························
Calories 140 | Carbohydrate 22g (Sugars 19g) | Total Fat 2g (Sat Fat 1g) | Protein 7g | Fiber 4g | Cholesterol 0mg | Sodium 60mg | Food Exchanges: 1 Fruit, ½ Low-Fat Milk | Carbohydrate Choices: 1 | Weight Watcher Smart Point Comparison: 6

Pumped Up
Peanut Butter Smoothie

Protein powder "pumps" up the protein in this incredible kid-pleasing peanut butter-flavored banana smoothie that drinks like a meal—with or without the protein powder. When choosing a protein powder, check the nutrition label carefully before you buy because many protein powders, especially flavored ones, contain added sugars. A pure protein powder should have no more than 2 grams of carbohydrate in each 2-tablespoon scoop.

MAKES 1 SERVING

2 tablespoons chunky or
  smooth peanut butter

½ small banana, frozen

½ cup low-fat milk

1½ tablespoons granulated
  no-calorie sweetener
  (or 2 packets)*

2 tablespoons vanilla or
  chocolate protein powder

¼ teaspoon vanilla extract

1 cup crushed ice

1. Place all the ingredients, except the ice, in a blender. Blend to mix.

2. Add crushed ice and blend on high until the ice is completely incorporated.

DARE *TO* COMPARE ·····················

A small-size Peanut Butter Moo'd® at Jamba Juice, also made with soy milk, frozen bananas, and peanut butter contains only 13 grams of protein, but 85 grams of carbohydrate (with 75 of them coming from sugars) and 490 calories. A step up to the "original" size will give you 21 grams of protein, 800 calories, and a staggering 115 grams of sugar!

*See page 382 for sweetener options.

NUTRITION INFORMATION PER SERVING ································
Calories 320 | Carbohydrate 25g (Sugars 13g) | Total Fat 16g (Sat Fat 3g) | Protein 28g | Fiber 4g | Cholesterol 0mg | Sodium 125mg | Food Exchanges: 3 Lean Fat Meat, 2 Fat, 1 Fruit, ½ Low-Fat Milk | Carbohydrate Choices: 2 | Weight Watcher Smart Point Comparison: 9

Easy Frosty Strawberry Fruit Shake

Bursting with fruit flavor, this creamy, frosty shake is one of my favorites. I love that it can be whipped up quickly with ingredients that you most likely already have on hand. Big and filling, it's also irresistibly low in calories and adds both a serving of fruit and calcium to your diet. For a richer shake, substitute ¼ cup light, no-sugar-added ice cream for the yogurt.*

MAKES 1 SERVING

½ cup low-fat milk

½ cup frozen strawberries

¼ cup light strawberry yogurt

2 tablespoons granulated
no-calorie sweetener*

½ cup crushed ice

1. Place all the ingredients, except the ice, in a blender. Blend to mix.

2. Add crushed ice and blend on high until the ice is completely incorporated.

Or try this: Any combination of berries or fruit and yogurt will do. For example try blueberries with blueberry yogurt, peaches with peach yogurt, or mix and match to create your own great combos.

* Adds 20 calories, 2.5 grams of fat, and 2 grams of carbohydrates.

*See page 382 for sweetener options.

NUTRITION INFORMATION PER SERVING
Calories 110 | Carbohydrate 18g (Sugars 15g) | Total Fat 1.5g (Sat Fat 1g) | Protein 8g | Fiber 2g | Cholesterol 5mg | Sodium 105mg | Food Exchanges: ½ Low-Fat Milk, ½ Fruit | Carbohydrate Choices: 1 | Weight Watcher Smart Point Comparison: 5

Frozen Hot Chocolate Frosty

My sons love drinking these! If you are a fan of the Original Chocolate Frosty ™ at Wendy's®, you are sure to love this, too. The biggest difference between a Wendy's frosty and this version is that this one has approximately one-half the calories, fat, and carbs, but double the protein and calcium. And I absolutely love that!

MAKES 1 SERVING

1 packet sugar-free hot cocoa mix

½ cup light, no-sugar-added ice cream

½ cup low-fat milk

½ to ¾ cup crushed ice

1. Place all the ingredients, except the ice, in a blender. Blend to mix.

2. Add crushed ice and blend on high until the ice is completely incorporated.

Family Focus: It's no surprise that those who frequent fast-food restaurants consume excessive amounts of fat, calories, sugar, and salt. But that doesn't mean you can't eat there *occasionally.* To do so without going overboard:

1. **Don't supersize**—it's not a better value to eat more than you should.
2. **Choose more healthful drinks** such as low-fat milk or diet soft drinks.
3. **Mix and match heavier foods with healthier ones.** If you must have fries, choose a smaller or lower-fat sandwich or burger. If you are craving a big cheeseburger, order a side salad with low-fat dressing instead of fries.

NUTRITION INFORMATION PER SERVING
Calories 160 | Carbohydrate 22g (Sugars 13g) | Total Fat 4.5g (Sat Fat 3g) | Protein 9g | Fiber 2g | Cholesterol 15mg | Sodium 190mg | Food Exchanges: 1 Carbohydrate, 1 Fat, ½ Low-Fat Milk | Carbohydrate Choices: 1½ | Weight Watcher Smart Point Comparison: 6

Vanilla Cake Batter Milkshake

When developing this recipe, I expected a double dose of vanilla flavor but was pleasantly surprised to find it actually tasted more like something I really love—cake batter ice cream. Yum. The secret to the "cake" flavor, and to making this thick and creamy with a mere ½ cup of ice cream, is the addition of sugar-free instant pudding mix. For a super-special treat, top this shake with a squirt of light whipped cream and some sprinkles—even if it's not your birthday.

MAKES 1 SERVING

⅔ cup low-fat milk

1 rounded tablespoon sugar-free instant vanilla pudding mix

½ cup light, no-sugar-added vanilla ice cream

⅔ cup crushed ice

1. Place all the ingredients, except the ice, in a blender. Blend to mix.

2. Add crushed ice and blend on high until the ice is completely incorporated and the shake is thick and creamy.

DARE *TO* COMPARE •••••••••••••••••••••••
A small Cake 'n Shake™ milkshake at Cold Stone Creamery® contains a dizzying 1140 calories, 60 grams of fat (including almost 2 days' worth of saturated fat), and a whopping 140 grams of carbohydrate (including the equivalent of 26 teaspoons of sugar)!

NUTRITION INFORMATION PER SERVING ••••••••••••••••••••••••
Calories 175 | Carbohydrate 27g (Sugars 10g) | Total Fat 4g (Sat Fat 2.5g) | Protein 7g | Fiber 4g | Cholesterol 15mg | Sodium 500mg | Food Exchanges: 1 Carbohydrate, ½ Low-Fat Milk | Carbohydrate Choices: 1½
Weight Watcher Smart Point Comparison: 7

Double Chocolate Pudding Milkshake

This rich-tasting ultra-chocolate milkshake is for all my chocolate-loving readers, including my son, Stephen, who dubbed this recipe his favorite. Following the formula of my Vanilla Cake Batter Milkshake, this also uses a touch of instant pudding to make it thick and creamy. For even more Sensational Pudding Milkshake variations, see page 72.

MAKES 1 SERVING

⅔ cup low-fat milk

1 rounded tablespoon sugar-free instant chocolate pudding mix

½ cup light, no-sugar-added chocolate ice cream

⅔ cup crushed ice

1. Place all the ingredients, except the ice, in a blender. Blend to mix.

2. Add crushed ice and blend on high until the ice is completely incorporated and the shake is thick and creamy.

NUTRITION INFORMATION PER SERVING
Calories 175 | Carbohydrate 27g (Sugars 10g) | Total Fat 4g (Sat Fat 2.5g) | Protein 7g | Fiber 4g | Cholesterol 15mg | Sodium 500mg | Food Exchanges: 1 Carbohydrate, ½ Low-Fat Milk | Carbohydrate Choices: 1½ | Weight Watcher Smart Point Comparison: 7

Sensational Pudding Milkshakes

It's not every day that a dietitian says you can guiltlessly enjoy a dolled-up milkshake, but you can with these delicious pudding milkshakes. Use the master recipe with one of the four great variations provided or feel free to get creative and make your own sensational flavor combination.

MAKES 1 SERVING

⅔ cup low-fat milk

1 rounded tablespoon sugar-free instant pudding mix

⅓ cup light, no-sugar-added ice cream

⅔ cup crushed ice

1. Place all the ingredients, except the ice, in a blender. Blend to mix.

2. Add crushed ice and blend on high until the ice is completely incorporated and the shake is thick and creamy.

Banana Cream Pie Milkshake
- Prepare the shake using sugar-free instant banana cream pudding mix and light, no-sugar-added vanilla ice cream.
- Top, if desired, with 2 tablespoons light whipped topping and garnish with 1 tablespoon crushed graham cracker crumbs. (Adds 45 calories, 7 carbs, and 1.5 grams of fat.)

Strawberry Cheesecake Milkshake
- Melt 1 tablespoon of sugar-free strawberry jam with 1 tablespoon of water in the microwave. Stir and let cool.
- Prepare the shake using sugar-free cheesecake pudding mix and light, no-sugar-added vanilla ice cream. Pour shake into a glass. Stir in strawberry sauce. (Adds 10 calories and 2 grams of carbs.)

Marvelous Mocha Milkshake
- Prepare the shake using sugar-free chocolate pudding mix and light, no-sugar-added coffee ice cream.
- If desired, top with 2 tablespoons of light whipped topping and a dusting of cocoa powder. (Adds 25 calories, 3 carbs and 1 gram of fat.)

Chocolate Cookie Milkshake
- Prepare the shake using sugar-free chocolate fudge pudding mix and light no-sugar-added cookies and cream ice cream.
- Top, if desired, with 2 tablespoons light whipped topping and a maraschino cherry. (Adds 30 calories, 4 carbs, and 1 gram fat.)

NUTRITION INFORMATION PER SERVING
Calories 150 | Carbohydrate 23g (Sugars 10g) | Total Fat 3.5g (Sat Fat 2.5g) | Protein 7g | Fiber 1g | Cholesterol 15mg | Sodium 500mg | Food Exchanges: 1 Carbohydrate, ½ Low-Fat Milk | Carbohydrate Choices: 1½
Weight Watcher Smart Point Comparison: 6

Pumpkin Pie Milkshake

If you like pumpkin pie you will love this milkshake. Better yet, with four grams of heart-healthy fiber, a healthy dose of cinnamon, and more than a day's worth of vitamin A, this is my best great-tasting, good-for-you shake ever!

MAKES 1 SERVING

⅓ cup canned pumpkin

½ cup low-fat milk

½ cup light, no-sugar-added vanilla ice cream

½ teaspoon ground cinnamon

Scant ¼ teaspoon nutmeg

Pinch of ginger

½ cup crushed ice

1. Place all the ingredients, except the ice, in a blender. Blend to mix.

2. Add crushed ice and blend on high until the ice is completely incorporated.

NUTRITION INFORMATION PER SERVING
Calories 180 | Carbohydrate 28g (Sugars 12g) | Total Fat 4.5g (Sat Fat 3g) | Protein 8g | Fiber 4g | Cholesterol 15mg | Sodium 135mg | Food Exchanges: 1 Carbohydrate, 1 Vegetable, ½ Low-Fat Milk | Carbohydrate Choices: 2 | Weight Watcher Smart Point Comparison: 7

Marvelous Muffins, Quick Breads, and Coffee Cakes

EVERYDAY BLUEBERRY MUFFINS

CINNAMON APPLESAUCE MUFFINS

FRESH ZUCCHINI MUFFINS

BANANA CHOCOLATE CHIP MUFFINS

TWO-BITE DOUBLE CHOCOLATE MUFFINS

BREAKFAST OATMEAL SQUARES

OLD-FASHIONED PUMPKIN BREAD

WHOLESOME BANANA BREAD

LUSCIOUS LEMON LOAF

QUICK SOUR CREAM COFFEE CAKE

BLUE RIBBON SOUR CREAM COFFEE CAKE

CHERRY ALMOND COFFEE CAKE

AMAZING APPLE COFFEE CAKE

QUICK RASPBERRY CREAM CHEESE TWIST

WHOLESOME BUTTERMILK BISCUITS

The only thing that beats waking up to the smell of fresh-baked muffins, sweet breads, and homemade coffee cakes is the pleasure you get from eating them. If you're looking for a sweet way to start the day, this chapter shows you sixteen wonderful ways to do so. The truth is, this chapter features some of my personal favorites as well as a number of recipes I am the most proud of. Creating reduced-fat *and* reduced-sugar baked goods that are every bit as moist and tender as their high-calorie counterparts takes a lot of trial and error, but when you sample these perfect muffins, breads, and coffee cakes, I'm sure you'll agree that it was worth the trouble.

All of the recipes in this chapter are classified as "quick" breads because instead of yeast they use baking soda and/or baking powder for leavening, so there is no rising time required. I like to think of them as quick because they are so quick and easy to make. I kick off the chapter with the most popular quick bread of all—muffins. Muffins are not only quick (and easy), they're great for grabbing on-the-go. It may surprise you to know that the "healthy" blueberry muffin from the local bakery or coffee shop has as many calories as three pancakes smothered in a quarter cup of maple syrup. And while reduced-fat muffins may tempt you with their promise of less fat and fewer calories, they still contain just as much sugar (and often more) than a traditional muffin. In comparison, my healthy Everyday Blueberry Muffins have only half the fat, a third of the calories and carbohydrates, and a fraction of the added sugar of those found at the bakery or coffee shop.

Here you will also find wonderful quick-bread loaves, including two all-time favorites: Wholesome Banana Bread and Old-Fashioned Pumpkin Bread, along with picture-perfect coffee cakes. I find lazy Sunday mornings the perfect time to serve the crumb-topped Quick Sour Cream Coffee Cake, and for hurried weekdays nothing is better than the Amazing Apple Coffee Cake on page 93. It cooks in just eight minutes! And finally, a breakfast bread chapter wouldn't be complete without a recipe for biscuits. Using the winning combination of all-purpose and white whole wheat flours, my light-textured Wholesome Buttermilk Biscuits on page 95 will make you love adding whole grains to your diet.

For the Love of Gluten-Free Recipes!

If you or someone you love is avoiding gluten, the good news is that most of mother nature's finest (and healthiest) foods are naturally gluten-free, including fruits, vegetables, lean meats, seafood, beans, nuts, and eggs—along with nutrient-rich dairy products and oils. And while foods like bread, cakes, and cookies made with wheat or barley or rye-based flour fill store shelves, fortunately, there are plenty of gluten-free products that make it easier than ever to eat, and cook, gluten free! Here are some tips on how to eat (and drink) G-free with this book:

BEVERAGES, QUICK BREADS AND BREAKFAST

- All of the beverages, shakes and smoothies—excepting the Chocolate Cookie and Banana Cream Pie Milkshake variations—are gluten-free. There are 33 to choose from!
- For pancakes and baked goods, substitute a gluten-free flour blend or baking mix 1:1. Pamela's brand is great for pancakes. Cup4Cup brand is my choice for muffins and breads.
- Gluten-free breads, tortillas and pizza crusts make it easy to enjoy a Breakfast BLT (page 103), South of the Border Wrap (page 101), or Breakfast Pizza (page 105). The frittata and oatmeal recipes, including Cinnamon Roll Oatmeal (page 99) are already G-free.

SOUPS, SALADS AND SANDWICHES

- In the Quick-Fix Soups and Chili's chapter, the soups on pages 149, 150, 153-160, and both chilis are gluten-free when made with gluten-free broth. A switch to gluten-free pasta renders the noodle-laced soups on (pages 151 and 161) G-free. For thickening recipes like the Chicken Corn Chowder, use gluten-free flour or ½ as much cornstarch mixed with a little water.
- Seventeen of the twenty-three recipes in the salad chapter, including the Red White and Blue Potato Salad (page 188), are already gluten-free! To enjoy the rest, simply opt for gluten-free bread for the croutons in the Everyday Chicken Caesar Salad (page 195), gluten-free pasta for the Pasta Primavera and Creamy Macaroni Salad Three Ways (pages 189 and 190), and Tamari sauce instead of soy.
- A simple swap to gluten-free bread makes the sandwich chapter an easy go-to for G-free meals. (Or, skip the bread altogether and wrap sandwich fillings in lettuce leaves.)

SIDES AND ENTREES

- There are over 30 easy gluten-free recipes in the *For the Love of Vegetables and Starchy Sides* chapters. Veggies, rice, potatoes, and beans are all gluten-free! To convert the Oven-Baked Onion Rings (page 249) use store-bought gluten-free breadcrumbs, for the Stovetop Macaroni and Cheese (page 274) your favorite gluten-free pasta, and for the Country Cornbread Muffins (page 290), gluten-free flour. Cornmeal is gluten-free. (Couscous contains gluten.)
- For pasta dishes, use your favorite gluten-free pasta or pour pasta sauces over cooked rice, spaghetti or butternut squash, or even baked potatoes.
- You'll find plenty of chicken, beef, pork, and fish entrees like Garlic Lime Chicken (page 298), All-American Meatloaf Minis (page 323), and Sweet-and-Sour Shrimp Stir Fry (page 356) that are already gluten-free. The rest can be made so easily by using cornstarch or gluten-free flour for thickening or dusting, gluten-free breadcrumbs for coating, and Tamari instead of soy sauce. (For thickening, use half as much cornstarch as you would regular flour).

DELECTABLE DESSERTS

- The Amazing Peanut Butter Cookies (page 383), Simple Meringue Cookies (page 387), Creamy Old-Fashioned Vanilla Pudding (pages 411), Hot Apple Stir Fry (page 376), and Easy Ultra-Rich Chocolate Mousse (page 424) along with those on pages 368-370, 375, 388, 390, 406, 407, 412, 421, 423, 425, and 428 are gluten-free recipes.
- Purchase ready-made gluten-free crusts for the pies and gluten-free graham crackers or cookie crumbs, and the dozen recipes on page 363-366, 373-374, 392, 413-416 and 426 will also be will be gluten-free.
- For baked goods made with wheat flour, store-bought gluten-free "flour" is the easy way to go. There are many brands to choose from, however they vary greatly in taste and texture. Cup4Cup is the best replacement for all-purpose flour I have found. It works great for cookies, cupcakes and cakes including my Unbelievable Chocolate Cake (page 404)!
- Note: Sugar-free pudding, Jello®, ice cream, cocoa powder, whipped topping, jam, cream cheese, most oats, coconut and sucralose- and stevia-based sweeteners are all G-free.

Note: Experts agree that there is no need to avoid wheat if you do not have celiac disease or gluten sensitivity. A gluten-free diet does not guarantee weight loss or better health. Many gluten-free foods are higher in sugar, fat, and calories, as well as lower in nutrients such as fiber, B vitamins and iron. Consult a physician or registered dietitian before starting a gluten-free diet. *Gluten Free Diet: A Comprehensive Resource Guide* by Shelley Case RD is an excellent resource.

Everyday Blueberry Muffins

A slight hint of orange lends a new twist to this American morning favorite. Bursting with blueberries and deliciously sweet, you'd never guess there's less than one teaspoon of sugar in each muffin. Leftovers can be wrapped and frozen for busy mornings and reheated by popping one in the microwave for about 30 seconds for that just-baked warmth.

MAKES 12 SERVINGS

1 cup low-fat plain yogurt

⅓ cup light orange juice

1 large egg

3 tablespoons margarine or butter, melted

1½ teaspoons vanilla extract

2 cups all-purpose flour

½ cup granulated no-calorie sweetener*

3 tablespoons granulated sugar

1 tablespoon baking powder

½ teaspoon baking soda

1 cup fresh blueberries

1. Preheat the oven to 400°F. Lightly spray 12 muffin cups with nonstick baking spray (paper or foil liners may be added before spraying).

2. In a medium bowl, whisk together the first five ingredients (yogurt through vanilla extract). Set aside.

3. In a large bowl, stir together the next five ingredients (flour through baking soda). Add blueberries and stir lightly to coat with flour mixture. Make a well in center of the dry ingredients and pour in the yogurt mixture. Using a large spoon or spatula, stir just until the dry ingredients are moistened.

4. Spoon the batter evenly into prepared muffin tins, filling each cup ⅔ full. Bake for 15 minutes or until the center springs back when lightly touched. Cool for 5 minutes before removing to a wire rack.

DARE TO COMPARE..................................

Mimi's®, a popular breakfast chain, is known for their tasty low-fat Blueberry Muffin. The problem is that for many baked goods, when the fat goes down—the sugar goes up! With 439 calories and 101 grams of carbohydrate, one of these "healthy" muffins has as much sugar as is recommended for an entire day.

*See page 382 for sweetener options

NUTRITION INFORMATION PER SERVING ···

Calories 150 | Carbohydrate 23g (Sugars 7g) | Total Fat 3.5g (Sat Fat 1g) | Protein 4g | Fiber 1g | Cholesterol 20mg | Sodium 160mg | Food Exchanges: 1½ Starch, ½ Fat | Carbohydrate Choices: 1½ | Weight Watcher Smart Point Comparison: 5

Cinnamon Applesauce Muffins

Nice and cinnamony, these tender applesauce muffins are one of my kids' favorites. What I love is the wonderful aroma of cinnamon that fills my kitchen and draws everyone out of bed with smiles on their faces.

MAKES 12 SERVINGS

¼ cup margarine or butter, softened

2 tablespoons dark brown sugar

2 large eggs

¾ cup unsweetened apple-sauce

1 teaspoon vanilla extract

1 cup all-purpose flour

1 cup white whole wheat flour

⅔ cup granulated no-calorie sweetener*

1 teaspoon baking soda

1 teaspoon baking powder

1 tablespoon plus ½ teaspoon ground cinnamon

2 teaspoons granulated sugar

1. Preheat the oven to 400°F. Lightly spray 12 muffin cups with nonstick baking spray (paper or foil liners may be added before spraying).

2. In a large bowl, cream the margarine and brown sugar for 3 to 4 minutes until fluffy. Beat in the eggs, applesauce, and vanilla extract.

3. In a medium bowl, stir together the flours, sweetener, baking soda, baking powder, and 1 tablespoon cinnamon. Using a large spoon or spatula, stir the flour mixture into the creamed butter mixture just until the dry ingredients are moistened.

4. Spoon the batter evenly into muffin tins, filling each cup two-thirds full.

5. In a small bowl, combine the granulated sugar and ½ teaspoon cinnamon. Sprinkle evenly over muffins. Bake the muffins for 20 minutes or until the center springs back when lightly touched. Cool for 5 minutes before removing to a wire rack.

Marlene Says: According to some studies, cinnamon may help regulate blood sugar levels. Adding a sweet pinch of cinnamon to your day may just help keep the doctor away.

*See page 382 for sweetener options

NUTRITION INFORMATION PER SERVING
Calories 140 | Carbohydrate 23g (Sugars 5g) | Total Fat 4.5g (Sat Fat 1.5g) | Protein 4g | Fiber 2g | Cholesterol 35mg | Sodium 160mg | Food Exchanges: 1½ Starch, 1 Fat | Carbohydrate Choices: 1½ | Weight Watcher Smart Point Comparison: 5

Fresh Zucchini Muffins

These cake-like muffins are a real treat, even if you don't like zucchini! Unlike many zucchini muffins that are dark and heavy, these are light and tender. Like magic, the grated zucchini disappears into the fragrant baked muffins but keeps the finished product nice and moist. (When my friend PJ tried them on her finicky husband, she said the hardest part was keeping him from eating them all!)

MAKES 12 SERVINGS

1 cup grated zucchini

½ cup low-fat buttermilk

1 large egg

1 large egg white

1 teaspoon vanilla extract

1 cup all-purpose flour

½ cup white whole wheat flour

⅔ cup granulated no-calorie sweetener*

2 tablespoons light brown sugar

1 teaspoon baking soda

2 teaspoons baking powder

1½ teaspoons ground cinnamon

¾ teaspoon ground nutmeg

¼ cup shortening

1. Preheat the oven to 375°F. Lightly spray 12 muffin cups with nonstick baking spray (paper or foil liners may be added before spraying).

2. In a medium bowl, stir together the first 5 ingredients (zucchini through vanilla extract). Set aside.

3. In a large bowl, combine the next 8 ingredients (all-purpose flour through nutmeg). Using your fingertips, a pastry blender, or two knives, cut the shortening into flour mixture until the shortening is thoroughly incorporated. Make a well in the center and add the zucchini mixture. Using a large spoon or spatula, stir just until the dry ingredients are moistened.

4. Spoon the batter evenly into muffin tins, filling each cup two-thirds full. Bake for 12 to 15 minutes or until the center springs back when lightly touched. Cool for 5 minutes before removing to a wire rack.

> **DARE *TO* COMPARE** ·····························
> When it comes to muffins, those containing fruits or vegetables may seem to be healthier choices, but this is often not the case. Even the Mini Zucchini Walnut Muffin at Starbucks® for example, will set you back 390 calories, 23 grams of fat, and 42 grams of carbohydrate, including 22 grams of sugar.

*See page 382 for sweetener options

NUTRITION INFORMATION PER SERVING ··
Calories 120 | Carbohydrate 16g (Sugar 2g) | Total Fat 5g (Sat Fat 1.5g) | Protein 3g | Fiber 1g | Cholesterol 20mg | Sodium 210mg | Food Exchanges: 1 Starch, 1 Fat | Carbohydrate Choices: 1 | Weight Watcher Smart Point Comparison: 4

Banana Chocolate Chip Muffins

Here's another favorite flavor combination baked into a delectable, but better-for-you, muffin. To make the most of the chocolate chips, put them right up on top where you get the most bang for your buck (so to speak). A kid favorite? You bet.

MAKES 12 SERVINGS

1 cup mashed banana

¼ cup plain low-fat yogurt

½ cup granulated no-calorie sweetener*

1 large egg

1 large egg white

3 tablespoons margarine or butter, melted

1 teaspoon vanilla extract

1¾ cups all-purpose flour

1½ teaspoons baking soda

1 teaspoon baking powder

6 tablespoons mini chocolate chips

1. Preheat the oven to 375°F. Lightly spray 12 muffin cups with nonstick baking spray (paper or foil liners may be added before spraying).

2. In a medium bowl, whisk together the first seven ingredients (banana through vanilla extract). Set aside.

3. In a large bowl, combine the flour, baking soda, and baking powder and stir. Make a well in the center and add the banana mixture. Using a large spoon or spatula, stir just until the dry ingredients are moistened.

4. Spoon the batter into prepared muffin tins, filling each cup two-thirds full. Sprinkle each muffin with 1 heaping teaspoon chocolate chips.

5. Bake for 15 minutes or until the center springs back when lightly touched. Cool for 5 minutes before removing to a wire rack.

Marlene Says: Instead of mini chocolate chips you may use regular ones and chop them a bit. The smaller-sized pieces allow for greater distribution and therefore you don't have to use as many.

*See page 382 for sweetener options

NUTRITION INFORMATION PER SERVING
Calories 155 | Carbohydrate 22g (Sugars 6g) | Total Fat 6g (Sat Fat 1.5g) | Protein 3g | Fiber 1g | Cholesterol 20mg | Sodium 190mg | Food Exchanges: 1½ Starch, 1 Fat | Carbohydrate Choices: 1½ | Weight Watcher Smart Point Comparison: 5

Two-Bite Double Chocolate Muffins

When it comes to baked goods, the good news is that small is now big! From mini-muffins to two-bite brownies, scones, and cupcakes, food manufacturers have finally found that sometimes a bite, or two, is all we need. Here I have taken a favorite recipe and scaled it down for when just a couple of bites will satisfy. These are also great for your little ones at snack time. Wrap leftovers tightly and store in the freezer; reheat for fifteen to thirty seconds in the microwave to bring back the fresh-baked aroma before serving.

MAKES 24 SERVINGS

¼ cup canola oil

2 large egg whites

1½ teaspoons vanilla extract

¾ cup granulated no-calorie sweetener*

½ cup unsweetened apple-sauce

¾ cup low-fat buttermilk

2 cups all-purpose flour

½ cup cocoa powder (preferably Dutch-process)

¼ cup packed dark brown sugar

1½ teaspoons baking powder

½ teaspoon baking soda

½ cup mini chocolate chips

1. Preheat the oven to 400°F. Lightly coat a nonstick 24 mini-muffin baking pan with nonstick baking spray.

2. In a medium bowl, whisk together the first 6 ingredients (oil through buttermilk). Set aside.

3. In a large bowl, combine the next 6 ingredients (flour through chocolate chips). Stir. Create a well in the center and add the buttermilk mixture. Using a large spoon or spatula, stir just until the dry ingredients are moistened.

4. Spoon the batter evenly into the prepared muffin tins, filling each cup two-thirds full.

5. Bake for 15 minutes or until the center springs back when lightly touched. Cool for 5 minutes before removing to a wire rack.

*See page 382 for sweetener options

⋮ **NUTRITION INFORMATION PER SERVING** ·····················
⋮ Calories 100 | Carbohydrate 15g (Sugars 5g) | Total Fat 3.5g (Sat Fat 1g) | Protein 2g | Fiber 1g | Cholesterol
⋮ 0mg | Sodium 70mg | Food Exchanges: 1 Starch, ½ Fat | Carbohydrate Choices: 1 | Weight Watcher Smart
⋮ Point Comparison: 3

Breakfast Oatmeal Squares

These oaty on-the-go squares are a snap to prepare in just one bowl. They make a great snack to send off with the kids and are a much healthier (and less expensive) alternative to pricey, high sugar, packaged-breakfast bars.

MAKES 12 SERVINGS

2 cups rolled quick oats

¼ cup all-purpose flour

1 teaspoon baking powder

½ teaspoon baking soda

2 teaspoons ground cinnamon

1 large egg

¾ cup pumpkin purée

¼ cup low-fat milk

¼ cup sugar-free maple syrup

⅓ cup granulated no-calorie sweetener

¼ cup packed light brown sugar

2 teaspoons vanilla extract

¼ cup raisins, chopped

1. Preheat the oven to 350°F. Lightly coat a 9-inch square baking pan with nonstick baking spray.

2. In a large bowl, combine the first 5 ingredients (oats through cinnamon). Stir. Add the remaining ingredients and stir until thoroughly combined.

3. Pour into prepared baking pan and smooth the top.

4. Bake for 25 to 30 minutes or until the center springs back when touched or an inserted toothpick comes out clean. Let cool on a wire rack for 5 minutes and then turn out of pan to cut (bottoms will become slightly wet if left in pan).

5. Cut into 12 portions and wrap individually, if desired.

> **DARE TO COMPARE** ··
> Don't be fooled. Several brands of breakfast bars, or cookies, can be found at your grocery store. Although higher in fiber and lower in sugar than some snack bars, they still range from 170 to 300 calories, and from 33 to 55 grams of carbohydrate, each. Read the label before you buy (or just make your own healthy squares!).

*See page 382 for sweetener options

NUTRITION INFORMATION PER SERVING ··
Calories 80 | Carbohydrate 16g (Sugars 5g) | Total Fat 1.5g (Sat Fat 0g) | Protein 3g | Fiber 2g | Cholesterol 20mg | Sodium 125mg | Food Exchanges: 1 Starch | Carbohydrate Choices: 1 | Weight Watcher Smart Point Comparison: 2

Old-Fashioned Pumpkin Bread

Moist and wonderfully spiced pumpkin bread is always a holiday favorite, but this quick and easy family favorite deserves to be enjoyed year round. As with all quick breads, the batter can easily be converted into muffins (see Or Try This below for baking instructions), and individual portions can be wrapped and frozen for anytime convenience.

MAKES 12 SERVINGS

¼ cup canola oil

1 cup canned solid pack pumpkin

1 large egg

2 large egg whites

½ cup low-fat buttermilk

3 tablespoons molasses

1 cup granulated no-calorie sweetener*

1 cup all-purpose flour

¾ cup white whole wheat flour

2 teaspoons baking powder

1 teaspoon baking soda

1½ teaspoons cinnamon

1 teaspoon ginger

½ teaspoon allspice (optional)

¼ teaspoon cloves

¼ teaspoon salt

1. Preheat the oven to 350°F. Lightly coat a 9 x 5-inch loaf pan with nonstick cooking spray.

2. In a medium bowl, whisk together the oil, pumpkin, whole egg, egg whites, buttermilk, molasses, and sweetener.

3. In a large bowl, combine the flours, baking powder, baking soda, spices, and stir. Make a well in the center and pour in the pumpkin mixture. With a large spoon or spatula, stir just until blended. Do not overmix.

4. Spoon the batter into the prepared loaf pan and smooth surface.

5. Bake for 40 to 45 minutes until the crack appears dry or toothpick or cake tester inserted into the center comes out clean. Cool on rack for 10 to 15 minutes and then remove from pan.

Or try this: To make *Pumpkin Muffins*, preheat the oven to 375°F, spoon batter into 12 prepared muffin cups. Bake for 16 to 18 minutes or until top springs back when lightly touched.

*See page 382 for sweetener options

NUTRITION INFORMATION PER SERVING ···
Calories 150 | Carbohydrate 22g (Sugars 4g) | Total Fat 4g (Sat Fat 0g) | Protein 4g | Fiber 2g | Cholesterol 35mg | Sodium 220mg | Food Exchanges: 1½ Starch, 1 Fat | Carbohydrate Choices: 1½ | Weight Watcher Smart Point Comparison: 5

Wholesome Banana Bread

When faced with too many ripe bananas—it's banana bread time! In fact, the great thing about ripe bananas is that the riper they are, the better the bread. In this recipe I use a mixture of white whole wheat and all-purpose flour for a wholesome, but light-textured, loaf. If you choose, however, you can use all white whole wheat flour for a slightly nuttier-tasting loaf with a bit more fiber. Once the bread is cool, I often slice the loaf and place each slice in its own baggie to freeze for later use. Then on busy mornings all I have to do to serve up a delicious piece of home-baked bread is to throw one in the microwave for about thirty seconds. (The frozen slices will stay fresh in the freezer for several weeks.)

MAKES 12 SERVINGS

2 large eggs

⅔ cup granulated no-calorie sweetener*

1⅓ cups mashed banana (about 3 medium ripe bananas)

¼ cup vegetable oil

1 tablespoon molasses

1½ teaspoons vanilla extract

1 cup white whole wheat flour

1 cup all-purpose flour

1½ teaspoons baking soda

½ cup chopped walnuts (optional)

1. Preheat the oven to 350°F. Lightly coat a nonstick 9 x 5-inch loaf pan with cooking spray.

2. In a large bowl, beat the eggs and sweetener together with an electric mixer until the eggs are pale yellow and have tripled in volume. Reduce the speed to low and add the mashed bananas, oil, molasses, and vanilla extract.

3. In a large bowl, combine the flours, baking soda, and nuts, if desired. Stir. Make a well in the center and add the banana mixture. Using a large spoon or spatula, stir just until the dry ingredients are moistened.

4. Scrape batter into the prepared loaf pan and smooth top.

5. Bake for 45 to 50 minutes or until a toothpick inserted into the middle of the loaf comes out clean. Cool on a wire rack for 10 to 15 minutes before removing from pan.

*See page 382 for sweetener options

NUTRITION INFORMATION PER SERVING ···
Calories 160 | Carbohydrate 24g (Sugars 5g) | Total Fat 6g (Sat Fat 0g) | Protein 4g | Fiber 2g | Cholesterol 35mg | Sodium 10mg | Food Exchanges: 1½ Starch, 1 Fat | Carbohydrate Choices: 1½ | Weight Watcher Smart Point Comparison: 4

Luscious Lemon Loaf

Whether served alone or on a plate surrounded with fresh berries, the versatility of fresh lemon bread can't be beat. I love how lemon extract imparts the wonderful, natural lemon flavor without the acidity of regular lemon juice. You'll find it in the baking aisle with the extracts. (Rather than serving the loaf with berries, you can also roll one cup of blueberries into the bread by adding them to the flour mixture.)

MAKES 12 SERVINGS

¼ cup canola oil

¼ cup granulated sugar

1 large egg

2 large egg whites

½ cup unsweetened applesauce

1 teaspoon vanilla extract

1 teaspoon lemon extract

1 teaspoon lemon zest

2 cups all-purpose flour

¾ cup plus 2 tablespoons granulated no-calorie sweetener*

2 teaspoons baking powder

½ teaspoon baking soda

¾ cup light sour cream

2 tablespoons lemon juice

1. Preheat the oven to 350 F. Coat a 9 x 5-inch loaf pan with nonstick baking spray.

2. In a medium bowl, whisk together the first 8 ingredients (oil through lemon zest) until well blended.

3. In a large bowl, combine the flour, sweetener, baking powder, and baking soda. Make a well in the center and pour in the wet mixture. With a large spoon or spatula, combine just until blended. Do not overmix.

4. Spoon the mixture into the prepared loaf pan and smooth the surface.

5. Bake for 50 to 55 minutes or until a toothpick or a cake tester inserted into the middle of the loaf comes out clean. Place loaf pan on a wire rack. In a small bowl, whisk together the lemon juice and remaining 2 tablespoons sweetener. Brush over the loaf while it is still warm and let cool before removing from the pan.

*See page 382 for sweetener options

NUTRITION INFORMATION PER SERVING ·······························
Calories 170 | Carbohydrate 24g (Sugars 7g) | Total Fat 6g (Sat Fat 1g) | Protein 5g | Fiber <1g | Cholesterol 25mg | Sodium 210mg | Food Exchanges: 1½ Starch, 1 Fat | Carbohydrate Choices: 1 | Weight Watcher Smart Point Comparison: 5

Quick Sour Cream Coffee Cake

With its signature crumb topping and rich taste of sour cream, this coffee cake is the real deal. To make it quicker, while still producing a moist and tender cake crumb, I cut the fat into the flour, which eliminates the need to use a mixer. Needless to say, it makes for a great Sunday morning treat.

MAKES 9 SERVINGS

CAKE BATTER

¾ cup light sour cream

¼ cup unsweetened apple-sauce

2 tablespoons brown sugar

1 large egg

1 large egg white

½ cup granulated no-calorie sweetener*

1½ cups all-purpose flour

¾ teaspoon baking soda

1 teaspoon baking powder

½ teaspoon ground cinnamon

3 tablespoons margarine or butter

TOPPING

¼ cup all-purpose flour

¼ cup rolled quick oats

2 tablespoons packed light brown sugar

2 tablespoons granulated no-calorie sweetener

2 tablespoons margarine or butter, melted

¾ teaspoon ground cinnamon

1. Preheat the oven to 350°F. Lightly coat an 8-inch square baking pan with nonstick cooking spray.

2. For the cake batter, in a medium bowl whisk together the sour cream, applesauce, brown sugar, egg, egg white, and sweetener. Set aside.

3. In a large bowl, combine the flour, baking soda, baking powder, and cinnamon. Using your fingertips, a pastry blender, or two knives, cut the margarine into the flour mixture until crumbly. Create a well in the center and pour in the sour cream mixture. Mix gently with a large spoon or spatula until blended. Spoon the batter into prepared baking pan.

4. For the topping, in a small bowl, combine all the ingredients with a fork, until mixture is crumbly. Sprinkle the topping evenly over the batter.

5. Bake for 25 minutes or until a toothpick inserted in the center comes out clean. Cool on a wire rack.

Perfect Pairing: A great healthy brunch partner would be a terrific veggie-filled frittata (you will find several to choose from in the Breakfast Entrées chapter), or for a fun-filled breakfast pop the coffee cake into the oven and while it bakes have the family create their own omelets using the Omelet in a Baggie recipe on page 106.

*See page 382 for sweetener options

NUTRITION INFORMATION PER SERVING
Calories 210 | Carbohydrate 28g (Sugars 7g) | Total Fat 8g (Sat Fat 3g) | Protein 5g | Fiber 1g | Cholesterol 30mg | Sodium 250mg | Food Exchanges: 2 Starch | Carbohydrate Choices: 2 | Weight Watcher Smart Point Comparison: 7

Blue Ribbon
Sour Cream Coffee Cake

If you are looking for a great coffee cake for a leisurely brunch, this is it! This light and tender cake is studded with beautiful fresh blueberries and topped with a buttery, sweet, crunchy topping. I like to think of it as dessert for breakfast. Pair it with your favorite breakfast frittata or one of those in the Breakfast Entrées chapter for a breakfast that is sure to please.

MAKES 9 SERVINGS

CAKE BATTER

¾ cup light sour cream

¼ cup unsweetened applesauce

2 tablespoons granulated sugar

1 large egg

1 large egg white

½ cup granulated no-calorie sweetener*

1½ cups all-purpose flour

¾ teaspoon baking soda

1 teaspoon baking powder

3 tablespoons margarine or butter

1 cup fresh blueberries (½ pint)

TOPPING

⅓ cup all-purpose flour

2 tablespoons brown sugar

2 tablespoons granulated no-calorie sweetener

2 tablespoons margarine or butter, melted

1. Preheat the oven to 350°F. Lightly coat an 8-inch square baking pan with nonstick baking spray.

2. For the cake batter, in a medium bowl whisk together the sour cream, applesauce, sugar, egg, egg white, and sweetener.

3. In a large bowl, combine the flour, baking soda, and baking powder. Using your fingertips, a pastry blender, or two knives, cut margarine into flour mixture until crumbly. Create a well in the center and pour in the sour cream mixture. Add blueberries and mix gently with a large spoon or spatula until blended. Spoon the batter into prepared baking pan.

4. For the topping, in a small bowl, combine all the ingredients with a fork until mixture is crumbly. Sprinkle the mixture evenly over the batter.

5. Bake for 25 minutes or until a toothpick inserted into the center comes out clean. Cool on a wire rack.

Marlene Says: It's hard not to be drawn to the bakery case at your local coffee shop but watch out. Even lower-fat versions can sabotage your diet. While the calories have been reduced, there is stil 8 teaspoons of sugar in each piece.

*See page 382 for sweetener options

Cherry Almond Coffee Cake

It took several tries to get this coffee cake just right, but it was worth it. The combination of dark sweet cherries, cream cheese, and almonds makes this very special. Of course, it would also be a beautiful addition to any holiday breakfast table.

MAKES 8 SERVINGS

CAKE BATTER

1 cup all-purpose flour

1½ teaspoons baking powder

½ teaspoon baking soda

3 tablespoons shortening

½ cup granulated no-calorie sweetener*

1 large egg

1 large egg white, beaten (reserve 2 tablespoons)

½ cup low-fat milk

½ teaspoon vanilla extract

½ teaspoon almond extract

TOPPING

½ cup light tub-style cream cheese

2 tablespoons granulated no-calorie sweetener*

2 teaspoons granulated sugar

¼ teaspoon almond extract

1 cup frozen unsweetened cherries, slightly thawed

¼ cup sliced almonds

2 teaspoons powdered sugar (optional)

1. Preheat the oven to 350° F. Lightly coat an 8-inch round cake pan with nonstick cooking spray.

2. For the cake batter, in a medium bowl, mix together the flour, baking powder, and baking soda. Set aside.

3. In a medium bowl, with an electric mixer, cream the shortening and sweetener. Add the egg, egg white, milk, and extracts to mixture. Add the creamed mixture to the dry ingredients using a spatula or wooden spoon. *Do not overmix*. Pour the batter into prepared cake pan and smooth out with a spatula.

4. For the topping, in a small bowl whisk the cream cheese until smooth. Add the reserved 2 tablespoons of egg white, sweetener, sugar and extract and whisk until combined. Drop teaspoonfuls of cream cheese randomly on top of cake batter. Drain the cherries. Swirl the mixture gently and press cherries into topping. Top with almonds.

5. Bake for 25 minutes, until a toothpick comes out clean when inserted into center of cake. Cool on cake rack and lightly dust cake with powdered sugar just before serving.

*See page 382 for sweetener options

NUTRITION INFORMATION PER SERVING ··

Calories 180 | Carbohydrate 22g (Sugars 8g) | Total Fat 7g (Sat Fat 2.5g) | Protein 5g | Fiber 1g | Cholesterol 35mg | Sodium 230mg | Food Exchanges: 1 Starch, ½ Fruit, 1 Fat | Carbohydrate Choices: 1 | Weight Watcher Smart Point Comparison: 7

Amazing Apple Coffee Cake

What's so amazing about this cake is that it takes only eight short minutes to . . . bake! Well, actually, to microwave. When I threw out the idea for this recipe to Sophia, my assistant (an accomplished pastry chef), she winced and told me that baking is meant to be done in a real oven. But when we gave it a try we were amazed. It proved to both of us that while the top does not brown like it does in a regular oven (which does not matter because it's topped with apples), a toothsome, warm coffee cake can indeed be produced in a microwave—in minutes.

MAKES 9 SERVINGS

CAKE BATTER

1½ cup-all-purpose flour

½ cup granulated no-calorie sweetener*

2 teaspoons baking powder

½ teaspoon baking soda

¼ cup brown sugar

¼ cup margarine or butter, softened

1 large egg

⅔ cup low-fat milk

TOPPING

1 cup apple slices, ⅛-inch thick

1 tablespoon granulated sugar

1 teaspoon ground cinnamon

1. Lightly coat an 8-inch square microwave-safe dish with non-stick baking spray.

2. For the cake batter, in a large bowl whisk together the flour, sweetener, baking powder, and baking soda. Set aside.

3. In a medium bowl, cream the sugar and margarine together until fluffy. Add the egg and beat until combined. Add the milk into butter mixture (it will appear separated). Add the creamed mixture to the dry ingredients, using a spatula or wooden spoon. *Do not overmix.* Pour the batter into prepared dish and smooth with a spatula.

4. For the topping, arrange the apple slices on top of the cake batter. In a small bowl, combine the sugar and cinnamon and sprinkle it over the apple slices.

5. Cover the dish with plastic wrap. Microwave on high for 4 minutes. Remove the plastic wrap and cook for another 4 minutes. Let sit for 5 minutes and serve warm. (This is at its best when freshly made.)

*See page 382 for sweetener options

NUTRITION INFORMATION PER SERVING ••••••••••••••••••••••••••••••
Calories 180 | Carbohydrate 25g (Sugars 9g) | Total Fat 7g (Sat Fat 2g) | Protein 4g | Fiber 1g | Cholesterol 45mg | Sodium 200mg | Food Exchanges: 1 Starch/Bread, 1½ Fat | Carbohydrate Choices:1½ | Weight Watcher Smart Point Comparison: 7

Quick Raspberry Cream Cheese Twist

This beautiful raspberry-filled pastry is one of my all-time favorites. Here, you can take advantage of a healthy reduced-fat baking mix to make your own homemade pastry in little more than thirty minutes. I find this especially nice to serve when I have overnight guests.

MAKES 8 SERVINGS

3 ounces light cream cheese

3 tablespoons margarine or butter

2 cups reduced-fat baking mix (like Bisquick Heart Smart)

4 tablespoons granulated no-calorie sweetener, divided (or 6 packets)*

⅓ cup low-fat milk

½ cup reduced-sugar raspberry preserves

1 cup fresh raspberries

1 large egg white (for wash)

1 teaspoon granulated sugar

1. Preheat the oven to 425°F.

2. In a large bowl, using a pastry blender or fork, cut the cream cheese and margarine into the Bisquick until crumbly. Blend in 2 tablespoons of the sweetener and the milk. Bring the dough together into a ball and turn onto a lightly floured surface. Knead the dough about 10 times, just until soft dough forms. Roll dough out into a 16 x 8-inch rectangle.

3. Carefully move the dough onto a cookie sheet. Spread preserves down the center of the dough lengthwise, about 4 inches wide. Top the preserves with the raspberries and sprinkle the remaining 2 tablespoons of sweetener over the berries. Cut slits 1½ inches apart and at a 45-degree angle along the outer edge of the dough, where there are no preserves. Fold these dough strips across the filling, alternating side to side. Brush the strudel with the egg white and sprinkle with sugar.

4. Bake for 15 minutes until golden brown.

> **DARE TO COMPARE**
> An average cheese Danish has 450 calories, 20 grams of fat, and 60 carbohydrates (with 36 of them, or 9 teaspoons, coming from sugar).

*See page 382 for sweetener options

NUTRITION INFORMATION PER SERVING
Calories 185 | Carbohydrate 28g (Sugars 9g) | Total Fat 6g (Sat Fat 2g) | Protein 4g | Fiber 3g | Cholesterol 65mg | Sodium 115mg | Food Exchanges: 1½ Starch/ Bread, ½ Fruit, 1 Fat | Carbohydrate Choices: 2
Weight Watcher Smart Point Comparison: 7

Wholesome Buttermilk Biscuits

Hot biscuits are always a welcome addition to any meal, but these have the added bonus of being good for you. Because they're drop biscuits, and require no rolling, they're also quick and easy. I serve them with reduced-sugar jam in the morning and with Best Oven-Fried Chicken (page 295) for dinner, but I'm sure you will find plenty of your own favorite ways of serving them.

MAKES 12 SERVINGS

1 cup all-purpose flour

1 cup white whole wheat flour

2 teaspoons baking powder

¼ teaspoon baking soda

1½ tablespoons shortening

1 cup plus 2 tablespoons
   low-fat buttermilk

1. Preheat the oven to 425°F. Line a baking sheet with parchment paper or nonstick baking spray.

2. In a large bowl, mix together the flours, baking powder, and baking soda.

3. Using your fingertips, a pastry blender, or two knives, cut the shortening into the flour mixture until the shortening is thoroughly incorporated. Create a well in the center of the flour and pour in the buttermilk. Mix by hand or with a spatula just until moistened. Do not overmix the batter; it will appear slightly loose.

4. Drop tablespoonfuls of batter evenly spaced apart onto the prepared baking sheet.

5. Bake 12 to 15 minutes or until the tops are dry and bottoms are lightly browned.

Marlene Says: The USDA recommends that at least half of all grains eaten are whole grains. Whole wheat bread products are one of the easiest ways to incorporate whole grains into your diet.

NUTRITION INFORMATION PER SERVING ·······················
Calories 100 | Carbohydrate 17g (Sugars 1g) | Total Fat 2g (Sat Fat 0g) | Protein 3g | Fiber 2g | Cholesterol 0mg | Sodium 130mg | Food Exchanges: 1 Starch | Carbohydrate Choices: 1 | Weight Watcher Smart Point Comparison: 3

Breakfast Entrées

CINNAMON ROLL OATMEAL

QUICK OVERNIGHT OATMEAL

SOUTH OF THE BORDER WRAP

BREAKFAST BLT SANDWICH

SCRAMBLED EGG AND HAM PANINI

BREAKFAST PIZZA

OMELET IN A BAGGIE

TURKEY BREAKFAST SAUSAGE

CLASSIC ITALIAN FRITTATA

GREEK FRITTATA

FAJITA FRITTATA

HAM AND CHEESE BISCUITS

EVERYDAY CINNAMON FRENCH TOAST

BROWN SUGAR CINNAMON FRENCH TOAST

EASY OVEN-BAKED FRENCH TOAST

BETTER-FOR-YOU BUTTERMILK PANCAKES

PUMPKIN PANCAKES

WHOLESOME BLUEBERRY PANCAKES

FRUIT AND YOGURT BREAKFAST SUNDAES

The most important meal of the day is breakfast. Eating breakfast gets your engine running and kick starts your metabolism. People who eat breakfast are stronger, smarter, thinner, and happier than those who don't. Moreover, eating breakfast can help you lose weight—and keep it off. According to the National Weight Control Registry, breakfast eaters tend to eat fewer calories, less saturated fat and cholesterol, and have better overall nutritional status than breakfast skippers.

The key is, of course, to select a breakfast that's both healthy and satisfying. Traditional rich pastries, sugar-loaded cereals, and fast-food sandwiches are not the breakfast of which they speak. Breakfast foods that are full of sugar and refined carbohydrates may give you a quick boost (while sending your blood sugar soaring), but they burn off quickly, leaving you dragging by mid-morning, while high-fat breakfasts will weigh you down before your day gets started. On the other hand a wholesome breakfast that is modest in calories and high in protein and fiber will satisfy your hunger and kick the day off right.

I'm excited to bring you a wonderful variety of mouth-watering breakfast options that will tempt even the most die-hard breakfast skipper. Sweet Cinnamon Roll Oatmeal takes just minutes to make and beats the over-sugared packaged variety any day. My three fabulous frittatas are packed with fresh vegetables to fill you up not out, and my guilt-free Ham and Cheese Biscuits, just right whether on a breakfast buffet or grabbed to go, are sure to please. You will also find traditional favorites made even better like my Better-for-You Buttermilk Pancakes and Brown Sugar Cinnamon French Toast. Last, if you're a fan of the breakfast drive-through you will love the two great grab-'n'-go breakfast sandwiches—the sensational Breakfast BLT and the South of the Border Wrap. Breakfast has never tasted better!

For the Love of Eggs

The poor egg has been condemned for too long. Eggs are egg–ceptional when it comes to providing both taste and good nutrition. The truth is that hundreds of studies now support that eggs can be part of any healthy diet because the cholesterol in eggs raises blood cholesterol far less than the saturated fats found in other foods such as milk, butter, cheese and meat.

EIGHT EGG-CITING REASONS TO LOVE EGGS:

1. **Eggs are an economical source of high-quality protein.** One large egg supplies 10% of the recommended daily allowance of protein for a 2,000-calorie diet.

2. **Eggs are nutrient rich.** Eggs are packed with 13 essential nutrients, including iron, vitamins A, D, B12, riboflavin, and choline, an essential nutrient for heart health.

3. **Eggs can help you lose weight.** In a study that compared eating either eggs or bagels for breakfast, the egg eaters lost almost twice as much weight along with a greater decrease in waist circumference.

4. **Eggs can help control blood sugar.** The protein and fat in eggs digest slowly and don't spike blood sugar, so adding eggs to a meal can help moderate carbs and keep blood sugar steady.

5. **Eggs are great for your eyes.** Eggs yolks contain lutein and zeaxanthin, which have been shown to reduce the risk of age-related blindness (macular degeneration).

6. **Egg whites are fabulous.** Egg whites are virtually fat free, contain more than half of the protein of the egg, and none of the cholesterol. To enjoy eggs without the fat and cholesterol substitute 2 egg whites, or ¼ cup liquid egg substitute for each whole egg.

7. **Eggs are egg-quisite for cooking and baking.** Eggs bind ingredients and thicken sauces, enable coatings, add color and flavor, and help cakes and soufflés to rise. Separated, egg whites foam to make meringues while yolks emulsify and add creamy texture to sauces.

8. **Eggs are delicious!**

Cinnamon Roll Oatmeal

If you want to add more whole grains to your diet, eating oatmeal is the perfect place to start. Oats are inexpensive and easy to prepare, and when done up right they taste nothing like "health" food. Moreover, a bowl of oatmeal with its unique mixture of protein, fiber, and complex carbohydrates keeps you satisfied longer and won't cause the rapid rise in blood sugar found with sweetened cereals. To finish off your "cinnamon roll" top it off with a tablespoon of raisins* or a tablespoon of chopped nuts.** My oatmeal-loving husband always does both.

MAKES 1 SERVING

½ cup rolled oats

1 cup water

1 tablespoon granulated no-calorie sweetener*

½ teaspoon ground cinnamon

½ teaspoon vanilla extract

Pinch of salt

Splash of low-fat milk or nonfat half-and-half (optional)

1. In a medium-size microwave-safe bowl (at least 2-cup capacity), combine all the ingredients except milk and stir.

2. Microwave on high for 2 minutes. Remove and stir again. Add milk if desired.

Family Focus: Studies done on school-age children show that they perform better on tests when they eat a bowl of oatmeal instead of a high-sugar cereal for breakfast.

• Adds 30 calories, 7 grams of carb, ½ fruit, and ½ additional carbohydrate choice.

• Adds 50 calories, 5 grams of fat, 1 fat, and 0 additional carbohydrate choices.

*See page 382 for sweetener options

NUTRITION INFORMATION PER SERVING
Calories 160 | Carbohydrate 28g (Sugars 1g) | Total Fat 2.5g (Sat Fat 0g) | Protein 7g | Fiber 5g | Cholesterol 0mg | Sodium 150mg | Food Exchanges: 1½ Starch, ½ Fat | Carbohydrate Choices: 1½ | Weight Watcher Smart Point Comparison: 4

Quick Overnight Oatmeal

Also known as Irish or pinhead oats, steel-cut oats are the least refined of the oat cereals and are chopped instead of rolled. This process results in a wonderful nutty flavor and chewier texture than that of the more familiar rolled oats. The downside of this marvelous oat is a much longer cooking time, which can be difficult on harried midweek mornings, but you can cut the cooking time from twenty-five minutes to five by soaking the oats overnight and microwaving them in the same bowl in the morning. (P.S.: Eat them Oprah's way by adding a handful of blueberries and a few whole almonds.)

MAKES 1 SERVING

¼ cup steel-cut oats

1 cup water

Pinch of salt

1 tablespoon sugar-free maple syrup

Splash of low-fat milk or nonfat half-and-half (optional)

1. In a medium-size microwave-safe bowl (four-cup capacity to allow for boiling), combine the oats and water. Cover and set aside overnight.

2. To cook the oatmeal, add pinch of salt and place in microwave. Microwave on high for 5 minutes. Remove, stir again, and drizzle with sugar-free maple syrup. Add milk if desired.

Or try this: To make *Quick Overnight Oatmeal for 4,* place 1 cup of steel cut oats and 4 cups of water in a medium-size saucepan. Set aside to soak overnight. To cook, add ¼ teaspoon salt, and place over medium heat. Bring to simmer and cook for 5 to 7 minutes. Serve with sugar-free maple syrup and milk if desired.

NUTRITION INFORMATION PER SERVING ·······························
Calories 140 | Carbohydrate 27g (Sugars 2g) | Total Fat 2.5g (Sat Fat 0g) | Protein 6g | Fiber 4g | Cholesterol 0mg | Sodium 100mg | Food Exchanges: 1½ Starch, ½ Fat | Carbohydrate Choices: 1½ | Weight Watcher Smart Point Comparison: 4

South of the Border Wrap

Tortillas that are higher in fiber and lower in carbohydrates are one of the best new foods to come out of the low-carb craze. The ones I used in this recipe contain 80 calories, 13 grams of carbohydrate, and 10 grams of fiber. It's important to read the nutrition label on regular flour tortillas because some burrito-size ones can contain as much as 35 grams of carbohydrate with very little fiber and appreciable amounts of fat.

MAKES 4 SERVINGS

4 large eggs (or 2 large eggs and ½ cup liquid egg substitute)

2 large egg whites

Salt and pepper to taste

Dash Tabasco, or other hot sauce

¼ cup diced onion

¼ cup diced green bell pepper

4 (8-inch) reduced-carb high-fiber tortillas

½ cup shredded light Mexican Blend cheese

⅓ cup prepared salsa

1. In a small bowl, beat the eggs and egg whites. Add the salt, pepper, and hot sauce to taste.

2. Spray a medium-size skillet with nonstick cooking spray and place over medium heat. Add the onions and peppers and sauté until soft, 3 to 4 minutes. Add the eggs and scramble, cooking for 2 to 3 minutes or until eggs are set. Set aside.

3. Warm the tortillas in the microwave for 30 seconds. Divide egg scramble among each of the four tortillas. Top each evenly with cheese and salsa.

4. Fold over one side, then the bottom, and then the last side of the tortilla, burrito style.

DARE TO COMPARE

One of the most popular breakfast burritos served is the McSkillet® Burrito at McDonald's®. It combines eggs, onions, peppers, cheese, salsa, potatoes and sausage in a warm tortilla. The hefty nutritional price for all this: 610 calories, 36 grams of fat (including almost ⅔ of your daily allotment for saturated fat), 44 grams of carbohydrate, 1400 mg of sodium, and more than a day's worth of cholesterol.

NUTRITION INFORMATION PER SERVING
Calories 220 | Carbohydrate 18g (Sugars 2g) | Total Fat 10g (Sat Fat 3.5g) | Protein 16g | Fiber 10g
Cholesterol 220mg | Sodium 580mg | Food Exchanges: 1 Starch, 1 Medium-Fat Meat, 1 Low-Fat Meat, 1Vegetable | Carbohydrate Choices: 1 | Weight Watcher Smart Point Comparison: 5

Breakfast BLT Sandwich

Wow, a BLT for breakfast! This filling and satisfying egg sandwich is *so* good you will never believe you are eating a breakfast sandwich that is better for you. But with half the calories, carbs, and sodium, only one-third the fat, and a load more fiber than a sausage and egg biscuit, you definitely are. Short on time? Wrap it up to go and avoid the line at the local fast-food drive-through.

MAKES 1 SERVING

1 Light Multigrain Thomas' English muffin (or 2 slices light wheat bread)

2 slices center cut bacon

1 large egg, beaten (or ¼ cup liquid egg substitute)

2 mounded teaspoons light mayonnaise

2 leaves of lettuce

2 slices tomato

1. Spray a small skillet with nonstick cooking spray and place over medium heat.

2. Place bacon on a paper towel and microwave according to instructions on the package (usually about 2 to 3 minutes), or until desired crispiness.

3. While the bacon is cooking, place English muffin halves in toaster. Pour the beaten egg into the preheated skillet and use a spatula to push the cooked portion to the center and allow uncooked egg to flow to the edges. As the egg continues to cook, move to the center of the pan and shape to fit the size of the muffin. When the egg is just firm enough, flip and briefly cook second side. Remove from the heat.

4. Spread mayonnaise evenly over each half of toasted muffin. Place a lettuce leaf on one muffin half. Add one slice tomato, then egg, bacon slices, then remaining tomato and lettuce. Top with second muffin half.

Perfect Pairing: Pair your BLT with an 8-ounce glass of fortified light orange juice and this tasty meal will give you over 100% of the daily value of vitamin C and 70 % of the calcium along with a whopping 9 grams of fiber.

NUTRITION INFORMATION PER SERVING ·······························
Calories 260 | Carbohydrate 26g (Sugars 2g) | Total Fat 12g (Sat Fat 4g) | Protein 17g | Fiber 9g | Cholesterol 230mg | Sodium 570mg | Food Exchanges: 1 Starch, 1½ Medium-Fat Meat, ½ Vegetable, 1 Fat | Carbohydrate Choices: 1 | Weight Watcher Smart Point Comparison: 8

Scrambled Egg and Ham Panini

This has become my kids' new favorite good-to-go breakfast. *They tell me that it keeps them satisfied for hours. I use a regular large egg for them, and the egg substitute for myself when I'm looking to lower the fat and calories. (Using the liquid egg substitute saves you 40 calories, 5 grams of fat (1.5 of them saturated), and 210 grams of cholesterol.)*

MAKES 1 SERVING

1 large egg, beaten (or ¼ cup liquid egg substitute)

3 tablespoons part-skim mozzarella cheese or any reduced-fat variety, shredded

3 slices lean deli-style ham, thinly sliced (about ½ ounce)

2 pieces sourdough bread (thinly sliced)

1. Spray a small nonstick skillet with cooking spray and place over medium heat. Pour the egg into the preheated skillet and use a spatula to push the cooked portion to the center and allow uncooked egg to flow to the edges. As the egg continues to cook, move to the center of the pan and shape to fit the size of the bread.

2. When the underside is cooked, flip the egg and top it immediately with the cheese and then the ham. Cook for an additional minute or until the egg is cooked through and then remove from the pan with the spatula.

3. Lightly spray the pan with cooking spray again and place one piece of bread in the pan. Place the egg stack on top of the bread and top with remaining bread slice. Using the lid of a small pot, press firmly down on the top of the sandwich. Allow the panini to cook for about 2 minutes or until lightly browned; then flip and press again. Cook remaining side until brown.

Marlene Says: If you are on a strict low-sodium diet use reduced-sodium ham.

NUTRITION INFORMATION PER SERVING ································
Calories 250 | Carbohydrate 23g (Sugars 1g) | Total Fat 9g (Sat Fat 3g) | Protein 20g | Fiber 1g | Cholesterol 230mg | Sodium 510mg | Food Exchanges: 1½ Starch, 1½ Medium-Fat Meat, ½ Very Lean Meat, | Carbohydrate Choices: 1½ | Weight Watcher Smart Point Comparison: 7 (6 with egg substitute)

Breakfast Pizza

I don't know about your kids, but my boys never, ever, tire of eating pizza. The inspiration for this recipe came from a friend who delighted us with a breakfast pizza one morning when we were spending a weekend at her home. Since then I have made this many times for my family and guests and hope you will enjoy it, too.

MAKES 6 SERVINGS

- 1 large (12-inch) thin, partially baked pizza crust, such as Boboli
- ⅔ cup prepared salsa
- 6 large eggs and 4 large egg whites (or 4 large eggs and 1 cup liquid egg substitute)
- ¾ cup shredded light Mexican Blend Cheese
- ½ green bell pepper, cut into rings
- 1 green onion, chopped

1. Preheat the oven to 450°F. Place the partially baked crust on a pizza pan or baking sheet and spread the salsa over it with the back of a spoon. Set aside.

2. Spray a medium-size nonstick skillet with cooking spray and place over medium heat. In a small bowl, whisk together the eggs and egg whites (or eggs and egg beaters) until blended. Scramble the eggs in preheated skillet until eggs are just set. Do not overcook.

3. Spread the scrambled eggs over salsa. Top with cheese, green pepper rings, and sprinkle with green onions.

4. Bake for 12 minutes until the cheese is melted and the edges of the crust are browned. Cut into wedges to serve.

Marlene Says: Swapping out the regular crust for a 12-inch whole wheat crust will save you 15 calories and add 3 grams of fiber to each serving.

NUTRITION INFORMATION PER SERVING
Calories 260 | Carbohydrate 26g (Sugars 1g) | Total Fat 9g (Sat Fat 4g) | Protein 17g | Fiber 2g | Cholesterol 26mg | Sodium 580mg | Food Exchanges: 1½ Starch, 2 Medium-Fat Meat, ½ Vegetable
Carbohydrate Choices: 1½ | Weight Watcher Smart Point Comparison: 7

Omelet in a Baggie

My good friend PJ asked me what I thought about this rather interesting idea of creating an omelet by placing all of the ingredients in a baggie and boiling it. It was intriguing enough for me to try and here is the result. This is a very fun thing to do as the ingredients really do turn into an omelet that rolls out of the baggie quite nicely. You can also do this as a family. Simply line up all your usual omelet fillings (adding or subtracting from my Denver omelet version below), put out enough eggs and baggies for everyone, and start cooking. Use a permanent marker to write your names on each of the baggies before filling, and then boil them all together. A large pot of boiling water will hold four omelets.

MAKES 1 SERVING

1 large egg

2 large egg whites

2 tablespoons reduced-fat sharp cheddar

2 tablespoons lean ham

2 tablespoons onion, chopped

2 tablespoons green bell pepper, diced

Salt and pepper to taste

1. Fill a large saucepan three-quarters full of water and bring to a low boil.

2. Place the egg and egg whites into a sealable plastic baggie that zips shut, and mix the eggs together by gently squeezing and shaking the sealed bag.

3. Once the eggs are well mixed, add the remaining ingredients, and reseal the bag tightly, making sure to remove as much excess air as possible. Shake the bag gently to evenly distribute the ingredients.

4. Place the baggie into the water, and cook for 12 minutes.

5. Using tongs, remove the bag from the water. Open the baggie and slide the omelet out onto a plate and serve immediately.

Marlene Says: Although I have never had a problem with the baggies, be sure to only use ones that are durable.

NUTRITION INFORMATION PER SERVING
Calories 180 | Carbohydrate 5g (Sugars 3g) | Total Fat 7g (Sat Fat 3g) | Protein 22g | Fiber 1g | Cholesterol 225mg | Sodium 510mg | Food Exchanges: 1½ Medium-Fat Meat, 2 Lean Meat, 1 Vegetable | Carbohydrate Choices: ½ | Weight Watcher Smart Point Comparison: 5

Turkey Breakfast Sausage

Making your own sausage may seem an intimidating prospect at first, but there really isn't anything to fear. In this recipe, all the ingredients are mixed together in one bowl and then formed into patties. It couldn't be easier. The key to this savory breakfast classic is a perfect combination of spices. Pork sausage can be very high in fat, but this version uses lean turkey, which cuts 75 percent of the fat, while reducing the calories and sodium by half! Better yet, when these patties are cooked to golden-brown perfection, even the most discriminating sausage lover will relish them.

MAKES 8 SERVINGS

1 pound lean ground turkey
¼ cup rolled quick oats
½ teaspoon salt
½ teaspoon pepper
½ teaspoon fennel, crushed
½ teaspoon garlic powder
½ teaspoon dried thyme
½ teaspoon ground sage
Pinch of red pepper flakes
1 teaspoon light brown sugar

1. In a medium-size bowl, mix all the ingredients thoroughly with your hands.

2. Separate mixture into 8 equal portions. Roll each portion into a ball and press flat to form a 4-inch round patty. Continue forming patties with the remaining mixture.

3. Spray a large, nonstick skillet with cooking spray and place over medium-high heat. Add patties to pan and cook for about 2 minutes on each side, until there is no pink left in the center. Be careful not to overcook. The patties will shrink slightly during the cooking process.

DARE TO COMPARE
A two-ounce pork sausage patty (precooked) has 200 calories, 17 grams of fat (5 of them saturated), and 8 grams of protein.

NUTRITION INFORMATION PER SERVING
Calories 80 | Carbohydrate 2g (Sugars 1g) | Total Fat 2.5g (Sat Fat 1.5g) | Protein 12g | Fiber 0g | Cholesterol 40mg | Sodium 190mg | Food Exchanges: 2 Lean Meats | Carbohydrate Choices: 0 | Weight Watcher Smart Point Comparison: 2

Classic Italian Frittata

A frittata is an Italian open-faced omelet that's easy to make and large enough to serve an entire family of four. Packed with vegetables and herbs, and topped with cheese, frittatas are also wonderfully versatile. You can vary the ingredients to suit your taste and serve it cold, at room temperature, or straight from the oven. They can even be cooked ahead and reheated. This one includes meaty mushrooms and Italian squash, but for meat lovers be sure to check out the crowd-pleasing sausage variation.

MAKES 4 SERVINGS

4 large eggs

4 large egg whites

1 tablespoon water

¼ teaspoon salt

Pepper to taste

1 tablespoon olive oil

½ small onion, sliced

1 garlic clove, minced

½ teaspoon dried thyme

2 small zucchini, sliced (about 1½ cups)

1½ cups mushroom slices

⅓ cup freshly grated Parmesan cheese

1. Preheat the broiler.

2. In a medium bowl, whisk together the eggs, egg whites, water, salt, and pepper.

3. Place a large ovenproof nonstick skillet over medium heat. Add the olive oil and heat for about 20 seconds; then add the onion and cook for 2 to 3 minutes to soften. Add the garlic, thyme, and zucchini and cook for 3 to 4 minutes longer or until zucchini begins to soften. Add the mushrooms and cook the entire vegetable mixture for an additional 2 to 3 minutes, just until the mushrooms start to soften, but are not cooked down. Reduce the heat to low and pour in the beaten egg mixture. Push the cooked egg edges to the center, gently allowing the uncooked egg portion to flow to the outside edges. Continue to cook over medium-low heat for another 4 to 5 minutes until the eggs are almost set.

4. Sprinkle the cheese evenly over the eggs and place under the preheated broiler for about 3 minutes to finish cooking the egg and to slightly brown the cheese. Remove the pan from the oven. Use a spatula to loosen the edges and cut into four portions.

Or try this: To make an *Italian Sausage and Mushroom Frittata* sauté 8 ounces Italian turkey sausage with the onion. Omit zucchini, if desired. Adds 70 calories, 2.5 grams of fat, and 12 grams of protein per serving.

NUTRITION INFORMATION PER SERVING ·········
Calories 190 | Carbohydrate 6g (Sugars 3g) | Total Fat 11g (Sat Fat 3.5g) | Protein 17g | Fiber 2g | Cholesterol 220mg | Sodium 440mg | Food Exchanges: 1 Medium-Fat Meat, 1 Lean Meat, 1 Vegetable, 1 Fat | Carbohydrate Choices: ½ | Weight Watcher Smart Point Comparison: 5

Greek Frittata

The incredible flavors of Greece get star treatment here, showing how easy it is to mix and match ingredients when making frittatas. I find this version particularly delicious even when served cold. Sliced tomatoes make a nice accompaniment.

MAKES 4 SERVINGS

4 large eggs

4 large egg whites

1 tablespoon water

¼ teaspoon salt

Pepper to taste

1 tablespoon olive oil

½ red onion, diced

¼ cup chopped kalamata or black olives

1 cup artichoke hearts, chopped

¾ teaspoon dried oregano

¼ cup light or reduced-fat feta cheese

1. Preheat the broiler.

2. In a medium bowl, whisk together the eggs, egg whites, water, salt, and pepper.

3. Heat a large, ovenproof nonstick skillet over medium heat. Heat the tablespoon of oil, then add the onion, and cook for 2 to 3 minutes to soften. Add the olives, artichoke hearts, and oregano and cook for 2 to 3 minutes to warm the vegetables. Reduce the heat to low and pour in the beaten egg mixture. Push the cooked egg edges to the center, allowing the uncooked egg portion to flow to the outside edges to finish cooking. Continue to cook over medium-low heat for another 4 to 5 minutes until the eggs are almost set.

4. Sprinkle the cheese evenly over the eggs and place under the preheated broiler for about 3 minutes to finish cooking the egg and warming the cheese.

5. Remove the pan from the broiler. Use a spatula to loosen the edges and slide the frittata out onto a plate. Cut into four portions.

NUTRITION INFORMATION PER SERVING •••

Calories 180 | Carbohydrate 8g (Sugars 3g) | Total Fat 10g (Sat Fat 2.5g) | Protein 14g | Fiber 3g | Cholesterol 215mg | Sodium 550mg | Food Exchanges: 1 Medium-Fat Meat, 1 Low-Fat Meat, 1 Vegetable, 1 Fat | Carbohydrate Choices: ½ | Weight Watcher Smart Point Comparison:5

Fajita Frittata

While testing frittatas and thinking of all the possible variations, I thought it might be nice to take one south of the border! (The sound of the name alone had me hooked.) A sprinkling of fresh cilantro and/or a dollop of light sour cream make nice garnishes, as would the addition of a lovely twist of orange on the plate. Olé!

MAKES 4 SERVINGS

4 large eggs

4 large egg whites

1 tablespoon water

¼ teaspoon salt

Pepper to taste

1 tablespoon olive oil

1 cup sliced yellow onion

1½ cups sliced red and green bell peppers

½ teaspoon ground cumin

½ cup black beans, drained and rinsed

½ cup prepared salsa

½ cup reduced-fat Mexican cheese blend

1. Preheat the broiler.

2. In a medium bowl, whisk together the eggs, egg whites, water, salt, and pepper.

3. Heat a large, ovenproof nonstick skillet over medium heat. Heat the tablespoon of oil; then add the onions, bell pepper, and cumin and cook for 5 to 6 minutes or until the vegetables are softened. Sprinkle the beans evenly across the pan and gently mix them in to warm them. Reduce the heat to low and pour in the beaten egg mixture. Push the cooked egg edges to the center, allowing the uncooked egg portion to flow to the outside edges. Continue to cook over medium-low heat for another 4 to 5 minutes until the eggs are almost set.

4. Lightly spoon the salsa across the egg mixture, cover evenly with the cheese and place under the preheated broiler for about 3 minutes to finish cooking the egg and melting the cheese.

5. Remove the pan from the broiler. Use a spatula to loosen the edges and slide the frittata out onto a plate if desired. Cut into four portions.

NUTRITION INFORMATION PER SERVING
Calories 220 | Carbohydrate 13g (Sugars 4g) | Total Fat 12g (Sat Fat 3.5g) | Protein 17g | Fiber 4g | Cholesterol 225mg | Sodium 550mg | Food Exchanges: 1 Medium-Fat Meat, 1 Low-Fat Meat, 1 Vegetable, 1 Fat, ½ Starch Carbohydrate Choices: ½ | Weight Watcher Smart Point Comparison: 6

Ham and Cheese Biscuits

My son Stephen went through a phase during which he thought the best thing in the world to eat was a McDonald's® sausage biscuit with cheese. It didn't take him long to realize that he never felt as good after he ate it as he did while he ate it! With close to 500 calories and 30 of them coming from artery-clogging fat, it's not hard to figure out why. Even worse, the sodium clocks in at 1200 milligrams (which explains the need for those large drinks). The appeal of that version of biscuit sandwich quickly faded, but the appeal of a biscuit with meat and cheese did not. Here is a terrific substitute. Low in fat and calories, with a nice punch of protein, this is one tasty alternative.

MAKES 12 SERVINGS

2 cups all-purpose flour

2 teaspoons baking powder

¼ teaspoon baking soda

1½ tablespoons shortening

¾ cup reduced-fat sharp cheddar, shredded

¾ cup lean ham, cubed

1 cup plus 2 tablespoons low-fat buttermilk

1. Preheat the oven to 425°F. Spray a large nonstick cookie sheet with cooking spray.

2. In a large bowl, mix together the flour, baking powder, and baking soda.

3. Using your hands or a pastry cutter, cut in the shortening until all the pieces are pea size. The flour mixture will look crumbly. Toss in the cheese and ham and blend well.

4. Add the buttermilk and use a spatula to mix just until the dry ingredients are thoroughly moistened.

5. Drop heaping tablespoonfuls of batter onto a prepared cookie sheet 2 inches apart. Bake for 13 to 15 minutes, or until golden brown.

Marlene Says: Because my boys usually grab at least two of these at a time, I occasionally make them double the size. Use twice the batter for each one and cook for 15 to 17 minutes. To add fiber, you may replace 1 cup of the all-purpose flour with white whole wheat if you choose.

NUTRITION INFORMATION PER SERVING
Calories 130 | Carbohydrate 18g (Sugars 1g) | Total Fat 3g (Sat Fat 1.5g) | Protein 8g | Fiber 1g | Cholesterol 10mg | Sodium 300mg | Food Exchanges: 1 Starch, 1 Medium-Fat Meat | Carbohydrate Choices: 1 | Weight Watcher Smart Point Comparison: 4

Everyday Cinnamon French Toast

French toast is usually an unhealthy splurge because traditional French toast is often made with cream, fried in butter, and then topped with more butter as well as syrup. But it doesn't have to be. When lightened up, French toast can be a healthy balance of protein, fiber, fat, and carbohydrates that will satisfy you for hours. If you cannot find cinnamon-swirl bread, white whole wheat and sourdough are also healthy choices.

MAKES 4 SERVINGS

1 large egg

2 large egg whites

1 cup low-fat milk

2 tablespoons granulated no-calorie sweetener*

¾ teaspoon vanilla extract

½ teaspoon ground cinnamon

8 slices whole grain cinnamon-swirl bread (like Pepperidge Farm)

Sugar-free syrup (optional)

1. Coat griddle or large skillet with nonstick cooking spray and place over medium heat.

2. In a shallow bowl, whisk together all the ingredients except the bread and syrup. Place slices of bread into the egg mixture, turning to coat both sides.

3. Place the bread onto the hot griddle and cook until the underside is golden brown. Turn and cook until the second side is golden brown. Serve immediately.

*See page 382 for sweetener options

NUTRITION INFORMATION PER SERVING (2 SLICES)
Calories 220 | Carbohydrate 32g (Sugars 1g) | Total Fat 7g (Sat Fat 2g) | Protein 11g | Fiber 4g | Cholesterol 10mg | Sodium 300mg | Food Exchanges: 2 Starch, 1 Medium-Fat Meat, ½ Fat | Carbohydrate Choices: 2
Weight Watcher Smart Point Comparison: 6

Brown Sugar Cinnamon French Toast

One of the most persistent myths about diabetes is that you cannot eat any sugar, which is simply not true. What is true is that we should all limit our intake of added sugars. This recipe is a great example of how a mere teaspoon of sugar (per serving) can be very satisfying. Pair this French toast with a drizzle of sugar-free syrup, a couple slices of lean Canadian bacon, and a half cup of fresh berries and you have a sweet and healthy breakfast.

MAKES 4 SERVINGS

1 large egg

2 large egg whites

¾ cup low-fat milk

¾ teaspoon vanilla extract

1½ tablespoons brown sugar

1 tablespoon granulated no-calorie sweetener (optional)

1 teaspoon ground cinnamon

4 slices thick-sliced bread (like Texas toast)

1. In a shallow bowl, whisk together the egg, egg whites, milk, and vanilla extract until combined. Set aside.

2. In a small bowl, mix together the brown sugar, Splenda, and cinnamon.

3. Spray a medium nonstick skillet with cooking spray and place over medium heat.

4. Dip the bread slices in the egg mixture, coating both sides evenly. Place the bread into the hot skillet. While the underside is cooking, sprinkle 1 teaspoon of cinnamon sugar mixture evenly onto top of toast (pressing it through a mesh sieve makes for a nice even coating). Flip and finish cooking for 3 minutes, checking occasionally, while being careful not to overcook cinnamon sugar-coated underside.

Family Focus: This is a great recipe for cooking with kids. It entails breaking eggs (which all kids adore), measuring, whisking, and flipping. Best of all, it has a great sweet finish. What more could you ask?

NUTRITION INFORMATION PER SERVING ·······································
Calories 150 | Carbohydrate 26g (Sugars 9g) | Total Fat 2.5g (Sat Fat 0g) | Protein 7g | Fiber 2g | Cholesterol 55mg | Sodium 240mg | Food Exchanges: 1½ Starch, ½ Lean Meat | Carbohydrate Choices: 1½ | Weight Watcher Smart Point Comparison: 6

Easy Oven-Baked French Toast

There are a lot of recipes that try to make baking French toast for a crowd easy, but this casserole-style recipe for French toast is one of my favorites because it's so simple. Just prepare the casserole the night before and pop it into the oven in the morning. When done, the top of this luscious cinnamon and maple-scented casserole has a golden brown crust while the center is soft and sweet. Furthermore, the addition of the fragrant maple extract gives the impression that syrup has already been incorporated, making the need for additional syrup optional.

MAKES 10 SERVINGS

1 cup liquid egg substitute

2 large eggs

2½ cups low-fat milk

⅔ cup granulated no-calorie sweetener*

1 teaspoon vanilla extract

½ teaspoon maple extract

1½ teaspoons cinnamon

12 ounces French bread, cut into 10 1½-inch thick slices

2 teaspoons powdered sugar (optional)

1. Spray a 13 x 9-inch baking dish with nonstick cooking spray.

2. In a large bowl, whisk together the egg substitute, eggs, milk, sweetener, extracts, and cinnamon until well mixed. Soak the bread slices in the egg mixture, arrange snuggly in a baking dish, and pour any remaining egg mixture over the bread. Cover and refrigerate the casserole overnight (or for at least one hour).

3. Preheat the oven to 350°F. Bake for 40 to 45 minutes, until puffed in center and lightly browned.

4. Remove from the oven and lightly dust with powdered sugar before serving, if desired.

Or try this: Take Oven-Baked French Toast to new heights by serving it with *Easy Quick Raspberry Sauce.* Thaw one 12-ounce bag of frozen, unsweetened raspberries. Place raspberries in a bowl and mash with 2 to 4 tablespoons granulated no-calorie sweetener to taste. Serve at room temperature or heat in the microwave until warm.

*See page 382 for sweetener options

NUTRITION INFORMATION PER SERVING
Calories 150 | Carbohydrate 22g (Sugars 3g) | Total Fat 2.5g (Sat Fat1.0g) | Protein 9g | Fiber 1g | Cholesterol 45mg | Sodium 290mg | Food Exchanges: 1 Starch, ½ Low-Fat Milk, ½ Lean Meat | Carbohydrate Choices: 1½ | Weight Watcher Smart Point Comparison: 4

Better-for-You Buttermilk Pancakes

It's not simple to sneak whole grains into an Aunt Jemima® pancake-loving family, but white whole wheat flour makes it easy to do. These Better–for-You Buttermilk Pancakes cook up light and tender just like the classic, yet they have half the fat and twice the fiber. They are good enough to make even Aunt Jemima envious.

MAKES 6 SERVINGS

¾ cup all-purpose flour

¾ cup white whole wheat flour

1½ tablespoons granulated no-calorie sweetener*

1 teaspoon baking powder

½ teaspoon baking soda

1 large egg

2 large egg whites

1½ cups low-fat buttermilk

1 teaspoon vanilla extract

1. In a medium bowl, combine the flours, sweetener, baking powder, and baking soda.

2. In a separate bowl, whisk together the eggs, buttermilk, and vanilla extract. Pour the liquid ingredients into the dry ingredients and stir until well combined. Make sure not to overmix the batter.

3. Spray a nonstick skillet or griddle with cooking spray and place over medium heat. Pour ¼ cup of batter per pancake onto skillet and spread into a 4-inch circle. Cook the pancake for 3 to 4 minutes on the first side, or until golden on the bottom. Flip the pancake just once more and cook for an additional 2 to 3 minutes. Serve hot.

*See page 382 for sweetener options

NUTRITION INFORMATION PER SERVING (2 PANCAKES)
Calories 185 | Carbohydrate 30g (Sugars 5g) | Total Fat 2g (Sat Fat 0g) | Protein 8g | Fiber 2g | Cholesterol 40mg | Sodium 280mg | Food Exchanges: 2 Starch, ¼ Low-Fat Milk | Carbohydrate Choices: 2 | Weight Watcher Smart Point Comparison: 5

Pumpkin Pancakes

There is nothing better than waking up to the smell of hot pancakes. These fabulous pancakes bring the wonderful aroma of pumpkin pie to breakfast throughout the year, and because they are already perfectly spiced they are terrific with, or without, syrup. Speaking of syrup, these days the sugar-free options are better than ever. If you haven't found one you like, keep trying or switch to a "light" version (with 50 percent less sugar) and use it as a drizzle rather than a drench.

MAKES 7 SERVINGS

1½ cups all-purpose flour

½ cup wheat bran

2 teaspoons baking powder

½ teaspoon baking soda

1½ teaspoons ground cinnamon

½ teaspoon ground ginger

¼ teaspoon ground nutmeg

¼ cup granulated no-calorie sweetener*

1 large egg

½ cup canned pumpkin purée

1¾ cup low-fat milk

Sugar-free maple syrup (optional)

1. In a medium bowl, combine the flour, bran, baking powder, baking soda, spices, and sweetener.

2. In a separate bowl, beat the egg and add the pumpkin and milk. Mix until thoroughly combined.

3. Pour the liquid ingredients into the dry ingredients and stir until the dry ingredients are just moistened. Make sure not to overmix the batter.

4. Spray a nonstick skillet or griddle with cooking spray and place over medium heat. Pour ¼ cup of batter per pancake onto the skillet and spread into a 4-inch circle. Cook the pancake for 3 to 4 minutes on the first side, or until golden on the bottom. Flip the pancake just once more and cook for an additional 2 to 3 minutes. Serve hot.

> **DARE TO COMPARE** ·
> A typical restaurant serving of pancakes ranges from as low as 500 calories for a short stack to as high as 900 calories for a full-size order (4 to 8 carb servings respectively). Three pancakes at Denny's® have 510 calories and 102 grams of carbohydrate (and, yes, that's without syrup).

*See page 382 for sweetener options

NUTRITION INFORMATION PER SERVING (2 PANCAKES) ·
Calories 150 | Carbohydrate 29g (Sugars 4g) | Total Fat 2g (Sat Fat 0g) | Protein 7g | Fiber 3g | Cholesterol 35mg | Sodium 110mg | Food Exchanges: 2 Starch, ¼ Low-Fat Milk | Carbohydrate Choices: 2 | Weight Watcher Smart Point Comparison: 4

Wholesome Blueberry Pancakes

These are a bit different than your typical all-flour pancakes as they include cottage cheese, which gives them a delicious, healthy new twist by lowering the refined carbohydrate and increasing the protein. The small curds of cheese melt just slightly during cooking to give each pancake a creamy, delectable texture while plump fresh blueberries add a sweet taste of fruit from the inside out. Wholesome has never tasted better!

MAKES 5 SERVINGS

½ cup all-purpose flour

½ cup white whole wheat flour

2 teaspoons baking powder

½ teaspoon baking soda

½ teaspoon ground cinnamon

¼ cup granulated no-calorie sweetener*

½ cup low-fat milk

1 cup low-fat cottage cheese

2 large eggs, well beaten

1 teaspoon vanilla extract

¾ cup fresh blueberries

1. In a medium bowl, mix together the flours, baking powder, baking soda, cinnamon, and sweetener.

2. In another bowl, whisk together the milk, cottage cheese, eggs, and vanilla extract.

3. Whisk the wet ingredients into the dry, being careful not to overmix. Fold in the blueberries.

4. Preheat a nonstick griddle or skillet over medium heat. Allow the pancake batter to rest while the griddle is preheating. Spray the griddle lightly with cooking spray.

5. Pour ¼ cup of batter per pancake and spread into a 4-inch circle. Cook the pancake for 3 to 4 minutes on the first side, until edges appear dry, some of the bubbles have popped, and the underside is browned. Flip the pancake and cook for another 2 to 3 minutes. The centers will puff and remain moist. Serve hot.

*See page 382 for sweetener options

NUTRITION INFORMATION PER SERVING (2 PANCAKES)
Calories 180 | Carbohydrate 27g (Sugars 5g) | Total Fat 3g (Sat Fat 1g) | Protein 12g | Fiber 3g | Cholesterol 90mg | Sodium 540mg | Food Exchanges: 1½ Bread, 1 Medium-Fat Meat | Carbohydrate Choices: 1½ | Weight Watcher Smart Point Comparison: 5

Fruit and Yogurt Breakfast Sundaes

There's no need to buy these pre-made when you can make them so easily right at home. Substituting the usual granola and sugar-sweetened yogurt with a less dense cereal and light yogurt more than halves the carbs and calories while allowing you to mix and match your own favorite berries and yogurt flavors. To make them "to go," layer the ingredients in 12-ounce plastic cups.

MAKES 2 SERVINGS

2 (6-ounce) containers of light Greek yogurt

1 cup fresh, sliced strawberries, raspberries, or mixed berries (or frozen thawed)

6 tablespoons flake and oat cluster cereal

1. Distribute one container of yogurt evenly between two glasses or cups.

2. Top yogurt with berries and cover with remaining container of yogurt.

3. Sprinkle 3 tablespoons of cereal over each of the sundaes.

DARE TO COMPARE.......................................

If you were to use regular low-fat yogurt, sweetened strawberries, and granola to make your sundae (as most restaurants do), the calories would soar to 300, the carbs would climb to 60 grams, and the fat would increase to 5 grams.

Marlene Says: To get a real fiber boost try sprinkling your sundae with 3 tablespoons of FiberOne cereal. It will add another 5 grams of fiber per serving.

NUTRITION INFORMATION PER SERVING ································
Calories 130 | Carbohydrate 21g (Sugars 14g) | Total Fat 1g (Sat Fat 0g) | Protein 13g | Fiber 2g | Cholesterol 5mg | Sodium 120mg | Food Exchanges: ½ Low-Fat Milk, ½ Starch, ½ Fruit | Carbohydrate Choices: 1 | Weight Watcher Smart Point Comparison: 3

Winning Appetizers

SKINNY DIP AND CHIPS

TOMATO BASIL BRUSCHETTA

HEALTHY HUMMUS

"HOMEMADE" SALSA IN A FLASH

SPICY JALAPEÑO CARROTS

CREAMY GUACAMOLE

CREAMY TUSCAN WHITE BEAN DIP

SMOKY BLUE CHEESE BACON DIP

SENSATIONAL SPINACH DIP

CLASSIC HOT ARTICHOKE DIP

SALMON MOUSSE SPREAD

HOMEMADE PITA CHIPS

OVEN-FRIED ZUCCHINI ROUNDS

STEAMED ARTICHOKES WITH CREAMY MUSTARD DIP

EASY SWEET-AND-SOUR MEATBALLS

BBQ CHICKEN QUESADILLAS

PEPPERONI PIZZA POPPERS

BUFFALO CHICKEN STRIPS WITH BLUE CHEESE DIP

SPICY SHRIMP WITH ASIAN APRICOT DIPPING SAUCE

SWEET 'N' SPICY NUTS AND BOLTS PARTY MIX

The right appetizer can set the perfect tone for a meal or make the party. And while most of us realize that appetizers are not always healthy, the phrase "killer appetizer" is far more accurate than you might expect. From eateries ranging from Denny's® to Chili's® to Outback Steakhouse®, appetizers are bigger, greasier, and more calorically dense than ever. To be specific, an Awesome Blossom™ fried onion appetizer serves up 2,700 calories, 203 grams of fat, 194 grams of carbohydrates, and 6,360 milligrams of sodium; a warm bowl of cheesy spinach and artichoke dip averages 1200 calories and 82 grams of fat (with half of them saturated); and even a "healthy" bruschetta appetizer can tack on over 700 calories, 40 grams of fat, and 80 grams of carbohydrate—all before your meal!

The wonderful news is that you do not need to give up your favorite appetizers for the sake of your health. The winning collection found in this chapter includes many of today's most popular appetizers along with traditional favorites and brand-new creations. As a dietitian I couldn't (nor would I want to) leave out the requisite healthy vegetables and dip, but this collection goes so much further—cheesy, creamy, gooey, sweet, and fried—whatever you crave it's all here (and now it's guilt-free).

Nothing says party like chips and dip, and this chapter is chock-full of your all-time favorites, starting with Creamy Guacamole with a sneaky mayonnaise substitute that makes it creamy with less fat and more protein. My cheesy Classic Hot Artichoke Dip tastes as decadent as ever, and easy man-pleasing Smoky Blue Cheese Bacon Dip is rich only in flavor. Beyond dips you will find crispy Oven-Fried Zucchini Rounds, Easy Sweet-and-Sour Meatballs, made sweet without the sugar, and Pepperoni (yes, pepperoni) Pizza Poppers that can send anyone into a pizza popping frenzy. For entertaining, the Tomato Basil Bruschetta has all the right moves, while the elegant Salmon Mousse Spread is sure to impress. I also find the Oven-Baked Onion Rings on page 249 and the Express Beef Lettuce Wraps on page 212 are sure-fire winners when served as appetizers.

Skinny Dip and Chips

A walk through the produce aisle inspired this healthy dip and chips combination. Ready-to-go pre-cut carrot "chips" caught my eye; along with cool cucumber slices that I thought would make the perfect healthy "chips" for everyone's favorite dip. After noting that the best-selling brand of reduced-fat buttermilk ranch dip has around thirty ingredients (including sugar and artificial colors and flavors) and costs a bundle, I decided to make my own. The result is a delicious ranch-style dip you can make in just minutes for a fraction of the cost and ingredients. This dip and chips combo is sure to become a new party favorite.

MAKES 8 SERVINGS

½ cup buttermilk

⅓ cup light mayonnaise

¼ cup plain nonfat yogurt

¾ teaspoon dried dill

½ teaspoon garlic powder

½ teaspoon onion powder

¼ teaspoon pepper

⅛ teaspoon salt

1 (16-ounce) package fresh carrot chips

1 medium cucumber, sliced into ¼-inch "chips"

1. In a small bowl, whisk the buttermilk, mayonnaise, yogurt, dill, garlic powder, onion powder, pepper, and salt together. Cover and place in the refrigerator to chill for 30 minutes before serving.

2. Serve the dip with vegetable chips.

DARE *TO* COMPARE
Regular potato chips and ranch-style dressing have five times the calories and ten times the fat as my Skinny Dip and Chips! A large handful of chips (1-ounce) and 2 tablespoons dip contain a staggering 340 calories, 18 grams of carbohydrate, and 30 grams of fat! (And, of course, none of the healthy vitamin C or fiber.)

NUTRITION INFORMATION PER SERVING (1 CUP CHIPS AND 2 TABLESPOONS DIP)
Calories 65 | Carbohydrate 8g (Sugars 4g) | Total Fat 3g (Sat Fat 0g) | Protein 2g | Fiber 2g | Cholesterol 0mg | Sodium 160mg | Food Exchanges: 1 Vegetable, ½ Fat | Carbohydrate Choices: ½ | Weight Watcher Smart Point Comparison: 2

Tomato Basil Bruschetta

This simple Italian starter is perfect when you're having guests and are not sure what to serve. It's easy to make, delicious, and, most important, everyone loves it. I make the tomato topping ahead of time and keep it in the fridge. I also prep my bread ahead of time for the crostini (little toasted breads in Italian), and lay them out on a sheet pan. All I have to do before my guests arrive is quickly bake or broil the bread and place my ready-to-go topping on the warm crostini. (To make it even easier, simply serve the tomato topping in a pretty bowl with a small spoon and the crostini in a basket alongside and let your guests do the rest.) Feel free to double the recipe as I often do.

MAKES 6 TO 8 SERVINGS

3 small fresh tomatoes, seeded and diced

2 tablespoons julienned fresh basil

1 tablespoon finely chopped shallot or onion

2 teaspoons minced garlic (2 cloves)

2 teaspoons extra-virgin olive oil

1 teaspoon balsamic vinegar

Pinch of salt

Black pepper to taste

½ of a sourdough or regular French baguette (22 to 24 inches long)

2 garlic cloves, peeled and cut in half

1. In a medium bowl, mix together the tomatoes, basil, shallot, garlic, olive oil, vinegar, salt, and pepper. Cover and place in the refrigerator.

2. Slice the bread on the diagonal to make 20 ½-inch slices. Lay the bread flat on a large sheet pan and spray lightly with nonstick cooking spray (olive oil flavor is nice).

3. When ready to serve, preheat the oven to 425°F. Bake for 5 minutes, or until lightly brown. (Or, you may place the bread under the broiler for 1 to 2 minutes.) Remove the bread from the oven and rub the sliced garlic across the surface of the crostini. Spoon about 1 tablespoon of the tomato topping on each slice and serve.

Marlene Says: Summer is the best time of year to find fresh, fragrant tomatoes and basil. To julienne the basil, first stack several leaves on top of one another and roll them together like a cigar. Then slice across the basil with a sharp knife to create long, slender, beautiful ribbons.

NUTRITION INFORMATION PER SERVING (4 PIECES)
Calories 85 | Carbohydrate 12g (Sugars 2g) | Total Fat 2g (Sat Fat 0g) | Protein 2g | Fiber 1g | Cholesterol 0mg Sodium 140mg | Food Exchanges: 1 Starch | Carbohydrate Choices: 1 | Weight Watcher Smart Point Comparison: 2

Healthy Hummus

This simple, savory Middle Eastern spread made with beans is both healthy and versatile. Although eaten most often as a dip with vegetables or pita chips, it also makes a great spread for sandwiches and can be flavored a number of ways. Here I keep true to the popular classic recipe and flavor it with just the essentials, but a couple of tablespoons of either roasted red pepper or sun-dried tomatoes also can be added. To give it some kick, try adding roasted garlic or jalapeño peppers. Covered tightly in the refrigerator hummus keeps well for up to two weeks!

MAKES 7 SERVINGS

1 (15-ounce) can garbanzo beans, drained and rinsed

2 tablespoons lemon juice

2 tablespoons tahini

1 teaspoon minced garlic (1 clove)

¼ teaspoon salt

Pinch of cayenne pepper

1 tablespoon olive oil

3 to 4 tablespoons warm water

1. Place the garbanzo beans, lemon juice, tahini, garlic, salt, and cayenne pepper in a food processor and begin to process. Slowly add the olive oil and continue to process for 1 to 1½ minutes, or until smooth, or almost smooth.

2. Add 3 tablespoons of water and continue to process until hummus is completely smooth, scraping down the sides of the bowl as necessary. Add remaining water as needed to reach the desired thickness. Remove the hummus from the food processor and place in a bowl.

3. Cover and chill until ready to serve.

Marlene Says: All hummus is not created equal. While hummus can be a healthy choice, some brands contain far more fat (and therefore calories) than others. If you purchase pre-made hummus instead of making your own, look for a brand that has no more than 7 grams of fat in each 3-tablespoon serving.

NUTRITION INFORMATION PER SERVING (3 TABLESPOONS)
Calories 95 | Carbohydrate 10g (Sugars 0g) | Total Fat 5g (Sat Fat 0g) | Protein 3g | Fiber 3g | Cholesterol 0mg | Sodium 90mg | Food Exchanges: ½ Starch, 1 Fat | Carbohydrate Choices: ½ | Weight Watcher Smart Point Comparison: 2

"Homemade" Salsa in a Flash

When it comes to dips, salsa is the most popular good-for-you choice there is. I once worked for a catering company where we made lots of salsa. It was there where I learned this quick method for making salsa that looks and tastes completely homemade but takes only minutes to prepare. Combining just a few fresh ingredients with your favorite store-bought salsa is the behind-the-scenes trick.

MAKES 16 SERVINGS

1 (15-ounce) tub or jar salsa

4 medium ripe tomatoes (about 1 pound)

¼ cup diced red onion

3 tablespoons chopped fresh cilantro

Squeeze of fresh lime juice (optional)

1. Place the store-bought salsa in a medium bowl.

2. Cut the tomatoes in half. Gently squeeze out most of the seeds into a small dish and discard. Chop the tomato into small pieces and add to the salsa.

3. Add the onion, cilantro, and lime juice and mix well.

4. Serve with your favorite Mexican entrée or as a dip with low-fat tortilla chips or fresh vegetables.

NUTRITION INFORMATION PER SERVING (¼ CUP)
Calories 15 | Carbohydrate 2g (Sugars 1g) | Total Fat 0g (Sat Fat 0g) | Protein 1g | Fiber 1g | Cholesterol 0mg | Sodium 160mg | Food Exchanges: 1 Free Food | Carbohydrate Choices: 0 | Weight Watcher Smart Point Comparison: 0

Spicy Jalapeño Carrots

One of my favorite features at our local Mexican restaurant is their lovely salsa bar. While the salsa is good, it's the spicy pickled carrots that keep bringing me back. If you have never eaten pickled carrots, you are in for a real treat! Biting into one, you taste vinegar combined with a touch of sweetness followed by a pleasing bite of heat—all mingled with the naturally sweet flavor of tender crisp carrot. Serve a bowl of these before or with the meal. They pair well with a Mexican or Southwestern meal and just about any barbeque menu. (These will keep for several weeks stored in the fridge.)

MAKES 6 SERVINGS

½ cup white vinegar

1 tablespoon granulated sugar

2 garlic cloves, chopped

¾ teaspoon dried oregano

½ teaspoon salt

½ teaspoon whole black peppercorns

1 (6½-ounce) can sliced jalapeño peppers, liquid reserved

2¼ cups peeled, sliced carrots (about 4 medium carrots sliced diagonally)

1 cup sliced onion

1. In a medium saucepan, combine the vinegar, sugar, garlic, oregano, salt, and peppercorns. Spoon half of the jalapeños with 2 tablespoons liquid from the can into the saucepan.

2. Add the carrots and onion and bring to a simmer over medium heat. Cook for 3 minutes and remove from heat.

3. Cool to room temperature, cover, and refrigerate (preferably overnight). Serve cold.

Marlene Says: Vinegar has been found to lower the rate at which your blood sugar rises. Adding vinegar to carrots lowers their glycemic index and makes them more blood-sugar friendly.

NUTRITION INFORMATION PER SERVING (⅓ CUP)
Calories 35 | Carbohydrate 8g (Sugars 4g) | Total Fat 0g (Sat Fat 0g) | Protein 1g | Fiber 2g | Cholesterol 0mg | Sodium 130mg | Food Exchanges: 1 Vegetable | Carbohydrate Choices: ½ | Weight Watcher Smart Point Comparison: 1

Creamy Guacamole

It's not a fiesta until you serve the guacamole! Avocados are one of nature's healthiest foods because they are full of heart-healthy monounsaturated fats, contain natural antioxidants good for your skin and hair, and offer a surprisingly high dose of fiber. This recipe uses the fabulous trick of sneaking a touch of blended cottage cheese into the dish to create a luscious creamy guacamole that's lower in fat while higher in protein (and no one but you will know). Red pepper strips and baby carrots are great tortilla chip alternatives to serve with guacamole.

MAKES 6 SERVINGS

1 ripe avocado, peeled and pitted

⅓ cup low-fat cottage cheese

2 tablespoons fresh lime juice

2 tablespoons chopped red onion

1 small tomato, seeded and diced

Salt to taste

Few dashes Tabasco sauce

2 tablespoons chopped cilantro (optional)

1. Scoop the pulp of the avocado* and the cottage cheese into a food processor and process for 1 minute, scraping down sides of the bowl as necessary, until the mixture is smooth and creamy. (There should be no visible cottage cheese curds left.)

2. Place the creamed avocado mixture into a bowl. Add the lime juice, onion, tomato, salt, Tabasco, and cilantro and mix well. Taste and adjust the salt and cilantro as needed.

3. Serve immediately, or press plastic wrap onto surface of the dip and refrigerate until ready to serve.

   * To add texture, you may reserve some of the avocado and hand mash it into the creamed mixture before adding the other ingredients.

NUTRITION INFORMATION PER SERVING (¼ CUP)
Calories 70 | Carbohydrate 4g (Sugars 1g) | Total Fat 5g (Sat Fat 1g) | Protein 2g | Fiber 2g | Cholesterol 0mg | Sodium 150mg | Food Exchanges: 1 Fat | Carbohydrate Choices: 0 | Weight Watcher Smart Point Comparison: 2

Creamy Tuscan White Bean Dip

Cannellini beans are akin to a white kidney bean and are a popular staple in Italian cooking. Their mild flavor and creamy texture make them perfect to use as a dip base without the need for lots of added oil. Keeping true to Italian tradition, I have infused this dip with the great flavors of garlic, oregano, and rosemary.

MAKES 8 SERVINGS

1 (15-ounce) can white cannellini beans, rinsed and drained

⅓ cup low-fat cottage cheese

2 garlic cloves

2 tablespoons lemon juice

2½ tablespoons olive oil, separated

1 teaspoon minced fresh rosemary

1 teaspoon dried oregano

¼ teaspoon salt

1. Place the beans, cottage cheese, garlic, lemon juice, 1½ tablespoons of oil, herbs, and salt in a food processor and process for 1 to 1½ minutes until smooth, scraping down sides of bowl as necessary.

2. Transfer the dip to a serving bowl, cover, and refrigerate for 30 minutes or more to let flavors meld.

3. When ready to serve, remove the dip from refrigerator and let come to room temperature for best flavor. Garnish by drizzling the last tablespoon of olive oil across the top of the dip.

Marlene Says: Beans just keep getting better! New studies show that some of the starch in beans is resistant to digestion if they are cooked and then served cooled. Natural resistant starch, as it is called, acts like fiber rather than starch. In this recipe, an additional 2 grams of fiber in the form of natural resistant starch are found in each serving.

NUTRITION INFORMATION PER SERVING (3 TABLESPOONS)
Calories 90 | Carbohydrate 8g (Sugars 1g) | Total Fat 3g (Sat Fat .5g) | Protein 3g | Fiber 2g | Cholesterol 0mg | Sodium 210mg | Food Exchanges: ½ Starch, 1 Fat | Carbohydrate Choices: ½ | Weight Watcher Smart Point Comparison: 2

Smoky Blue Cheese Bacon Dip

No, you're not dreaming, this delectable, man-pleasing dip with the rich flavor of blue cheese and the smoky taste of bacon can now be a part of your healthy diet. Serve with a platter of crudités such as broccoli and cauliflower florets along with sticks of celery and carrots.

MAKES 12 SERVINGS

⅓ cup light mayonnaise

¼ cup crumbled blue cheese

½ cup light sour cream

½ cup plain low-fat yogurt

2 teaspoons white vinegar

¼ teaspoon liquid smoke

2 tablespoons real bacon bits

1 tablespoon finely chopped green onion (optional for garnish)

1. In a medium bowl, mix together the mayonnaise and the blue cheese. Mash some of the cheese into the mayonnaise with a fork for flavor, and leave some crumbles for texture.

2. Stir in the sour cream, yogurt, vinegar, liquid smoke, and 1 tablespoon of the bacon bits. Cover, place in refrigerator, and chill for 30 minutes to meld the flavors.

3. To serve, transfer the dip to a serving bowl and sprinkle with the last tablespoon of bacon bits and green onion if desired. (This is best served the same day it is made.)

NUTRITION INFORMATION PER SERVING (2 TABLESPOONS)
Calories 50 | Carbohydrate 2g (Sugars 1g) | Total Fat 4g (Sat Fat 1.5g) | Protein 2g | Fiber 0g | Cholesterol 5mg | Sodium 120mg | Food Exchanges: 1 Fat | Carbohydrate Choices: 0 | Weight Watcher Smart Point Comparison: 3

Sensational Spinach Dip

When I was growing up *one dish my mother was very proud of was her spinach dip. She referred to it as her "secret ingredients" dip. The secret ingredients were finely diced water chestnuts that melded into the dip for a secret crunch, and soy sauce that added a depth of flavor without revealing itself. Over the years I have made this dip on many occasions to rave reviews, but I was never comfortable with its high fat content. Now I am pleased to say that I have created a sensational low-fat version of this party staple—while keeping all of its flavorful secrets intact.*

MAKES 12 SERVINGS

½ cup light sour cream

½ cup light mayonnaise

¾ cup or 1 (8-ounce) container plain low-fat yogurt

½ teaspoon minced garlic

2 teaspoons reduced-sodium soy sauce

1 (8-ounce) can water chestnuts, drained and finely chopped

1 (10-ounce) package frozen chopped spinach, thawed and squeezed dry

¼ cup dried parsley

¼ cup dried minced onion

¾ teaspoon dried dill

1. In a medium bowl, whisk together the sour cream, mayonnaise, and yogurt. Add the garlic and mix well. Stir in the soy sauce and water chestnuts.

2. Add the spinach, parsley, onion, and dill and mix thoroughly.

3. Cover the dip and refrigerate until ready to serve.

DARE *TO* COMPARE
Traditional spinach dip recipes can contain as much as 210 calories and 22 grams of fat (5 grams of them saturated) in each serving.

NUTRITION INFORMATION PER SERVING (¼ CUP)
Calories 70 | Carbohydrate 4g (Sugars 2g) | Total Fat 4.5g (Sat Fat 1.5g) | Protein 3g | Fiber 1g | Cholesterol 5mg | Sodium 115mg | Food Exchanges: 1 Fat, 1 Vegetable | Carbohydrate Choices: 0 | Weight Watcher Smart Point Comparison: 2

Classic Hot Artichoke Dip

When it comes to hot dip recipes, hot artichoke dip is king. A perennial favorite at both restaurants and holiday parties, there's plenty to love about a dip that's so rich and creamy. Unfortunately, hot artichoke dip also tops the lists of dips not to eat if you are concerned about your health. This recipe, creamy as ever and rich in taste only, solves the dilemma. Place it in the oven just before your guests arrive and serve warm.

MAKES 10 SERVINGS

⅓ cup light tub-style cream cheese

⅓ cup light mayonnaise

⅓ cup light sour cream

1 teaspoon minced garlic (1 clove)

¼ teaspoon black pepper

½ cup white onion, finely diced

½ cup plus 2 tablespoons freshly grated Parmesan cheese

1 (10-ounce) package frozen artichoke hearts, thawed and chopped or 1 (14-ounce) can water-packed artichoke hearts, drained and chopped

1 (10-ounce) package chopped frozen spinach, thawed and squeezed dry

1. Preheat the oven to 350°F.

2. In a medium bowl, mix together the cream cheese, mayonnaise, sour cream, garlic, and black pepper.

3. Mix in the onion, ½ cup Parmesan, artichoke hearts, and spinach until well combined.

4. Spread the dip mixture into an 8-inch square baking dish.

5. Sprinkle the remaining 2 tablespoons of Parmesan over the top of the dip and bake for 20 to 25 minutes, or until the dip is hot. Serve warm.

Or try this: To make *Hot Artichoke Crab Dip,* substitute 1 cup lump crab meat for spinach (decreases carbohydrate content by 1.5 grams and increases protein content by 1.5 grams).

NUTRITION INFORMATION PER SERVING (¼ CUP)
Calories 100 | Carbohydrate 5g (Sugars 2g) | Total Fat 6g (Sat Fat 2.5g) | Protein 5g | Fiber 1g | Cholesterol 10mg | Sodium 290mg | Food Exchanges: 1 Vegetable, 1 Lean Meat, 1 Fat | Carbohydrate Choices: ½ | Weight Watcher Smart Point Comparison: 2

Salmon Mousse Spread

It's easy to get sidetracked and fall back on comforting rich foods when entertaining. Thus I adapted this super slim recipe from a recipe by Julee Rosso, one of the authors of The Silver Palate Cookbook. Here, I have converted her famous salmon mousse into a delectable, creamy salmon mousse spread that's just as delicious. I love that this is so easy to make, yet positively guest worthy. My favorite way to serve it is with unpeeled, sliced cucumber rounds, but crackers and flatbreads work beautifully as well.

MAKES 16 SERVINGS

2 tablespoons cold water

1 teaspoon unflavored gelatin (½ of a 1-ounce package)

¼ cup light tub-style cream cheese

½ cup low-fat cottage cheese

½ cup plain low-fat yogurt

¼ cup buttermilk

1 (6-ounce) can pink salmon, packed in water, well-drained (or ¾ cup flaked, cooked salmon)

1 tablespoon fresh lime juice

2 tablespoons minced fresh dill

½ tablespoon chopped fresh parsley or chervil

Pinch of cayenne pepper

1. Place the water in a very small microwavable cup or bowl. Sprinkle the gelatin evenly over the water. Set aside.

2. Place the cream cheese and cottage cheese in a food processor and process for 1 minute, or until completely smooth. Add the yogurt and buttermilk and process an additional 30 seconds.

3. Microwave the gelatin on high for 30 seconds, or until completely melted. Pour the gelatin into the food processor along with the salmon, lime juice, dill, parsley, and cayenne pepper. Process for 15 to 30 seconds, or until smooth.

4. Pour into a serving dish, cover, place in the refrigerator, and chill for at least 2 hours before serving. Garnish with additional fresh dill if desired.

NUTRITION INFORMATION PER SERVING (2 TABLESPOONS)
Calories 35 | Carbohydrate 1g (Sugars 1g) | Total Fat 1.5g (Sat Fat 0g) | Protein 5g | Fiber 0g | Cholesterol 20mg | Sodium 115mg | Food Exchanges: 1 Lean Meat | Carbohydrate Choices: 0 | Weight Watcher Smart Point Comparison: 1

Homemade Pita Chips

My son James recently fell in love with store-bought pita chips. Although the idea of these chips may sound healthy, a quick glimpse at the nutrition label reveals that some varieties of baked pita chips actually have more fat and calories than fried potato chips. The good news is that it's very easy to make wholesome pita chips at home. This basic recipe results in a crunchy, lightly seasoned chip that's great for dipping or spreads. Feel free to create your own unique flavors by sprinkling your favorite spices or herbs on the chips before baking.

MAKES 4 SERVINGS

2 (8-inch) whole wheat pita pockets

½ teaspoon garlic salt*

Cooking spray

* May omit or reduce to lower sodium content

1. Preheat the oven to 350°F.

2. Split each pita pocket in half by cutting along the seam and separating it into two thin rounds. Stack 2 rounds at a time and cut into six wedges (like a pie).

3. Spray a baking sheet with cooking spray. Place the pita pieces on the sheet and spray with an even coating of the cooking spray. Sprinkle evenly with the garlic salt.

4. Bake for 8 minutes, or until pita is crisp and golden brown.

Marlene Says: Plain pita bread can also vary quite a bit. Choose a whole wheat pita for extra fiber and check the label to be sure each pita has about 18 grams of carbohydrate per serving to keep the carbs down.

NUTRITION INFORMATION PER SERVING (6 CHIPS)
Calories 85 | Carbohydrate 17g (Sugars 1g) | Total Fat 1g (Sat Fat 0g) | Protein 3g | Fiber 2g | Cholesterol 0mg
Sodium 440mg | Food Exchanges: 1 Starch | Carbohydrate Choices: 1 | Weight Watcher Smart Point
Comparison: 3

Oven-Fried Zucchini Rounds

The trick to making crispy, healthy zucchini chips is to bake them in a hot oven on a wire rack. Baking them on the rack exposes all sides of the breaded rounds to the heat, crisping the seasoned breadcrumb Parmesan coating. One word of caution: you may want to double the recipe. When I was testing these I asked my husband to take a batch out of the oven while I ran an errand and when I returned, there were none left to taste! My "I don't really care for zucchini" husband had eaten the entire batch!

MAKES 4 SERVINGS

⅓ cup plain breadcrumbs

¼ cup freshly grated Parmesan cheese

½ teaspoon dried oregano

½ teaspoon garlic salt

2 large egg whites, lightly beaten

1 tablespoon water

2½ cups zucchini slices, cut ⅛-inch thick on the diagonal (about 2 medium zucchini)

1. Preheat the oven to 400°F. Place a wire rack on top of a baking sheet and spray with cooking spray.

2. In a wide, shallow bowl, mix together the breadcrumbs, Parmesan, oregano, and garlic salt.

3. In a separate bowl, beat together the egg white and water.

4. Dip each zucchini slice into the egg mixture; then roll in breadcrumbs. Place onto the wire rack and repeat until all of the zucchini has been coated.

5. Lightly spray with cooking spray and bake for 8 minutes. Serve hot.

DARE TO COMPARE

A single small serving of Fried Zucchini at Carl's Junior® contains almost twice as much sodium, four times the carbohydrates and calories, and eight times the fat as my Oven-Fried Zucchini Rounds.

NUTRITION INFORMATION PER SERVING (½ CUP)

Calories 80 | Carbohydrate 9g (Sugars 2g) | Total Fat 2.5g (Sat Fat 1.5g) | Protein 6g | Fiber 1g | Cholesterol 5mg | Sodium 350mg | Food Exchanges: ½ Vegetable, ½ Starch | Carbohydrate Choices: ½ | Weight Watcher Smart Point Comparison: 2

Steamed Artichokes with Creamy Mustard Dip

Steamed artichokes make a terrific appetizer. Modest in calories and high in fiber, eating artichokes adds a bit of fun before the meal as kids of all ages love to scrape the meat off the tender leaves with their teeth. Here, the microwave works fantastic for a quick-steam of the artichoke, and the mustard-tinged mayonnaise is not only healthier, but far more delicious than using mayonnaise or melted butter as a dip.

MAKES 4 TO 6 SERVINGS

2 large artichokes
⅓ cup light mayonnaise
⅓ cup light sour cream
1 tablespoon warm water
1 tablespoon yellow mustard
1 teaspoon cider vinegar
2 teaspoons granulated sugar

1. To prepare the artichokes, pull off any small or tough leaves near the base. Destem the artichoke. Trim the choke by slicing about 1 inch off the top. For the best presentation and to keep your fingers from getting pricked, trim off the thorny tips of the petals with a pair of scissors or kitchen shears. Rinse the artichokes.

2. Place the artichokes leaves side down into large microwavable dish and add about 1 inch of water. Cover the dish tightly with plastic wrap and microwave on high for about 10 minutes or until a knife easily pierces the stems and the leaves can be easily pulled off.

3. While the artichokes are steaming, prepare the dipping sauce by whisking together the mayonnaise, sour cream, water, mustard, vinegar, and sugar in a small bowl.

4. To eat the artichokes, peel off the leaves—one at a time—and dip the meaty underside into the dip and scrape off the meat with your teeth. When all of the fleshy outer leaves have been eaten, pull out the center core of thin immature leaves. Using a small spoon scrape out the thicket of fuzz, and discard. Beneath it lies the delicious heart of the artichoke.

NUTRITION INFORMATION PER SERVING (½ ARTICHOKE AND 3 TABLESPOONS DIP)
Calories 100 | Carbohydrate 12g (Sugars 4g) | Total Fat 5g (Sat Fat 1.5g) | Protein 2g | Fiber 4g | Cholesterol 10mg | Sodium 280mg | Food Exchanges: 1 Vegetable, 1 Fat, ½ Carbohydrate | Carbohydrate Choices: 1 | Weight Watcher Smart Point Comparison: 2

Easy Sweet-and-Sour Meatballs

The first time I used Splenda sweetener to create savory dishes was in my book, Fantastic Foods with Splenda. *Sweet-and-sour sauce was a natural for a makeover. Here I pair it with cocktail meatballs for a family favorite that quickly disappears at every party. I've provided an easy meatball recipe, but in a pinch you can use a pre-packaged brand. Be sure to check the nutrition label as many packaged brands are high in both fat and fillers.*

MAKES 10 SERVINGS

MEATBALLS

½ pound lean ground beef

½ pound lean turkey breast

½ cup milk

1 large egg

2 tablespoons dried minced onion

⅓ cup unseasoned bread-crumbs

2 tablespoons minced fresh parsley

½ teaspoon salt

¼ teaspoon pepper

SAUCE

⅓ cup ketchup

¼ cup cider vinegar

¼ cup granulated no-calorie sweetener*

2 teaspoons Worcestershire sauce

⅔ cup cold water

1 tablespoon plus 1 teaspoon cornstarch

1. Preheat the oven to 350°F.

2. To make the meatballs, in a large bowl, combine the ground beef, turkey, milk, egg, onion, breadcrumbs, parsley, salt, and pepper. Using slightly wet hands, roll the mixture into 1-inch balls and place on an ungreased baking sheet.

3. Bake for 15 minutes, or until the centers are no longer pink.

4. To make the sauce, in a small saucepan, combine the ketchup, vinegar, sweetener, Worcestershire sauce, water, and cornstarch. Place over medium heat and simmer until thickened and clear. Place the meatballs in the sauce, or pour sauce over meatballs and serve hot.

Marlene Says: A fun and less messy mixing technique is to simply place all of the meatball ingredients in a large, resealable plastic bag; close it, and knead ingredients together until it is well mixed. It's also a great way to get your kids into the kitchen!

*See page 382 for sweetener options

NUTRITION INFORMATION PER SERVING (3 MEATBALLS)·······················
Calories 130 | Carbohydrate 9g (Sugars 5g) | Total Fat 5g (Sat Fat 2g) | Protein 12g | Fiber 0g | Cholesterol 10mg | Sodium 480mg | Food Exchanges: 2 Lean Meat, ½ Carbohydrate | Carbohydrate Choices: ½ | Weight Watcher Smart Point Comparison: 3

BBQ Chicken Quesadillas

I originally developed this recipe for a cooking class for children with diabetes. My goal was to create something fun to make that would be easy, delicious, and nutritious. These cheesy, chicken-filled quesadillas with a BBQ twist are high in protein, calcium, and fiber, but low in fat and calories. Moreover, they satisfy picky kids and cheese-craving adults alike. Enjoy them as an appetizer, or serve them whole as a light lunch entrée or an afternoon snack. (If you eat the entire quesadilla, be sure to double the nutritional information.)

MAKES 4 SERVINGS

4 (8-inch) reduced-carb high-fiber flour tortillas

2 tablespoons barbeque sauce, divided

1 cup shredded cooked chicken breast, divided

⅔ cup reduced-fat Mexican cheese blend, divided

1. Spray a large nonstick skillet with cooking spray and place over medium-high heat.

2. Place 1 tortilla in the skillet and spread half the barbecue sauce over it. Add half the chicken to the tortilla. Sprinkle half the cheese on top. Cover with another tortilla. Cook for 2 minutes, or until the cheese begins to melt and the bottom of the tortilla is golden brown. Carefully flip the quesadilla and cook for another 2 to 3 minutes.

3. Repeat the steps with the remaining ingredients.

4. Cut each quesadilla into eight portions before serving.

Marlene Says: I use Mission Carb Balance Tortillas to make my quesadillas. The Fajita size fits perfectly in the bottom of a 9-inch skillet and has only 80 calories, 2 grams of fat, and 13 grams of carbohydrate. Better yet, each tortilla has a whopping 10 grams of fiber, making them an excellent addition to any diet.

NUTRITION INFORMATION PER SERVING (½ QUESADILLA OR 4 WEDGES)
Calories 140 | Carbohydrate 14g (Sugars 2g) | Total Fat 4.5g (Sat Fat 1g) | Protein 18g | Fiber 10g | Cholesterol 30mg | Sodium 460mg | Food Exchanges: 2 Lean Meat, ½ Starch | Carbohydrate Choices: 1 | Weight Watcher Smart Point Comparison: 3

Pepperoni Pizza Poppers

Not everything I make is popular with my two hungry boys, but they can't get enough of these soft pillows of biscuit dough filled with melted cheese and pepperoni. I have also taken a bit of license with the recipe title. Although they bear little resemblance to the popular deep-fried appetizers called poppers—the way my boys popped them in their mouths, I just had to call them "poppers."

MAKES 5 SERVINGS

Flour for dusting

1 (7.5-ounce) can refrigerated buttermilk biscuits

⅔ cup marinara sauce, divided

20 turkey pepperoni slices, divided

¾ cup shredded part-skim mozzarella cheese, divided

1 tablespoon grated Parmesan cheese

2 teaspoons dried oregano

1. Preheat the oven to 450°F.

2. Dust a cutting board with a small amount of flour. Place the biscuits on the board and use a rolling pin to flatten to a generous 2½-inch circle, using additional flour as needed to prevent sticking.

3. Spread 1 teaspoon of marinara sauce on one-half of each circle, avoiding the edges. Lay two slices of pepperoni on top of the sauce. Sprinkle 2 teaspoons of mozzarella over the pepperoni. Fold in half by bringing the empty side over the filling. Seal each popper by pressing down on the dough of the exposed edge with the tines of a fork.

4. Spray a cookie sheet with cooking spray. Place the poppers 1 inch apart on the baking sheet and spray the tops lightly with additional cooking spray. Sprinkle the tops with Parmesan and oregano.

5. Bake for 8 minutes, or until golden brown. Pop 'em while they're hot!

NUTRITION INFORMATION PER SERVING (2 POPPERS)
Calories 160 | Carbohydrate 22g (Sugars 4g) | Total Fat 4g (Sat Fat 1g) | Protein 8g | Fiber .5g | Cholesterol 10mg | Sodium 640mg | Food Exchanges: 1½ Starch, 1 Lean Meat | Carbohydrate Choices: 1½ | Weight Watcher Smart Point Comparison: 5

Buffalo Chicken Strips with Blue Cheese Dip

Spicy chicken wings are reported to have been invented back in 1964 when the owner of a bar in Buffalo, New York, had a few too many leftover wings and a handful of hungry mouths to feed. Boy, have chicken wings gained in popularity ever since! My husband and boys are all devout wing aficionados and they devour these. I serve these true to the original with blue cheese dip and crunchy celery and carrot sticks.

MAKES 4 SERVINGS

BLUE CHEESE DIP

¼ cup nonfat plain yogurt

¼ cup light sour cream

2 tablespoons light mayonnaise

3 tablespoons crumbled blue cheese

1 teaspoon white vinegar

BUFFALO CHICKEN STRIPS

¼ teaspoon garlic powder

¼ teaspoon onion powder

1½ tablespoons hot sauce (more if you like them HOT)

2 teaspoons vegetable oil

½ pound boneless chicken breasts or tenders, cut into ¼-inch strips

2 teaspoons butter

Black pepper to taste

3 celery stalks, cut into sticks

2 carrots, cut into sticks (or ¾ cup baby carrots)

1. To make the dip, in a small bowl, whisk together the yogurt, sour cream, mayonnaise, blue cheese, and vinegar. Cover and refrigerate.

2. For the strips, in another small bowl, mix the garlic and onion powders with the hot sauce and set aside.

3. Heat the oil in a large nonstick skillet over medium-high heat. Add the chicken and cook 3 to 4 minutes, turning frequently, until browned and almost cooked through. Add the hot sauce mixture and butter to the skillet. Swirl the chicken in the sauce and cook for 1 to 2 additional minutes, or until the sauce completely coats the chicken. Season with black pepper.

4. Place the bowl of blue cheese dip in the center of a platter and surround it with the chicken, celery, and carrot sticks. Provide toothpicks or small forks to dip the chicken into the dip.

> **DARE *TO* COMPARE** · · · · · · · · · · · · · · · · · · ·
> It's hard to believe just 5 little chicken wings could have so many calories. At Ruby Tuesday®, even if you *share* an order of Buffalo Chicken Strips, you are gobbling down 472 calories and a staggering 28 grams of fat before you even get your entrée.

NUTRITION INFORMATION PER SERVING (¼ RECIPE) ·
Calories 180 | Carbohydrate 7g (Sugars 5g) | Total Fat 10g (Sat Fat 4g) | Protein 15g | Fiber 2g | Cholesterol 45mg | Sodium 230mg | Food Exchanges: 2 Lean-Meat, 1 Vegetable, 1 Fat | Carbohydrate Choices: ½ Weight Watcher Smart Point Comparison: 5

Spicy Shrimp with Asian Apricot Dipping Sauce

If you're looking for an easy recipe with tons of flavor, try these spicy, garlicky shrimp paired with an incredible dipping sauce. This recipe combines the sweetness of apricots with soy sauce and sesame oil for an authentic Asian flavor that can't be beat. High in protein and low in calories, these make a great addition to any appetizer spread.

MAKES 6 SERVINGS

24 extra-large shrimp (about 1 pound, 21 to 26 count), peeled with tails on

¼ teaspoon red chili flakes (½ teaspoon for extra spicy)

1 teaspoon minced garlic (1 clove)

2 teaspoons olive oil

¼ cup reduced-sugar apricot jam

2 tablespoons reduced-sodium soy sauce

1 tablespoon natural rice wine vinegar

1 teaspoon ketchup

½ teaspoon sesame oil

Chopped cilantro for garnish

1. Place the shrimp in a medium bowl and toss thoroughly with chili flakes, garlic, and olive oil. Set aside.

2. In a small microwavable serving bowl, combine the jam, soy sauce, vinegar, ketchup, and sesame oil. Mix well. (The jam will not completely mix in.) Microwave for 30 to 45 seconds, or until jam melts. Remove, stir, and set aside.

3. Spray a large nonstick sauté pan with cooking spray and place over high heat. When the pan is hot, lay the shrimp in the pan, leaving space around each shrimp. (This will need to be done in two batches.) Sear for 1 to 1½ minutes per side, pressing down on the shrimp as necessary to ensure nice browning.

4. Place the sauce in the middle of a platter and surround it with the shrimp. Garnish with the chopped cilantro.

DARE *TO* COMPARE ....
Outback Steakhouse® is famous for their coconut shrimp. Just three shrimp (half of an appetizer order) contain 345 calories, 15 grams of fat, 19 grams of carbohydrate, but only 6 grams of protein. Shrimp can be a caloric bargain, but breading, oil, and coconut are not.

NUTRITION INFORMATION PER SERVING (4 SHRIMP) ·····················
Calories 80 | Carbohydrate 4g (Sugars 0g) | Total Fat 1.5g (Sat Fat 0g) | Protein 13g | Fiber 0g | Cholesterol 120mg | Sodium 450mg | Food Exchanges: 1 Lean Meat | Carbohydrate Choices: 0 | Weight Watcher Smart Point Comparison: 2

Sweet 'n' Spicy Nuts and Bolts Party Mix

While new reduced-fat versions of snack mixes abound, it doesn't necessarily mean they are healthy (especially when you need to control your blood sugar). To lower the fat and calories, manufacturers usually remove heart-healthy nuts and add refined cereals. To create a more blood-sugar friendly mix, I combined wholesome grains, peanuts, and pretzels to create a snack that is higher in protein and fiber and lower in sugar and carbohydrates than most commercial brands.

MAKES 12 SERVINGS

1 cup Wheat Chex®

1½ cups Cheerios® cereal

2 cups pretzel sticks

1½ cups roasted, unsalted peanuts

1 large egg white

½ cup granulated no-calorie sweetener*

1 tablespoon Cajun seasoning

¼ teaspoon dried thyme

1 tablespoon butter

1. Preheat the oven to 350°F.

2. In a large bowl, mix together the Chex, Cheerios, pretzels sticks, and peanuts.

3. In a small saucepan, whisk together the egg white, sweetener, and Cajun seasoning. Crush the thyme between your fingers as you add it to pan. Whisk and place over low heat. Add the butter and heat gently just until the butter is melted and the egg white liquefies (do not heat too high, or the egg white will cook).

4. Pour the egg white mixture over the cereal mixture and toss well to coat all pieces evenly. Spread evenly on a baking sheet and bake for 30 minutes. Remove from the oven and cool.

*See page 382 for sweetener options

NUTRITION INFORMATION PER SERVING (½ CUP)
Calories 180 | Carbohydrate 18g (Sugars 1g) | Total Fat 10g (Sat Fat 2g) | Protein 7g | Fiber 3g | Cholesterol 0mg | Sodium 290mg | Food Exchanges: 1 Starch, 1 High-Fat Meat, 1 Fat | Carbohydrate Choices: 1 | Weight Watcher Smart Point Comparison: 5

Quick-Fix Soups and Chilis

CHICKEN TORTILLA SOUP

CREAMY BROCCOLI CHEDDAR SOUP

ROTISSERIE CHICKEN NOODLE SOUP

ANY DAY BEEF BARLEY VEGETABLE STOUP

5-MINUTE EGG DROP SOUP

SPEEDY BLACK BEAN SOUP WITH JALAPEÑO CREAM

"CREAM" OF BUTTERNUT SQUASH SOUP

CHUNKY CHICKEN MINESTRONE SOUP

ITALIAN SAUSAGE AND ESCAROLE SOUP

CREAMY BASIL TOMATO SOUP

SPAGHETTI AND MEATBALL SOUP

"CUP OF RED" CLAM CHOWDER

CREAMY SEAFOOD CHOWDER

CHICKEN CORN CHOWDER

SUPER CHILI

QUICK-FIX WHITE CHICKEN CHILI

Cookbook authors Carla Snyder and Meredith Deeds describe soup as "comfort in a bowl, love on a spoon, and satisfaction simmering on the stove"—I could not say it better. Soup is the original one-pot meal because it often requires no more than a few ingredients and a nice sturdy pot. There are few aromas that whet the appetite like a simmering soup. It's no wonder that Americans consume ten billion bowls of soup a year.

You just can't go wrong with soup. That said, many of us have abandoned making soups because we perceive they take too long to make. While developing this chapter I once again realized, and you will too, that making the flavorful, decadent-tasting soups you love can be both easy and quick! In fact, more than half of those in this chapter can be on the table—from start to finish—in less than 30 minutes. The remaining soups take only a few minutes longer.

In this section you will find fourteen scrumptious soups and two nutritious chilis that are perfect for a quick meal or last-minute gatherings. I am thrilled to bring you some of my all-time favorites: Chicken Tortilla Soup, Speedy Black Bean Soup with a luscious Jalapeño Cream, and an incredible curried "Cream" of Butternut Squash Soup along with quick-'n'-healthy versions of restaurant classics, such as Creamy Broccoli Cheddar Soup (this delectable version boasts 75 percent less fat and calories than typical restaurant versions), "Cup of Red" Clam Chowder, and Chunky Chicken Minestrone. If you enjoy belly-warming chilis, the meat-and-bean chili is delivered with a whisper of barbecue flavor, and the fabulous white chicken chili with canned green chilies is the quickest chili you will ever find.

When comparing nutritional information please note while manufacturers and many healthy soup recipes always use one cup as the serving size, I do not. For cream soups and those that are likely to accompany a meal, such as 5-Minute Egg Drop Soup, a one-cup serving is fine, but for soups that are more likely to be eaten as a meal, such as the Chunky Chicken Minestrone or Spaghetti and Meatball Soup, the serving size (and the corresponding nutrition information), is for a meal-size serving—a bowlful (or at least 1½ cups).

Chicken Tortilla Soup

Because this is one of my favorite soups, I much prefer to make it at home rather than risk being disappointed with restaurant versions that dilute the authentic flavor by adding thickeners like flour, loads of melted cheese (or worse, cheese spreads), and heaps of fried tortilla chips. When left simple, this is a vibrant and satisfying soup that can be made in just minutes. Part of the fun (and a traditional ritual in our house) is adding the extra garnishes. I usually top each bowl of soup with tortilla strips before serving, but feel free to serve the strips in a bowl next to a plate of fresh cilantro and lime wedges, so everyone can choose their own garnishes.

MAKES 4 SERVINGS

3 corn tortillas

1 tablespoon olive oil

1 small onion, diced

¾ teaspoon cumin

⅛ teaspoon turmeric

2 teaspoons finely chopped jarred jalapeño slices (or 1 fresh jalapeño seeded and diced)

½ cup corn niblets (frozen or canned, drained)

2 (14-ounce) cans, or 4 cups, reduced-sodium chicken broth

¾ pound skinless, boneless chicken breast

1 tomato, seeded and diced

Fresh cilantro, for garnish

Fresh lime wedges, for garnish

Grated reduced-fat Monterey Jack cheese (optional)

1. Preheat the oven to 400°F. Slice the tortillas into thin strips and place on a baking sheet. Spray with cooking spray and sprinkle lightly with salt if desired. Place the strips in the oven and cook for 10 minutes, or until browned and crisp, turning once during cooking.

2. Heat the oil in a medium soup pot over medium heat. Add the onion and sauté for 3 to 4 minutes, or until soft. Add the cumin, turmeric, and jalapeño, and sauté for 1 minute. Add the corn and broth and cook for 10 minutes to integrate flavors. Add the chicken, cover and simmer on medium low for 20 minutes.

3. Remove the chicken and stir in the tomato. Shred chicken with fork and divide among four bowls. Ladle the soup over the chicken and top with tortilla strips. Serve cilantro, lime wedges, and cheese if desired along side soup.

Marlene Says: A jar of sliced jalapeños is a good pantry staple. Unlike fresh jalapeños they do not require seeding before using and are soft, which allows them to quickly meld into soups or stews. For a mild chili-flavored broth with less heat, substitute one 4-ounce can of diced green chiles for the jalapeños.

NUTRITION INFORMATION PER SERVING (1½ CUPS) ···
Calories 230 | Carbohydrate 19g (Sugars 4g) | Total Fat 6g (Sat Fat 1g) | Protein 23g | Fiber 3g | Cholesterol 30mg | Sodium 590mg | Food Exchanges: 3 Lean Meat, 1 Starch, 1 Vegetable, ½ Fat | Carbohydrate Choices: 1 | Weight Watcher Smart Point Comparison: 5

Creamy Broccoli Cheddar Soup

Most creamy, cheesy soups contain too much fat to ever be considered healthy, but this soup is a delicious exception! The secret is using reduced-fat sharp cheddar cheese and nonfat half-and-half to create the taste and texture of "rich and creamy" without the fat or calories. This belly-filling soup also delivers a healthy dose of the antioxidant vitamins A and C along with bone-building calcium. To make it vegetarian, simply use reduced-sodium vegetable broth instead of chicken broth.

MAKES 6 SERVINGS

2 teaspoons olive oil

¾ cup chopped green onion

2 garlic cloves, minced

¾ teaspoon dried thyme

2 (14-ounce) cans, or 4 cups, reduced-sodium chicken broth

12 ounces (or about 5 cups) fresh broccoli florets

1½ tablespoon cornstarch

⅔ cup nonfat half-and-half

Pinch of cayenne

½ teaspoon salt (optional)

¾ cup shredded reduced-fat sharp cheddar cheese

1. Heat the oil in a medium pot over medium-low heat. Add the green onion and garlic and cook for 3 to 4 minutes, or until the onion is soft. With your fingers, crush the thyme into the pot, and stir.

2. Add the broth and broccoli. Cover and simmer for 8 to 10 minutes, or until the broccoli is tender but not mushy. Transfer the soup to a blender or food processor, and purée until smooth. Pour the soup back into the pot.

3. In a small bowl, whisk together the cornstarch and half-and-half. Pour the mixture into the soup. Add the cayenne pepper and additional salt if desired. Gently heat to a low simmer for 5 minutes, or until soup thickens slightly. Stir the cheese into the soup, cook for 1 minute, and serve.

DARE *TO* COMPARE

The average cup of broccoli cheddar soup at your local sandwich shop contains 280 calories, 18 grams of fat (with 9 of them saturated), 18 grams of carbohydrate, and 1,000 milligrams of sodium.

NUTRITION INFORMATION PER SERVING (1 CUP)
Calories 110 | Carbohydrate 10g (Sugars 4g) | Total Fat 4.5g (Sat Fat 2g) | Protein 10g | Fiber 3g | Cholesterol 10mg | Sodium 460mg | Food Exchanges: 1 Lean Protein, 1½ Vegetable, ½ Fat | Carbohydrate Choices: ½ | Weight Watcher Smart Point Comparison: 3

Rotisserie Chicken Noodle Soup

Now you can have all the goodness of home-style chicken noodle soup in just 30 minutes—without the fuss! Loaded with chunky carrots and celery, freshly cooked noodles, and plenty of chicken, this flavorful meal-in-a-bowl kicks its competitors to the curb. The trick to giving this soup the taste and texture of slow-cooked in just minutes is a store-bought rotisserie chicken. You may never go back to making chicken soup the old-fashioned way again.

MAKES 6 SERVINGS

1 tablespoon olive oil

2 medium carrots, sliced thick on the diagonal (about 1 cup)

2 celery stalks, sliced thick on the diagonal

1 small onion, diced

2 garlic cloves, minced

1 teaspoon dried thyme

3 (14-ounce) cans, or 6 cups, reduced-sodium chicken broth

2 cups uncooked wide noodles

1 store-bought rotisserie chicken

¼ teaspoon black pepper

1. Heat the oil in a large soup pot over medium-high heat. Add the carrots, celery, onion, and garlic and sauté for 5 to 6 minutes, or until the onion is softened and vegetables are beginning to brown. Use your fingers to crush the thyme into the vegetables, and stir.

2. Add the chicken broth, cover, and simmer for 5 minutes. Remove the lid and add the noodles. Cover and cook for 10 minutes, or until the noodles are tender.

3. While the noodles are cooking, remove the skin from the chicken breasts and thighs and shred the meat to equal about three cups. (Save legs and wings for another use.) Add the shredded chicken and black pepper to the pot and simmer for 5 minutes.

NUTRITION INFORMATION PER SERVING (1 ¼ CUPS)
Calories 215 | Carbohydrate 13g (Sugars 3g) | Total Fat 6g (Sat Fat 1g) | Protein 26g | Fiber 2g | Cholesterol 75mg | Sodium 550mg | Food Exchanges: 3 Lean Meat, 2 Vegetable, ½ Starch | Carbohydrate Choices: 1 | Weight Watcher Smart Point Comparison: 4

Any Day Beef Barley Vegetable Stoup

Barley is a terrific grain choice for anyone concerned with type 2 diabetes or pre-diabetes. It's an excellent source of dietary fiber, including beta-glucan, a soluble fiber that helps to lower blood sugar. Adding it to your diet is easy with this hearty, warming, stick-to-your ribs "stoup" (a cross between a stew and a soup). Tender canned beef and frozen vegetables and instant or quick-cooking barley make this stoup a snap to prepare even on the busiest of days.

MAKES 6 SERVINGS

1 tablespoon olive oil

1 small onion, chopped

2 stalks celery, chopped

2 teaspoons garlic powder

2 teaspoons dried thyme

1 (28-ounce) can whole tomatoes

2 (14-ounce) cans, or 4 cups, reduced-sodium beef broth

⅓ cup quick-cooking pearled barley*

1 (12-ounce) can beef with gravy

1 (10-ounce) bag frozen mixed vegetables

½ teaspoon black pepper

1 tablespoon Worcestershire sauce

*For regular pearl barley add an additional 20 to 30 minutes to cooking time.

1. Heat the oil in a large soup pot over medium heat. Add the onion and celery and cook for 5 minutes, or until slightly softened. Add the garlic powder. Using your fingers, crush the thyme into the pot, and cook for 1 minute.

2. Use your hands to break apart the tomatoes before adding them to the pot. Add the tomato liquid and all the remaining ingredients. Bring to a boil, cover and simmer for 20 minutes.

Marlene Says: Although convenient, canned foods are often high in sodium. You may reduce the sodium in this dish by substituting no-salt-added canned tomatoes (subtract 160 mg per serving) and/or low-sodium beef broth (subtract 220 mg per serving).

NUTRITION INFORMATION PER SERVING (1½ CUPS)
Calories 180 | Carbohydrate 23g (Sugars. 4g) | Total Fat 4g (Sat Fat 1g) | Protein 16g | Fiber 5g | Cholesterol 70mg | Sodium 820mg | Food Exchanges: 2 Lean Meat, 2 Vegetable, ½ Starch | Carbohydrate Choices: 1½ | Weight Watcher Smart Point Comparison: 3

5-Minute Egg Drop Soup

A steaming bowl of egg drop soup is the perfect accompaniment to any Asian meal. Fortunately, egg drop soup is one of the easiest and quickest soups you can make. To keep the egg strands from getting tough or rubbery be sure to take the soup off the heat soon after stirring in the egg.

MAKES 4 SERVINGS

½ teaspoon canola oil

1 teaspoon minced fresh or jarred ginger

2 (14-ounce) cans reduced-sodium chicken broth

2 teaspoons cornstarch

2 teaspoons water

1 large egg

4 green onions, sliced

Fresh cracked black pepper to taste

1. Heat the oil in a medium pot over medium-high heat. Add the ginger and sauté until warmed. Add the chicken broth and heat until simmering. In a small bowl or cup, dissolve the cornstarch into the water. Stir into the soup and cook until soup clears, about 1 minute.

2. In a small bowl whisk the egg until well beaten. Slowly stream the egg into the simmering soup. As soon as the egg sets, stir gently and remove from the heat. Add the green onions and ladle into bowls. Add the fresh pepper to each bowl to taste.

Fit Tip: Adding clear broth, low-calorie soups to meals has been shown to help reduce the total calories consumed and aid in weight loss.

NUTRITION INFORMATION PER SERVING (1 CUP)
Calories 50 | Carbohydrate 3g (Sugars 0g) | Total Fat 2.5g (Sat Fat 1.5g) | Protein 4g | Fiber 0g | Cholesterol 55mg | Sodium 490mg | Food Exchanges: 1 Fat | Carbohydrate Choices: 0 | Weight Watcher Smart Point Comparison: 1

Speedy Black Bean Soup with Jalapeño Cream

This soup is fast, fit, and fantastic! Convenient canned beans complemented with fresh ingredients and savory seasonings make a thick bean soup that's short on preparation time but long on flavor. Although it can be served without the jalapeño cream, adding it really makes the soup look and taste extra special. You can also try a light sprinkling of cheese, light sour cream, a squeeze of fresh lime, and/or thin slices of fresh avocado as additional (or alternate) garnishes.

MAKES 4 SERVINGS

2 teaspoons olive oil

2 garlic cloves, minced

1 small red onion, diced

½ red bell pepper, diced

2 (15-ounce) cans black beans, drained and rinsed

1 (14-ounce) can, or 2 cups, reduced-sodium chicken broth

2 tablespoons finely chopped cilantro

1½ teaspoon cumin

1½ dried oregano

Pinch of cayenne

¼ cup light sour cream

¼ cup low-fat plain yogurt

1 tablespoon minced cilantro, plus additional for garnish

1 teaspoon finely chopped jalapeño chili (fresh or jarred)

2 tablespoons sherry

½ teaspoon liquid smoke

1. Heat the olive oil in a large soup pot over medium heat. Add the garlic, onion, and bell pepper, and cook about 5 minutes, until the onion and pepper are tender.

2. Add the black beans, broth, chopped cilantro, cumin, oregano, and cayenne and bring to a boil. Reduce heat and simmer covered for 20 minutes, stirring occasionally.

3. To make the jalapeño cream, combine the sour cream, yogurt, minced cilantro, and jalapeño in a small bowl. Set aside.

4. After 20 minutes, add the sherry and liquid smoke to the soup. Stir well and remove the soup from the heat. Ladle half (or more if desired) of the soup into a blender (or use an immersion blender), and purée the soup. Return the puréed soup to the pot and heat for 5 more minutes.

5. To serve, top each bowl of soup with a dollop of the jalapeño cream and additional cilantro garnish, if desired.

Marlene Says: Beans are jam-packed with fiber. The fiber in beans not only reduces "bad" cholesterol, but helps to keep blood sugar in check. A healthy goal is to eat at least 25 grams of fiber daily.

NUTRITION INFORMATION PER SERVING (1¼ CUPS)
Calories 240 | Carbohydrate 36g (Sugars 9g) | Total Fat 5g (Sat Fat 1.5g) | Protein 15g | Fiber13g | Cholesterol 5mg | Sodium 475mg | Food Exchanges: 2 Lean Meat, 2 Starch, ½ Fat | Carbohydrate Choices: 2 | Weight Watcher Smart Point Comparison:5

"Cream" of Butternut Squash Soup

This "sneaky" soup will wow the entire family with its rich taste and creamy texture, and I guarantee that no one will ever guess the secret ingredient: heart-healthy silken tofu. And while tofu is what gives this soup its thick and creamy texture, it's the flavor of butternut squash, curry, and ginger that really stand out. (To omit tofu, stir 1 tablespoon cornstarch into an additional ¾ cup nonfat half-and-half and add in step 4.)

MAKES 6 SERVINGS

1 tablespoon olive oil

1 medium onion, diced

1 (2½-pound) butternut squash (or 2 to 2½ cups mashed butternut squash)

8 ounces lite silken tofu

½ cup nonfat half-and-half

2½ cups reduced-sodium chicken broth

2 teaspoons curry powder

1½ teaspoons fresh ginger, grated or from a jar

1½ teaspoons brown sugar

½ cup sherry

Salt and pepper to taste

1. Heat the olive oil in a soup pot over medium heat. Add the onions and sauté for 15 minutes, or until soft and caramelized.

2. While the onions are cooking, place the whole squash in the microwave and cook for 5 minutes. Remove from microwave and cut in half. Scoop out the seeds and place halves, cut side down, in a glass or ceramic baking dish. Pour 2 tablespoons of water in the bottom of the dish and cover with plastic wrap. Microwave for 10 more minutes, or until squash is soft when pricked with a fork.

3. Scoop out the flesh of the squash and place it in a blender or food processor. Add the tofu and half-and-half to the blender. When the onions are caramelized, add the broth to the pot and stir. Scoop out a couple ladles of the broth and add to the blender. Pulse until smooth, adding more broth as necessary. Work in batches, if necessary, to purée all of the squash mixture with all of the broth.

4. Pour the soup back into the pot. Add the curry powder, ginger, and brown sugar. Stir well and simmer for 10 minutes. Pour in the sherry and cook for 5 more minutes. Add salt and pepper to taste.

NUTRITION INFORMATION PER SERVING (1 CUP)
Calories 110 | Carbohydrate 15g (Sugars 5g) | Total Fat 2g (Sat Fat 0g) | Protein 5g | Fiber 3g | Cholesterol 0mg | Sodium 280mg | Food Exchanges: 1 Starch, ½ Lean Meat | Carbohydrate Choices: 1 | Weight Watcher Smart Point Comparison: 2

Chunky Chicken Minestrone Soup

I find this pot of soup perfect for any family gathering, whether it's a casual Sunday supper or enjoying a favorite sport on television. Just be sure to use a large pot because this recipe makes a generous twelve cups of soup. Chock full of vegetables, it has all the great flavors of the Italian classic, but here the addition of chicken in place of pasta creates a meal-worthy soup that truly satisfies with far less starch (meaning you can guiltlessly enjoy that must-have roll or breadstick). The Everyday Mixed Greens Salad with Italian Vinaigrette on page 173 would round out the meal nicely.

MAKES 8 SERVINGS

1 tablespoon olive oil

2 boneless, skinless chicken breasts, cut into bite-size pieces (about 12 ounces)

1 medium onion, diced

4 garlic cloves, minced

1 teaspoon dried basil

1 teaspoon dried oregano

2 medium carrots, sliced

½ small cabbage, shredded (about 3 cups)

2 medium zucchini, sliced on the diagonal

2 (14-ounce) cans, or 4 cups, reduced-sodium chicken broth

1 (15-ounce) can, or 2 cups, reduced-sodium beef broth

1 (28-ounce) can Italian crushed tomatoes

1 (15-ounce) can Great Northern beans, drained and rinsed

2 tablespoons minced fresh parsley

⅓ cup grated Parmesan cheese

1. Heat the olive oil in a large soup pot over medium heat. Add the chicken and sauté for 2 to 3 minutes, or until slightly browned. Add the onion and cook for 2 more minutes, or until the onions are slightly softened. Add the garlic, spices, carrots, cabbage, and zucchini. Sauté, stirring for 5 to 8 minutes, or until all the vegetables are coated with oil and the zucchini is softened.

2. Add the broths and tomatoes, cover, and simmer for 30 minutes. Add the beans and parsley, and simmer uncovered for 10 additional minutes.

3. Serve with Parmesan cheese or top each bowl with 2 teaspoons before serving.

Family Focus: This soup is the perfect way to sneak more veggies into your kids' diets. Loaded with great Italian flavor and topped with cheese it's hard to resist. It's also an excellent source of vitamin A (providing more than an entire day's worth), vitamin C, iron, and calcium.

NUTRITION INFORMATION PER SERVING (1½ CUPS)

Calories 180 | Carbohydrate 23g (Sugars 9g) | Total Fat 4.5g (Sat Fat 1.5g) | Protein 19g | Fiber 6g | Cholesterol 25mg | Sodium 690mg | Food Exchanges: 2 Lean Meat, 2 Vegetables, ½ Starch | Carbohydrate Choices: 1½ | Weight Watcher Smart Point Comparison: 5

Italian Sausage and Escarole Soup

If you've ever been to the Olive Garden restaurants and enjoyed a bowl of their Toscana soup, you've already experienced the delicious combination of potatoes, kale, and Italian sausage. My rendition of this extremely flavorful soup is both lighter and faster but doesn't forsake any of the fabulous taste. To reduce the fat I use low-fat evaporated milk thickened with a touch of cornstarch; for extra flavor I add lean smoked sausage; and to reduce the cooking time tender escarole replaces longer cooking kale. The fact that just a few healthy ingredients can combine so quickly into something as delicious as this soup is amazing.

MAKES 4 SERVINGS

6 ounces lite smoked sausage

2 (14-ounce) cans, or 4 cups, reduced-sodium chicken broth

¼ teaspoon red pepper flakes

1 large russet potato (about ½ pound)

4 cups washed and chopped escarole

½ cup low-fat evaporated milk

2 teaspoons cornstarch

1. Cut the sausage at an angle into slices about ½-inch thick and place into a medium soup pot. Add the broth and red pepper flakes and place over medium heat.

2. Slice the unpeeled potato into ¼-inch slices, then quarter each slice and add to the pot. Bring the soup to a simmer, cover, and cook for 10 minutes. Remove the lid, add the escarole, and simmer for 5 more minutes.

3. Whisk together the evaporated milk and cornstarch in a small cup and add to the soup. Simmer for 3 to 4 minutes, stirring occasionally, until slightly thickened.

Marlene Says: A simple switch from cream to low-fat evaporated milk and regular Italian sausage to lean turkey sausage reduced the fat (including the saturated fat) of the original recipe by almost 75 percent. It also cut 100 unhealthy calories per serving.

NUTRITION INFORMATION PER SERVING (1½ CUPS)
Calories 180 | Carbohydrate 16g (Sugars 9g) | Total Fat 4.5g (Sat Fat 1.5g) | Protein 19g | Fiber 6g | Cholesterol 25mg | Sodium 690mg | Food Exchanges: 2 Lean Meat, 2 Vegetable, 1 Starch | Carbohydrate Choices: 1½ | Weight Watcher Smart Point Comparison: 5

Creamy Basil Tomato Soup

Move over canned soup. This soup is so quick and easy to make and so delicious that I don't be-lieve my family will ever see a can of tomato soup in the house again! Serve it as the first course of a meal or with your favorite grilled cheese sandwich. It's terrific.

MAKES 8 SERVINGS

2 tablespoons margarine or butter

½ medium red onion, finely chopped

1 teaspoon garlic powder

1 teaspoon dried basil

2 tablespoons all-purpose flour

1 (12-ounce) can evaporated 2% milk

1 (46-ounce) bottle low-sodium tomato juice

Black pepper to taste

1. Melt the margarine in a medium pot over medium heat. Add the onion and sauté for 5 minutes, or until translucent.

2. Add the garlic and basil, and sprinkle in the flour. Whisk in the evaporated milk and cook until the mixture thickens and bubbles, about 3 to 4 minutes. Whisk in the tomato juice and cook for 10 minutes, stirring occasionally. Add black pepper to taste and serve.

Or try this: For *Creamy Pizza Soup*: Reduce the basil to ¾ teaspoon and add ¾ teaspoon dried oregano. To serve, place a heaping tablespoon of shredded part-skim mozzarella cheese in each bowl before ladling in soup. Garnish each bowl with a sprinkle of Parmesan. (Adds 35 calories, 2 grams of fat, and 4 grams of protein per bowl.)

NUTRITION INFORMATION PER SERVING (1 CUP)
Calories 100 | Carbohydrate 14g (Sugars 11g) | Total Fat 2.5g (Sat Fat 1g) | Protein 5g | Fiber 1g | Cholesterol 10mg | Sodium 630mg | Food Exchanges: 2 Vegetable, ½ Fat | Carbohydrate Choices: 1 | Weight Watcher Smart Point Comparison: 3

Spaghetti and Meatball Soup

This soup has great kid appeal, but it's not just for kids! Inspired by a recipe by Chef Emeril Lagasse, this soup definitely kicks it up a notch with a richly flavored tomato broth, homemade meatballs, and a smattering of baby spinach. I use pasta shells, but if you want a true "spaghetti" and meatball soup, feel free to substitute three ounces of dry broken spaghetti (which is fun but not very spoon friendly) for the shells.

MAKES 6 SERVINGS

1 tablespoon olive oil

1 small onion, chopped

1 stalk celery, finely chopped

1½ teaspoons minced garlic

¾ teaspoon dried basil

½ dried oregano

1 (28-ounce) can crushed tomatoes

2 (14-ounce) cans, or 4 cups, reduced-sodium beef broth

½ teaspoon black pepper

1 recipe Italian Meatballs (page 324) shaped into 24 meatballs, uncooked

2 tablespoons Parmesan cheese

¾ cup dry medium pasta shells

2 cups baby spinach leaves

3 tablespoons grated Parmesan cheese, for garnish

1. Heat the olive oil in a large soup pot over medium-high heat. Add the onion and celery and cook for 3 to 4 minutes, or until the vegetables are soft. Add the garlic, basil, and oregano and cook for 1 minute. Add the crushed tomatoes, broth, and black pepper. Bring to a slow boil, reduce the heat, cover, and simmer on low for 15 minutes.

2. While the broth simmers, make the meatballs.

3. Carefully add the meatballs to the simmering broth. Gently stir. Add the Parmesan and simmer for 10 more minutes.

4. Add the pasta and spinach, stir well, and cook for 10 to 15 minutes, or until the pasta is cooked through. Serve each bowl garnished with 2 teaspoons of Parmesan cheese, if desired.

NUTRITION INFORMATION PER SERVING (1½ CUPS)
Calories 290 | Carbohydrate 26g (Sugars 7g) | Total Fat 10g (Sat Fat 3g) | Protein 23g | Fiber 5g | Cholesterol 45mg | Sodium 810mg | Food Exchanges: 2½ Lean Meat, 2 Vegetable, 1 Starch, 1 Fat | Carbohydrate Choices: 1½ | Weight Watcher Smart Point Comparison: 7

"Cup of Red" Clam Chowder

*If you ever pause to remember if Manhattan-style clam chowder is the "red one" or the "white one,"
you are not alone. A favorite seafood restaurant of mine solved the confusion when it named its Manhattan-style clam chowder (yes, the red one) simply Joe's Red Clam Chowder. At its busy take-out
counter customer after customer would line up and shout, "I'll take a cup of red." This soup is my trib-
ute to that fabulous clam chowder.*

MAKES 8 SERVINGS

1 tablespoon olive oil

1 small onion, chopped

2 stalks celery, chopped

1 small green pepper, diced

2 garlic cloves, minced

1 teaspoon dried thyme

½ teaspoon dried oregano

4 small red-skinned potatoes,
cut into eighths (about ½
pound)

1 (28-ounce) can crushed
tomatoes

1 (8-ounce) bottle clam juice

2 (6.5-ounce) cans chopped
clams

1 (14-ounce) can reduced-
sodium chicken broth

½ cup white wine

Pinch of red pepper flakes

¼ teaspoon black pepper

1. Heat the oil in a large soup pot over medium-high heat.
   Add the onion, celery, and bell pepper and cook for 5 minutes, or until slightly softened.

2. Add the garlic and cook for an additional minute. Using
   your fingers crush the thyme and oregano into the pot. Add
   the potatoes and stir.

3. Add all the remaining ingredients and bring to a boil. Cover
   and simmer for 30 minutes, stirring occasionally. Remove
   the lid and simmer uncovered for 10 additional minutes and
   serve.

NUTRITION INFORMATION PER SERVING (1 CUP) ·······················
Calories 120 | Carbohydrate 15g (Sugars 4g) | Total Fat 2g (Sat Fat 0g) | Protein 9g | Fiber 3g | Cholesterol
15mg | Sodium 420mg | Food Exchanges: 1 Lean Meat, 1 Vegetable, ½ Starch | Carbohydrate Choices: 1 |
Weight Watcher Smart Point Comparison: 2

Creamy Seafood Chowder

The only word to describe this soup is "impressive." Rich and creamy and studded with potatoes and generous chunks of fish, it's absolutely everything New England-style fish chowder should be, but with a mere fraction of the fat. I highly recommend this recipe to **any** *fan of luscious chowders. You can vary the fish, but be sure to choose one that is mild in flavor and firm in texture like cod, haddock, or snapper. You may also substitute a 6.5-ounce can of drained chopped clams or scallops for the shrimp.*

MAKES 6 SERVINGS

1 tablespoon margarine
or butter

1 medium onion, chopped

1 stalk celery, chopped

1 garlic clove, minced

4 small red-skinned potatoes,
diced

1 (8-ounce) bottle clam juice

1 (14-ounce) can, or 2 cups,
reduced-sodium chicken
broth

2 cups low-fat milk

½ cup nonfat half-and-half

3 tablespoons all-purpose flour

¼ teaspoon Old Bay seasoning

⅛ teaspoon liquid smoke

1 pound 1-inch-thick white fish
fillets such as cod cut into
1½-inch pieces

½ pound peeled uncooked
shrimp

Freshly ground black pepper

1. Heat the margarine in a large soup pot over medium heat. Add the onion and celery and cook for 5 minutes, or until slightly softened. Add the garlic, red potatoes, clam juice, broth, and milk. Cover and simmer for 10 minutes, or until the potatoes are almost tender.

2. Whisk together the half-and-half and flour. Stir the mixture into the soup along with the Old Bay seasoning and liquid smoke. Simmer soup for 2 to 3 minutes to thicken.

3. Add the fish to the soup and simmer for 5 minutes. Add the shrimp and simmer for an additional 5 minutes, or until seafood is cooked through. Add black pepper to taste and serve.

DARE *TO* COMPARE
Rich in butter, bacon, and lots of heavy cream, it's no wonder that a typical bowl of New England chowder served in a restaurant can have over 500 calories, 35 grams of fat, and more than a day's worth of saturated fat.

NUTRITION INFORMATION PER SERVING (1½ CUPS)
Calories 210 | Carbohydrate 17g (Sugars 5g) | Total Fat 3.5g (Sat Fat 1g) | Protein 26g | Fiber 1g | Cholesterol 85mg | Sodium 520mg | Food Exchanges: 3 Lean Meat, ½ Low-Fat Milk, ½ Starch | Carbohydrate Choices: 1 | Weight Watcher Smart Point Comparison: 5

Chicken Corn Chowder

When I teach cooking classes, one of the things I really like to do is introduce products that make life easier. Instant flour is one of those products because it's formulated to dissolve quickly in hot and cold liquids, making it exceptional for thickening anything without lumps. It's great to have on hand for sauces, gravies, and especially for this soup because it dissolves seamlessly into the liquid, eliminating the need for a flour slurry or butter-based roux. This hearty soup brings a taste of summer to a cold winter's day.

MAKES 4 SERVINGS

1 tablespoon margarine or butter

2 stalks celery, chopped

¾ pound skinless, boneless chicken breast, cut into ½-inch pieces

1 cup canned or frozen corn niblets

½ cup chopped green onion

1 teaspoon dried thyme

¼ teaspoon salt

1 (14-ounce) can, or 2 cups, reduced-sodium chicken broth

1½ cups cups low-fat milk

½ cup nonfat half-and-half

4 tablespoons instant flour (like Wondra)

⅛ teaspoon cayenne pepper

1. Melt the margarine in a medium pot over medium heat. Add the chopped celery and sauté for 3 to 4 minutes to slightly soften. Add the chicken and cook while stirring for 3 to 4 minutes or until the chicken is no longer pink. Add the corn and green onions to the chicken and celery. Using your fingers, crush the thyme into the mixture and add the salt.

2. Add the broth, milk, and half-and-half and stir. Sprinkle the instant flour into the soup and stir until soup is smooth. Add the cayenne pepper to the soup and simmer for 10 minutes.

DARE *TO* COMPARE

Be sure to read the label before picking up a tub of "homemade" Chicken Corn Chowder at your local market or club store. Each cup contains as many as 350 calories and over 20 grams of fat (with half of them saturated). The only thing "slim" is the chicken but with 11 grams of protein per cup it offers only one-fourth of the belly-filling chicken found in my hearty Chicken Corn Chowder.

NUTRITION INFORMATION PER SERVING (1½ CUPS)
Calories 235 | Carbohydrate 20g (Sugars 8g) | Total Fat 5g (Sat Fat 1.5g) | Protein 27g | Fiber 2g | Cholesterol 45mg | Sodium 510mg | Food Exchanges: 3½ Lean Meat, 1 Starch, ½ Low-Fat Milk | Carbohydrate Choices: 1 | Weight Watcher Smart Point Comparison: 6

Super Chili

Among chili aficionados debates rage about the meat, the beans, the spices, and just about everything else that could possibly go into a chili recipe. I like to keep my chili simple, because for me it's often a last-minute dinner choice. A fan of the Southwest, my chili includes black beans and is tinged with a smoky barbecue flavor my family just loves. It contains the perfect nutritional balance of ingredients. All-meat chili recipes are low in carbohydrates but are often high in fat and ignore the incredible health benefits of fiber-rich beans. In contrast, all-bean chilies are healthful but can wreak havoc for those who must watch their carbohydrate intake. This chili combines lean meat, black beans, and plenty of vegetables for a super mix of good nutrition and great taste.

MAKES 6 SERVINGS

2 teaspoons canola oil

1 medium onion, finely chopped

1 medium red bell pepper, diced

1 teaspoon minced garlic

½ pound each lean ground beef and turkey (or 1 pound lean ground beef or turkey)

1 (15-ounce) can black beans, drained and rinsed

2 (14-ounce) cans stewed tomatoes

2 teaspoons chili powder

1 teaspoon cumin

⅛ teaspoon red pepper flakes (or more to taste)

1 tablespoon molasses

1 tablespoon white vinegar

1 tablespoon Worcestershire sauce

½ teaspoon liquid smoke

1. Heat the oil in a large saucepan over medium-high heat. Add the onion and bell pepper and sauté for 3 to 4 minutes, or until slightly softened.

2. Add the garlic and meat and cook, turning to break up the meat, until it is browned.

3. Add the black beans, tomatoes, chili powder, cumin, red pepper flakes, molasses, vinegar, Worcestershire sauce, and liquid smoke. Stir well and simmer for 15 minutes.

Or try this: For a *Super Vegetarian Chili*, substitute 1 package of Morningstar Farms Meal Starters Crumbles in place of the ground meat. (Subtracts 40 calories, 6 grams of protein, and 3 grams of fat and adds 4 grams of carbohydrate and 3 grams of fiber per serving.)

NUTRITION INFORMATION PER SERVING (1 CUP) ·······················
Calories 230 | Carbohydrate 24g (Sugars 10g) | Total Fat 6g (Sat Fat 2g) | Protein 20g | Fiber 5g | Cholesterol 40mg | Sodium 510mg | Food Exchanges: 2 Lean Meat, 2 Vegetable, 1 Starch | Carbohydrate Choices: 1½ | Weight Watcher Smart Point Comparison: 6

Quick-Fix White Chicken Chili

This white wonder of a chili couldn't be easier—or faster—especially if you have leftover chicken or turkey meat on hand. Even if no leftovers are at hand, you can quickly prepare shredded chicken using the Perfect Poached Chicken recipe on page 301. Prepare as directed and shred the chicken with two forks while still warm.

MAKES 6 SERVINGS

2 teaspoons canola oil

1 medium onion, diced

1 teaspoon minced garlic

1½ teaspoons ground cumin

¾ teaspoon dried oregano

⅛ teaspoon cayenne pepper

1 (14-ounce) can, or 2 cups, reduced-sodium chicken broth

1 (4-ounce) can chopped green chilies

2 (15-ounce) cans white beans (Great Northern or cannellini), drained

3 cups shredded skinless chicken breast

⅓ cup fresh chopped cilantro, for garnish

1 cup reduced-fat Mexican blend shredded cheese (optional)

1. Heat the oil over medium heat in a large saucepan. Add the onion and sauté for 4 to 5 minutes or until slightly softened.

2. Add the garlic, cumin, oregano, and cayenne pepper and sauté for 1 minute.

3. Stir in the chicken broth, green chilies, beans, and chicken. Reduce heat to low and simmer for 15 minutes. Ladle into bowls and top with the cilantro and cheese if desired.

NUTRITION INFORMATION PER SERVING (1 CUP)
Calories 210 | Carbohydrate 17g (Sugars 3g) | Total Fat 6g (Sat Fat 1.5g) | Protein 21g | Fiber 6g | Cholesterol 85mg | Sodium 80mg | Food Exchanges: 3 Lean Meat, 1 Starch | Carbohydrate Choices: 1 | Weight Watcher Smart Point Comparison: 5

Sensational Side and Entrée Salads

SIDE SALADS

EVERYDAY MIXED GREENS WITH ITALIAN VINAIGRETTE

WEDGE SALAD WITH BUTTERMILK RANCH DRESSING

ROMAINE SALAD WITH AVOCADO RANCH DRESSING

BALSAMIC SALAD WITH PEARS, BLUE CHEESE, AND PECANS

SHREDDED SPINACH, LETTUCE, AND FRESH ORANGE SALAD

STRAWBERRY SPINACH SALAD
WITH BUTTERMILK POPPY SEED DRESSING

5-MINUTE SKINNY SLAW

APPLE JICAMA CRANBERRY SLAW

CLASSIC CREAMY COLESLAW

FRESH BROCCOLI AND WALNUT SALAD

FAMILY-FRIENDLY ITALIAN TOMATO SALAD

BEST EVER THREE BEAN SALAD

RED, WHITE, AND BLUE POTATO SALAD

PASTA PRIMAVERA SALAD

CREAMY MACARONI SALAD THREE WAYS

WARM SPINACH SALAD WITH OLIVE OIL AND GARLIC

ENTRÉE SALADS

THAI SHRIMP SALAD
EVERYDAY CHICKEN CAESAR SALAD
BUFFALO CHICKEN AND BLUE CHEESE SALAD
CHINESE CHICKEN SALAD WITH CRUNCHY RAMEN NOODLES
FAJITA BEEF SALAD
SPINACH, TUNA, AND WHITE BEAN SALAD
SOUTHWEST CHICKEN SALAD

I try to eat healthy most of the time. Sometimes I succeed, and some-
times I don't. The one healthy eating habit that effortlessly works in my favor is
that I genuinely love salads. Adding salads to your diet is a great way to cut
calories and add nutrients—if you do it right.

I once had a client that was trying to shed a few pounds. He was delighted to
share with me that he too had become a "salad lover"—as he had found the perfect salad swap for his usual burger. But when we looked a bit closer at what was
really in his salad bowl, we saw that in addition to the lean lettuce and bits of
healthy tomato, the buffalo chicken salad he had become so fond of also piled on
"lightly" fried pieces of buffalo chicken, cheddar cheese, and a hefty dose of blue
cheese dressing. And in fact an analysis proved his newfound wonder contained
over 1,000 calories (and more than half of them came from unhealthy fat). The
reality is, when ordered at a restaurant, scooped up at the deli, or even picked up
at a "healthy" grocery store, salads can pack in more calories than you expect,
with the biggest culprits being the add-ons—cheese, bacon, nuts, croutons, and,
of course, dressings, which are often high in fat and sugar.

But let's face it—those add-ons are often what make a salad so darn tasty.
With that well in mind, I have created an array of good-for-you salads that cut
the excess fat and calories, but never the flavor. From super-slim plate fillers like
Everyday Mixed Greens with homemade zesty Italian Vinaigrette and 5-Minute
Skinny Slaw to salad bar favorites like my Best Ever Three Bean Salad and
creamy macaroni salad, made not one but three ways, these salads are sure to
please. If it's a sweet salad you crave look no further than the beautiful Strawberry Spinach Salad with Poppy Seed Dressing. If creamy is your thing, the Classic Creamy Coleslaw will hit the mark, and if it's sweet, creamy, and a
bit-o-bacon, the Fresh Broccoli and Walnut Salad will not disappoint!

Last, but not least, you will find seven fantastic entrée salads. Pumped up with
protein, these salads make the perfect light meal. Personally, I could eat the
Everyday Chicken Caesar Salad every day, but it would be a shame to miss out
on the warm Fajita Beef and yes, Buffalo Chicken and Blue Cheese Salads.

For the Love of Dressings

A great salad needs a great dressing, but dressings loaded with sugar, fat, and calories can derail even the healthiest of salads. A typical restaurant ladle of dressing can cost you as many as 350 calories, contain more fat than a Quarter Pounder with Cheese, or more sugar than a full-sized chocolate bar. Here are my best tricks for creating crowd-pleasing, better-for-you dressings:

TO REDUCE THE FAT IN VINAIGRETTES

- Substitute less acidic vinegars, such as balsamic, rice wine, or flavorful red wine for plain white or cider vinegar, and reduce the oil (needed to balance the acid) by one-half.

- Substitute fruit juices, broth, or brewed tea for up to one-half the oil.

- When using less oil, select it wisely. With stronger flavored oils such as extra-virgin olive oil, sesame oil, and flavored nut oils like walnut and hazelnut, a little goes a long way.

- Pump up the flavor but not the fat of dressings by whisking in minced garlic, chopped herbs, and lemon or orange zest. Mustard does double duty as an emulsifier.

TO CREATE DELIGHTFUL CREAMY DRESSINGS

- Substitute buttermilk for one-half the mayonnaise. Contrary to its name buttermilk has no butter in it, but its creamy texture and tangy taste are perfect for lower calorie classics like ranch dressing.

- An equal combination of light mayonnaise and plain low-fat yogurt is the perfect healthy swap-out for mayonnaise in any dressing recipe.

- Strong cheeses like blue and Parmesan deliver big flavor in small amounts.

TO CREATE SWEET DRESSINGS WITH LESS SUGAR

- Use a sugar substitute for all or part of the sugar in the recipe.

- Add tomato juice or tomato juice blends to create extra body when reducing sugar.

- Substitute reduced-calorie juices for some of the oil or vinegar.

Side Salads

Everyday Mixed Greens with Italian Vinaigrette

A basic green salad is always welcome, especially when it's tossed with delicious homemade Italian dressing. This dinner staple is terrific served with everything from Italian favorites to good ol' American hot dogs and hamburgers. I have purposely kept the salad ingredients to a minimum, but feel free to add your own favorite veggies to the bowl.

MAKES 4 SERVINGS

DRESSING

2 tablespoons extra-virgin olive oil

2 tablespoons water

1 tablespoon white or red wine vinegar

1 tablespoon balsamic vinegar

1 teaspoon Dijon mustard

1 teaspoon minced garlic (1 clove)

1 teaspoon dried oregano

½ teaspoon dried basil

Salt to taste

Pepper to taste

SALAD

6 cups mixed greens

2 medium tomatoes, cored and cut into wedges

½ medium cucumber, peeled, cut in half lengthwise, and sliced

1. To make the dressing, in a medium bowl whisk together all the oil, water, vinegars, mustard, garlic, oregano, basil, salt, and pepper.

2. For the salad, in a large bowl, combine the greens, tomato wedges, and cucumber slices. Pour the dressing on top of the salad mix and toss lightly.

NUTRITION INFORMATION PER SERVING (1½ CUPS SALAD)
Calories 90 | Carbohydrate 7g (Sugars 1g) | Total Fat 7g (Sat Fat 1g) | Protein 1g | Fiber 2g | Cholesterol 0mg | Sodium 35mg | Food Exchanges: 1½ Fat, 1 Vegetable | Carbohydrate Choices: ½ | Weight Watcher Smart Point Comparison: 2

Wedge Salad with Buttermilk Ranch Dressing

Something about a wedge salad is just plain fun, making this a favorite for kids of all ages. This modern version is dressed with a luscious, reduced-fat ranch dressing, bacon, and hard-boiled egg. Don't forget to serve this salad with a knife.

MAKES 6 SERVINGS

DRESSING

½ cup buttermilk

¼ cup light mayonnaise

¼ cup plain nonfat yogurt

1½ teaspoons fresh parsley
   (½ teaspoon dried)

½ teaspoon onion powder

½ teaspoon garlic powder

¼ teaspoon dried dill

⅛ teaspoon salt

¼ teaspoon black pepper

SALAD

1 head iceberg lettuce

2 tablespoons real bacon bits

3 hard-boiled eggs, peeled
   and cut into quarters

1. To make the dressing, in a medium bowl whisk together the buttermilk, mayonnaise, yogurt, parsley, onion powder, garlic powder, dill, salt, and pepper.

2. For the salad, place the lettuce on a large cutting board. Cut in half lengthwise. Cut each half into three wedges, and carefully cut out the core.

3. Place each wedge onto a plate. Pour the dressing (about 2½ tablespoons) over the wedges. Sprinkle 2 teaspoons bacon bits over each wedge and garnish with egg.

Marlene Says: To keep the wedges cold and crisp, do not dress them until serving time. If you prefer to prepare this ahead of time, place the wedges on serving plates or in a shallow bowl and cover them with moistened paper towels. Store in the refrigerator.

NUTRITION INFORMATION PER SERVING (1 WEDGE AND 2½ TABLESPOONS DRESSING)
Calories 100 | Carbohydrate 4g (Sugars 4g) | Total Fat 6g (Sat Fat 1.5g) | Protein 4g | Fiber 2g | Cholesterol 110mg | Sodium 270mg | Food Exchanges: 1 Vegetable, 1 Fat | Carbohydrate Choices: 0 | Weight Watcher Smart Point Comparison: 3

Romaine Salad with Avocado Ranch Dressing

Some salads, like this one, are all about the dressing. Here, buttery avocado is combined with tradi-tional ranch-style flavors for a creamy dressing that will become a family favorite. Crisp romaine, roasted red peppers, and a smattering of black beans are the perfect complements. You may also add cilantro to either the dressing or the salad for a great flavor boost. (Note: You will only use one-half the dressing, so cover and refrigerate the remainder for another time or simply double the salad ingredients if you are serving a larger crowd. The extra dressing will keep for several days.)

MAKES 4 SERVINGS

DRESSING

½ medium avocado, pitted and peeled

½ cup buttermilk

¾ cup plain nonfat yogurt

½ teaspoon garlic powder

½ teaspoon onion powder

⅛ teaspoon salt

¼ teaspoon pepper

SALAD

6 cups chopped romaine lettuce or hearts of romaine

½ cup roasted red peppers (jarred), cut into ½-inch pieces

¼ cup black beans, drained and rinsed

1. To make the dressing, combine the avocado, buttermilk, yogurt, garlic powder, onion powder, salt, and pepper in a food processor or blender. Process until smooth.

2. For the salad, in a large bowl, toss together the romaine let-tuce, peppers, and black beans. Add one-half (about ¾ cup) of the dressing and toss lightly.

Marlene Says: When buying avocados for dressings and dips, pebbly textured, dark-skinned Haas avocados have a creamier, richer flesh and work best. Light-skinned Fuerte avo-cados have a higher water content and are terrific for sand-wiches and salads.

NUTRITION INFORMATION PER SERVING (1½ CUPS)
Calories 130 | Carbohydrate 16g (Sugars 7g) | Total Fat 4.5g (Sat Fat 1g) | Protein 8g | Fiber 5g | Cholesterol 15mg | Sodium 360mg | Food Exchanges: 1 Vegetable, ½ Carbohydrate, 1 Fat | Carbohydrate Choices: 1 | Weight Watcher Smart Point Comparison: 3

Balsamic Salad with Pears, Blue Cheese, and Pecans

The first time I encountered this delicious salad combination was when I lived in Columbus, Ohio. We often ate at a restaurant that was well known for its signature balsamic salad, which was topped with blue cheese and candied pecans. Although delicious, it didn't take me long to realize that eating it was a major health hazard, so I set out to develop my own signature version. Here is my take on this now-familiar salad that has allowed us (and now you) to enjoy it healthfully right at home.

MAKES 4 SERVINGS

DRESSING

3 tablespoons balsamic vinegar

2 tablespoons chicken broth

2 tablespoons extra-virgin olive oil

2 teaspoons Dijon mustard

Pinch of salt

Pepper to taste

SALAD

4 cups packed mixed greens

6 tablespoons blue cheese crumbles

⅓ cup chopped pecans

1 large pear, cored and cut into thin slices (or 1 large apple)

1. To make the dressing, in a small bowl whisk together the vinegar, chicken broth, oil, mustard, salt, and pepper.

2. For the salad, place the greens in a large bowl. Pour the dressing over the greens and toss lightly.

3. Arrange the greens on plates. Divide the blue cheese and pecans evenly among the plates, sprinkling on top of the greens. Garnish plates with the pear slices and serve.

DARE *TO* COMPARE ·······················

With over 500 calories and 50 grams of fat, the restaurant version of this salad contains all the calories and twice the fat of an entire healthy meal. It also contains 28 grams of carbohydrate, 15 of them from sugar.

NUTRITION INFORMATION PER SERVING (1 SALAD) ························

Calories 210 | Carbohydrate 12g (Sugars 7g) | Total Fat 16g (Sat Fat 3.5g) | Protein 4g | Fiber 3g | Cholesterol 10mg | Sodium 260mg | Food Exchanges: 1 Vegetable, ½ Fruit, ½ High-Fat Meat, 2 Fat | Carbohydrate Choices: ½ | Weight Watcher Smart Point Comparison: 7

Shredded Spinach, Lettuce, and Fresh Orange Salad

This is one of my all-time favorite salads, and I have served it to everyone I know. The combination of shredded spinach and iceberg lettuce offers a nice cool crunch along with great color and flavor, while cold bits of fresh orange, tangy green onions, and a quick 'n' easy sweet-and-sour dressing complete this perfect mix.

MAKES 4 SERVINGS

DRESSING

3 tablespoons natural rice wine vinegar

2 tablespoons canola oil

2 tablespoons orange juice

¼ teaspoon dried mustard

2 tablespoons granulated no-calorie sweetener (or 3 packets)*

Dash of salt

Pinch of black pepper

GREENS

4 cups shredded iceberg lettuce

1½ cups spinach leaves

2 green onions, sliced on the diagonal

1 large cold orange, peeled and sectioned

1. To make the dressing, in a small bowl whisk together the vinegar, oil, orange juice, mustard, sweetener, salt, and pepper.

2. For the salad, place the lettuce in a large bowl.

3. Stack the spinach leaves on top of each other and slice across them to make long shreds. Add to the lettuce. Add the green onions and orange sections.

4. Pour on the dressing and toss lightly.

Perfect Paring: Although I serve this with most anything, I find it to be the ideal complement to Mexican dishes. Try it with Creamy Chicken Enchiladas (page 313), Beef Fajitas (page 329), Snapper Vera Cruz (page 346), or your favorite take-out tacos.

*See page 382 for sweetener options

NUTRITION INFORMATION PER SERVING (1¼ CUPS) Calories 100 | Carbohydrate 8g (Sugars 6g) | Total Fat 6g (Sat Fat 0.5g) | Protein 1g | Fiber 2g | Cholesterol 0mg | Sodium 20mg | Food Exchanges: 1 Vegetable, 1 Fat, ½ Fruit | Carbohydrate Choices: ½ | Weight Watcher Smart Point Comparison: 2

Strawberry Spinach Salad with Buttermilk Poppy Seed Dressing

This is one of the prettiest and healthiest salads you will ever eat. The contrast of beautiful red strawberries against dark green spinach leaves is simply stunning, but as if that weren't enough, it also offers a substantial serving of both fiber and vitamin C in sixty slim calories. The creamy, sweet, white poppy seed dressing adds the crowning touch.

MAKES 4 SERVINGS

DRESSING

¼ cup plain nonfat yogurt

¼ cup buttermilk

1 tablespoon granulated sugar

1 teaspoon lemon juice

¾ teaspoon poppy seeds

Dash salt

Pepper to taste

SALAD

6 cups spinach leaves

1½ cups sliced fresh strawberries

1. To make the dressing, in a small bowl, whisk together the yogurt, buttermilk, sugar, lemon juice, poppy seeds, salt, and pepper.

2. For the salad, in a large bowl, place the spinach and strawberries. Pour the dressing on top, and toss together lightly. Serve immediately.

NUTRITION INFORMATION PER SERVING (ABOUT 1½ CUPS)
Calories 60 | Carbohydrate 11g (Sugars 8g) | Total Fat 1g (Sat Fat 0g) | Protein 3g | Fiber 3g | Cholesterol 0mg | Sodium 135mg | Food Exchanges: ½ Fruit, 1 Vegetable | Carbohydrate Choices: ½ | Weight Watcher Smart Point Comparison: 1

5-Minute Skinny Slaw

This super-easy, super-quick, and super-skinny slaw is a fantastic side dish salad that is good-to-go in five minutes. Perfect for busy weeknights, this slaw is a great plate filler. If you prefer a slaw with a kick of heat, try the Asian variation; it's just as easy and just as delicious.

MAKES 6 SERVINGS

DRESSING

⅓ cup natural rice vinegar

3 tablespoons granulated no-calorie sweetener (or 4 packets)*

2 tablespoons canola oil

1 teaspoon celery seed

2 teaspoons Dijon mustard

Black pepper to taste

SLAW

1 (10-ounce) bag of shredded cabbage

1 large carrot, peeled and grated

3 green onions, chopped

1. To make the dressing, in a small bowl, whisk together the vinegar, sweetener, oil, celery seed, mustard, and pepper.

2. For the slaw, in a large bowl, place the cabbage, carrot, and green onions in a bowl and toss together. Pour the dressing on top of the cabbage mixture and toss well to coat. Serve immediately, or chill until serving time.

Or try this: For *5-Minute Asian Skinny Slaw:* Substitute 1 tablespoon sesame oil for 1 of the tablespoons of canola oil. Replace the celery seed with ½ teaspoon minced ginger and add ⅛ teaspoon crushed red pepper. Toss as directed.

*See page 382 for sweetener options

NUTRITION INFORMATION PER SERVING (ABOUT 1 CUP) ·······················
Calories 70 | Carbohydrate 5g (Sugars 2g) | Total Fat 5g (Sat Fat 0g) | Protein 1g | Fiber 2g | Cholesterol 0mg | Sodium 55mg | Food Exchanges: 1 Vegetable, 1 Fat | Carbohydrate Choices: ½ | Weight Watcher Smart Point Comparison: 2

Apple Jicama Cranberry Slaw

This slaw gets rave reviews from family members every time I serve it. If you are not familiar with jicama, it is a deliciously crunchy, slightly sweet root vegetable from Mexico that is sometimes referred to as a Mexican potato. It pairs perfectly with sweet apples and crunchy carrots to produce this delightful "slaw." This slaw is best served chilled. To serve immediately make sure the apples, jicama, and carrots are cold before slicing.

MAKES 8 TO 10 SERVINGS

DRESSING

1½ tablespoons honey

3 tablespoons lime juice (about 2 small limes)

1½ tablespoons extra-virgin olive oil

¼ teaspoon salt

¼ teaspoon black pepper

SLAW

3 cups julienned (long thin slices) jicama

2 large Fuji apples, cored and cut into thin strips (about 2 cups)

1 cup julienned carrot

⅓ cup dried cranberries

⅓ cup chopped fresh parsley or cilantro

1. To make the dressing, in a small microwavable bowl heat the honey for 5 seconds, just until runny. Remove from the microwave, add the lime juice, oil, salt, and pepper and whisk until mixed.

2. For the slaw, in a large bowl, combine the jicama, apples, carrots, cranberries, and parsley or cilantro. Pour the dressing on top, and toss together to coat.

3. Cover and place in the refrigerator. Serve chilled.

Marlene Says: Fresh uncut jicama will keep in your refrigerator for up to three weeks. Once cut, wrap it in plastic wrap, refrigerate, and use within one week. To peel, cut off the ends with a knife and use a vegetable peeler to scrape off the thin brown skin.

NUTRITION INFORMATION PER SERVING (¾ CUP) ⋯⋯⋯⋯⋯⋯⋯⋯⋯⋯⋯
Calories 80 | Carbohydrate 16g (Sugars 11g) | Total Fat 2.5g (Sat Fat 0g) | Protein 1g | Fiber 3g | Cholesterol 0mg | Sodium 70mg | Food Exchanges: 1 Vegetable, ½ Fruit, ½ Fat | Carbohydrate Choices: 1 | Weight Watcher Smart Point Comparison: 2

Classic Creamy Coleslaw

There are probably as many different coleslaws as there are cooks. This version of a classic sweet and creamy slaw is made with the twist of both red and green cabbage. The red cabbage lends a great boost of color, as well as contributing powerful antioxidants proven to reduce the risk for heart disease. (If you prefer your slaw more like the Colonel's, use only finely chopped green cabbage, eliminate the celery seed, and substitute horseradish for the mustard powder.)

MAKES 8 SERVINGS

DRESSING

½ cup light mayonnaise

⅓ cup light sour cream

4 tablespoons white vinegar

3 to 4 tablespoons low-fat milk

2 tablespoons granulated sugar or granulated no-calorie sweetener*

1 teaspoon celery seed

½ teaspoon mustard powder

¼ teaspoon salt

⅛ teaspoon black pepper

SLAW

8 cups shredded green and red cabbage

1 large carrot, shredded

3 green onions, chopped

* Subtract 3 grams of carbohydrate and sugar and 12 calories with sweetener

1. To make the dressing, in a medium bowl, whisk together the mayonnaise, sour cream, vinegar, milk, sugar, celery seed, mustard powder, salt, and pepper.

2. For the slaw, in a large bowl, combine the cabbage, carrot, and onion. Pour dressing over cabbage mixture and toss well to coat.

3. Cover and place in the refrigerator. Serve chilled.

DARE TO COMPARE ....
It's hard to believe that just ½ cup of deli coleslaw can contain as much as 230 calories and 23 grams of fat—that's almost twice the calories of most ice creams! A single side portion of the slaw at KFC® will set you back 180 calories, 10 grams of fat, and 22 grams of carbohydrate (18 of them from sugar).

*See page 382 for sweetener options.

NUTRITION INFORMATION PER SERVING (1 CUP SHREDDED, ¾ CUP CHOPPED) ··············
Calories 70 | Carbohydrate 11g (Sugars 8g) | Total Fat 3.5g (Sat Fat 0.5g) | Protein 2g | Fiber 3g | Cholesterol 5mg | Sodium 225mg | Food Exchanges: 1 Vegetable, ½ Fat | Carbohydrate Choices: ½ | Weight Watcher Smart Point Comparison: 2

Fresh Broccoli and Walnut Salad

If you want a surefire way to convert someone from a broccoli hater to a broccoli lover, serve them this salad! Whether it's made extra sweet with plump raisins or savory with bacon bits (or both!), this salad is an unparalleled crowd pleaser. To toast the walnuts, place them on an ungreased baking pan and bake at 325°F for 5 to 8 minutes, or until lightly browned and fragrant.

MAKES 5 SERVINGS

DRESSING

¼ cup light mayonnaise

6 tablespoons plain nonfat yogurt

2 tablespoons cider vinegar

2 teaspoons granulated sugar or granulated no-calorie sweetener

SALAD

4 cups broccoli florets

½ cup thinly sliced red onion

⅓ cup toasted walnut pieces

¼ cup raisins or 3 tablespoons real bacon bits

1. To make the dressing, in a medium bowl whisk together the mayonnaise, yogurt, vinegar, and sugar.

2. For the salad, in a large bowl, toss the broccoli, onion, walnuts, and raisins. Pour the dressing over the broccoli and mix well.

3. Cover and place in the refrigerator for at least 4 hours to meld the flavors and slightly soften the broccoli before serving. Just before serving, toss in the bacon bits.

Marlene Says: If you eliminate the raisins and substitute bacon, you will reduce the carbohydrates by 4 grams and the calories by 10. You will also add 2 grams of protein and 125 mg of sodium.

NUTRITION INFORMATION PER SERVING (¾ CUP) ⋯⋯⋯⋯⋯⋯⋯⋯⋯⋯⋯⋯⋯
Calories 130 | Carbohydrate 13g (Sugars 4g) | Total Fat 7g (Sat Fat 1g) | Protein 4g | Fiber 3g | Cholesterol 0mg | Sodium 120mg | Food Exchanges: 1 Vegetable, ½ High-Fat Meat, ½ Fruit | Carbohydrate Choices: 1 | Weight Watcher Smart Point Comparison: 3

Family-Friendly Italian Tomato Salad

Garden-fresh tomato salads are a delicious ritual of summer when tomatoes are at peak of flavor. This twist on the Italian classic Insalata Caprese also layers tomatoes with cheese, but instead of fresh mozzarella I substitute reduced-fat provolone with a bit of smoky flavor for kid-pleasing results. If you choose to make a traditional Caprese salad, use four ounces of sliced fresh mozzarella instead of the provolone, which will add 20 calories and 2 grams of fat to each serving.

MAKES 4 SERVINGS

DRESSING

1½ tablespoons extra-virgin olive oil

1 tablespoon balsamic vinegar

Pinch of salt

Pinch of dried oregano (optional)

SALAD

2 large ripe tomatoes (about 1 pound)

6 slices reduced-fat provolone cheese

¼ cup fresh basil

1. To make the dressing, in a small bowl whisk together the oil, vinegar, salt, and oregano.

2. For the salad, on a cutting board, slice the tomatoes into ¼- to ½-inch thick slices. Cut the cheese slices in half. Set aside.

3. Reserve a couple of basil sprigs for garnish. Remove the rest of the basil leaves from the stems. Stack the leaves on top of each other and roll tightly, like a cigar. Slice thinly to resemble long ribbon strips and then shake apart.

4. Arrange the salad on a plate in a fanned-out design, alternating the tomato with the cheese slices. Sprinkle the basil on top. Drizzle the dressing over the salad and use the reserved basil to garnish the plate.

Family Focus: Kids love to cook. Younger children can help to alternate the layers of tomatoes and cheese (reinforcing learning about shapes), while older children can hone their dexterity and knife skills slicing the tomatoes and creating the thin ribbons of basil.

NUTRITION INFORMATION PER SERVING (ABOUT 2 SLICES TOMATO, 1½ SLICES CHEESE)
Calories 150 | Carbohydrate 5g (Sugars 3g) | Total Fat 11g (Sat Fat 4g) | Protein 9g | Fiber 1g | Cholesterol 15mg | Sodium 230mg | Food Exchanges: 1 Vegetable, 1 Medium Fat-Meat, 1 Fat | Carbohydrate Choices: ½ | Weight Watcher Smart Point Comparison: 4

Best Ever Three Bean Salad

For my book Fantastic Food with Splenda, *I created a delicious Classic Three Bean Salad reduced in carbohydrates, calories, and fat. But I've managed to improve on it with this updated version that was declared by those who enjoyed it at a recent barbecue to be the best three bean salad ever. The deliciously unique dressing absolutely makes this incredibly good-for-you salad.*

MAKES 8 SERVINGS

DRESSING

1 small red onion

3 tablespoons canola oil

2 tablespoons ketchup

2 tablespoons granulated no-calorie sweetener (or 3 packets)*

2 tablespoons apple cider vinegar

2 teaspoons Worcestershire sauce

2 teaspoons soy sauce

½ teaspoon liquid smoke

Freshly ground black pepper

SALAD

1 (15-ounce) can cut green beans, drained

1 (15-ounce) can yellow wax beans, drained

1 (15-ounce) can red kidney beans, rinsed and drained

1 small green bell pepper, diced

1 small red bell pepper, diced

1 small red onion, diced

1. To make the dressing, peel and grate the red onion with a cheese or box grater into a small bowl. Add the oil, ketchup, sweetener, vinegar, 2 tablespoons water, Worcestershire sauce, soy sauce, liquid smoke, and pepper and whisk to combine.

2. For the salad, in a large bowl gently mix together the beans, peppers, and red onion.

3. Pour the dressing over the bean mixture and toss to coat. Cover and refrigerate 1 hour or more to meld flavors (overnight is great).

DARE *TO* COMPARE ·····································

Traditional three-bean salad recipes, like the one in the *Joy of Cooking* (with ½ cup of salad oil and ¾ cup sugar in the dressing), can turn a healthy salad into a fat- and sugar-filled nutritional fiasco that delivers 270 calories, 15 grams of fat, and 35 grams of carbohydrate (with 22 of them from sugar) in a one-half cup serving.

*See page 382 for sweetener options

NUTRITION INFORMATION PER SERVING (½ CUP) ·····················
Calories 130 | Carbohydrate 17 (Sugars 4g) | Total Fat 5 (Sat Fat 0g) | Protein 4g | Fiber 5g | Cholesterol 15mg | Sodium 360 | Food Exchanges: 1 Starch, ½ Vegetable, 1 Fat | Carbohydrate Choices: 1 | Weight Watcher Smart Point Comparison: 3

Red, White, and Blue Potato Salad

My mother taught me that the secret to great potato salad was marinating the hot cooked potatoes with vinaigrette. As always, she was right. What my mom didn't realize was that the vinaigrette also permitted the creamy dressing to slide easily over the potatoes, making it possible to use less mayonnaise (and less fat). To create my "Red, White, and Blue Potato Salad," I leave the red potato skins on for extra texture, fiber, and color, and add blue cheese for a big burst of flavor. This salad is fantastic paired with any grilled lean beef (including burgers!).

MAKES 6 SERVINGS

2 pounds small red potatoes, skins on

3 tablespoons apple cider vinegar

1 tablespoon canola oil

1 tablespoon Dijonnaise

1 tablespoon water

½ teaspoon salt

⅓ cup chopped green onions, plus extra for garnish

3 hard-boiled eggs, peeled, and coarsely chopped (discard 2 of the yolks)

1 cup chopped celery

⅓ cup light sour cream

3 tablespoons light mayonnaise

1 tablespoon milk

⅓ cup crumbled blue cheese

Ground black pepper to taste

2 slices center cut bacon, cooked and crumbled for garnish (optional)

1. Place the potatoes in a large pot of cold water and bring to a boil over medium-high heat. Cook the potatoes until fork tender but not mushy, about 20 minutes.

2. While the potatoes are cooking, whisk together the vinegar, oil, Dijonnaise, water, and salt in a small bowl. Add the green onions.

3. When the potatoes are just tender, drain and rinse with cool water. Quarter the potatoes and place in a medium bowl. Pour the green onion marinade over warm potatoes. Cover and place in the refrigerator until chilled. (This can sit overnight.)

4. Dice the eggs. Add the eggs and celery to the cooled potato mixture.

5. In a small bowl, whisk together the sour cream, mayonnaise, milk, blue cheese, and pepper. Spoon over the potatoes and stir gently. Garnish with the chopped eggs, extra green onion, and bacon, if desired. Refrigerate and serve chilled.

NUTRITION INFORMATION PER SERVING (¾ CUP)
Calories 170 | Carbohydrate 23g (Sugars 3g) | Total Fat 6g (Sat Fat 2g) | Protein 6g | Fiber 4g | Cholesterol 35mg | Sodium 370mg | Food Exchanges: 1½ Starch, 1 Fat | Carbohydrate Choices: 1½ | Weight Watcher Smart Point Comparison: 5

Pasta Primavera Salad

Homemade Italian vinaigrette and gorgeous fresh vegetables elevate this salad from a high-carb potluck no-no into something that can be enjoyed frequently. Try some of the new blends of multi-grain pastas to add extra fiber and protein to this already-healthy salad that packs an entire serving of vegetables with every serving.

MAKES 8 SERVINGS

2 cups broccoli florets

4 cups cooked rotini, penne, or fusilli pasta (3 cups dry)

1 cup halved cherry tomatoes

1 large yellow bell pepper, cut into strips

½ cup thinly sliced red onion (½ small)

1 recipe Italian Vinaigrette (page 173)

1 tablespoon red wine vinegar

1 tablespoon extra-virgin olive oil

2 tablespoons freshly grated Parmesan cheese

1. Place the broccoli florets in a small microwavable casserole dish with ½ inch of water. Cover and microwave on high for 1½ minutes. Rinse with cold water to stop the cooking process and set aside to cool.

2. In a large bowl, mix together the cooled broccoli, pasta, tomatoes, pepper, and onion. Add Italian Vinaigrette, vinegar, and olive oil and mix well.

3. Top with the Parmesan cheese. Cover and chill for at least two hours or overnight before serving.

Or try this: This very versatile salad is great for leftovers and can easily make a meal. Simply double the portion size and add your favorite protein such as grilled chicken or shrimp. For a vegetarian entrée, try adding garbanzo beans or strips of low-fat cheese.

NUTRITION INFORMATION PER SERVING (¾ CUP)
Calories 160 | Carbohydrate 23g (Sugars 3g) | Total Fat 6g (Sat Fat 1g) | Protein 5g | Fiber 3g | Cholesterol 0mg | Sodium 55mg | Food Exchanges: 1 Starch, 1 Vegetable, 1 Fat | Carbohydrate Choices: 1½ | Weight Watcher Smart Point Comparison: 4

Creamy Macaroni Salad Three Ways

Creamy homemade macaroni salad is a great comfort food that pleases any crowd. This simple wholesome recipe can be easily altered to accommodate different tastes or the ingredients you have on hand. The three ways I suggest are: the traditional Southern version with cheddar cheese and peas, a slightly sweeter Kid's Favorite variation, and a delicious Seafood variation that's terrific as a light meal.

MAKES 8 SERVINGS

½ cup light mayonnaise

⅓ cup light sour cream or plain low-fat yogurt

¼ teaspoon salt, or to taste

¼ teaspoon black pepper

½ cup reduced-fat sharp cheddar cheese

3 cups cooked large elbow multigrain pasta (2 cups dry)

1½ cups finely diced celery

1 cup small diced red bell pepper

½ cup frozen green peas

½ cup chopped green onion

1. In a small bowl, combine the mayonnaise, yogurt, salt, and pepper.

2. In a large bowl, combine the remaining ingredients. Add the mayonnaise mixture and gently stir until well mixed. Refrigerate and serve chilled.

Kid's Favorite Variation: Add 2 tablespoons each apple cider vinegar and granulated no-calorie sweetener to the ingredients in step 1. Omit the cheese. (Subtract 1 gram fat and 10 calories per serving.)

Seafood Variation: Increase the light sour cream or yogurt to ½ cup and add 1 teaspoon chopped fresh dill in step 1. Add 1 cup halved cherry tomatoes and 2 (6-ounce) cans water-packed tuna, drained, or 1 pound small cooked shrimp to ingredients in step 2. Omit the cheese. (Adds 50 calories, 9 grams of protein, and .5 grams of fat for a 1 cup serving.)

DARE *TO* COMPARE ·
A ⅔ cup serving of traditional home-style mayonnaise-laden macaroni salad has over 400 calories.

NUTRITION INFORMATION PER SERVING (⅔ CUP) ·
Calories 150 | Carbohydrate 19g (Sugars 3g) | Total Fat 6g (Sat Fat 1.5g) | Protein 6g | Fiber 3g | Cholesterol 5mg | Sodium 260mg | Food Exchanges: 1 Starch, 1 Fat | Carbohydrate Choices: 1 | Weight Watcher Smart Point Comparison: 4

Warm Spinach Salad with Olive Oil and Garlic

I modeled this recipe after one my spinach- and garlic-loving husband often orders at his favorite Italian restaurant. My goal was to find an easy and healthful way to make it at home without sacrificing its great flavor. To make preparation easier I replaced the whole garlic cloves with fresh minced garlic, and to make it lower in fat I substituted chicken broth for a portion of the olive oil. I then added a bit more balsamic vinegar to kick up the original flavor. My husband says that this version is better than the one he used to order. Mission accomplished!

MAKES 2 SERVINGS

¼ cup chicken broth

2 teaspoons minced garlic (4 cloves)

1 tablespoon olive oil

2 tablespoons balsamic vinegar

Pinch of salt

Pepper to taste

8 cups spinach

2 tablespoons grated Parmesan cheese

1. Add the chicken broth and garlic to a large sauté pan and place over medium heat. Bring to a simmer. Reduce the heat to medium low, cover, and cook for 10 minutes to soften and mellow the garlic. (The chicken broth should reduce by no more than half.)

2. Whisk in the olive oil, balsamic vinegar, salt, and pepper. Turn off the heat and add the spinach. Using tongs, quickly toss the spinach in warm dressing just until coated. Immediately transfer to serving plates.

3. Top with the grated Parmesan cheese and serve.

Marlene Says: This big restaurant-style salad delivers a whopping 160 percent of your daily vitamin A, 60 percent of your vitamin C, and 20 percent each of calcium and iron.

NUTRITION INFORMATION PER SERVING (½ RECIPE)
Calories 140 | Carbohydrate 9g (Sugars 3g) | Total Fat 9g (Sat Fat 2g) | Protein 7g | Fiber 3g | Cholesterol 5mg | Sodium 350mg | Food Exchanges: 2 Vegetables, 1 Medium-Fat Meat, 1 Fat | Carbohydrate Choices: ½ Weight Watcher Smart Point Comparison: 4

Entrée Salads

Thai Shrimp Salad

This simple salad is bursting with traditional Thai flavor. The dressing is made with fish sauce, or nam pla, a common ingredient in Thai cooking. If you have not cooked with this pungent, salty condiment before, do not fret when you open the bottle and smell its strong aroma. It will dissipate and impart its distinctive taste, adding a wonderful depth to the dressing. However, if you prefer to leave it out, the dressing will still have a delicious Asian flavor.

MAKES 2 SERVINGS

DRESSING

2 tablespoons lime juice (1 lime)

2 tablespoons natural rice wine vinegar

2 teaspoons reduced-sodium soy sauce

2 teaspoons fish sauce

½ teaspoon minced garlic (about 1 clove)

¼ teaspoon grated fresh ginger

1½ tablespoons granulated sugar or granulated no-calorie sweetener*

2 tablespoons chopped fresh cilantro

SALAD

2½ cups mixed greens

¾ cup sliced cucumber

½ cup halved cherry tomatoes

¼ cup chopped fresh mint

8 ounces cooked and peeled shrimp

2 tablespoons chopped green onions

1. To make the dressing, in a small bowl whisk together all the lime juice, vinegar, soy sauce, fish sauce, garlic, ginger, sugar, and cilantro.

2. For the salad, in a large bowl, combine the greens, cucumber, tomatoes, mint, shrimp, and green onions.

3. Pour the dressing on top and toss together lightly. Serve immediately.

Marlene Says: Asian foods tend to be high in sodium. If you choose to omit the fish sauce completely, the sodium will be reduced by 400 mg per serving.

*See page 382 for sweetener options

NUTRITION INFORMATION PER SERVING (1 SALAD)
Calories 160 | Carbohydrate 10g (Sugars 3g) | Total Fat 1.5g (Sat Fat 0g) | Protein 27g | Fiber 3g | Cholesterol 220mg | Sodium 1040mg | Food Exchanges: 4 Lean Meat, 1½ Vegetables | Carbohydrate Choices: ½ | Weight Watcher Smart Point Comparison: 2

Everyday Chicken Caesar Salad

Chicken Caesar Salad is undoubtedly one of the most popular (if not the most popular) entrée salad featured on restaurant menus. But what most people don't realize is that most recipes for Chicken Caesar Salads contain more fat and calories than a loaded Big Mac—that's a big problem, especially if you enjoy this salad as much as I do. So here's an easy way to create a delicious and healthful restaurant-quality Chicken Caesar salad at home. To enjoy it as a side salad, simply leave out the chicken.

MAKES 4 SERVINGS

DRESSING

2 tablespoons lemon juice

3 tablespoons low-fat plain yogurt

2 teaspoons Dijon mustard

1½ teaspoons minced garlic (3 cloves)

1 teaspoon Worcestershire sauce

1 teaspoon anchovy paste*

2 tablespoons extra-virgin olive oil

3 tablespoons grated Parmesan cheese

½ teaspoon ground black pepper, or to taste

SALAD

8 cups romaine lettuce

3 cups shredded cooked skinless chicken breast

1 cup croutons

Parmesan for garnish (optional)

1. To make the dressing, in a food processor combine the lemon juice, yogurt, mustard, garlic, Worcestershire sauce, and anchovy paste and pulse briefly. With the processor running, slowly add in the olive oil until the dressing is creamy and smooth. Add the Parmesan and pepper and pulse briefly.

2. For the salad, in a large bowl combine the lettuce, chicken, and croutons.

3. Pour the dressing on top, and toss together to combine.

> **DARE *TO* COMPARE**··
> Order a Chicken Caesar Salad at the Old Spaghetti Factory® instead and be prepared to eat 990 calories, 75 grams of fat, 30 grams of carbohydrate and 2400 mg of sodium.

* Even if you think you don't like anchovies, you'll find that a touch of the paste really makes the dressing taste authentic, with no fishy taste.

NUTRITION INFORMATION PER SERVING (GENEROUS 2 CUPS)··
Calories 325 | Carbohydrate 9g (Sugars 1g) | Total Fat 14g (Sat Fat 3g) | Protein 39g | Fiber 2g | Cholesterol 105mg | Sodium 360mg | Food Exchanges: 4 Lean Meat, 1 Vegetable, 1 Fat, ½ Starch | Carbohydrate Choices: ½
Weight Watcher Smart Point Comparison: 8

Buffalo Chicken and Blue Cheese Salad

Nipping at the heels of Caesar salad in popularity, this newcomer to the salad-as-a-meal arena has a flavor combination that's hard to beat. Here, spicy buffalo-wing flavored chicken combines with cool and crunchy carrots, celery, and romaine lettuce, and then is topped with a luscious blue cheese dressing.

MAKES 4 SERVINGS

DRESSING

¼ cup buttermilk

¼ cup light sour cream

2 tablespoons light mayonnaise

¼ cup crumbled blue cheese

1 tablespoon apple cider vinegar

¼ teaspoon garlic powder

Pepper to taste

SALAD

5 cups chopped romaine lettuce

½ cup chopped carrot

¾ cup chopped celery (2 stalks)

2 teaspoons vegetable oil

1 pound boneless, skinless chicken breasts or tenders, cut into ½-inch cubes

½ teaspoon garlic powder

½ teaspoon onion powder

3 tablespoons (or more) hot sauce

4 teaspoons butter or margarine

¾ cup chopped green onion

1. To make the dressing, in a small bowl whisk together the buttermilk, sour cream, mayonnaise, blue cheese, cider vinegar, garlic powder, and pepper. Cover and place in the refrigerator.

2. For the salad, in a large bowl combine the lettuce, carrot, and celery. Set aside.

3. Heat the oil in a large nonstick skillet over medium-high heat. Add the chicken and cook, stirring frequently, until browned and almost cooked through, 3 to 4 minutes.

4. Combine the garlic powder, onion powder, and hot sauce. Add the hot sauce mix and butter to the skillet. Swirl the chicken in the sauce and cook 1 to 2 additional minutes, or until sauce completely coats chicken.

5. Add the chicken to the lettuce mix to combine. Portion the salad onto four plates. Divide the dressing among the salads, spooning across the top. Sprinkle with the green onions.

Or try this: Add some fiber and take it to go. To create a *Buffalo and Blue Wrap*, smear 3 tablespoons of the blue cheese dressing onto a large reduced-carb tortilla, add the salad mix and green onions, and wrap it up burrito style.

NUTRITION INFORMATION PER SERVING (1 SALAD) ·······························
Calories 280 | Carbohydrate 6g (Sugars 4g) | Total Fat 14g (Sat Fat 6g) | Protein 31g | Fiber 2g | Cholesterol 90mg | Sodium 370mg | Food Exchanges: 4 Lean Meat, 1 Vegetable, 1 Fat | Carbohydrate Choices: ½ | Weight Watcher Smart Point Comparison: 7

Chinese Chicken Salad with Crunchy Ramen® Noodles

This salad is positively addictive. The first time I had it was at a potluck dinner and I enjoyed it so much I asked the host to make it for my bridal shower. When I finally saw a copy of the original recipe, with its large amounts of oil, nuts, and sugar, I knew I would have to find a way to make it healthier if I wanted to keep enjoying it. I now have a version I enjoy every bit as much as the original that contains one-half the original calories and carbs and one-third the fat. Enjoy.

MAKES 4 SERVINGS

DRESSING

2 tablespoons canola oil

¼ cup natural wine vinegar

¼ cup granulated no-calorie sweetener (or 6 packets)*

1½ tablespoons reduced-sodium soy sauce

1 tablespoon sesame oil

SALAD

¼ cup slivered almonds

5 cups shredded cabbage (preferably Napa)

1 large carrot, shredded (about ¾ cup)

½ cup diced green onion

1 (8-ounce) can sliced water chestnuts, drained

1 (3-ounce) package plain ramen noodles, broken into medium-size pieces

2 cups chopped cooked skinless chicken breast

1. To make the dressing, in a small bowl, whisk together the canola oil, vinegar, sweetener, soy sauce, and sesame oil.

2. For the salad, place the almonds in a dry small skillet and toast over low heat for about 2 to 3 minutes, until the almonds are browned. Set aside.

3. In a large bowl, combine the cabbage, carrot, green onion, and water chestnuts. Add the ramen noodles and lightly toss.

4. Pour the dressing over the salad and toss well to coat. Let stand 10 minutes, top with the almonds and serve.

DARE TO COMPARE ·······················
Made with the original recipe, this entrée salad contained 850 calories, 57 grams of fat, 52 grams of carbohydrate, and 1,000 mg of sodium!

*See page 382 for sweetener options

NUTRITION INFORMATION PER SERVING (1½ CUPS) ·······················
Calories 380 | Carbohydrate 25g (Sugars 6g) | Total Fat 18g (Sat Fat 3g) | Protein 23g | Fiber 7g | Cholesterol 50mg | Sodium 400mg | Food Exchanges: 3 Lean Meat, 2 Fat, 1 Starch, 1 Fat | Carbohydrate Choices: 1 | Weight Watcher Smart Point Comparison: 9

Fajita Beef Salad

I find it exciting to create new flavor and texture combinations. I am delighted with this recipe, which pairs the cold freshness of a salad with the warm smoky flavor of grilled fajitas. Quickly stir-frying the beef rather than grilling also makes this dish not only delicious but also all-weather friendly.

MAKES 4 SERVINGS

MARINADE

2 tablespoons lime juice
  (1 lime)

2 teaspoons olive oil

1 garlic clove, minced

¼ teaspoon liquid smoke

½ teaspoon dried oregano

¼ teaspoon ground cumin

¼ teaspoon salt

⅛ teaspoon cayenne pepper

SALAD

12 ounces well-trimmed beef
  top sirloin steak

6 cups chopped romaine
  lettuce

½ cup carrot slices

1 large red onion, sliced thickly
  (2 cups)

1 large red bell pepper, cut
  into thick strips

1¼ cups salsa, divided

¼ cup low-fat Mexican blend
  cheese

1. To make the marinade, in a small bowl whisk together the lime juice, oil, garlic, liquid smoke, oregano, cumin, salt, and cayenne pepper.

2. For the salad, slice the steak across the grain into very thin strips, about ¼ inch thick. Place the beef in a glass dish, cover with the marinade, and let sit for 15 to 20 minutes.

3. While the beef is marinating, toss together the lettuce and carrot in a large bowl.

4. Spray a large nonstick skillet with cooking spray and place over medium-high heat. Sauté the onion and pepper for 5 to 6 minutes, or until softened and slightly browned. Transfer to a bowl and cover to keep warm.

5. Turn the heat to high and spray the skillet again. Add the beef to the pan in a single layer, and sauté for 2 to 3 minutes, stirring until cooked through and browned. (This may take two batches.) Combine the onions and peppers with the beef.

6. To assemble, toss the salad with ¾ cup salsa. Divide the salad among four plates and top with the beef mixture. Divide the remaining ½ cup salsa among the salads and sprinkle with the cheese. Serve immediately.

Or try this: For restaurant-style Chili's®-Style Grilled Beef Fajitas, see page 329.

NUTRITION INFORMATION PER SERVING (1 SALAD) ·······················
Calories 230 | Carbohydrate 15g (Sugars 6g) | Total Fat 9g (Sat Fat 3g) | Protein 24g | Fiber 5g | Cholesterol 55mg | Sodium 230mg | Food Exchanges: 3 Lean Meat, 3 Vegetables | Carbohydrate Choices: ½ | Weight Watcher Smart Point Comparison: 5

Spinach, Tuna, and White Bean Salad

The combination of white cannellini beans and canned tuna is a classic Tuscan dish known as Fagioli Toscanelli con Tonno. *In this salad I have combined the traditional ingredients with spinach, red onion, and juicy, ripe red tomatoes to create a large, satisfying meal. The ingredients are layered rather than mixed, creating a beautiful presentation that's a snap to arrange.*

MAKES 2 SERVINGS

DRESSING

2 tablespoons lemon juice

1½ tablespoons extra-virgin olive oil

1 tablespoon water

1 tablespoon balsamic vinegar

½ teaspoon minced garlic (1 clove)

¾ teaspoon dried dill

Salt to taste

Pepper to taste

SALAD

4 cups spinach

½ red onion, sliced

¾ cup white cannellini beans (½ of a 15-ounce can), rinsed and drained

1 (6-ounce) can albacore tuna, packed in water

2 medium tomatoes, cut into wedges, or 8 to 10 cherry tomatoes

1. For the dressing, in a small bowl whisk together the lemon juice, olive oil, water, vinegar, garlic, dill, salt, and pepper. Cover and set aside in the refrigerator to chill.

2. For the salad, divide the spinach leaves between two plates. Divide the onion slices and beans between the plates, on top of the spinach. Place half of the tuna on top of each salad and arrange the tomato around the edges of the plates.

3. Divide the dressing between the salads.

NUTRITION INFORMATION PER SERVING (1 SALAD)
Calories 330 | Carbohydrate 26g (Sugars 9g) | Total Fat 12g (Sat Fat 1g) | Protein 29g | Fiber 7g | Cholesterol 25mg | Sodium 400mg | Food Exchanges: 4 Lean Meat, 1 Starch, 1 Vegetable, 1 Fat | Carbohydrate Choices: 1 | Weight Watcher Smart Point Comparison: 7

Southwest Chicken Salad

One of my favorite on-the-go meals is the Southwest Chicken Salad at McDonald's®. Full of flavor and texture, it's a satisfying taste of the Southwest with less fat and fewer calories than many other fast foods. Using it as my inspiration, I have developed my own version to share with the whole family for a fraction of the cost (and the temptations that come with eating in a fast food restaurant).

MAKES 4 SERVINGS

DRESSING

¼ cup red wine vinegar

3 tablespoons lime juice (about 2 limes)

3 tablespoons seasoned rice wine vinegar

2 tablespoons canola oil

1 teaspoon cumin

½ teaspoon chili powder

½ teaspoon minced garlic

¼ cup finely chopped fresh cilantro

SALAD

1 medium red bell pepper, chopped

1 cup canned black beans, drained and rinsed

½ cup corn niblets, drained

2 cups chopped or shredded cooked skinless chicken breast (about 12 ounces)

8 cups chopped romaine lettuce

¼ cup crushed baked tortilla chips (optional)

1. To make the dressing, in a small bowl whisk together the red wine vinegar, lime juice, rice wine vinegar, oil, cumin, chili powder, garlic, and cilantro. Set aside.

2. For the salad, gently toss the pepper, beans, corn, and chicken with the dressing.

3. Place 2 cups chopped lettuce on each of four plates and top with the chicken mixture. Pour any remaining dressing over the salads and top with the crushed tortilla chips, if using.

NUTRITION INFORMATION PER SERVING (1 SALAD)
Calories 310 | Carbohydrate 21g (Sugars 5g) | Total Fat 13g (Sat Fat 2g) | Protein 30g | Fiber 6g | Cholesterol 55mg | Sodium 390mg | Food Exchanges: 4 Lean Meat, 1 Starch, 1 Vegetable, 1 Fat | Carbohydrate Choices: 1 | Weight Watcher Smart Point Comparison: 7

Food in Hand

DILLY OF A TUNA SANDWICH

NUTTY CHICKEN SALAD SANDWICH

STUFFED SEAFOOD SALAD ROLLS

GREEK PITA POCKET

DELI-STYLE ROAST BEEF SANDWICH
WITH HORSERADISH SAUCE

VERY VEGGIE WRAP

CHICKEN CAESAR WRAP

EXPRESS BEEF LETTUCE WRAPS

WAY BETTER FOR YOU TUNA MELT

TURKEY PESTO PANINI

CRISPY, SPICY CHICKEN SANDWICH

JUST RIGHT MEATBALL HEROES

QUICK PITA PIZZAS

TURKEY BURGERS ITALIANO

SURPRISE TURKEY JOES

BAJA FISH TACOS

Hand-held food is the perfect choice when it comes to convenience and fun—after all there is no fork, no knife, and often no plate required! The sandwich is a prime example. It was born in eighteenth-century England, where John Montague, the fourth Earl of Sandwich, was such a passionate card player that rather than stop the game to eat he had his servants place meat between two slices of bread. Today sandwiches are not only the number one on-the-go meal but also America's favorite dinner. But traditional hot and cold sandwiches aren't the only hand-held foods we love to grab. Tacos, pizza, and the popular "wrap" have all been created as our love for quick, casual fare has grown.

Unfortunately, when it comes to good health there is nothing fun about the nutritional content of many of the hand-held foods we love to eat. In the effort to satisfy our cravings for all things crispy, cheesy, and creamy, much of the casual fare we enjoy has gotten out of hand (so to speak), when it comes to fat and calories. The case in point is easily made with one of my stepdaughter Colleen's favorite sandwiches—the regular tuna melt at Schlotzsky's® sandwich shop. When faced with choosing the sandwich she loved, with it's staggering 1399 calories, 54 grams of fat (with 25 of them saturated), and 159 grams of carbohydrate, or sticking to her meal plan, Colleen was torn. Her dilemma inspired us to create the Way Better for You Tuna Melt on page 213. Served on toasted sourdough, it's creamy, cheesy, and melty, just like Schlotzsky's, but contains only 330 calories, 12 grams of fat, and 28 grams of carbohydrate. Now not only can she enjoy her favorite sandwich guilt-free, so can you.

In this chapter you will find a large selection of today's most popular hand-held foods with all the flavor and flair of the originals, simply without the extra fat, calories, carbohydrates—or cost! From the creamy Stuffed Seafood Salad Rolls and slightly sweet Express Beef Lettuce Wraps, to cheesy Quick Pita Pizza's and Crispy, Spicy Chicken Sandwiches, I guarantee there is something here for everyone and every taste. P.S.: In the Breakfast Entrées chapter you will find several wonderful hand-held breakfast recipes, including my favorite—the Breakfast BLT.

For the Love of Bread

It seems ironic that bread, one of life's greatest staples, is often the first to go when we try to lose weight or limit carbohydrates. One ounce of plain bread averages just 80 calories, but variations in size, density, and ingredients can vastly alter the nutrient content of bread choices. For example, eating a large bagel is the equivalent to eating four regular slices of bread (or eight pieces of "light bread"!). When it comes to ingredients, added oils and sugars add calories, while whole grains and added fiber reduce calories and lower the glycemic index (or blood sugar impact) of bread.

This handy guide highlights the breads you will find in my bread-containing creations throughout the book. It also highlights the positive nutritional difference choosing light and whole grain breads, tortillas, and English muffins can make for any bread lover!

VARIETY	CALORIES	CARBS	FAT	PROTEIN	FIBER	CARB CHOICES	POINT COMPARISON
Regular White Slice, 1 oz.	80	14g	1g	3g	0g	1	1
Light Wheat or White, Slice	45	9g	0g	3g	3g	½	1
White Pita Pocket 6" diameter	165	33g	1g	5g	1g	2	3
Whole Wheat Pita Pocket 4" diameter	80	15g	0.5g	3g	2g	1	1
Whole Wheat Hamburger Bun	130	20g	2g	2g	2g	1	2
Hot Dog Roll	110	21g	1g	3g	1g	1½	2
Submarine or Hoagie Roll	210	39g	3g	5g	2g	2½	4
Subway 6-inch Wheat Sub Roll	250	48g	3.5g	10g	4g	3	5
Corn Tortilla	60	12g	1g	1g	1g	1	1
Flour Tortilla (8-inch round)	150	25g	1.5g	4g	1g	1½	3
High-Fiber Tortilla (8-inch) round)	110	18g	2.5g	5g	11g	½	2
English Muffin	120	25g	1g	4g	1g	1½	2
Light English Muffin	100	24g	1g	6g	8g	1	1
Large Bagel (Bagel store variety)	300	60g	1g	12g	4g	4	6
Mini Whole Wheat Bagel	120	22g	1g	5g	3g	1	2

*White whole wheat bread is a whole grain with the look and taste of white.

Dilly of a Tuna Sandwich

No need to hit the deli when you can make great tasting, dill-icious sandwiches right at home. This carb-conscious healthy sandwich uses light bread, which is higher in fiber and lower in carbohydrates than regular bread. You can substitute your favorite bread or eliminate it altogether and wrap the tuna filling in large lettuce leaves. (Just remember that two slices of light wheat bread contain 90 calories, 18 grams of carbohydrate, and 5 grams of fiber, so you can adjust the nutrition content and carbs accordingly.)

MAKES 2 SERVINGS

1 (6-ounce) can water-packed white albacore tuna, drained and rinsed

1 tablespoon light mayonnaise

1 tablespoon low-fat plain yogurt

1 small carrot, grated

2 green onions, minced

¾ teaspoon fresh minced or ½ teaspoon dried dill

Pepper to taste

2 large lettuce leaves, washed and dried

4 slices light wheat or white bread

1. Place the tuna in a small bowl and flake with a fork.

2. Mix in the mayonnaise, yogurt, carrot, onions, dill, and pepper.

3. Place the lettuce on two slices of the bread. Pile half of the tuna mixture onto each sandwich. Top each with another piece of lettuce and bread.

Marlene Says: To quickly reduce the sodium content of canned tuna, open the can with a can opener but do not remove the lid. Place the can over the sink and while holding the lid down drain the can of the water. With the lid still intact, refill the can with fresh water. Swirl the water into the tuna and then drain one more time.

NUTRITION INFORMATION PER SERVING (1 SANDWICH)
Calories 230 | Carbohydrate 21g (Sugars 5g) | Total Fat 5g (Sat Fat 1g) | Protein 25g | Fiber 8g | Cholesterol 35mg | Sodium 510mg | Food Exchanges: 3 Lean Meat, 1 Starch, ½ Fat | Carbohydrate Choices: 1 | Weight Watcher Smart Point Comparison: 5

Nutty Chicken Salad Sandwich

My nut-loving husband and I had a lengthy discussion on whether or not slivered or sliced almonds should be used in this mouth-watering, creamy chicken salad to give it the proper nutty crunch. We finally agreed that the slivered version provided a heftier crunch, but if you prefer to use sliced, by all means do! Either way, don't forget to toast the nuts. The extra flavor and crunch are well worth this brief step.

MAKES 4 SERVINGS

¼ cup slivered almonds

2 cups diced cooked chicken

3 tablespoons light mayonnaise

3 tablespoons low-fat plain yogurt

⅓ cup finely diced celery

⅛ teaspoon garlic powder

⅛ teaspoon onion powder

⅛ teaspoon salt, or to taste

⅛ teaspoon black pepper, or to taste

¼ cup finely diced red onion (optional)

8 slices light white bread

1 cup shredded lettuce

1. Place the almonds in a small dry skillet over medium heat and toast for 3 to 4 minutes, or until the almonds are lightly browned and fragrant. Remove from heat and cool.

2. In a large bowl, combine the chicken, mayonnaise, yogurt, celery, spices, and red onion, if desired. Add the toasted almonds and mix well.

3. To assemble the sandwiches, scoop ½ cup of chicken salad onto half of the bread slices. Top each with ¼ cup shredded lettuce and a remaining slice of bread.

Or try this: For a terrific old-fashioned chicken salad plate place ½ cup of chicken salad atop of a bed of fresh greens. Garnish with cucumber and tomato slices and a handful of whole wheat crackers.

NUTRITION INFORMATION PER SERVING (1 SANDWICH) ⋯⋯⋯⋯⋯⋯⋯⋯⋯⋯⋯⋯
Calories 280 ∣ Carbohydrate 23g (Sugars 6g) ∣ Total Fat 10g (Sat Fat 1.5g) ∣ Protein 27g ∣ Fiber 8g ∣ Cholesterol 35mg ∣ Sodium 420mg ∣ Food Exchanges: 3 Lean Meat, 1 Starch, 1 Fat ∣ Carbohydrate Choices: 1 ∣ Weight Watcher Smart Point Comparison: 7

Stuffed Seafood Salad Rolls

My inspiration for this recipe came from the ever-popular crab stands dotted along Fisherman's Wharf in San Francisco where locals and visitors line up for fresh walk-a-way seafood specialties and sourdough bread. In my version of this local specialty I combine both crab and shrimp with Old Bay seasoning and a couple drops of Tabasco to create a creamy seafood filling stuffed into partially hollowed out sourdough rolls. These are definitely worth lining up for!

MAKES 4 SERVINGS

1 cup lump crabmeat or imitation crabmeat (about 6 ounces)

1 cup cooked baby shrimp (about 6 ounces)

⅓ cup finely diced celery

3 tablespoons light mayonnaise

2 tablespoons low-fat plain yogurt

¼ teaspoon Old Bay seasoning

2 to 3 drops Tabasco sauce

¼ cup chopped green or red onion (optional)

4 sourdough rolls (about 2.25 ounces each)

1. In a large bowl, mix together the crab, shrimp, celery, mayonnaise, and yogurt. Add the Old Bay seasoning, Tabasco sauce, and onion if desired, and mix well.

2. Using a serrated knife, cut near the top third of each of the rolls, taking care not to cut all the way through the rolls. Pull out part of the bread from bottom half of the roll to form a "well." Discard the extra bread. Spoon the seafood salad mixture into each of the rolls.

> **DARE TO COMPARE** ·····································
> Both the crab stand rolls and mine are made with sourdough bread, which has a lower glycemic index (the rate at which food will raise your blood sugar) than other white breads. Unfortunately the crab stand rolls are packed with a lot more than low-fat crab. Each stuffed roll is estimated to contain over 700 calories, 400 of which, or 45 grams, are from fat!

NUTRITION INFORMATION PER SERVING (1 SANDWICH) ·····························
Calories 250 | Carbohydrate 25g (Sugars 2g) | Total Fat 6g (Sat Fat 1.5g) | Protein 22g | Fiber 2g | Cholesterol 100mg | Sodium 590mg | Food Exchanges: 3 Lean Meat, 1½ Starch, 1 Fat | Carbohydrate Choices: 1½ | Weight Watcher Smart Point Comparison: 6

Greek Pita Pocket

These delectable, heart-healthy pita pockets serve up all the fabulous flavors of a Greek salad—right in the palm of your hand. When choosing a pita bread, be sure to read the nutrition label because the nutrient content varies from brand to brand. Some brands contain considerably more calories and carbohydrates than others.

MAKES 4 SERVINGS

2 whole wheat pita pockets,*
   cut in half

4 red or green leaf lettuce
   leaves

2 tomatoes, sliced thick
   (2 to 3 slices per tomato)

½ cup peeled and sliced
   cucumber

6 tablespoons crumbled,
   reduced-fat feta cheese

¼ cup slivered red onion

8 kalamata olives, cut in half

GREEK DRESSING:

2 tablespoons virgin olive oil

2 tablespoons red wine
   vinegar

1 teaspoon dried oregano

1 garlic clove, crushed

¼ teaspoon black pepper

Pinch of salt

* Each serving contains 80
   calories, 17 grams of carb, and
   2 grams of fiber.

1. Open each pita with a small knife. Tuck one piece of lettuce inside each pocket pushing it up against one side. Add two slices of tomato and then tuck in several slices of cucumber. Sprinkle each pocket with 1 heaping tablespoon of crumbled feta and ¼ of the onion.

2. In a small bowl whisk together all of the dressing ingredients. Drizzle each pocket with dressing. Garnish with four olive halves.

Perfect Pairing: Add a cup of Creamy Basil Tomato Soup and a fresh orange to complete your meal.

NUTRITION INFORMATION PER SERVING (1 SANDWICH)
Calories 210 | Carbohydrate 23g (Sugars 2g) | Total Fat 10g (Sat Fat 1g) | Protein 7g | Fiber 4g | Cholesterol 100mg | Sodium 575mg | Food Exchanges: 1 Medium-Fat Meat, 1 Starch, 1 Vegetable, 1 Fat | Carbohydrate Choices: 1½ | Weight Watcher Smart Point Comparison: 6

Deli-Style Roast Beef Sandwich with Horseradish Sauce

This sandwich is delicious proof that even red meat and cheese can be part of a healthy diet when properly selected and prepared. Here, two hungry-man favorites, beef and cheese, are complemented with a creamy homemade horseradish sauce on wholesome pumpernickel bread, creating a sandwich that's too good to miss.

MAKES 2 SERVINGS

1½ tablespoons light mayonnaise

1½ tablespoons low-fat plain yogurt

2 teaspoons horseradish

½ teaspoon granulated sugar

4 slices pumpernickel bread

2 large red lettuce leaves

1 medium tomato, sliced

Sliced red onion (optional)

4 ounces thin-sliced deli roast beef

2 slices reduced-fat cheddar cheese

1. In a small bowl combine the mayonnaise, yogurt, horseradish, and sugar. Set aside.

2. Line two slices of bread with lettuce, tomato, and sliced onion, if using. Top with roast beef and cheese. Spread horseradish sauce on remaining slice of bread and close the sandwiches.

Marlene Says: Most deli roast beef is cut from the eye of the round and is low in fat and high in nutrients, including iron, zinc, and B-vitamins thiamin, riboflavin, niacin, and B12. If you are uncertain if it is lean, ask before you buy.

NUTRITION INFORMATION PER SERVING (1 SANDWICH)
Calories 310 | Carbohydrate 28g (Sugars 3g) | Total Fat 9g (Sat Fat 4g) | Protein 19g | Fiber 2g | Cholesterol 45mg | Sodium 680mg | Food Exchanges: 3 Lean Meat, 2 Starch, ½ Fat | Carbohydrate Choices: 2 | Weight Watcher Smart Point Comparison: 8

Very Veggie Wrap

Move over meat; this super vegetable wrap weighs in at almost half a satisfying pound. Loaded with good-for-you vegetables, creamy hummus, and awesome fresh flavor, each wrap also packs a hefty amount of nutrition by delivering more than an entire day's worth of vitamins A and C, and half your daily fiber needs. This wrap packs well to go.

MAKES 4 SERVINGS

4 (9-inch) reduced-carbohydrate high-fiber tortillas

Fresh ground black pepper to taste (optional)

4 large lettuce leaves

1 cup hummus (page 125)

¼ cup crumbled, reduced-fat feta

1 large red bell pepper, sliced

½ cup shredded carrot

⅓ cup slivered red onion

1 medium cucumber, peeled, halved and sliced

¾ cup alfalfa sprouts

1. Heat 1 tortilla in the microwave for 15 seconds to soften.

2. To assemble each wrap, spread ¼ cup hummus onto the middle section of the tortilla (to within 1½ inches of all sides). Add pepper if desired. Press the lettuce onto the hummus in the middle of the tortilla. Sprinkle the feta cheese, and arrange the pepper, carrot, onion, and cucumber on top of the lettuce. Top with the alfalfa sprouts. Fold the bottom 1½ inches of the wrap upward to cover filling and then fold in sides. Place a toothpick in the center of the wrap to hold it shut. Repeat with the remaining ingredients.

DARE *TO* COMPARE

A seemingly "healthy" 12-inch Blimpie Veggie Supreme packs on 1,106 calories, 56 grams of fat (33 of them saturated), 96 grams of carbohydrate, 2,800 milligrams sodium, and 6 grams of fiber.

NUTRITION INFORMATION PER SERVING (1 SANDWICH)
Calories 270 | Carbohydrate 37g (Sugars 3g) | Total Fat 10g (Sat Fat 4g) | Protein 18g | Fiber 17g | Cholesterol 5mg | Sodium 550mg | Food Exchanges: 2 Lean Meat, 1½ Starch, 1 Vegetable, 1 Fat | Carbohydrate Choices: 2
Weight Watcher Smart Point Comparison: 6

Chicken Caesar Wrap

Chicken Caesar wraps are popular and people pleasing, and just like a Caesar salad they are often loaded with excessive fat and calories, especially when you add an oversized carbohydrate-packed tortilla. Substituting a reduced-fat, high-fiber tortilla and a healthy chicken Caesar mix delivers the same great taste with less fat, fewer calories, lower carbs, and more belly-filling protein and fiber.

MAKES 4 SERVINGS

2 tablespoons olive oil

2 tablespoons lemon juice

2 tablespoons plain low-fat yogurt

3 tablespoons grated Parmesan cheese

2 teaspoons Dijon mustard

1 teaspoon Worcestershire sauce

1½ teaspoon minced garlic

½ teaspoon black pepper, or to taste

6 cups shredded romaine lettuce

2 cups shredded cooked skinless chicken breast

4 (9-inch) reduced-carbohydrate high-fiber tortillas

4 teaspoons grated Parmesan cheese

1. In a small bowl, whisk together the olive oil, lemon juice, yogurt, Parmesan cheese, mustard, Worcestershire sauce, and minced garlic. Add black pepper to taste and set aside.

2. In a large bowl, toss together the romaine and chicken. Pour the dressing on top and toss together.

3. To assemble the wraps, heat 1 tortilla in the microwave for 15 seconds to soften. Spoon about ¾ cup of the chicken salad mixture onto the middle of the wrap. Top with 1 teaspoon Parmesan cheese. Fold the bottom 1½-inches of the wrap upward to cover filling and then fold in sides. Place a toothpick in the center of the wrap to hold it shut. Repeat with the remaining ingredients.

Fit Tip: Look for a tortilla that has approximately 80-100 calories, and 10 to 13 grams of fiber. Two easy to find brands are Mission Carb Balance and La Tortilla Factory Smart and Delicious.

NUTRITION INFORMATION PER SERVING (1 SANDWICH)
Calories 350 | Carbohydrate 22g (Sugars 2g) | Total Fat 12g (Sat Fat 3g) | Protein 36g | Fiber 13g | Cholesterol 70mg | Sodium 490mg | Food Exchanges: 3 Lean Meat, 1 Starch, 2 Fat | Carbohydrate Choices: 1 | Weight Watcher Smart Point Comparison: 6

Express Beef Lettuce Wraps

When you need to "shed the bread" but don't want to sacrifice taste, you can't beat these delicious, sweet and spicy Asian lettuce wraps. They are modeled after those on the menu at P. F. Chang's China Bistro®, which is famous for its incredible Chinese chicken lettuce wraps. (P.S.: Although the ingredient list may look long, these really are quick and take just three easy steps.)

MAKES 4 SERVINGS

2 tablespoons reduced-sodium soy sauce

3 tablespoons granulated no-calorie sweetener

2 tablespoons natural rice wine vinegar

2 tablespoons hoisin

2 teaspoons sesame oil

½ teaspoon red chili flakes

1½ teaspoons cornstarch

1 tablespoon canola oil

1 pound lean ground beef

1 (8-ounce) can water chestnuts, drained and minced

1 cup chopped mushrooms

½ medium red bell pepper, finely chopped

4 green onions, chopped

1 small carrot, grated

1 large head butter lettuce, washed, dried, and separated

½ cucumber, thinly sliced, for garnish

1 small grated carrot, for garnish

Fresh mint leaves, for garnish

1. Place ¼ cup of water in a small saucepan. Whisk in the soy sauce, sweetener, vinegar, hoisin, sesame oil, red chili flakes, mustard, and cornstarch. Place over medium heat and bring to a low boil. Cook for 1 to 2 minutes, or until the sauce has thickened and clears. Set aside.

2. In a large nonstick skillet, heat oil until hot but not smoking. Add the beef and sauté, using a spoon to stir and break up the meat. Cook for 7 to 8 minutes or until the beef is just no longer pink. Add the water chestnuts, mushrooms, bell pepper, and green onions and cook for 3 to 4 minutes or until all vegetables are incorporated and the mushrooms are cooked.

3. Pour the warm sauce into beef. Stir to combine. Toss in the grated carrot and remove from the heat. Spoon the meat onto lettuce leaves, or place in a bowl and serve with lettuce leaves and garnishes.

DARE *TO* COMPARE ···
An appetizer order of chicken lettuce wraps at P. F. Chang's China Bistro® has 612 calories, 28 grams of fat, and 60 grams of carbohydrate. (A switch to ground chicken breast here will save you 35 calories and 7 grams of fat.)

NUTRITION INFORMATION PER SERVING (4 WRAPS) ·····························
Calories 295 | Carbohydrate 18g (Sugars 4g) | Total Fat 13g (Sat Fat 4g) | Protein 26g | Fiber 5g | Cholesterol 65mg | Sodium 640mg | Food Exchanges: 4 Lean Meat, 2 Vegetable, ½ Starch | Carbohydrate Choices: 1 | Weight Watcher Smart Point Comparison: 6

Way Better for You Tuna Melt

My stepdaughter, Colleen, adores tuna melts, but shortly after she was diagnosed with type 2 diabetes the reality sunk in that her melty cheesy American staple was a dietary disaster! To remedy this situation, Colleen and I were inspired to create the first of our many recipe "makeovers." I'll never forget how stunned Colleen was to learn that four of our versions matched the calorie count of only one of the restaurant versions she used to order (never mind the fat or the carbohydrates!). Most important, our recipe is just as creamy and filled with the traditional melty goodness we all expect in a tuna melt.

MAKES 2 SERVINGS

1 (6-ounce) can water-packed white albacore tuna, drained and rinsed

1½ tablespoons light mayonnaise

1½ tablespoons low-fat plain yogurt

4 slices sourdough bread

2 slices reduced-fat American cheese

2 teaspoons margarine or butter

1. Combine the tuna, mayonnaise, and yogurt and mix. Divide the tuna mix between two of the slices of bread. Lay the cheese on top of the tuna and cover with the remaining piece of bread.

2. Heat 1 teaspoon of the margarine in a large nonstick skillet over medium-low heat. Place the sandwiches in the skillet cheese side down. Cook for 3 to 4 minutes, or until underside is golden brown.

3. Lift the sandwiches out of the way, add the remaining margarine to the pan, and flip the sandwiches. Cook for 3 more minutes, or until the underside is golden brown and the cheese is melted.

> **DARE TO COMPARE** ·······················
> Schlotzsky's® tuna melt served on a sourdough bun with "fat-free dressing" clocks in at 1399 calories, 54 grams of fat (25 of them saturated), 159 grams of carbohydrate, and 4342 mgs of sodium.

NUTRITION INFORMATION PER SERVING (1 SANDWICH) ·····························
Calories 300 | Carbohydrate 25g (Sugars 2g) | Total Fat 10 (Sat Fat 2g) | Protein 26g | Fiber 0g | Cholesterol 25mg | Sodium 750mg | Food Exchanges: 3 Lean Meat, 1 Lean Meat, 2 Starch, 1 Fat | Carbohydrate Choices: 2 | Weight Watcher Smart Point Comparison: 7 (Schlotzsky's® 32)

Turkey Pesto Panini

The popularity of Italian "pressed" sandwiches, called panini, can be seen in restaurants and sandwich shops and by the plethora of fancy "presses" now available at cooking stores. But here's the kicker: you don't need any special equipment to make wonderfully flavorful panini. All you need is a nonstick grill pan or a basic nonstick skillet and a pot lid. This recipe will give you twice the pesto you will need, so you can easily double this recipe or you can store any leftover pesto, covered, in the refrigerator for up to one week. Pesto is a great-tasting pizza topping and is delicious tossed with pasta.

MAKES 2 SERVINGS

1 cup fresh spinach

1 cup fresh basil

2 tablespoons pine nuts or chopped walnuts

1 tablespoon extra-virgin olive oil

1 tablespoon chicken broth

2 garlic cloves, minced

¼ cup grated Parmesan cheese

4 slices foccacia bread (¼-inch thick for 1-ounce slices)

4 spinach leaves, washed and dried

6 ounces sliced, reduced-sodium turkey breast

2 (¾-inch) slices part-skim mozzarella cheese

1. To make the pesto, place the spinach and basil in a food processor. Add the nuts, oil, chicken broth, and garlic, and pulse to mix. Add the Parmesan and process until smooth.

2. Build the panini by spreading 1 rounded tablespoon of the pesto on two of the slices of foccacia. Layer the spinach, turkey, and mozzarella on top of the pesto and top with the remaining slice of bread.

3. Spray a nonstick grill pan or skillet with cooking spray and heat over medium-high heat.

4. Place the panini in the hot skillet. Using the bottom of a pot lid, press firmly down on the top of the panini. Cook it for about 3 minutes, or until the underside is golden brown, and then lift the panini, spray the skillet, flip, and press again. Cook for 3 more minutes or until the cheese is melted and underside is golden brown.

Fit Tip: To lower the sodium content of this panini by one-third, use reduced-sodium turkey, usually found sliced to order in the deli.

NUTRITION INFORMATION PER SERVING (1 PANINI)
Calories 330 | Carbohydrate 33g (Sugars 3g) | Total Fat 10g (Sat Fat 4.5g) | Protein 28g | Fiber 2g | Cholesterol 50mg | Sodium 850mg | Food Exchanges: 3 Lean Meat, 1 Medium-Fat Meat, 2 Starch, 1 Fat | Carbohydrate Choices: 2 | Weight Watcher Smart Point Comparison: 8

Crispy, Spicy Chicken Sandwich

In an effort to make their menu selections seem "healthier," fast food restaurants often include chicken sandwiches. The problem is that the best tasting of these chicken sandwiches, not surprisingly, are those that are deep-fried. The great news is that now you can enjoy the same great taste without ever having to buy the high-fat version of this sandwich in a restaurant again.

MAKES 4 SERVINGS

2 tablespoons reduced-fat mayonnaise

2 tablespoons low-fat plain yogurt

¼ teaspoon garlic powder

½ teaspoon Tabasco chipotle sauce, or less to taste

4 boneless, skinless chicken breasts (about 1-pound)

2 tablespoons all-purpose flour

2 tablespoons breadcrumbs

¾ teaspoon salt

½ teaspoon black pepper

¼ teaspoon onion powder

¼ teaspoon garlic powder

1 egg white, beaten

4 whole wheat hamburger buns

4 lettuce leaves

1 large tomato, sliced

1. In a small bowl, whisk the mayonnaise, yogurt, garlic powder, and Tabasco. Cover and place in the refrigerator.

2. Wrap each chicken breast in plastic wrap and gently pound them with a mallet on a cutting board to an even thickness (about ½-inch thick). Set aside. Place the egg white in a large flat bowl, and whisk until slightly airy.

3. Combine the flour, breadcrumbs, salt, pepper, onion powder, and garlic powder in another flat bowl.

4. Spray a large nonstick skillet with cooking spray and place over medium-high heat. Dip the chicken in the egg, and then roll in the breadcrumbs to coat. Place the chicken in the skillet and cook for 3 to 4 minutes on each side or until outside is browned and the inside is cooked through.

5. Remove the chipotle sauce from the refrigerator and spread about 1 tablespoon on the bottom half of each bun. Top with the chicken breast, lettuce, and tomato.

DARE *to* COMPARE
The spicy chicken sandwich at Jack in the Box® has 620 calories, 31 grams of fat, and 64 grams of carbohydrates.

NUTRITION INFORMATION PER SERVING (1 SANDWICH)
Calories 300 | Carbohydrate 24g (Sugars 4g) | Total Fat 12 (Sat Fat 2g) | Protein 29g | Fiber 3g | Cholesterol 65mg | Sodium 750mg | Food Exchanges: 4 Lean Meat, 2 Starch, 1 Fat | Carbohydrate Choices: 2 | Weight Watcher Smart Point Comparison: 7

Just Right Meatball Heroes

The only thing better than eating a meatball is eating a meatball sandwich! My hungry boys love meatball subs. What I don't like, though, is how unhealthy the sub shop meatball sandwiches can be. A small 6-inch meatball sub averages 800 calories and contains over 35 grams of fat. If you're watching carbohydrates, the rolls are often the equivalent of at least four pieces of bread. If you are watching your sodium intake, let's just say it is a whole day's worth! For this sub I take my Everyday Italian Meatballs (page 324) and top them with marinara sauce and Parmesan cheese to create a homemade meatball sandwich that makes me the hero.

MAKES 6 SERVINGS

1 recipe Everyday Italian Meatballs (page 324)

1½ cups marinara sauce*

6 hot dog rolls

6 tablespoons Parmesan cheese

* For delicious homemade marinara see page 244. When buying jarred sauce look for one that contains no more than 5 grams of sugar in each ½ cup.

1. Place the meatballs and marinara sauce in a medium saucepan over medium heat. Bring to a low simmer and cook for 3 to 4 minutes, or until both meatballs and sauce are warm.

2. Split the rolls and place 3 meatballs in each roll. Spoon the marinara over each and top with 1 tablespoon Parmesan cheese.

Or try this: To make it melty and toasty, pass on the Parmesan and top each sandwich with either 3 tablespooons or a ¾-ounce slice of shredded part-skim mozzarella cheese. Place heros on a baking pan and broil for 1 minute or until the cheese melts and bread toasts. (Adds 30 calories, 2 grams of fat, and 2 grams of protein to each sandwich.)

NUTRITION INFORMATION PER SERVING (1 SANDWICH)
Calories 320 | Carbohydrate 32g (Sugars 4g) | Total Fat 10 (Sat Fat 4g) | Protein 26g | Fiber 3g | Cholesterol 65mg | Sodium 750mg | Food Exchanges: 2½ Lean Meat, 1½ Starch, ½ Vegetable | Carbohydrate Choices: 2 | Weight Watcher Smart Point Comparison: 9

Quick Pita Pizzas

I make these pizzas whenever my sons want a speedy snack or light meal (and I usually make one for myself, too!) Pita bread makes for an amazingly easy pizza like crust. For variety, add different toppings such as veggies or lean turkey pepperoni slices.

MAKES 1 PIZZA

2 tablespoons pizza sauce

1 whole wheat pita

¼ cup shredded part-skim mozzarella cheese

1. Preheat the oven to 400°F.

2. Spread the sauce on top of the pita, and top with the cheese.

3. Bake for 8 to 10 minutes, until cheese is melted.

Or try this: For an extra crispy crust with less carb, carefully separate the 2 layers that form the pocket with a knife. Use only one of the layers, add toppings, and bake as directed. Reduces the carbohydrate by 14 grams and the calories by 56.)

NUTRITION INFORMATION PER SERVING (1 SANDWICH) ·······················
Calories 240 | Carbohydrate 34g (Sugars 4g) | Total Fat 7 (Sat Fat 3.5g) | Protein 14g | Fiber 5g | Cholesterol 15mg | Sodium 750mg | Food Exchanges: 2½ Lean Meat, 1½ Starch, ½ Vegetable | Carbohydrate Choices: 2 | Weight Watcher Smart Point Comparison: 7

Turkey Burgers Italiano

If turkey burgers conjure up images of dry plain burgers that pale in comparison to their beefy counterparts, you are in for a very pleasant surprise. These moist, flavorful burgers are made moist by adding breadcrumbs and tasty with "Italian-style" seasoning. Topped with marinara sauce and cheese, they may just become your new family favorite.

MAKES 4 SERVINGS

1 pound lean ground turkey

¼ cup breadcrumbs

½ teaspoon garlic salt

1 teaspoon dried oregano

1 large egg white

¼ teaspoon onion powder

⅛ teaspoon black pepper

¾ cup marinara sauce

4 (¾-inch) slices part-skim mozzarella cheese slices

4 whole wheat hamburger buns

1. In a large bowl, mix together the turkey, breadcrumbs, garlic salt, oregano, egg white, onion powder, and black pepper until all ingredients are thoroughly incorporated

2. Evenly separate the turkey into 4 balls and flatten to form burger patties.

3. Spray a large nonstick skillet with cooking spray and place over medium-high heat. Add the patties to the pan and cook turkey burgers about 4 minutes on each side, or until just cooked through. With burgers still in the pan, top each burger with the marinara and a slice of the cheese.

4. Cover the pan with a lid or foil and turn off the heat. Let sit for 3 to 4 minutes to allow the cheese to melt. Warm buns, if desired, and top with burgers.

Perfect Pairing: Round out your meal with Everyday Mixed Greens with Italian Vinaigrette (page 173).

NUTRITION INFORMATION PER SERVING (1 SANDWICH)
Calories 360 | Carbohydrate 33g (Sugars 4g) | Total Fat 11 (Sat Fat 4g) | Protein 30g | Fiber 4g | Cholesterol 70mg | Sodium 710mg | Food Exchanges: 3½ Lean Meat, 2 Starch, ½ Vegetable | Carbohydrate Choices: 2 | Weight Watcher Smart Point Comparison: 8

Surprise Turkey Joes

While quite content with the sloppy joe recipe I developed several years back, I couldn't help but be intrigued one night when I came across a recipe on the internet that had garnered rave reviews. The recipe used a rather unusual ingredient—diet cola. So my family and I had our own sloppy taste test: my old sloppy joe recipe against the new version. Well, as you can see from the ingredient list below, I now have a new recipe. After several follow-up tastings, we unanimously agreed that diet Dr. Pepper was even better than diet cola.

MAKES 6 SERVINGS

1 pound lean ground turkey
  (or half turkey and half beef)

½ cup diced onion

1 small green bell pepper, diced

3 stalks celery, diced

2 teaspoons all-purpose flour

¾ cup diet Dr. Pepper (or cola)

½ cup low-sugar ketchup*

1 tablespoon vinegar

1 tablespoon Worcestershire sauce

Pinch of salt

6 whole wheat hamburger buns

* Regular ketchup will add 5 grams of carbohydrate and 20 calories to each Joe.

1. In a medium skillet over medium heat brown the turkey with the onion, bell pepper, and celery.

2. When the meat is cooked through, drain the excess liquid and add the remaining ingredients except the buns; mix thoroughly. Reduce the heat, and simmer for 15 to 20 minutes or until thickened.

3. Serve a scant ¼ cup on each bun.

NUTRITION INFORMATION PER SERVING (1 SANDWICH)
Calories 270 | Carbohydrate 22g (Sugars 4g) | Total Fat 9 (Sat Fat 2.5g) | Protein 22g | Fiber 4g | Cholesterol 15mg | Sodium 510mg | Food Exchanges: 2½ Lean Meat, 1 Starch, 1 Vegetable | Carbohydrate Choices: 1½ | Weight Watcher Smart Point Comparison: 6

Baja Fish Tacos

The story goes that the first restaurant to specialize in Baja-style fish tacos opened in San Diego in 1983 after a college student went to Baja Mexico for spring break and came home not with a sunburn but rather with a passion for the local fish tacos. I must admit that I was a bit hesitant at first to try fish in a taco, but I too was hooked at first bite. My only criticism was that over 50 percent of the calories in each taco was from fat. I am thrilled to say that my version of these tasty tacos has half the fat, calories, carbs, and sodium yet is every bit as addictive as the original. And there are two tacos per serving because no one can eat just one!

MAKES 4 SERVINGS

3 tablespoons light mayonnaise

3 tablespoons low-fat plain yogurt

2 tablespoons low-fat milk

⅛ teaspoon Tabasco sauce

¾ teaspoon garlic salt, divided

1 pound white fish fillets, such as cod or tilapia, cut into four pieces

2 tablespoons all-purpose flour

½ teaspoon chili powder

¾ lime, cut into wedges

1 tablespoon vegetable oil

8 (6-inch) corn tortillas

2 cups finely shredded cabbage

Fresh cilantro for garnish

½ cup salsa (optional)

Lime wedges (optional)

1. In a small bowl, whisk together the mayonnaise, yogurt, milk, Tabasco sauce, and ⅛ teaspoon of the garlic salt.

2. Pat the fish fillets dry. In a shallow bowl, mix together the flour, chili powder, and remaining garlic salt. Squeeze the lime wedges over the fillets, and dredge in the flour mixture.

3. Heat the oil in a large nonstick skillet over medium-high heat. Pan-fry for 3 minutes on each side, or until slightly browned and fully cooked.

4. Wet the tortillas with a very small amount of water. Wrap them tightly in either a clean dish towel or a paper towel and microwave for 1 minute.

5. Assemble the tacos by dividing each piece of fish into two tortillas and drizzling 1 tablespoon of sauce on the fish. Tuck the cabbage into the tacos, and garnish with cilantro. If desired, serve with salsa and lime wedges.

DARE *to* COMPARE
Two World Famous Fish Tacos from Rubio's® have 540 calories, 26 grams of fat, 62 grams of carbohydrate, 18 grams of protein, and 960 mgs of sodium.

NUTRITION INFORMATION PER SERVING (2 TACOS)
Calories 300 | Carbohydrate 31g (Sugars 4g) | Total Fat 7 (Sat Fat 1g) | Protein 27g | Fiber 5g | Cholesterol 55mg | Sodium 500mg | Food Exchanges: 3 Very Lean Meat, 1½ Starch, ½ Vegetable, 1 Fat | Carbohydrate Choices: 2 | Weight Watcher Smart Point Comparison: 7

Great Pasta-bilities

COWBOY SPAGHETTI

PASTA PRIMAVERA

CHICKEN FAJITA PASTA

CREAMY SEAFOOD LINGUINE

PENNE AND SHRIMP IN SPICY TOMATO SAUCE

CORKSCREW CHICKEN AND BROCCOLI ALFREDO

GREEK CHICKEN BOWTIE PASTA

ASIAN BEEF NOODLE BOWL

LAZY PORK LO MEIN

SPICY CHICKEN ORIENTAL PRIMAVERA

RIGATONI, WHITE BEANS, AND SAUSAGE

FAST FIX LASAGNA BAKE

NUTTY BEEFY NOODLES

NEW-AGE TUNA NOODLE CASSEROLE

QUICK TURKEY BOLOGNESE

EVERYDAY SPAGHETTI AND ITALIAN MEATBALLS

Who doesn't love delicious, satisfying, and extremely versatile pasta?
Sadly, for many, pasta has been tainted with claims that it contributes to weight gain and high blood sugar. Well, I am here to say that pasta is a healthy, wholesome food that everyone can enjoy! Pasta is an excellent source of carbohydrates and a good source of protein, vitamins, and minerals. When it comes to gaining weight, calorie for calorie pasta is no more likely to make you gain weight than any other food. As for its effect on raising blood sugar, traditional Italian pasta has a dense compact structure, which actually causes it to digest more slowly than most refined grain foods, thus giving it a low glycemic index (the rate at which a food raises blood sugar).

That said, pasta can be challenging to fit into weight loss and diabetes diets. Why? First, although pasta's glycemic index is not high, pasta is still a very dense source of carbohydrates, which can be of concern for those who count carbs. And second, pasta is one of those foods we tend to overeat. A single serving of cooked pasta, according to the UDSA Food Pyramid, is a mere one-half cup. For those with diabetes, a carbohydrate choice or serving of cooked pasta is only one-third of a cup. When you consider that most restaurants serve up at least two cups of pasta in the average pasta dish (and that's before it's topped with even weightier sauces), it's easy to see why pasta can be a bit difficult.

That's why I am thrilled to tell you that in this chapter you will find more pasta-bilities than you have ever imagined for seamlessly fitting delectable pasta dishes into any healthy, calorie- or carbohydrate-conscious diet. I have s-t-r-e-t-c-h-e-d the calories and carbohydrates by adding flavorful fresh vegetables and lean protein to each recipe to create entrées with the perfect balance of carbohydrates, protein, and fat in portion sizes that will truly satisfy. From restaurant favorites, such as creamy Alfredo-style Corskscrew Chicken and Broccoli Pasta and Creamy Seafood Linguine, to quick-and-easy creations, such as Lazy Pork Lo Mein and Quick Turkey Bolognese, and of course good ol' Everyday Spaghetti and Meatballs, these pastas are too good to ever give up. (P.S.: Please feel free to mix and match the type of pasta you prefer, being sure to try some of the new healthy whole grain blends.)

For the Love of Pasta

For many years the only real variety found in pasta has been its shape. White refined pastas dominated the shelves with the exception of a smattering of whole wheat pastas known as much for their dark color, gritty texture, and pronounced wheaty taste as for their health qualities.

Today, a new generation of whole wheat, whole wheat blend, and whole-grain blend pastas line the shelves. The great news is that these new pastas, which also come in a myriad of shapes and sizes, deliver superior whole-grain nutrition without sacrificing taste.

Today's whole wheat pastas offer more fiber, vitamins, and minerals than refined pastas, but, unlike the whole wheat pastas of yesterday, they have a milder flavor and smoother texture. New "whole wheat blend" pastas also offer more fiber than white but have an even milder taste than that of whole wheat. Last, healthful whole-grain blends are the latest pasta sensation. Made with a varying mix of grains, they are more nutritious than refined pasta (with more fiber and protein) but are proud to boast a look and taste very similar to the refined pastas we all love.

MARLENE'S TIPS FOR PREPARING WHOLESOME PASTA

1. **Read the cooking instructions carefully.** Cooking times vary and most varieties are at their best served al dente. Overcooking can result in a gummy texture.

2. **Partner whole wheat and strong-flavored pastas with stronger-flavored sauces.** Spicy tomato sauces, nutty Asian sauces, and fragrant pesto are fantastic.

3. **Use creamy or traditional tomato-based sauces to soften the taste and conceal the color of whole-grain blend pastas.** "Plain" reveals the grain. Toss whole-grain blend pastas with your favorite sauces to please even the pickiest of pasta eaters.

4. **Add fresh vegetables and lean meats for flavor and texture.** Doing so places the focus on the entire dish while allowing you to reduce the amount of pasta.

5. **Keep trying until you find a brand you love.** Because the taste and texture of pasta varies considerably by brand (with new ones coming out all the time), try a few to find the one you and your family enjoy the best.

Cowboy Spaghetti

A few slices of lean center-cut bacon impart a ranch-worthy flavor to this hearty spaghetti dish adapted from Rachael Ray. Made even healthier with lean ground beef, turkey, and a mild-tasting multi-grain pasta, this rendition still has all the memorable flavors that have made it a family favorite. Keep the hot sauce nearby for those who really enjoy the heat.

MAKES 6 SERVINGS

8 ounces spaghetti

3 slices center-cut bacon, chopped

1 medium onion, chopped

1 medium green bell pepper, chopped

3 to 4 garlic cloves, minced

2 teaspoons dried oregano

½ pound lean ground beef

½ pound lean ground turkey

⅛ teaspoon black pepper

1 teaspoon hot sauce (like Tabasco)

2 teaspoons Worcestershire sauce

1 (14-ounce) can fire-roasted chopped tomatoes

1 (15-ounce) can tomato sauce

¾ cup (3 ounces) reduced-fat shredded cheddar cheese

1. Cook the pasta according to the package directions while preparing the sauce, and set aside.

2. Add the bacon to a large sauté pan over medium-high heat and cook 5 to 6 minutes, or until slightly crisp. Add the onion, bell pepper, garlic, and oregano and cook for 3 to 4 minutes, or until vegetables are slightly softened. Add the ground beef and turkey. Break the meat up as it cooks for 5 to 7 minutes, or until browned.

3. Add the black pepper, hot sauce, Worcestershire, chopped tomatoes, and tomato sauce. Stir and allow to simmer for 10 minutes.

4. Serve the hot spaghetti topped with the cowboy sauce and shredded cheese.

Family Focus: Feeding a family with different individual dietary needs can be tough. With this dish for those watching carbohydrates, you can cut back on the amount of pasta per serving and add extra sauce. And for those strictly counting calories (or points), serve ½ cup pasta with ½ cup sauce for a savings of 117 calories and 3 points. And don't forget to serve with a family-size green salad for everyone.

NUTRITION INFORMATION PER SERVING (1½ CUPS)
Calories 350 | Carbohydrate 39g (Sugars 6g) | Total Fat 9 (Sat Fat 3g) | Protein 29 | Fiber 6g | Cholesterol 33g | Sodium 600mg | Food Exchanges: 3 Lean Meat, 2 Vegetable, 1½ Starch | Carbohydrate Choices: 2½ | Weight Watcher Smart Point Comparison: 8

Pasta Primavera

Chock-full of fresh vegetables, this terrific pasta dish will fill you up but not out! I have included a colorful assortment to offer a variety of tastes and textures, but feel free to use any combination you like. Another great option is to include fresh, seasonal vegetables, such as substituting asparagus for broccoli in the spring and zucchini for the mushrooms in the summer. The best primavera recipes use only fresh vegetables, but thawed frozen broccoli florets also work quite nicely in a pinch.

MAKES 4 SERVINGS

6 ounces linguine

2 teaspoons olive oil

1 cup chopped onion

1 teaspoon dried thyme

½ teaspoon fresh cracked black pepper

Pinch of crushed red pepper (optional)

3 garlic cloves, minced

1 cup chopped carrot

2 cups broccoli florets

½ cup water

1 small red bell pepper, julienned

1 cup sliced mushrooms

1 cup reduced-sodium chicken or vegetable broth

2 teaspoons cornstarch

¼ cup nonfat half-and-half

¼ cup freshly grated Parmesan cheese

Salt to taste

1. Cook the pasta according to the package directions while preparing the sauce, and set aside.

2. Heat the oil in a large sauté pan over medium-high heat. Add the onion and sauté for 2 to 3 minutes, or slightly softened. Add the thyme, black pepper, red pepper, and garlic, and stir well.

3. Add the carrot and broccoli to the pan, and sauté to coat with seasonings. Add the water, cover, and allow the vegetables to steam for 3 to 4 minutes, or until the carrots begin to soften.

4. Add the bell pepper and mushrooms and stir. Add the broth to the pan. Whisk the cornstarch into the half-and-half, and add to the pan. Cook for 3 to 4 minutes, or until the sauce clears and the peppers are tender. Toss in the pasta and stir well to coat.

5. Add about half of the Parmesan cheese to the mixture and toss well. Season with salt to taste and top with the remaining Parmesan cheese.

Marlene Says: This is a great vegetarian recipe to have on hand. Be sure to use the vegetable broth option, and before serving, check to see if your guests eat dairy products. If not, there are many wonderful non-dairy cheeses that can replace the Parmesan.

NUTRITION INFORMATION PER SERVING (1½ CUPS)
Calories 250 | Carbohydrate 42 (sugars 7g) | Total Fat 5g (Sat Fat 1g) | Protein 13g | Fiber 8g | Cholesterol 5mg | Sodium 390mg | Food Exchanges: 2 Starch, 2 Vegetables, 1 Fat | Carbohydrate Choices: 2½ | Weight Watcher Smart Point Comparison: 6

Chicken Fajita Pasta

Everyone loved my idea for this colorful dish, which takes the great flavors of chicken fajitas and infuses them into an even more fabulous-tasting pasta dish. I love this recipe because not only is it easy to make and serve, it offers the flavor of fajitas while eliminating the need for all of the fattening fajita toppings, making it way healthier than its grilled counterpart. Feel free to substitute red sweet peppers for the green bell pepper.

MAKES 4 SERVINGS

6 ounces (about 2¼ cups dry) penne or fettuccine pasta

2 teaspoons vegetable oil

1 medium white onion, sliced into strips

2 medium green bell peppers, sliced into strips

2 to 3 garlic cloves, minced

12 ounces boneless, skinless chicken breast, sliced into ½-inch thick strips

1 teaspoon cumin

1 teaspoon dried oregano

½ teaspoon salt

¼ teaspoon black pepper

Pinch of red pepper flakes

1 cup low-sodium chicken broth

Juice of 1 large lime

2 teaspoons cornstarch

2 medium tomatoes, seeded and chopped

3 tablespoons chopped fresh cilantro

½ cup reduced-fat Mexican blend cheese (optional)

1. Cook the pasta according to the package directions while preparing the sauce, and set aside.

2. Heat the oil in a large sauté pan over medium-high heat. Add the onion and peppers and sauté for 3 to 4 minutes, or until slightly softened. Add the garlic and chicken strips and sauté for 3 to 4 more minutes, or until chicken is mostly cooked through. Sprinkle the cumin, oregano, salt, pepper, and red pepper flakes over the chicken.

3. In a small bowl, whisk together the chicken broth, lime juice, and cornstarch. Pour over the chicken and vegetables and cook for 2 more minutes, or until the sauce is slightly thickened and the chicken is no longer pink in the center.

4. Add the cooked pasta, chopped tomato, and cilantro to the pan. Turn off the heat and toss well to coat. Sprinkle with the cheese, if using, and serve.

DARE to COMPARE ··················
An order of chicken fajitas at Baja Fresh®, including rice, beans, flour tortillas, guacamole, and sour cream delivers a hefty 1140 calories, 33 grams of fat, 3240 milligrams of sodium, and 147 grams of carbohydrate! (Weight Watcher Plus Point Comparison: 25 points!)

NUTRITION INFORMATION PER SERVING (1½ CUPS) ··················
Calories 330 | Carbohydrate 40g (Sugars 7g) | Total Fat 5g (Sat Fat 1) | Protein 30 | Fiber 6g | Cholesterol 45mg | Sodium 510mg | Food Exchanges: 3 Lean Meat, 2 Starch, 1 Vegetable, 1 Fat | Carbohydrate Choices: 2½ | Weight Watcher Smart Point Comparison: 5

Creamy Seafood Linguine

The problem with most creamy sauces is that the cream often comes from artery-clogging, high-calorie heavy whipping cream. This lovely creamy sauce, on the other hand, uses nonfat half-and-half and a touch of cornstarch to mimic cream with delightful results. Feel free to use either all shrimp or all scallops or even substitute your favorite fish for one or both.

MAKES 4 SERVINGS

6 ounces linguine

½ cup reduced-sodium chicken broth

½ cup nonfat half-and-half

1 tablespoon cornstarch

2 teaspoons olive oil

¾ cup finely chopped onion

3 to 4 garlic cloves, minced

½ teaspoon dried basil

¼ cup dry white wine or sweet vermouth*

1 (6.5-ounce) can chopped clams, broth included

6 ounces raw bay scallops

8 ounces raw shrimp, peeled

Fresh parsley, for garnish

* Adds a rich flavor, 2 grams of carbohydrate, and 10 calories

1. Cook the pasta according to the package directions while preparing the sauce, and set aside.

2. Combine the chicken broth, half-and-half, and cornstarch. Set aside.

3. In a large sauté pan, heat the oil over medium-high heat. Add the onion and cook for 2 minutes. Add the garlic and basil and cook for 3 more minutes, or until the onion is soft. Stir in the wine, clams, scallops, and shrimp.

4. Immediately add the broth mixture and bring to a low boil. Reduce heat to medium and simmer for 4 to 5 minutes, or until sauce is thickened and seafood is cooked.

5. Serve the pasta topped with the sauce and garnished with fresh chopped parsley.

NUTRITION INFORMATION PER SERVING (1½ CUPS)
Calories 300 | Carbohydrate 34g (Sugars 7g) | Total Fat 4.5g (Sat Fat .5g) | Protein 27g | Fiber 2g | Cholesterol 95mg | Sodium 400mg | Food Exchanges: 3 Lean Meat, 2 Starch | Carbohydrate Choices: 2 | Weight Watcher Smart Point Comparison: 7

Penne and Shrimp in Spicy Tomato Sauce

Growing up with an Italian mother has made me such a pasta lover that I can't imagine pasta ever not being part of my diet! What most people don't know about pasta is that it has a low glycemic index (the rate at which it will raise your blood sugar) and that it can be included in moderation in any diet (even when you are trying to lose weight). This dish combines a mild-tasting, fiber-rich whole wheat blend pasta and balances it with a bold red sauce made with America's favorite seafood, shrimp. This meal is easily completed with the addition of a well-chilled mixed green salad.

MAKES 5 SERVINGS

8 ounces (about 3 cups dry) whole wheat blend penne pasta

1 tablespoon olive oil

3 garlic cloves, minced

¼ teaspoon red pepper flakes, or more to taste

1 (28-ounce) can plum tomatoes, drained

1 pound large raw shrimp, shelled and deveined

2 tablespoons sweet vermouth (optional)

Salt and pepper to taste

¼ cup finely chopped fresh parsley

½ cup grated Romano or Parmesan cheese

1. Cook the pasta according to the package directions while preparing the sauce, and set aside.

2. Heat the oil in a large nonstick saucepan over low heat. Add the garlic and red pepper flakes. Stir for 1 minute to soften the garlic. Add the tomatoes, crushing them with a fork. Bring to a simmer and heat for about 5 minutes, until mixture reduces slightly. Add the shrimp and vermouth, and cook for 5 more minutes.

3. When the pasta is cooked, drain and add to the tomato mixture. Toss together over low heat. Season with salt and pepper and gently mix in the parsley.

4. Divide the pasta among serving dishes. Spoon any remaining sauce over the top. Sprinkle each portion with 2 tablespoons of the grated cheese.

Chef's Tip: All shrimp is frozen and then thawed, so buying it frozen in bags is the same as buying it thawed from the fish case (only less expensive). Look for uncooked, easy to peel or unpeeled shrimp. Once home, move the shrimp to the fridge one day before it is to be used.

NUTRITION INFORMATION PER SERVING (1¾ CUPS) ·········
Calories 345 | Carbohydrate 45g (Sugars 3g) | Total Fat 8g (Sat Fat 3.0g) | Protein 25g | Fiber 9g | Cholesterol 140mg | Sodium 480mg | Food Exchanges: 2½ Lean Meat, 2 Starch, 2 Vegetables, ½ Fat | Carbohydrate Choices: 2½ | Weight Watcher Smart Point Comparison: 8

Corkscrew Chicken and Broccoli Alfredo

This is a terrific family favorite. *The thick and velvety Parmesan cream sauce that adorns this dish mimics rich Alfredo sauce (only without the requisite butter and cream). If you don't have rotini on hand, substitute any similar shaped pasta. Bowties are really fun.*

MAKES 6 SERVINGS

8 ounces (3 cups dry) rotini, or bowties

5 cups broccoli florets

1 cup low-fat milk

1½ tablespoons cornstarch

1 cup reduced-sodium chicken broth

¼ cup light cream cheese

½ teaspoon garlic powder

¼ teaspoon pepper, or more to taste

½ cup grated Parmesan cheese

2 cups shredded cooked boneless, skinless chicken breast

1. Cook the pasta according to the package directions while preparing the sauce, and set aside.

2. Place the broccoli in a large microwave-safe dish. Add 3 tablespoons of water, cover, and microwave for 4 minutes, or until crisp tender.

3. In a medium saucepan, whisk the milk and cornstarch until smooth. Whisk in the broth and place over low heat. Add the cream cheese, garlic powder, and pepper. Bring to a low simmer and cook until the sauce thickens, about 4 minutes. Whisk in the Parmesan and cook for 1 to 2 more minutes, or until sauce is smooth.

4. Toss the cooked pasta, broccoli, and chicken together in a large serving dish. Pour the sauce on top, and toss gently to combine.

> **DARE to COMPARE** ·······················
> The restaurant version of this dish is described as white meat chicken and steamed broccoli "lightly" tossed with pasta in an Alfredo-style sauce. It averages over 1200 not-so- light calories. It also contains an entire day's worth of fat and carbohydrates, two days' worth of saturated fat, and a whopping 2,000 mg of sodium.

NUTRITION INFORMATION PER SERVING (1½ CUPS)··
Calories 330 | Carbohydrate 36g (Sugars 5g) | Total Fat 7g (Sat Fat 3.5g) | Protein 27g | Fiber 4g | Cholesterol 50mg | Sodium 400mg | Food Exchanges: 3 Lean Meat, 2 Starch, 1 Vegetable, ½ Fat | Carbohydrate Choices: 2 | Weight Watcher Smart Point Comparison: 8

Greek Chicken Bowtie Pasta

Infused with the flavors of the Mediterranean, this is one of my favorite pasta dishes. Artichoke hearts are not only easy to keep on hand but a great bargain when it comes to good nutrition. Low in calories and carbohydrates, they are nutritional powerhouses packed with vitamin C, disease-fighting antioxidants, and fiber. Because the ingredients for this dish are those I commonly have on hand, I often throw it together when I have leftover cooked chicken. If you do the same, eliminate step 2 and add the cooked chicken along with the artichoke hearts and oregano in step 3.

MAKES 6 SERVINGS

8 ounces (3 cups dry) farfalle "bowtie"

4 teaspoons olive oil, divided

2 to 3 garlic cloves, minced

1 pound skinless, boneless chicken breast, cut into 1-inch pieces

¾ cup sliced red onion

1 (14-ounce) can artichoke hearts, drained quartered (or 1 cup frozen, thawed)

1 teaspoon dried oregano

2 large tomatoes, seeded and chopped

Juice of 1 lemon

2 teaspoons cornstarch

¾ cup reduced-sodium chicken broth

¼ teaspoon salt

Pepper to taste

3 tablespoons chopped fresh parsley

¾ cup crumbled reduced-fat feta cheese

1. Cook the pasta according to the package directions while preparing the sauce, and set aside.

2. Heat 2 teaspoons of the olive oil in a large sauté pan over medium-high heat. Add the garlic and sauté for 30 seconds. Add the chicken and cook for 2 to 3 minutes until lightly browned; then add the onion and cook for another 3 minutes, or until onion starts to soften.

3. Reduce the heat to medium and add the artichokes and oregano.

4. Add the tomatoes, lemon juice, and remaining 2 teaspoons olive oil. Whisk the cornstarch into the broth and add to the pan. Bring the mixture to a simmer and cook until sauce clears. Add the cooked pasta, salt, pepper, and parsley, and toss well.

5. Sprinkle the feta across top of pasta and serve.

Or try this: A few large handfuls of fresh spinach make a beautiful and nutritious addition to this dish. Add either baby spinach leaves or chopped fresh spinach to the cooked pasta and toss until the spinach wilts.

NUTRITION INFORMATION PER SERVING (1½ CUPS)
Calories 355 | Carbohydrate 37g (Sugars 5g) | Total Fat 9g (Sat Fat 2g) | Protein 31g | Fiber 7g | Cholesterol 50mg | Sodium 640mg | Food Exchanges: 3½ Lean Meat, 2 Starch, 1 Vegetable | Carbohydrate Choices: 2
Weight Watcher Smart Point Comparison: 7

Asian Beef Noodle Bowl

This fragrant dish is best described as a cross between a soup and a pasta dish. Lots of tasty broth and bean sprouts, which are great pasta extenders, help to keep this filling "pasta" bowl slim in carbs while heavy in taste. To make this recipe an absolute snap, I use quick-cooking fresh fettuccine noodles, jarred garlic and ginger, and bagged shredded carrots. To keep it authentic, be sure to include either the fresh mint or basil. Both are delicious.

MAKES 4 SERVINGS

12 ounces top sirloin steak, sliced very thin across the grain

1 tablespoon rice wine vinegar

1 teaspoon plus 2 teaspoons fresh grated ginger

2 (14-ounce) cans, or 4 cups, reduced-sodium beef broth

1 cup water

2 tablespoons reduced-sodium soy sauce

1 teaspoon minced garlic

Dash of hot pepper flakes

2 teaspoons granulated sugar

4½ ounces fresh fettuccini

1 cup shredded carrots

¼ cup chopped green onions

1½ cups bean sprouts

4 tablespoons fresh chopped cilantro

¼ cup fresh chopped mint or basil (optional)

1. Place the sliced meat into a bowl or resealable bag. Sprinkle with the rice wine vinegar and add 1 teaspoon of the ginger. Toss and set aside.

2. Add the remaining ginger, broth, water, soy sauce, garlic, pepper flakes, and sugar to a large pot. Bring to a boil and let simmer 5 minutes.

3. While cooking, shred the carrots (if needed), and chop the green onions and herbs. After 5 minutes, add the noodles, carrots, and green onions. Cook for 3 minutes. Stir in the beef, bean sprouts, and half of the cilantro. Cook for 1 to 2 minutes, or until beef is no longer pink.

4. Remove from heat. Using tongs, portion the noodles, beef, and vegetables into four bowls. Then ladle the hot broth over the noodle mixture in the bowls. Top with the remaining cilantro and fresh mint or basil if desired.

NUTRITION INFORMATION PER SERVING (2 CUPS)
Calories 280 | Carbohydrate 23g (Sugars 6g) | Total Fat 10g (Sat Fat 4g) | Protein 23g | Fiber 3g | Cholesterol 50mg | Sodium 570mg | Food Exchanges: 3 Lean Meat, 1 Starch, 1 Vegetable | Carbohydrate Choices: 1½ | Weight Watcher Smart Point Comparison: 7

Lazy Pork Lo Mein

No more need for greasy Chinese take-out with this recipe! Pork lo mein is one of the most popular Chinese take-out dishes—and one of the least healthy. This recipe delivers the same great flavor you'd expect from the best Asian restaurants, only it's quicker, less expensive, and far healthier than eating out. Be sure to use the fresh bean sprouts, because they give this dish great texture as well as provide extra bulk, fiber, and a nice dose of vitamin C.

MAKES 4 SERVINGS

6 ounces spaghetti or linguine

2 teaspoons canola oil

12 ounces pork tenderloin, cut into ½-inch strips

1½ cups shredded carrots

1 (8-ounce) package, or 2 cups, sliced mushrooms

2 cups fresh bean sprouts

½ cup water or reduced-sodium chicken broth

2 tablespoons reduced-sodium soy sauce

2 tablespoons oyster sauce

1 tablespoon rice vinegar

2 tablespoons ketchup

1 teaspoon fresh grated ginger

2 teaspoons sesame oil

1 teaspoon cornstarch

¼ teaspoon crushed red pepper flakes (optional)

1. Cook the pasta according to the package directions while preparing the sauce, and set aside.

2. Heat the oil in a large sauté pan over medium-high heat. Add the pork and cook 4 to 5 minutes, until lightly browned and almost cooked through.

3. Reduce heat to medium, and add the carrots, mushrooms, and bean sprouts. Stir and cook for 2 minutes.

4. In a small bowl or measuring cup, whisk together the remaining ingredients and pour over the pork mixture. Cook until the sauce comes to a simmer and thickens. Add the cooked pasta and toss well.

> **DARE to COMPARE**
>
> An order of pork lo mein at P.F. Chang's China Bistro® delivers 1419 calories, 72 grams of fat, an entire day's worth of carbs (168 grams), and two days worth of the recommended allowance for sodium (5,337 milligrams).

NUTRITION INFORMATION PER SERVING (GENEROUS 1½ CUPS)
Calories 320 | Carbohydrate 35g (Sugars 10g) | Total Fat 9g (Sat Fat 1.5g) | Protein 27g | Fiber 5g | Cholesterol 55mg | Sodium 1140mg | Food Exchanges: 3 Lean Meat, 2 Vegetable, 1½ Carbohydrate | Carbohydrate Choices: 2 | Weight Watcher Smart Point Comparison: 7

Spicy Chicken Oriental Primavera

This recipe is one of my most treasured, and most requested, creations. For years I have served it (minus the chicken) as a side dish, alongside grilled meat or fish. It's easy to set it up ahead of time for last-minute cooking. (See Marlene Says.) The exceptional, richly flavored sauce is both sweet and spicy from the combination of fresh orange zest, hoisin sauce, and chilies. It never fails to wow. The addition of chicken turns my winning side dish into a fabulous one-dish meal that you and your family are guaranteed to enjoy.

MAKES 5 SERVINGS

6 ounces linguine

2 cups shredded cooked chicken

1 red bell pepper, julienned

1 yellow bell pepper, julienned

2 cups sliced mushrooms (1 8-ounce package)

8 green onions, chopped

1 tablespoon canola oil

1 cup reduced-sodium chicken broth

¼ cup sherry

2 rounded tablespoons hoisin sauce

2 tablespoons seasoned rice wine vinegar

2 tablespoons reduced-sodium soy sauce

1 tablespoon fresh orange zest

½ teaspoon chili flakes

1 tablespoon cornstarch

1 tablespoon sesame oil

2 garlic cloves, minced

1. In a large pot, cook the pasta al dente according to package directions. Drain and return to the pot. Stir in the chicken, bell peppers, mushrooms, green onions, and canola oil, and cover with lid.

2. In a large measuring cup, whisk together all the remaining ingredients except garlic. Spray a very large skillet or sauté pan with nonstick cooking spray and add garlic. Heat for 30 seconds and then add sauce. Simmer over medium-high heat for 2 to 3 minutes, or until sauce is fragrant and slightly thickened.

3. Pour the pasta, vegetable, and chicken mixture into the skillet and stir gently. Cook for 2 to 3 minutes, until noodles are well coated and vegetables are crisp tender.

Marlene Says: Prepare the pasta, vegetables, and sauce ahead of time. Lightly rinse the pasta with warm water after cooking and return it to the pot as directed in the recipe (omitting the chicken). Whisk together the sauce ingredients and set aside. Just prior to serving heat the skillet and cook sauce as directed in step 2. Add chicken along with pasta and vegetables.

NUTRITION INFORMATION PER SERVING (1½ CUPS)
Calories 315 | Carbohydrate 35g (Sugars 6g) | Total Fat 7g (Sat Fat 1.5g) | Protein 26g | Fiber 5g | Cholesterol 50mg | Sodium 660mg | Food Exchanges: 3 Lean Meat, 2 Starch, 1 Vegetable | Carbohydrate Choices: 2 | Weight Watcher Smart Point Comparison: 7

Rigatoni, White Beans, and Sausage

This dish is as simple to make as it is beautiful. White beans, sausage, and rigatoni medley with deep green spinach, ruby red tomatoes, and a kick of garlic to create a rustic pasta dish filled with fabulous flavor. If tomatoes are in season, by all means feel free to substitute two large ones, seeded and diced, for the canned.

MAKES 6 SERVINGS

8 ounces rigatoni

2 cups reduced-sodium chicken broth

3 garlic cloves, minced

¾ pound turkey kielbasa sausage, sliced thin

1 teaspoon dried oregano

1 tablespoon olive oil

1 (14-ounce) can white cannellini beans, drained

1 (14-ounce) can no-salt-added diced tomatoes, well drained

6 ounces (6 cups) baby spinach leaves

6 tablespoons finely grated fresh Parmesan cheese

Freshly cracked black pepper

1. Cook the pasta according to package directions in a large pot. Drain and set aside.

2. Pour the chicken broth and garlic into the same pot. Place over medium-high heat and bring to a simmer. Add the sausage, oregano, and olive oil. Stir well.

3. Stir in the beans, tomatoes, and cooked pasta to the pot. Place the spinach on top of mixture. Cover with a lid and turn off the heat. Allow to steam for about 1 minute, just until spinach has begun to wilt. Stir mixture.

4. Serve with a heaping tablespoon of Parmesan cheese on top and seasoned with black pepper to taste.

Fit Tip: Because the broth and sausage add plenty of sodium to this dish, I recommend using no-salt-added tomatoes. Many brands now offer no-salt-added versions, some of which have as little as one-tenth of the sodium in the regular variety.

NUTRITION INFORMATION PER SERVING (1½ CUPS) ⋯⋯⋯⋯⋯⋯⋯⋯⋯⋯
Calories 300 | Carbohydrate 40g (Sugars 4g) | Total Fat 8g (Sat Fat 2g) | Protein 17g | Fiber 6g | Cholesterol 40mg | Sodium 720mg | Food Exchanges: 2 Lean Meat, 2 Carbohydrate, 2 Vegetable, ½ Fat | Carbohydrate Choices: 2½ | Weight Watcher Smart Point Comparison: 8

Fast Fix Lasagna Bake

Campanelle, which means bellflowers in Italian, is also the name of a bite-size pasta that has curled edges similar to a lasagna noodle. I find them the perfect substitute for the much larger lasagna noodle in this much quicker—and far healthier—lasagna bake. This is like a typical lasagna in that it's a great cook-once, eat-twice dish with leftovers keeping for several days in the refrigerator. The Italian turkey sausage in the sauce is a big hit in my house, but lean ground beef can be substituted.

MAKES 12 SERVINGS

12 ounces campanelle noodles

1 tablespoon olive oil

1 small white onion, chopped

3 garlic cloves, minced

8 ounces Italian turkey sausage, bulk or removed from casings

1 (14-ounce) can reduced-sodium beef broth

⅓ cup dry red wine

1 (28-ounce) can crushed tomatoes

1 (6-ounce) can tomato paste

2 teaspoons granulated sugar

1½ teaspoons each dried basil and dried oregano

¼ teaspoon black pepper

1½ cups low-fat cottage cheese

1 (15-ounce) package reduced-fat ricotta cheese

2 tablespoons water

2 cups shredded part-skim mozzarella cheese

¼ cup grated Parmesan cheese

1. Preheat the oven to 350°F. Coat an 13 x 9-inch square casserole dish with nonstick cooking spray.

2. Cook the pasta according to the package directions while preparing the sauce, and set aside.

3. Marinara sauce: In a large saucepan, heat the oil over medium-high heat. Add the onion and sauté for 2 minutes, or until tender. Add the garlic and sausage and cook until meat is slightly browned. Deglaze the pan by pouring in the beef broth and wine and scraping the browned bits from the bottom. Add the tomatoes, tomato paste, sugar, herbs, and pepper. Simmer for 15 to 20 minutes.

4. In a medium bowl, mix together the cottage cheese and ricotta cheese. Add the water and a dash of black pepper. Set aside.

5. Toss half of the red sauce with the cooked pasta. Layer half of the pasta in the casserole dish. Top evenly with the cheese mixture. Pour ½ cup of sauce across cheese mixture and top with remaining pasta. Cover with remaining sauce and sprinkle top with mozzarella and Parmesan cheese.

6. Cover with foil and bake for 30 minutes, or until heated through. Serve.

NUTRITION INFORMATION PER SERVING (1½ CUPS)
Calories 320 | Carbohydrate 33g (Sugars 8g) | Total Fat 10g (Sat Fat 4g) | Protein 23g | Fiber 4g | Cholesterol 35mg | Sodium 640mg | Food Exchanges: 2 Medium-Fat Meat, 1½ Starch, 1 Vegetable, 1 Fat | Carbohydrate Choices: 2 | Weight Watcher Smart Point Comparison: 6

Nutty Beefy Noodles

This recipe, adapted from Laura's Lean Beef, is absolutely delicious when made with beef, but it's also great as a vegetarian option. When I tried the meatless version using soy crumbles my meat-loving husband devoured a plateful without even suspecting the soy switcheroo and my vegetarian assistant, Molly, was absolutely thrilled. Nutritionally speaking, making it with a beef alternative is a tradeoff. It adds heart-healthy soy and eliminates 35 calories per serving (3 grams of fat and 5 grams of protein), but it also adds 4 grams of carbohydrate and 220 milligrams of sodium.

MAKES 6 SERVINGS

8 ounces spaghetti

1 red bell pepper, chopped

1 yellow bell pepper, chopped

1 carrot, peeled and shredded

¼ cup peanut butter

2 tablespoons reduced-sodium soy sauce

2 tablespoons rice wine vinegar

2 tablespoons ketchup or reduced-sugar ketchup

1 tablespoon brown sugar

1 teaspoon minced ginger

½ teaspoon red pepper flakes

1 cup warm water

¾ teaspoons cornstarch

1 pound lean ground beef (or 12-ounces beef-flavored soy crumbles)

2 garlic cloves, minced

4 green onions, chopped

1. In a large pot, cook the pasta according to package directions. Drain and return to the pot. Mix in the bell peppers and carrot, cover, and set aside.

2. In a small bowl, whisk together the peanut butter, soy sauce, vinegar, ketchup, brown sugar, ginger, and red pepper flakes until smooth. Whisk in the warm water and cornstarch.

3. In a very large sauté pan over medium-high heat, brown the beef and garlic. Cook for 5 minutes, until the beef is browned.

4. Pour the sauce into the beef and bring to a simmer. Stir in the pasta and vegetables and cook for 5 to 7 minutes, until the vegetables are crisp tender. Serve topped with the green onions.

NUTRITION INFORMATION PER SERVING (SCANT 1½ CUPS)
Calories 350 | Carbohydrate 36g (Sugars 6g) | Total Fat 11g (Sat Fat 3.5g) | Protein 27g | Fiber 5g | Cholesterol 0mg | Sodium 470mg | Food Exchanges: 2 Lean Meat, 2 Starch, 1 Vegetable, 1 Fat | Carbohydrate Choices: 2 Weight Watcher Smart Point Comparison: 9

New-Age Tuna Noodle Casserole

This is a tuna noodle casserole for the twenty-first century! The chopped artichoke hearts give this classic casserole a tasty new twist, and the reduced-fat soup and cheddar cheese eliminate excess fat and calories common to many traditional tuna noodle recipes. Dare I say my husband came back for thirds?

MAKES 4 SERVINGS

1 (10¾-ounce) can reduced-fat cream of celery or mushroom soup (like Healthy Request)

¾ cup low-fat milk

½ cup shredded reduced-fat cheddar cheese

¾ teaspoon dried thyme

1 (14-ounce) can artichoke hearts, drained and slightly chopped

2 cups cooked wide noodles

2 (6-ounce) cans water-packed white albacore tuna, drained and rinsed

2 tablespoons grated Parmesan

1. Preheat the oven to 375°F. Spray a 9 x 9-inch casserole dish with cooking spray.

2. In a large bowl, gently mix together the soup, milk, cheddar, and thyme. Add the artichokes and noodles. Gently stir in the tuna.

3. Spoon the mixture into the prepared casserole dish. Sprinkle the Parmesan on top, and cover. Bake for 20 minutes, uncover, and bake for 5 more minutes. Allow to sit for 5 minutes before serving.

Or try this: If you prefer a more traditional taste, replace the artichokes with 1½ cups of canned and drained or frozen and slightly thawed peas and carrots. (Adds 15 calories and 4 grams of carbohydrate.)

⋮ NUTRITION INFORMATION PER SERVING (1⅓ CUPS) ··
⋮ Calories 315 ┃ Carbohydrate 26g (Sugars 6g) ┃ Total Fat 8g (Sat Fat 3.5g) ┃ Protein 33g ┃ Fiber 4g ┃ Cholesterol
⋮ 50mg ┃ Sodium 640mg ┃ Food Exchanges: 3 Very Lean Meat, 1 Medium-Fat Meat, 1 Starch, 1 Vegetable, 1 Fat ┃
⋮ Carbohydrate Choices: 1½ ┃ Weight Watcher Point Comparison: 7

Quick Turkey Bolognese

Named after the city of Bologna in northern Italy, this famous meat sauce dates back to the fifth century. Traditional Bolognese sauce takes hours to simmer, but in this "quick," better-for-you version I have cut the simmer time down to a manageable twenty minutes, making it perfect for a weeknight supper. Enjoy.

MAKES 8 SERVINGS

2 teaspoons olive oil

1 cup chopped onion

1 large celery stalk, finely chopped

2 garlic cloves, minced

2 medium carrots, peeled and grated

1 (20-ounce) package lean ground turkey

½ cup red wine

1 cup reduced-sodium beef broth

2 teaspoons Worcestershire sauce

1½ cups canned crushed tomatoes

9 ounces fettuccine

1. In a large pot, heat the oil over medium-high heat. Add the onion and celery and cook for 6 to 8 minutes, or until they are both softened. Stir in the garlic and carrots and cook for 2 minutes. Add the turkey and cook for 5 minutes, breaking up the meat as it cooks until it is browned. Pour in the wine and cook for 4 to 5 minutes, or until most of the liquid is evaporated.

2. Stir in all the remaining ingredients and bring to a low simmer. Reduce the heat, cover, and cook for 20 minutes.

3. Cook the fettuccine according to package directions while the sauce simmers. Pour the sauce over the fettuccine to serve.

NUTRITION INFORMATION PER SERVING (1½ CUPS) ·········
Calories 340 | Carbohydrate 39g (Sugars 7g) | Total Fat 8g (Sat Fat 2g) | Protein 25g | Fiber 5g | Cholesterol 50mg | Sodium 340mg | Food Exchanges: 3 Lean Meat, 2 Vegetable, 1½ Starch | Carbohydrate Choices: 2 | Weight Watcher Smart Point Comparison: 8

Everyday Spaghetti and Italian Meatballs

Soon after my stepdaughter, Colleen, was diagnosed with type 2 diabetes I realized that one of our regular Sunday dinners—a big platter of pasta with homemade marinara and a pile of garlic bread— was in need of an update. If we were still going to enjoy this dinner, the calories had to be curbed and the carbs needed to be s-t-r-e-t-c-h-e-d. Much to everyone's delight, I added tasty meatballs, and to Colleen's delight, we began pairing our more moderate healthy pasta platter with a big salad like the Wedge Salad with Buttermilk Ranch Dressing on page 174. The best part is that we all feel better after eating this newer healthier-than-ever spaghetti and Italian meatball dinner (and Colleen can still fit in a piece of garlic bread!) Bonus: You will use only one-half the marinara sauce, leaving you with 3 cups for another meal. Covered and stored in the refrigerator, it will keep for up to two weeks.

MAKES 6 SERVINGS

1 recipe uncooked Everyday Italian Meatballs (page 324)

12 ounces spaghetti

1 tablespoon olive oil

½ cup finely chopped onion

3 garlic cloves, minced

⅓ cup dry red wine or beef broth

1 (28-ounce) can crushed tomatoes

1 (6-ounce) can tomato paste

⅓ teaspoon sugar

1½ teaspoons dried basil leaves

1½ teaspoons oregano leaves

Pinch of red pepper flakes

¼ teaspoon black pepper

2 cups water

1. Prep the Everyday Italian Meatballs according to the directions, but do not cook. Set aside.

2. In a large saucepan, heat the oil over medium-high heat. Add the onion and sauté for 3 to 4 minutes, or until soft. Add the garlic and sauté for 1 additional minute. Deglaze the pan by pouring in the wine and scraping the browned bits from the bottom. Add the tomatoes, tomato paste, sugar, herbs, red pepper, black pepper, and water. Simmer for 15 to 20 minutes. (If you prefer your sauce smoother, blend to desired texture. Place sauce back in pot.)

3. Cook the pasta according to the package directions while the sauce simmers, drain, and set aside.

4. Gently stir the uncooked meatballs into the sauce and cover. Simmer for 15 to 20 minutes or until meatballs feel firm and are cooked through. Place pasta in a large bowl or platter. Pour 1 cup of sauce into pasta. Top with meatballs and serve with remaining sauce.

NUTRITION INFORMATION PER SERVING (1 CUP OF PASTA WITH ½ CUP SAUCE AND 3 MEATBALLS) Calories 420 | Carbohydrate 49g (Sugars 5g) | Total Fat 11g (Sat Fat 3.5g) | Protein 28g Fiber 7g | Cholesterol 45mg | Sodium 360mg | Food Exchanges: 3 Lean Meat, ½ Starch, 1 Vegetable Carbohydrate Choices: 3 | Weight Watcher Smart Point Comparison: 9

For the Love of Vegetables

It appears our Mothers were right when they told us to eat our vegetables because as we now know, vegetables contain powerful disease fighters. Research shows that the vitamins, minerals, and phytochemicals (powerful plant chemicals) found in vegetables can reduce everything from the risk of heart disease and diabetes to high blood pressure and cancer. Vegetables also help keep your weight down, your eyes bright, your hair shiny, and your skin beautiful. Clearly there are a lot of reasons to love vegetables, yet studies show that most of us eat far less than the recommended five servings (or 2½ cups) of a variety of vegetables each day. There are many reasons we don't eat vegetables, ranging from availability, to cost, to preparation time, but the number one reason—is taste. Plain vegetables simply do not have the flavor appeal of the other foods we love.

This chapter will convince you that vegetables can taste great with tantalizing recipes that you will be excited to eat and share—time and time again. From crispy Oven-Baked Onion Rings to Italian Zucchini Parmesan and Seared, Steamed, and Glazed Green Beans, you won't find a plain, tasteless vegetable in the bunch. While I include classic vegetable combinations like my Easy Cheesy Microwave Medley and Sautéed Sweet Peppers and Onions, there is also an array of brand new tastes and textures to entice you. Some that really wowed my testers were the beautiful buttery ribbons of fresh zucchini, the luscious Indian cabbage flavored with coconut and curry, the rich and creamy cauliflower faux-tatoes, and the Maple-Glazed Carrot Coins that are as sweet and fragrant as French toast. This may well be the beginning of a new love affair—with vegetables!

Oven-Baked Onion Rings

Just reading the name "onion rings" conjures up an image of golden-fried perfection. The problem with onion rings is that while the deep-fried ones are too high in fat, baked versions lack the taste and texture of fried. I am happy to say that after many attempts with multiple coating and seasoning combinations. I have come up with a recipe that produces crisp and delicious, better-for-you onion rings that are perfect in every way.

MAKES 4 SERVINGS

1 large sweet onion (about 1 pound) or 2 medium, peeled

6 tablespoons breadcrumbs

6 tablespoons finely crushed cornflakes (¾ cup whole flakes, crushed)

4 teaspoons cornmeal

½ teaspoon garlic powder

½ teaspoon onion powder

¼ teaspoon salt

Pinch of cayenne pepper

Pinch of black pepper

2 tablespoons flour

½ cup buttermilk

1. Preheat the oven to 400°F. Coat a wire rack with cooking spray and place on top of a baking sheet.

2. Turning the onion onto its side, cut 1-inch thick slices. Gently separate the onion slices into rings.

3. In a wide, shallow bowl, mix together the breadcrumbs, cornflakes, cornmeal, garlic powder, onion powder, salt, cayenne, and black pepper.

4. In a small bowl whisk the flour into the buttermilk. Dip each onion ring into the buttermilk mixture and then into the crumbs. Place on the wire rack. Repeat the process for all of the onion rings. Spray the onion rings thoroughly with cooking spray (a quick spray of cooking spray while coating will also help the crumbs to stick.)

5. Bake for 10 minutes. Flip the onion rings over and bake for an additional 12 minutes, or until crisp and golden brown.

DARE to COMPARE ···
A large order of onion rings at Burger King® has 440 calories, 22 grams of fat, 53 grams of carbohydrate, and 620 mg of sodium. Add the ounce of dipping sauce and the total is 590 calories, 37 grams of fat, and 56 grams of carbohydrate.

NUTRITION INFORMATION PER SERVING (¼ ONION)··
Calories 125 | Carbohydrate 25g (Sugars 9g) | Total Fat 2g (Sat Fat 0g) | Protein 4g | Fiber 3g | Cholesterol 0mg | Sodium 260mg | Food Exchanges: 1 Carbohydrate, 1 Vegetable | Carbohydrate Choices: 1½ | Weight Watcher Smart Point Comparison: 3

Quick "Pickle" Chips

These super-quick, super-easy "chips" are just the thing to spruce up any sandwich plate because they offer all the crunchy appeal of sweet pickles without the added sugars and calories found in commercial brands. For extra eye-appeal, cut off both ends of the cucumber and run a fork firmly down all sides to score the skin before cutting into slices. If you prefer your pickles extra crunchy, place the slices in a sieve, toss with one teaspoon of salt and two teaspoons of vinegar and let stand for one hour. Rinse and pat dry before adding them to the recipe.

MAKES 4 SERVINGS

¾ cup apple cider vinegar

6 tablespoons granulated no-calorie sweetener (or 9 packets)

1 teaspoon dried dill

½ teaspoon mustard powder

Pinch of salt

Pinch of black pepper

1 large cucumber or English cucumber, washed and cut into ⅛-inch thick slices

1. In a medium bowl, whisk together the vinegar, sweetener, dill, mustard, salt, and pepper. Add the cucumber slices and toss together.

2. Cover and place in the refrigerator for 30 minutes before serving. (The chips will continue to soften as they sit. To keep them crunchy longer, follow above directions before marinating.)

Family Focus: Encourage kids of all ages to eat their vegetables by making them fun. "Chips" like these make a great swap-out for high-fat potato chips, and the Oven-Baked Onion Rings on page 249 fill in for fast-food fare. Everybody (and every *body*) wins!

NUTRITION INFORMATION PER SERVING (½ CUP OR ABOUT 5 PICKLE CHIPS)
Calories 15 | Carbohydrate 4g (Sugars 0g) | Total Fat 0g (Sat Fat 0g) | Protein 0g | Fiber 1g | Cholesterol 0mg | Sodium 150mg | Food Exchanges: 1 Vegetable | Carbohydrate Choices: 0 | Weight Watcher Smart Point Comparison: 0

Sweet Sesame Broccoli

Sweet, flavorful, and slightly spicy, this recipe makes broccoli appealing to even those who claim they don't care for it. Long known for its healthful properties as a cancer and cardiac disease fighter, broccoli also shows promise as a diabetes fighter. It appears that sulforaphane, a phytochemical (or plant compound) found in broccoli (and also in bok choy), reduces the tissue damage that can be triggered by high blood sugar.

MAKES 4 SERVINGS

4 cups broccoli florets, washed and trimmed

½ cup water

2 tablespoons reduced-sodium soy sauce

2 tablespoons reduced-sodium chicken broth

1 tablespoon granulated sugar

1 teaspoon sesame oil

½ teaspoon grated ginger

Dash of red pepper flakes (optional)

1 tablespoon sesame seeds

1. Place the broccoli florets and water in a large microwavable dish. Cover with plastic wrap.

2. Steam the broccoli in the microwave for 2½ to 3 minutes, or until crisp tender. Drain the broccoli in a colander. Return the broccoli to the dish, and set aside.

3. Prepare the dressing in a small bowl. Whisk together the soy sauce, chicken broth, sugar, sesame oil, ginger, and red pepper flakes, if using.

4. Place a small skillet over medium-high heat. Toast the sesame seeds for 1 to 2 minutes, or until aromatic and slightly browned. Remove the seeds from the skillet.

5. Add the dressing to the skillet. Cook for 2 minutes, or until thickened, and pour over the broccoli. Add the sesame seeds and toss.

NUTRITION INFORMATION PER SERVING (¾ CUP)
Calories 60 | Carbohydrate 9g (Sugars 1g) | Total Fat 2.5g (Sat Fat 0g) | Protein 3g | Fiber 2g | Cholesterol 0mg | Sodium 240mg | Food Exchanges: 1 Vegetable, ½ Fat | Carbohydrate Choices: ½ | Weight Watcher Smart Point Comparison: 2

Seared, Steamed, and Glazed Green Beans

This recipe is one I have used often, both at home and in cooking demonstrations. The beans get treated to three great cooking techniques: searing, steaming, and glazing, and yet they are done in 10 minutes using only one pan! The best thing about this unique but simple preparation is that it ensures delicious, company-worthy beans every time.

MAKES 4 SERVINGS

1 teaspoon olive oil

1 teaspoon minced garlic

1 pound fresh green beans, washed and trimmed

1 tablespoon water

3 tablespoons sweet vermouth, divided

¼ teaspoon seasoned salt, or to taste

1. Heat the oil in a large nonstick skillet over medium-high heat. Add the garlic and cook for 10 to 15 seconds. Add the green beans and sear while stirring for one minute.

2. Pour in the water and 2 tablespoons of the sweet vermouth. Immediately cover. Steam for 4 to 5 minutes, or until crisp tender.

3. Remove the lid, add the remaining vermouth, and sprinkle with seasoned salt. Cook for 1 to 2 minutes longer, tossing, until the water evaporates and the vermouth has glazed the beans.

DARE to COMPARE
Fresh is best. A single serving of green bean casserole has over 200 calories and 11 grams of fat.

NUTRITION INFORMATION PER SERVING (¼ RECIPE)
Calories 60 | Carbohydrate 10g (Sugars 4g) | Total Fat 1.5g (Sat Fat 0g) | Protein 2g | Fiber 4g | Cholesterol 0mg | Sodium 150mg | Food Exchanges: 1 Vegetable | Carbohydrate Choices: ½ | Weight Watcher Smart Point Comparison: 1

Orange-Ginger Carrots

East meets West in these vibrant orange and ginger-laced carrots. Though they add great zip and color to any plate, they go particularly well with Asian-inspired dishes like Spicy Kung Pao Shrimp (page 353) or Pork Satay with Peanut Sauce (page 337).

MAKES 4 SERVINGS

½ cup water

3 cups sliced carrots

2 teaspoons brown sugar

½ teaspoon minced ginger

Zest from half of one orange

¼ cup light orange juice

2 teaspoons butter or margarine

Salt and pepper to taste

1. Bring the water to a boil in a medium sauté pan over medium-high heat. Add the carrots. Cover and cook for 5 to 8 minutes, or until the carrots are crisp tender.

2. Remove the lid. Add the brown sugar, ginger, orange zest, and orange juice and stir to evenly distribute. Add the butter and toss to coat. Season with salt and pepper.

NUTRITION INFORMATION PER SERVING (½ CUP)
Calories 70 | Carbohydrate 12g (Sugars 8g) | Total Fat 2g (Sat Fat 1g) | Protein 1g | Fiber 3g | Cholesterol 5mg | Sodium 30mg | Food Exchanges: 1½ Vegetables | Carbohydrate Choices: ½ | Weight Watcher Smart Point Comparison: 2

Maple-Glazed Carrot Coins

If you're looking for a vegetable dish your kids will absolutely love, try these quick 'n' easy maple-glazed carrots. This recipe takes advantage of packaged carrot chips and sugar-free syrup to create a dish that's kid friendly and Mom approved. To kick the carrots up a notch, add the cinnamon; you will be amazed at how great the carrots taste, while your kids will love that their carrots smell like French toast.

MAKES 4 SERVINGS

2 teaspoons butter or margarine

1 (10-ounce) bag of carrot chips (or 3 cups thinly-sliced, peeled carrots)

⅓ cup sugar-free maple-flavored syrup

Rounded ¼ teaspoon ground cinnamon (optional)

1. Melt the butter in a skillet over medium-high heat.

2. Add the carrots and sauté for 3 minutes. Pour the syrup and sprinkle the cinnamon, if desired, over the carrots. Stir well. Cover and continue to cook for 5 additional minutes, stirring occasionally, until the carrots are crisp tender. Remove the lid and stir to evenly coat the carrots with the glaze before serving.

Family Focus: Flavoring healthful foods with familiar, well-loved flavors is a great way to help kids make healthful food a regular part of their diets.

NUTRITION INFORMATION PER SERVING (½ CUP)

Calories 70 | Carbohydrate 13g (Sugars 6g) | Total Fat 2g (Sat Fat 1g) | Protein 1g | Fiber 3g | Cholesterol 5mg | Sodium 70mg | Food Exchanges: 1 Vegetable, ½ Carbohydrate | Carbohydrate Choices: ½ Carbohydrate | Weight Watcher Smart Point Comparison: 1

Curried Cabbage

Honestly, to think that just a touch of curry powder can make cabbage taste this delicious is nothing short of a miracle. My husband loves curried dishes and even he was amazed at how luscious the *Creamy Indian Curried Cabbage* variation tastes, where yogurt and a touch of coconut extract duplicate the rich taste of coconut milk. He said he could eat the entire recipe all by himself (and I think he did).

MAKES 4 SERVINGS

2 teaspoons canola oil

1 medium white onion, sliced

1½ teaspoons curry powder

½ teaspoon salt

4 to 5 cups (½ medium head) green cabbage, shredded

¼ cup water

1. Heat the oil in a large skillet over medium-high heat. When hot, sauté the onion for 5 minutes, or until slightly soft.

2. Add the curry powder and salt and cook an additional 30 seconds.

3. Add the cabbage and water to the skillet. Cover and cook an additional 3 minutes, or until liquid is evaporated and the cabbage is soft and tender.

Or try this: Creamy Indian Curried Cabbage: Once the cabbage is wilted, remove from heat and add ¼ cup low-fat plain yogurt, 1 teaspoon brown sugar, and ¼ teaspoon coconut extract. Mix to combine and serve. (Adds 10 calories, 2 grams of carbohydrate, and 1 gram of protein per serving.)

NUTRITION INFORMATION PER SERVING (½ CUP)
Calories 60 | Carbohydrate 8g (Sugars 5g) | Total Fat 2.5g (Sat Fat 0g) | Protein 2g | Fiber 3g | Cholesterol 0mg | Sodium 310mg | Food Exchanges: 1 Vegetables | Carbohydrate Choices: ½ | Weight Watcher Smart Point Comparison: 1

Roasted Asparagus with Parmesan Cheese

For years, the only way I cooked my asparagus was to steam it. It wasn't until I ventured out of my rut and tried roasting it that I learned roasting gives asparagus a firmer texture and more complex flavor than steaming, and it's just as easy. Freshly grated Parmesan cheese is the perfect finishing touch.

MAKES 4 SERVINGS

1½ pounds asparagus spears, washed and trimmed

2 teaspoons olive oil

Salt to taste

Fresh ground black pepper to taste

¼ cup freshly grated Parmesan cheese

1. Preheat the oven to 450°F.

2. Toss the asparagus spears with the olive oil, salt, and pepper.

3. Spread evenly into a single layer on a flat baking sheet. Roast for 10 to 11 minutes, or until fork tender.

4. Sprinkle with the Parmesan cheese just before serving.

   Variation: If you prefer your Parmesan slightly browned, sprinkle it on top of the spears during the last 3 minutes of baking.

NUTRITION INFORMATION PER SERVING (¼ RECIPE)
Calories 60 | Carbohydrate 3g (Sugars 2g) | Total Fat 4.5g (Sat Fat 1.5g) | Protein 4g | Fiber 1g | Cholesterol 5mg | Sodium 260mg | Food Exchanges: 1 Vegetable, 1 Fat | Carbohydrate Choices: 0 | Weight Watcher Smart Point Comparison: 2

High-Heat Roasted Vegetables

Roasted vegetables look and taste amazing. Roasting vegetables at high heat caramelizes their natural sugars and brings out the sweetness of the carrots, peppers, and onions; browns and crisps potatoes; and mellows the taste of zucchini and yellow squash. Feel free to add or substitute your own favorite vegetables into the mix. Eggplant, sweet potatoes, turnips, yellow beets, and green or yellow sweet peppers all work equally well and make the dish feel new every time it's made.

MAKES 6 SERVINGS

1 medium red onion

4 red potatoes (about ½ pound), washed and sliced into ¼-inch thick slices (skin on)

2 small yellow squash (about ½ pound), cut into ½-inch thick rounds

2 small zucchini (about ½ pound), cut into ½-thick rounds

1 medium red bell pepper, cut into ½-inch thick strips

1 large carrot, peeled and sliced into ½-inch thick slices

2 tablespoons olive oil

2 tablespoons balsamic vinegar

1 tablespoon minced fresh rosemary

½ teaspoon dried oregano

½ teaspoon garlic powder

½ teaspoon seasoned salt

Few shakes black pepper

1. Place a 15 x 10 x 1-inch baking sheet or a roasting pan in the oven, and preheat the oven and pan to 450°F.

2. Chop the onion into quarters, and then quarter again. Place onion in a very large bowl. Add the potatoes, squash, zucchini, bell pepper, carrot, oil, vinegar, rosemary, oregano, garlic powder, salt, and pepper and toss well.

3. Carefully remove the preheated pan from the oven and lightly spray with cooking spray.

4. Pour the vegetables evenly onto the pan and spread into a single layer. Lightly spray the vegetables with cooking spray and place back into the oven.

5. Bake for 20 minutes. Turn the vegetables with a spatula or tongs. Reduce the temperature to 400°F and bake for an additional 10 minutes, or until the vegetables are tender and slightly charred, and the potatoes are browned.

NUTRITION INFORMATION PER SERVING (¾ CUP)
Calories 110 | Carbohydrate 17g (Sugars 6g) | Total Fat 4g (Sat Fat .5g) | Protein 3g | Fiber 4g | Cholesterol 0mg | Sodium 125mg | Food Exchanges: 1 Vegetable, ½ Starch, 1 Fat | Carbohydrate Choices: 1 | Weight Watcher Smart Point Comparison: 3

Easy Cheesy Microwave Medley

If you enjoy your vegetables drenched in cheesy goodness, this recipe is for you. Though evaporated milk gives it extra creaminess, this easy-cheesy sauce delivers twice the protein at a fraction of the fat and sodium content of most other homemade versions. Green beans and Brussels sprouts are also delicious when smothered in cheese sauce.

MAKES 4 SERVINGS

2 tablespoons water

2 cups cauliflower florets

1 cup sliced carrots

2 cups broccoli florets

¾ cup low-fat evaporated milk

1 teaspoon cornstarch

½ teaspoon dry mustard powder

¼ teaspoon garlic powder

⅛ teaspoon salt

¾ cup reduced-fat shredded cheddar cheese

Pepper to taste (optional)

1. Place the water, cauliflower, and carrots in a large microwavable dish. Cover with plastic wrap and microwave on high for 4 minutes. Add the broccoli to the mix and microwave for 3 additional minutes, or until all the vegetables are crisp tender (or softened to your liking).

2. While the vegetables are cooking, thoroughly whisk together the milk, cornstarch, mustard, garlic powder, and salt in a small saucepan.

3. Place the pan over medium heat and cook, while whisking, until the mixture thickens and starts to bubble. Turn off the heat and whisk in the cheese until melted and sauce is creamy. Add pepper, if desired.

4. Place the vegetables on a serving platter. Pour the cheese sauce over the vegetables and serve.

DARE *to* COMPARE
A traditional cheese sauce recipe contains 220 calories, 20 grams of fat (most of it saturated), and close to 1,000 mg of sodium per serving.

NUTRITION INFORMATION PER SERVING (1 CUP)
Calories 120 | Carbohydrate 14g (Sugars 9g) | Total Fat 3g (Sat Fat 1.5g) | Protein 11g | Fiber 3g | Cholesterol 10mg | Sodium 290mg | Food Exchanges: 1 Vegetable, ½ Milk | Carbohydrate Choices: 1 | Weight Watcher Smart Point Comparison: 3

Sautéed Sweet Peppers and Onions

Whether tucked into an omelet, piled high on sausage, or sizzling on a platter of fajitas, a fabulous mix of sautéed sweet peppers and onions can be the perfect complement to just about any dish. Using a splash of sweet, or Italian, vermouth (or apple juice) and a bit of herbs adds great color and flavor to the mix. Take special note of the "Perfect Pairings" for some of my favorite herb and entrée combinations.

MAKES 4 SERVINGS

2 teaspoons olive oil

1 large white onion, cut into ¼-inch thick slices

1 garlic clove, minced

3 medium bell peppers (one of each color preferred), cut into ½-inch slices

2 tablespoons sweet vermouth

½ teaspoon seasoning salt or kosher salt

Black pepper to taste

½ teaspoon dried herbs (optional)

1. Heat the oil in a large sauté pan over medium-high heat Add the onion and garlic and sauté for 3 to 4 minutes, until slightly softened.

2. Add the peppers and continue cooking for 6 to 8 minutes, or until crisp tender. Add the vermouth, salt, pepper, and dried herbs, if desired. Continue cooking until onions are caramelized and peppers are soft tender.

Perfect Pairings: Dill works well when pairing peppers and onions with grilled fish or turkey sausages. Think basil for peppers and onions that top turkey burgers and low-fat mozzarella cheese, thyme for peppers and onions served with lean red meats, and tarragon or oregano for peppers and onions that blanket sautéed or baked chicken breasts.

NUTRITION INFORMATION PER SERVING (½ CUP)
Calories 70 | Carbohydrate 10g (Sugars 5g) | Total Fat 2.5g (Sat Fat 0g) | Protein 1g | Fiber 2g | Cholesterol 0mg | Sodium 180mg | Food Exchanges: 2 Vegetable, ½ Fat | Carbohydrate Choices: ½ | Weight Watcher Smart Point Comparison: 2

Stewed Italian Zucchini Parmesan

The way I see it, the more a vegetable tastes like a pizza, the more likely you are to get your family to try it. Thinking back to my own childhood, I'm convinced my Mom knew this, too, because when she smothered zucchini in tomatoes, garlic, oregano, and Parmesan cheese, we gobbled it up. This is good tasting—and good for you, too. Thanks, Mom!

MAKES 4 SERVINGS

2 teaspoons olive oil

1 small onion, sliced

1 large garlic clove, minced

2 medium green zucchini, cut into ⅜-inch-thick slices (about 2 cups)

1 teaspoon dried oregano or Italian seasoning

1 (14-ounce) can Italian-style stewed tomatoes

2 tablespoons dry red wine or sweet vermouth (optional)

¼ cup freshly grated Parmesan cheese

1. Heat the oil in a large skillet over medium-high heat. Add the onion and garlic and cook for three minutes, or until tender. Add the zucchini and oregano and cook for an additional 3 minutes, or until slightly browned.

2. Stir in the tomatoes and wine or vermouth, if desired, and bring to a simmer. Cover and cook 10 to 12 minutes, or until the zucchini is tender.

3. Remove from heat and transfer to a large serving bowl. Sprinkle the Parmesan on top.

NUTRITION INFORMATION PER SERVING (¾ CUP) ·······················
Calories 120 | Carbohydrate 14g (Sugars 9g) | Total Fat 4.5g (Sat Fat 1.5g) | Protein 7g | Fiber 3g | Cholesterol 5mg | Sodium 330mg | Food Exchanges: 2 Vegetable, 1 Fat | Carbohydrate Choices: 1 | Weight Watcher Smart Point Comparison: 2

Buttered Zucchini Ribbons

If you have never "ribboned" zucchini before, I highly recommend it. Unlike the usual slice and dice preparation, an ordinary vegetable peeler is used to peel the zucchini into long, thin, buttery slices, or "ribbons." In addition to the unusual and beautiful presentation, zucchini ribbons cook quickly and can be tossed with wide noodles or topped with your favorite sauce as a healthy pasta alternative.

MAKES 4 SERVINGS

3 small zucchini (about 1 pound)

1 tablespoon butter

½ teaspoon minced garlic (or ¼ teaspoon garlic powder)

2 tablespoons slivered fresh basil

2 tablespoons grated Parmesan cheese

Salt and pepper to taste

1. Remove the ends from the zucchini. Using a vegetable peeler, slice the zucchini by peeling them lengthwise (peeling through the entire zucchini), to form long flat "ribbons." Set aside.

2. Melt the butter in a large sauté pan over medium heat. Add the garlic and cook for 30 seconds. Add the zucchini and cook on medium-high heat 3 to 4 minutes, turning gently with tongs until just soft. Do not overcook.

3. Turn off the heat and gently stir in the basil and Parmesan cheese. Season with the salt and pepper and serve immediately.

Marlene Says: Nothing beats the flavor of butter. Adding a bit of butter at the end of a recipe or using it in recipes where a small amount can greatly contribute to its flavor gives you the taste of butter without excess fat.

NUTRITION INFORMATION PER SERVING (½ CUP)
Calories 50 | Carbohydrate 3g (Sugars 2g) | Total Fat 4g (Sat Fat 2.5g) | Protein 3g | Fiber 1g | Cholesterol 10mg | Sodium 160mg | Food Exchanges: 1 Vegetable, 1 Fat | Carbohydrate Choices: 0 | Weight Watcher Smart Point Comparison: 2

Sautéed Summer Vegetables

At a large family reunion in a mountain village a couple of years ago, I was given a last-minute assignment to prepare the vegetable for dinner. My greatest concern immediately turned to what would be available at the limited local market. Thus, I was both delighted and relieved to find a large bin of one of summer's most beautiful offerings: patty pan squash. This member of the summer squash family is known for its round shape and pretty scalloped edges. Like all summer squashes, it's low in calories and a good source of fiber and vitamin C. I am proud to say this preparation, which combines it with bright yellow sweet corn, was a huge hit. You may substitute sliced zucchini and/or yellow summer squash for the patty pan if you choose.

MAKES 4 SERVINGS

1 pound patty pan squash

2 teaspoons olive oil

½ teaspoon minced garlic (1 clove)

½ cup canned corn kernels or fresh from the cob if in season

½ teaspoon dried dill

½ teaspoon seasoned salt

1. Trim the ends from the patty pan and place flat on a cutting board. Slice vertically at ⅜-inch intervals to create oval slices.

2. Heat the oil in a large sauté pan over medium-high heat. Add the garlic and sauté for 1 minute. Add the squash and raise heat to high. Sauté for 5 minutes, or until squash browns and begins to caramelize.

3. Add the corn, dill, and salt. Stir well and cook for 3 to 4 minutes more, or until the squash is soft but not mushy and corn is cooked through.

NUTRITION INFORMATION PER SERVING (½ CUP) ·······························
Calories 60 | Carbohydrate 9g (Sugars 3g) | Total Fat 2.5g (Sat Fat 0g) | Protein 2g | Fiber 3g | Cholesterol 0mg | Sodium 220mg | Food Exchanges: 1 Vegetable, ½ Fat | Carbohydrate Choices: ½ | Weight Watcher Smart Point Comparison: 2

Spaghetti Squash Pomodoro

With its long spaghetti-like strands, the unusual texture of spaghetti squash makes it a spectacular and healthy stand-in for pasta. This recipe uses the traditional Italian combination of fresh tomatoes, basil, and Parmesan cheese to create a delectable dish that's absolutely intoxicating. For a tried-and-true kids favorite check out the "Spaghetti-ed" Spaghetti Squash on page 265.

MAKES 6 SERVINGS*

1 large spaghetti squash
(about 3½ pounds)

2 tablespoons olive oil

½ cup grated Parmesan cheese
(2 tablespoons reserved)

3 tablespoons fresh basil
leaves, sliced into thin ribbons

2 medium tomatoes, seeded
and diced

Salt to taste

Pepper to taste

1. Pierce the spaghetti squash with a fork in several places and place whole in the microwave. Microwave on high for 10 minutes. Remove and cut in half lengthwise. Scoop out and discard the seeds. Using a fork, lift and tease out strands of the squash to resemble spaghetti. Pile the squash strands into a large microwavable serving dish.

2. Toss the squash strands with the olive oil, Parmesan cheese, basil, tomatoes, salt, and pepper. Sprinkle the top with the reserved Parmesan.

3. Microwave on high an additional 2 minutes.

> **DARE *to* COMPARE** ••••••••••••••••••••••••••
> An entrée portion of Pasta Pomodoro made with capellini pasta from the Olive Garden® restaurant is estimated to contain 990 calories, 45 grams of fat, and over 100 grams of carbohydrate.

* For 2 large entrée portions triple all the nutritional information.

NUTRITION INFORMATION PER SERVING (¾ CUP) ••••••••••••••••••••••••••••••••••
Calories 120 | Carbohydrate 9g (Sugars 1g) | Total Fat 7g (Sat Fat 2.5g) | Protein 5g | Fiber 2g | Cholesterol 5mg | Sodium 270mg | Food Exchanges: 2 Vegetable, ½ Lean Meat, 1 Fat | Carbohydrate Choices: ½ Carbohydrate | Weight Watcher Smart Point Comparison: 3

"Spaghetti-ed" Spaghetti Squash

With a mere forty-two calories per cup, spaghetti squash just can't be beat as a lower calorie and carbohydrate replacement for pasta. Here I keep it simple for you, and the kids, by topping it with store-bought marinara sauce and Parmesan cheese.

MAKES 8 SERVINGS

1 large spaghetti squash
(about 3½ pounds)

2 cups jarred marinara sauce

½ teaspoon dried oregano

1 cup grated Parmesan cheese
(2 tablespoons reserved)

1. Pierce the squash with a fork in several places. Microwave on high for 10 minutes. Remove from the microwave and cut in half lengthwise. Scoop out and discard the seeds. Using a fork, lift and tease out strands of the squash to resemble spaghetti. Pile the squash into a microwavable serving dish.

2. Toss the squash strands with the marinara sauce, oregano, and Parmesan cheese. Sprinkle the reserved Parmesan cheese over the top.

3. Microwave on high an additional 2 minutes.

NUTRITION INFORMATION PER SERVING (¾ CUP)
Calories 110 | Carbohydrate 12g (Sugars 0g) | Total Fat 4g (Sat Fat 2.5g) | Protein 7g | Fiber 2g | Cholesterol 10mg | Sodium 260mg | Food Exchanges: 2 Vegetable, 1 Lean Meat, 1 Fat | Carbohydrate Choices: 1 | Weight Watcher Smart Point Comparison: 2

Thyme for Mushrooms

Sadly, mushrooms just don't get the same attention as other more brightly colored vegetables—and I think it's time they do! No vegetable is as low in carbs and calories, or more versatile, than mushrooms. This simple dish can be made with any type of mushrooms you choose. Be creative and adventurous and try other varieties of mushrooms if you please. White mushrooms work well, but so do brown mushrooms with their richer flavor, and portobellos with their meatier texture.

MAKES 4 SERVINGS

½ pound whole mushrooms, quartered

1 garlic clove, minced

Scant ½ teaspoon dried thyme

1 tablespoon sherry wine or sweet vermouth

1 teaspoon butter or margarine

⅛ teaspoon salt

Pepper to taste

1. Spray a medium sauté pan with nonstick cooking spray and place over medium-high heat.

2. Add the mushrooms and garlic and cook for 3 to 4 minutes, stirring often.

3. Crush the thyme with your fingers and stir into the mushrooms.

4. Add the sherry or sweet vermouth and continue to cook until most of the liquid is evaporated, about 3 or 4 more minutes. Add the butter, salt, and pepper. Toss to coat, and serve.

Marlene Says: In addition to being low in calories and carbohydrates, mushrooms are majestically fat-free, cholesterol-free, very low in sodium, and the only vegetable to contain vitamin D. They are also a good source of selenium, several essential B vitamins, and potassium.

NUTRITION INFORMATION PER SERVING (½ CUP)
Calories 30 | Carbohydrate 3g (Sugars 1g) | Total Fat 1g (Sat Fat .5g) | Protein 1g | Fiber 1g | Cholesterol 5mg | Sodium 75mg | Food Exchanges: 1 Vegetable | Carbohydrate Choices: 0 | Weight Watcher Smart Point Comparison: 1

Sour Cream and Cheddar Mashed Faux-tatoes

This "swap-out" for mashed potatoes became very popular during the low-carb diet rage for good reason. When done right, steamed cauliflower makes a delicious reduced-carbohydrate stand-in for starchy mashed potatoes. Here I cook the cauliflower until it is very tender, remove the excess water, and then add delicious "richness" with light sour cream and reduced-fat cheddar cheese. You can also reduce the carb and calories while creating a more traditional texture by adding a single potato to the mix as I have done in my Parmesan Garlic Cauliflower Potato Mash (page 268).

MAKES 4 SERVINGS

1 medium head cauliflower, (about 2 pounds), cut into florets (5 cups)

¼ cup light sour cream

⅓ cup reduced-fat cheddar cheese

Salt and pepper to taste

1. Bring 1½ quarts of water and the cauliflower to a boil in a large pot over high heat. Reduce the heat to medium low and simmer the cauliflower for 15 minutes, or until tender.

2. Drain the cauliflower into a colander. Remove excess water by pressing down on the florets with the lid of a pot or small plate. Transfer the cauliflower back to the pot.

3. Add the sour cream and cheese and process with a hand mixer or immersion blender until smooth. Add salt and pepper.

> **DARE to COMPARE** ·······················
> Made with half-and-half and butter, a single serving (⅔ cup) of creamy homemade mashed potatoes contains 300 calories and contains over 30 grams of carbohydrate. (And restaurants often serve double that amount.)

NUTRITION INFORMATION PER SERVING (¾ CUP) ························
Calories 80 | Carbohydrate 8g (Sugars 3g) | Total Fat 3g (Sat Fat 2g) | Protein 7g | Fiber 3g | Cholesterol 10mg | Sodium 230mg | Food Exchanges: 1 Vegetable, 1 Lean Meat | Carbohydrate Choices: ½ | Weight Watcher Smart Point Comparison: 2

Parmesan Garlic Cauliflower Potato Mash

The combination of potato and cauliflower takes "faux" mashed potatoes to a whole new level by giving this mash a more traditional potato texture, making it easy to satisfy even the pickiest potato lovers. (Be sneaky: Don't even tell 'em it's a swap, and watch your family gobble it up!) See Or Try This for two additional cheesy potato variations.

MAKES 6 SERVINGS

1 large russet potato (about ½ pound), peeled and cubed

2 garlic cloves

1 medium head cauliflower (about 2 pounds), cut into florets or 5 cups florets

¼ cup light sour cream

2 tablespoons reduced-fat milk

⅓ cup freshly grated Parmesan cheese

Salt and pepper to taste

1. Bring 1½ quarts of water to a boil over high heat. Add the potato and garlic and cook for 5 minutes.

2. Add the cauliflower and reduce the heat to medium low. Cook an additional 15 minutes, or until the potatoes and cauliflower are tender.

3. Drain the mixture into a colander. Remove excess water by pressing down on the mixture with the lid of a pot or small plate. Transfer the vegetables back to the pot.

4. Add the sour cream, milk, Parmesan cheese, and salt and pepper. Process with a hand mixer or immersion blender until smooth.

Or try this: See page 277 for Parmesan Garlic Smashed Potatoes. For a *Parmesan Garlic Cauliflower Potato Mash* omit the garlic cloves and replace all of the Parmesan with ½ cup reduced-fat cheddar cheese. (Adds 1 gram of protein and .5 grams of fat.)

NUTRITION INFORMATION PER SERVING (¾ CUP)
Calories 100 | Carbohydrate 13g (Sugars 3g) | Total Fat 2g (Sat Fat 2g) | Protein 5g | Fiber 3g | Cholesterol 10mg | Sodium 170mg | Food Exchanges: 1 Lean Meat, ½ Vegetable, ½ Starch | Carbohydrate Choices: 1 | Weight Watcher Smart Point Comparison: 3

Super Simple Sweet-and-Sour Red Cabbage

Growing up with a German father, sweet-and-sour red cabbage was a staple on our dinner table. This updated version offers all the same great taste I remember so well, but without all of the added sugar. Traditionally, braised red cabbage is served alongside pork, but this pairs equally well with roast chicken or veal or even a lean beef roast. Its rich red color also makes a great addition to any holiday table.

MAKES 4 SERVINGS

1 small head (about 1½ pounds) red cabbage, shredded

1 cup plus 1 tablespoon water, divided

⅓ cup balsamic vinegar

3 tablespoons granulated no-calorie sweetener (or 4 packets)

1½ teaspoons cornstarch

½ teaspoon salt

Pepper to taste

1. In a medium saucepan over medium heat, combine the cabbage, 1 cup water, vinegar, and sweetener. Bring to a simmer; then reduce the heat to low. Cover and cook for 30 minutes.

2. In a small bowl, whisk together the remaining tablespoon water and cornstarch to dissolve.

3. Tilt the saucepan to separate the juice to one side. Add the dissolved cornstarch to the juice and cook for 1 minute, or until the sauce thickens.

4. Mix the cabbage into the thickened sauce to coat. Season with salt and pepper to taste.

Marlene Says: Cabbage is fabulous when it comes to good nutrition. High in vitamins C and K, as well as fiber, it's a proven cancer fighter. Red cabbage not only has all the great benefits of green cabbage, but also offers six times the vitamin C and powerful anti-inflammatory and anti-aging antioxidants compliments of its beautiful red pigment.

NUTRITION INFORMATION PER SERVING (ABOUT ¾ CUP)
Calories 60 | Carbohydrate 13g (Sugars 7g) | Total Fat 0g (Sat Fat 0g) | Protein 2g | Fiber 4g | Cholesterol 0mg | Sodium 320mg | Food Exchanges: 1 Vegetable, ½ Carbohydrate | Carbohydrate Choices: 1 | Weight Watcher Smart Point Comparison: 1

Asian Stir-Fried Vegetables with Ginger and Garlic

If you're in a hurry, don't be deterred by the long list of ingredients. This is actually a very simple recipe. You won't be cooking all of the vegetables at once, but adding them one at a time, which ensures that each vegetable is cooked to perfection (no hard carrots or limp snow peas here). To make it super simple, you can use a bag of pre-prepped stir-fry vegetables in the produce section to save chopping and slicing.

MAKES 4 SERVINGS

2 teaspoons olive oil

1 teaspoon minced garlic

½ teaspoon grated ginger

2 medium carrots, thinly sliced on a bias

1 cup sliced onion

1 small red bell pepper, cut into strips

2 cups broccoli florets

1 cup snow peas, cut in half

SAUCE

2 tablespoons reduced-sodium soy sauce

2 tablespoons seasoned rice vinegar

2 tablespoons sherry

½ teaspoon cornstarch

1 teaspoon sesame oil

2 teaspoons sugar

1. Heat the oil in a large skillet or wok on high heat. Add the garlic, ginger, and carrots, and cook for 2 minutes. Cover and cook 3 more minutes. Add 2 tablespoons water. Cover, and cook 2 more minutes. Add ¼ cup more water and the broccoli. Recover and cook for 3 minutes. Uncover, stir in the onion, pepper, and snow peas and cook for 2 to 3 minutes.

2. While the vegetables are cooking, make the sauce. Combine the soy sauce, vinegar, sherry, cornstarch, sesame oil, and sugar in a small mixing bowl. Whisk to mix well.

3. Create a well in the center of the skillet by moving the vegetables to the outside edge. Add the sauce ingredients to the well, stirring to combine. Cook for 1 minute, or just until the sauce bubbles and thickens slightly.

4. Stir the vegetables back into the thickened sauce and toss until well coated.

NUTRITION INFORMATION PER SERVING (ABOUT 1 CUP)
Calories 90 | Carbohydrate 13g (Sugars 7g) | Total Fat 3.5g (Sat Fat 0g) | Protein 3g | Fiber 4g | Cholesterol 0mg | Sodium 320mg | Food Exchanges: 2 Vegetables, ½ Fat | Carbohydrate Choices: 1 | Weight Watcher Smart Point Comparison: 2

Starchy Sides

STOVETOP MACARONI AND CHEESE

SWEET POTATO WEDGES

PARMESAN GARLIC SMASHED POTATOES

SWEET POTATO PUFF

SWEET AND EASY ACORN SQUASH

RED POTATOES AND GREEN BEANS

SPANISH RICE

VEGGIE BROWN RICE PILAF

STEPHEN'S STIR-FRIED RICE

GREEK-STYLE COUSCOUS

STOVETOP BARBEQUED BEANS

SIMPLE SOUTHWEST BLACK BEANS

CURRIED LENTILS AND CARROTS

COUNTRY CORNBREAD MUFFINS

PERFECT GRILLED CORN ON THE COB

More than just plate fillers, a tasty side can provide variety and enhance the flavor and textures of the entire meal. In fact, the right side can make the entire meal. According to healthy eating guidelines a lunch or dinner plate should be divided into fourths with one-fourth of the plate filled with lean meat, half with fruits and non-starchy vegetables, and the final fourth reserved for carbohydrates or starches. If you are a carb lover, it should come as a relief to know that including some starch on your plate is important as starches (or carbs) are the body's preferred fuel for your muscles—and your brain. The trick when it comes to carbs and good health is to fill your plate with carbs you find delicious and satisfying, yet that are still wholesome and packed with nutrients, rather than with simply extra calories and fat.

Well, you need look no further. The healthy, yet incredibly flavorful starch sides in this chapter are ready to take their place on any plate, and with any diet. Not only are these starches tasty enough to make the meal, they may even have your family asking not what's for dinner, but what's *with* dinner (especially when the side dish is velvety macaroni and cheese). In addition to the quick and easy Stovetop Macaroni and Cheese, you'll find over a dozen pleasing sides to mix and match with your favorite entrées. The Sweet Potato Wedges are a perfect accompaniment for the Best Oven-Fried Chicken, while creamy Parmesan Garlic Smashed Potatoes complement Smothered Steak Burgers with Mushroom Gravy. Chili's®-Style Grilled Beef Fajitas taste even better when served with authentic-tasting Spanish Rice, and Greek-Style Couscous is the perfect full-flavored companion for simple Perfect Pan Seared Scallops. But let's not forget the healthiest starches of all, beans and legumes, which are jam-packed with fiber. My Stovetop Barbequed Beans are a sweet favorite when served with a simple burger, and the zesty Simple Southwest Black Beans, prepared in just minutes, round out any Mexican-inspired main course. Delicious and nutritious, these sides are just the thing to complete your plate.

Stovetop Macaroni and Cheese

There is no question that macaroni and cheese is an American staple. In fact, the first macaroni and cheese recipes date back to Thomas Jefferson. In my house, son Stephen is our mac 'n' cheese addict, but my stepdaughter Colleen, who has diabetes, is not far behind. Yet for her, and many others, it's not easy to fit a full-size entrée portion of this very carbohydrate-rich dish into a healthy meal plan, which is why I choose to feature it here—as a delicious side dish. This version comes together quickly and easily on the stovetop and requires no baking. It also retains all the rich and creamy goodness of the original recipe, with much less fat. When Stephen gobbled it up, I knew I had succeeded. I'm sure you will be as delighted as he is with this healthier version of one of America's favorite comfort foods.

MAKES 6 SERVINGS

8 ounces dry macaroni shells*

12 ounces low-fat evaporated milk

2 teaspoons cornstarch

1 teaspoon dry mustard

½ teaspoon garlic powder

¼ teaspoon salt

1½ cups (6 ounces) reduced-fat shredded sharp cheddar cheese

White or black pepper (optional)

* Using shells is a fun twist my family loves and makes for a slightly larger serving size due to their bulk. Of course, traditional elbow macaroni may be substituted.

1. Cook the pasta according to package directions. Be careful not to overcook. Drain the pasta and rinse with cold water.

2. In a medium saucepan, whisk together the evaporated milk and the next 4 ingredients over medium heat. Whisk until the mixture thickens and bubbles form. Turn off the heat and stir in the cheese until melted and creamy.

3. Add the pasta, stirring until well blended. Sprinkle with pepper, if desired.

Perfect Pairing: For a simple Sunday supper pair this up with roast chicken, steamed broccoli, and a Wedge Salad with Buttermilk Ranch Dressing (page 174). Or to create a healthful macaroni and cheese entrée fold steamed broccoli and/or cubed chicken into the macaroni and cheese before serving.

NUTRITION INFORMATION PER SERVING (¾ CUP)
Calories 280 | Carbohydrate 36g (Sugars 8g) | Total Fat 7g (Sat Fat 4.5g) | Protein 18g | Fiber 0g | Cholesterol 25mg | Sodium 390mg | Food Exchanges: 2 Starch, ½ Low-Fat Milk | Carbohydrate Choices: 2½ | Weight Watcher Smart Point Comparison: 8

Sweet Potato Wedges

Sweet potatoes are an excellent starch choice for a side dish. Full of beta carotene and vitamin A and easier on the blood sugar than white or yellow potatoes—they are both nutritious and delicious! I recommend buying the sweeter, darker-skinned variety that are commonly sold as yams. I also find that leaving the skin on enhances the dish by adding more fiber, as well as providing a beautiful contrast between the dark red-tinged skin and the bright orange flesh. For a fast 'n' fit meal, whip these up along with a salad and pair them with a store-bought rotisserie chicken.

MAKES 4 SERVINGS

2 medium sweet potatoes
    (about 1¼ pounds),
    unpeeled and scrubbed
1 tablespoon vegetable oil
¾ teaspoon seasoned salt

1. Preheat the oven to 425°F.

2. Cut each sweet potato in half crosswise and then again lengthwise. Turn the potatoes over, cut side down, and cut into wedges.

3. Toss the potato wedges with the oil and salt. Spread wedges in an even layer onto a flat baking sheet.

4. Bake for 20 minutes, turning once halfway through as the potatoes caramelize and brown on the underside. Wedges are done when they are tender on the inside.

NUTRITION INFORMATION PER SERVING (½ POTATO)
Calories 120 | Carbohydrate 21g (Sugars 10g) | Total Fat 3.5g (Sat Fat 0g) | Protein 2g | Fiber 2g | Cholesterol 0mg | Sodium 270mg | Food Exchanges: 1½ Starch, ½ Fat | Carbohydrate Choices: 1½ | Weight Watcher Smart Point Comparison: 3

Parmesan Garlic Smashed Potatoes

Let's face it, mashed potatoes rarely make it onto anyone's healthiest foods list (especially for those watching their weight or blood sugar), but that doesn't mean you can't still enjoy them. The trick is how to do it healthfully—and in moderation. This gratifying recipe helps you do both. The buttery flesh of Yukon Golds eliminates the need for added butter, while Parmesan cheese, garlic, and light sour cream make them so rich, flavorful, and creamy that one-half cup is ever-so-satisfying. (P.S.: You don't even need to peel the potatoes. The skin is a concentrated source of dietary fiber that cooks up tender and adds a touch of "smashed" texture to this otherwise creamy dish.

MAKES 6 SERVINGS

1½ pounds Yukon Gold potatoes, cubed (about 6 medium potatoes)

6 garlic cloves, peeled

¼ cup light sour cream

¼ cup freshly grated Parmesan (½ ounce)

⅓ cup nonfat half-and-half (or low-fat milk), warmed

Salt to taste

Pepper to taste

1. Place the potatoes and garlic in a large pot of water and bring to a boil. Simmer 20 minutes or until potatoes are fork tender. Drain the potatoes and garlic and place in a large bowl.

2. Add the sour cream, cheese, and most of the milk. Using a potato masher or large fork, smash until smooth. Add the remaining milk to reach desired consistency. Season with salt and pepper.

DARE to COMPARE

A chef friend gave me her restaurant recipe for mashed potatoes. A single ¾-cup portion (the smallest they serve) serves up a staggering 500 calories, 39 grams of fat (including more saturated fat than a quarter pounder with cheese), and 38 grams of carbohydrate.

NUTRITION INFORMATION PER SERVING (½ CUP)
Calories 140 | Carbohydrate 25g (Sugars 3g) | Total Fat 2.5g (Sat Fat 1.5g) | Protein 5g | Fiber 3g | Cholesterol 5mg | Sodium 190mg | Food Exchanges: 1½ Starch, ½ Fat | Carbohydrate Choices: 1½ | Weight Watcher Smart Point Comparison: 4

Sweet Potato Puff

This is the most heavenly way to whip up sweet potatoes. My assistant Sophia, who had never eaten them this way, swooned upon eating her first bite. Sweet and rich, scented with cinnamon and topped with pecans, this puff leaves the old sugary marshmallow sweet potato recipe out in the cold. Adding pumpkin not only creatively curbs the carbs, but also makes this dish extra creamy. If you prefer an even lower carb puff, substitute two cups of mashed butternut squash for the sweet potatoes for an equally delicious puff with only 110 calories and thirteen grams of carbohydrate (and two points a serving).

MAKES 8 SERVINGS

2 pounds dark sweet potatoes or yams (2 cups mashed)

1 cup canned pumpkin purée

1 large egg

3 large egg whites

½ cup light sour cream

⅔ cup granulated no-calorie sweetener*

1 tablespoon margarine or butter, melted

¾ teaspoon ground cinnamon

1 teaspoon baking powder

¼ teaspoon salt

1 teaspoon vanilla extract

¼ cup chopped pecans

1. To prepare the sweet potato or yams, pierce the sweet potato with a fork and place in microwave. Cook on high for 10 minutes, or until the flesh is soft.

2. Preheat the oven to 350°F. Coat a 2-quart casserole or soufflé dish with nonstick cooking spray.

3. Cut the sweet potatoes or yams in half and scoop out the flesh into a large bowl. Add the remaining ingredients, except the pecans, and beat until smooth. Spoon into the casserole dish and smooth the top. Sprinkle the top with nuts.

4. Bake for 25 to 30 minutes, or until the center slightly puffs.

DARE *to* COMPARE ···
A traditional recipe for whipped sweet potato puff delivers close to 400 calories, 20 grams of fat (12 of them saturated), and 60 grams of carbohydrate—or an entire meal's worth of carbs—per serving.

* See page 382 for sweetener options

NUTRITION INFORMATION PER SERVING (½ CUP) ···
Calories 140 | Carbohydrate 19g (Sugars 8g) | Total Fat 6g (Sat Fat 1.5g) | Protein 4g | Fiber 3g | Cholesterol 30mg | Sodium 210mg | Food Exchanges: 1 Starch, 1 Fat | Carbohydrate Choices: 1 | Weight Watcher Smart Point Comparison: 5

Sweet and Easy Acorn Squash

Cutting a raw acorn squash in half is difficult, as you may well know. When I was growing up my mother would have my father take the thick-skinned squash into the garage where he would use a small hacksaw to saw the squash in half. It was quite a process, but always worth it when the cavity, filled with lots of brown sugar and butter, cooked until the flesh could easily be spooned into your mouth. Now, with the help of the microwave and a touch of sugar-free maple syrup, you can produce an equally sweet, delicious squash side dish for your family in just minutes.

MAKES 4 SERVINGS

2 small acorn squash (about 1¼ pounds each)

½ cup sugar-free maple flavored syrup

4 teaspoons brown sugar (optional)

4 teaspoons butter

1. Prick the squash in several places with a sharp knife and place in the microwave whole.

2. Microwave on high for 5 minutes. Remove and cut squash in half lengthwise. When cool enough to handle, scoop out seeds with a spoon. Pour 2 tablespoons maple syrup into each half and place flesh side up in a microwave-safe baking dish.

3. Add a couple of tablespoons of water to the bottom of the dish and cover tightly with plastic wrap. Place back in the microwave for 3 to 4 more minutes or until flesh is very soft when poked with a fork. Remove plastic wrap and place 1 teaspoon of brown sugar, if desired, and 1 teaspoon of butter into each cavity.

NUTRITION INFORMATION PER SERVING (½ CUP) ···
Calories 95 | Carbohydrate 22g (Sugars 6g) | Total Fat 4g (Sat Fat 2.5g) | Protein 1g | Fiber 4g | Cholesterol 10mg | Sodium 100mg | Food Exchanges: 1 Starch, 1 Fat | Carbohydrate Choices: 1 | Weight Watcher Smart Point Comparison: 2

Red Potatoes and Green Beans

A great way to lighten up carbohydrate-rich potatoes is to pair them with lower-carb vegetables, as I do here with fresh green beans. To shorten the prep time throw a microwavable steamer bag of ready-to-cook fresh green beans (found in the produce department) into the microwave while cooking the potatoes. Canned or frozen beans will also work, but be sure to choose cut, not French-style, green beans for this recipe. To serve, toss the potatoes, beans, and dressing in a large bowl or arrange the potatoes and beans on a platter and pour the dressing over them. Either way they are delicious.

MAKES 4 SERVINGS

12 ounces unpeeled red potatoes, quartered

2 strips bacon

¼ cup chopped onion

2 tablespoons cider vinegar

2 tablespoons granulated no-calorie sweetener

¾ teaspoon dried thyme

⅛ teaspoon salt

¾ teaspoon cornstarch

⅓ cup water

1½ cups fresh green beans, cooked or 1 (15-ounce) can, drained

¼ teaspoon salt

1. Fill a large pot with water and bring to a boil. Boil the potatoes for 20 minutes or until fork tender. Drain and set aside.

2. In a sauté pan, cook the bacon over high heat until the fat is rendered and the bacon crisp. Remove the bacon and set aside. Add the onion and cook for 2 to 3 minutes, or until translucent. Add the vinegar, sweetener, thyme, and salt. Stir over low heat. Dissolve the cornstarch in water and add to the sauté pan. Cook for 1 to 2 minutes until sauce thickens.

3. Combine the potatoes and beans. Sprinkle with salt. Pour the sauce over the entire potato mixture, lightly toss, and top with crumbled bacon.

Marlene Says: When researchers in Sydney, Australia, tested foods to determine their satiety value (a measure of how a set amount of food satisfies your hunger), boiled potatoes were the runaway star. They filled the participants sooner, and kept them full longer, than every other food tested. Boiling, not baking, the potatoes is key.

NUTRITION INFORMATION PER SERVING (¼ RECIPE)
Calories 150 | Carbohydrate 20g (Sugars 3g) | Total Fat 7g (Sat Fat 2.5g) | Protein 3g | Fiber 3g | Cholesterol 10mg | Sodium 440mg | Food Exchanges: 1 Starch, 1 Vegetable, 1 Fat | Carbohydrate Choices: 1½ | Weight Watcher Smart Point Comparison: 4

Spanish Rice

High in sodium and low in authentic flavor, the Spanish rice packets you find at the grocery store are basically no more than tomato flavoring and salt. The good news is that it only takes a few simple ingredients to turn everyday rice into an authentic fiesta-worthy side dish. Spanish rice is a perfect accompaniment to simple grilled meats like the In-a-Flash Southwestern Chicken on page 310. Olé.

MAKES 8 SERVINGS

1 tablespoon olive oil

½ medium white onion, chopped (about ½ cup)

1 garlic clove, minced

1 cup long-grain white rice

1 (15-ounce) can chopped tomatoes

1½ cups reduced-sodium chicken broth

1 teaspoon ground cumin

Salt to taste

Pepper to taste

1. In a medium saucepan, heat oil over medium-high heat. Sauté the onion for 3 minutes. Add the garlic and continue cooking until the onion is translucent and tender. Add the rice and sauté for 3 to 4 minutes to coat with oil and lightly brown.

2. Pour in the tomatoes, chicken broth, and seasonings. Stir. Cover and bring to a boil. Reduce the heat to a simmer and cook for 20 minutes, or until the rice is tender. Fluff with a fork before serving.

NUTRITION INFORMATION PER SERVING (½ CUP) ···
Calories 120 | Carbohydrate 22g (Sugars 1g) | Total Fat 2g (Sat Fat 0g) | Protein 3g | Fiber .5g | Cholesterol 0mg | Sodium 140mg | Food Exchanges: 1 Starch, 1 Vegetable | Carbohydrate Choices: 1½ | Weight Watcher Smart Point Comparison: 3

Veggie Brown Rice Pilaf

If the extra cooking time required for regular brown rice keeps you reaching for the white stuff, this recipe is for you. In fact, eating healthier doesn't get much easier than substituting a package of instant brown rice whenever white rice is called for in a dish. Lighter in color, texture, and taste, instant brown rice (which cooks in half the time of regular white rice) makes this terrific veggie pilaf super quick—and super easy. In addition to the traditional onion and carrot found in most pilafs, you can also add mushrooms, zucchini, or red pepper to this dish. For a super veggie pilaf, use all three.

MAKES 8 SERVINGS

1 tablespoon olive oil

¾ cup chopped red onion

½ cup diced carrot

¾ cup chopped mushrooms, zucchini, or red pepper

1 cup cups instant brown rice

1¾ cups low-sodium chicken broth

¼ teaspoon salt, or to taste

Fresh ground black pepper to taste

1. In a medium saucepan, heat the oil on medium-high heat. Add the onion and carrots; sauté for 3 to 4 minutes, or until the onion is translucent and the carrots have begun to soften. Add the chopped mushrooms or vegetable of choice and sauté for an additional 3 to 4 minutes.

2. Add brown rice, stirring until slightly toasted. Add the remaining ingredients and bring to a boil. Cover, reduce the heat, and simmer for 5 minutes. Remove from heat and allow to rest for an additional 5 minutes, or until the broth is absorbed.

3. Fluff with a fork and serve.

DARE to COMPARE ·······················
One-half cup of cooked white rice has 120 calories, 27 grams of carbohydrate, and 0 grams of fiber. In a study by the International Journal of Food Sciences and Nutrition, it was found that consuming brown rice over white rice lowered the rate of rise in blood sugar by 12 percent in healthy individuals, and 35 percent in those with diabetes.

NUTRITION INFORMATION PER SERVING (½ CUP) ························
Calories 90 | Carbohydrate 18 g (Sugars 2g) | Total Fat 3.5g (Sat Fat 0g) | Protein 2g | Fiber 2g | Cholesterol 0mg | Sodium 130mg | Food Exchanges: 1 Starch, ½ Vegetable | Carbohydrate Choices: 1 | Weight Watcher Smart Point Comparison: 3

Stephen's Stir-Fried Rice

When my son Stephen was in third grade he came home and told me another Mom had come to school and made the best rice ever. It was stir-fried rice. Eventually, I learned to make stir-fried rice from an Asian cooking instructor willing to share her secrets. She taught me first to cook the eggs into a pancake that you thinly slice and add back to the rice, to use oyster sauce instead of soy sauce for a richer taste, and in the Chinese tradition, to use day-old white rice. I still use most of her techniques, but I now use instant brown rice to create a stir-fried rice that is both faster and more nutritious. I was recently called by the mother of one of Stephen's friends who wanted to know how I made the rice I fed her son. He, too, said it was the best rice ever.

MAKES 4 SERVINGS

1 large egg

2 large egg whites

1 tablespoon vegetable oil

¾ teaspoon chopped fresh ginger

¼ cup finely chopped carrots

1 (8-ounce) can sliced water chestnuts, drained

1 cup chopped fresh mushrooms

4 green onions, chopped (reserve green ends for garnish)

¾ cup instant brown rice, cooked, then cooled (or 2 cups leftover white rice)

1½ tablespoons oyster sauce

Fresh ground pepper

Frozen peas (optional)

Smoked turkey or ham (optional)

1. In a small bowl, whisk together the egg and egg whites. Lightly spray a large nonstick skillet with cooking spray, and place over medium heat. Pour in the eggs and swirl the pan to cook the eggs like a flat pancake. Turn once and cook until set. Remove from the pan and roll the egg pancake into the shape of a cigar. Slice across the egg to make thin strips.

2. Add the oil to the pan, and turn the heat to medium high. Add the ginger, carrots, water chestnuts, and mushrooms. Cook for 3 to 4 minutes, or until the vegetables are slightly soft. Add the white parts of the green onions and cook for one more minute.

3. Add the rice, oyster sauce, peas and/or meat, if desired, and stir well to coat. Cook on high for 1 to 2 minutes to "fry' rice and then reduce the heat to low and cook for about 5 more minutes or until rice and vegetables are thoroughly heated through. Add the pepper to taste and garnish with the green parts of the onion, if desired.

Family Focus: Sitting down and sharing a meal is a good thing. Family meals not only encourage healthy eating and result in better nutrition but have been found to foster many other positive behaviors from less depression to better grades.

NUTRITION INFORMATION PER SERVING (½ CUP)
Calories 150 | Carbohydrate 21g (Sugars 2g) | Total Fat 5g (Sat Fat.5g) | Protein 5g | Fiber 3g | Cholesterol 55mg | Sodium 290mg | Food Exchanges: 1 Starch, 1 Vegetable, 1 Fat | Carbohydrate Choices: 1 | Weight Watcher Smart Point Comparison: 4

Greek-Style Couscous

Couscous is an extremely quick-cooking side dish that makes it perfect for busy weeknight dinners. Couscous found in North America is made from semolina flour, and because it's pre-steamed and re-dried, it requires a mere five minutes of preparation time. This unique recipe plumps it up with all the tastes and textures of a wonderful Greek salad for a flavor combination that's hard to beat.

MAKES 6 SERVINGS

⅔ cup couscous*

¾ cup reduced-sodium chicken broth

½ cucumber, peeled, seeded, and chopped

1 large tomato, seeded and chopped

¼ cup chopped red onion

1½ tablespoons extra-virgin olive oil

1 teaspoon crushed oregano

½ teaspoon minced garlic (1 to 2 cloves)

⅛ teaspoon salt

⅛ teaspoon black pepper

⅓ cup reduced-fat feta cheese, crumbled and divided

* I use regular couscous for this dish. Whole wheat couscous would add 1 gram of fiber per serving.

1. In a medium glass bowl, mix together the couscous and chicken broth. Microwave on high for 3 minutes. Remove from microwave, cover, and let stand for 2 minutes. Use a fork to fluff the couscous, breaking up any lumps.

2. Add the cucumber, tomato, onion, oil, oregano, garlic, salt, pepper, and half the feta to the couscous and stir to combine. Return to microwave for 1 additional minute. Transfer to a serving bowl, top with the remaining feta, and serve.

Marlene Says: This fragrant dish can be served hot, cold, or at room temperature. When heated the cucumbers lose just a bit of their cool crunch and meld deliciously into the couscous. For more crunch, do not return to the microwave and serve at room temperature. This is wonderful with grilled meats like chicken or beef.

NUTRITION INFORMATION PER SERVING (½ CUP)···
Calories 130 | Carbohydrate 18g (Sugars 2g) | Total Fat 4g (Sat Fat 1g) | Protein 5g | Fiber 2.5g | Cholesterol 0mg | Sodium 290mg | Food Exchanges: 1 Starch, 1 Vegetable | Carbohydrate Choices: 1 | Weight Watcher Smart Point Comparison: 3

Stovetop Barbequed Beans

Beans are a super food for anyone watching their blood sugar, but quick-and-easy barbequed bean recipes generally rely heavily on sugar-laden barbeque sauces. Instead, this recipe takes advantage of the lip-smacking barbeque sauce I created for my Slow-Cooker Root Beer Barbequed Chicken on page 309, and eliminates the equivalent of almost eight tablespoons of sugar when compared with a store-bought brand. When you're watching the added sugar in your diet, there are better places to put it than in a barbeque sauce.

MAKES 6 SERVINGS

1 teaspoon olive oil

1 small onion, chopped (about 1 cup)

2 (15-ounce) cans pinto beans, drained and rinsed

¾ cup root beer barbeque sauce (page 309)

Salt to taste

Fresh ground pepper to taste

For smokier beans, add ¼ teaspoon liquid smoke

1. In a large saucepan, heat the oil over medium-high heat. When hot, add onion and sauté for about 3 minutes until tender and translucent.

2. Add the beans and barbeque sauce. Simmer on low for 15 to 20 minutes until the sauce blends with the beans.

NUTRITION INFORMATION PER SERVING (½ CUP) ······················
Calories 140 | Carbohydrate 25g (Sugars 4g) | Total Fat 1.5g (Sat Fat 0g) | Protein 8g | Fiber 8g | Cholesterol 0mg | Sodium 240mg | Food Exchanges: 1½ Starch | Carbohydrate Choices: 1½ | Weight Watcher Smart Point Comparison: 3

Simple Southwest Black Beans

These simple black beans are, well, simple. Using canned beans and prepared salsa, it only takes minutes to create this fresh-tasting, versatile, and highly nutritious side dish that has all but kicked refried beans to the curb in my house. And while black beans are a great accompaniment to Southwest and Mexican dishes, these beans also go great with eggs at breakfast or tossed onto fresh greens at lunch.

MAKES 4 SERVINGS

1 teaspoon olive oil

½ cup chopped onion

1 (15-ounce) can black beans, drained

½ cup prepared salsa

¼ teaspoon ground cumin

1 to 2 tablespoons finely chopped fresh cilantro

1. In a medium saucepan, heat the oil over medium-high heat. Sauté the onion until tender, about 3 minutes. Add the beans and salsa. Stir to warm the beans thoroughly. Add the cumin and continue to stir until hot.

2. Before serving, sprinkle with cilantro.

Marlene Says: When it comes to fiber, you just can't beat beans. With 6 grams of fiber in a mere half cup, they stand heads and shoulders above most foods, including wheat bread, brown rice, and even oatmeal—and that's no beans.

NUTRITION INFORMATION PER SERVING (½ CUP) ·······················
Calories 90 | Carbohydrate 18g (Sugars 3g) | Total Fat 1.5g (Sat Fat 0g) | Protein 5g | Fiber 6g | Cholesterol 0mg | Sodium 310mg | Food Exchanges: 1 Starch | Carbohydrate Choices: 1 | Weight Watcher Smart Point Comparison: 2

Curried Lentils and Carrots

Quick-cooking lentils are often overlooked by cooks, which is unfortunate because lentils are versatile, easy to prepare, and the only legume that requires no presoaking. They are also packed with folate, fiber, vitamin B, and iron. This one-pot dish pumps up the flavors and nutrients of lentils with the additions of curry, carrots, onions, and celery to create a noteworthy side dish. It also makes for great leftovers, as the flavors continue to meld when refrigerated overnight.

MAKES 8 SERVINGS

2 teaspoons olive oil

1 teaspoon minced garlic (2 cloves)

½ cup chopped onion

1 cup chopped carrot

1 cup chopped celery

1 cup brown or green lentils, rinsed and picked over

1 teaspoon curry powder

¼ teaspoon turmeric (optional)

1 (14-ounce) can reduced-sodium chicken broth

¼ teaspoon black pepper

½ teaspoon seasoned salt

1. Heat the oil in a large sauté pan over medium heat. Add the garlic, onion, carrot, and celery. Sauté for 4 to 5 minutes, or until the vegetables begin to soften.

2. Add the lentils, curry powder, and turmeric and stir to combine. Pour the chicken broth over lentils. Add the pepper and bring to a slow boil. Allow to boil for 1 minute; reduce the heat to simmer for 20 to 25 minutes or until lentils are tender, but not mushy. Season with salt and serve.

NUTRITION INFORMATION PER SERVING (½ CUP)
Calories 110 | Carbohydrate 17g (Sugars 3g) | Total Fat 1.5g (Sat Fat 0g) | Protein 8g | Fiber 8g | Cholesterol 0mg | Sodium 230mg | Food Exchanges: 1 Starch, ½ Vegetable | Carbohydrate Choices: 1 | Weight Watcher Smart Point Comparison: 2

Country Cornbread Muffins

It just wouldn't be right to ignore this beloved side dish. In the South, a piece of fluffy fresh cornbread accompanies almost every meal! Unfortunately, when it comes to your health, many Southern cornbread recipes contain just as much sugar and butter as a layer cake. This meal-worthy makeover keeps the tradition, but not the carbs and calories, by cutting back on the butter, adding white whole wheat flour for fiber, and swapping out the sugar—while retaining all the sweet Southern taste. I have made this recipe into muffins for fun and easy portion control, but you can also bake the batter in an eight-inch square greased pan (baking time will be 20 to 22 minutes). Y'all enjoy!

MAKES 12 SERVINGS

1 large egg

2 large egg whites

3 tablespoons margarine or
   butter, melted

1¼ cups buttermilk

1 teaspoon vanilla extract

1 cup cornmeal

½ cup white whole wheat flour

½ cup all-purpose flour

½ cup granulated no-calorie
   sweetener*

1 tablespoon baking powder

½ teaspoon baking soda

Pinch of salt

1. Preheat the oven to 375°F. Spray a 12-muffin-cup pan with nonstick baking spray.

2. In a medium bowl mix together the first 5 ingredients (egg through vanilla) until well combined.

3. In a separate large bowl, whisk together all the remaining ingredients. Pour the wet ingredients into the dry ingredients and mix with a spoon until all ingredients are combined.

4. Scoop the batter evenly into muffin cups and bake for 12 to 13 minutes, or until cornbread springs back when touched lightly in center.

Perfect Pairing: For a down-home Southern meal, pair these cornbread muffins with either Southern-Style Shrimp Creole (page 355) or Oven-Fried Chicken (page 295), your favorite sautéed greens, and Classic Creamy Coleslaw (page 183).

* See page 382 for sweetener options

NUTRITION INFORMATION PER SERVING (1 MUFFIN) ·······················
Calories 130 | Carbohydrate 18g (Sugars 2g) | Total Fat 3.5g (Sat Fat 2g) | Protein 4g | Fiber 2g | Cholesterol 25mg | Sodium 240mg | Food Exchanges: 1 Starch, 1 Fat | Carbohydrate Choices: 1 | Weight Watcher Smart Point Comparison: 4

Perfect Grilled Corn on the Cob

You're probably wondering why corn on the cob is in the starch chapter and not with the other vegetables. Corn is classified as a starch rather than a vegetable in food exchange lists due to its high starch content That's not to say you shouldn't eat corn. Corn is a very nutritious carbohydrate choice and a good source of thiamin, folate, fiber, and vitamin C. Better yet, corn on the cob comes with automatic portion control! And of course, corn is absolutely perfect for barbeques.

MAKES 4 SERVINGS

4 medium whole corncobs
   (about 7 inches)

Salt or seasoned salt to taste

Butter-flavored spray
   (like I Can't Believe It's
   Not Butter)

1. In a large, heavy pot, bring 2 quarts of water to a boil.

2. Add the corn, bring the water back to a boil, and cook for 5 to 6 minutes. Drain and grill for 3 to 4 minutes, rolling them until all sides are slightly charred.

Marlene Says: After cooking numerous ears of corn by boiling, grilling, and microwaving, we chose "boil and grill" as the best method for preparing corn. While grilling corn in the husk took a lot of work and the timing was unpredictable, grilling it without the husk tended to dry out the kernels. This led us to the boil then grill method, which produces perfectly tender "grilled" corn.

NUTRITION INFORMATION PER SERVING (1 CORNCOB)
Calories 80 | Carbohydrate 18g (Sugars 3g) | Total Fat 1g (Sat Fat 0g) | Protein 3g | Fiber 2g | Cholesterol 0mg | Sodium 15mg | Food Exchanges: 1 Starch | Carbohydrate Choices: 1 | Weight Watcher Smart Point Comparison: 2

Chicken and Turkey

BEST OVEN-FRIED CHICKEN

SKILLET CHICKEN PARMESAN

GARLIC-LIME CHICKEN

CHICKEN CURRY IN A HURRY

NO BONES CHICKEN CACCIATORE

20-MINUTE PERFECT POACHED CHICKEN

JAMMIN' CHICKEN

HONEY MUSTARD–GLAZED CHICKEN

QUICKER-THAN-TAKE-OUT ORANGE CHICKEN

ORANGE CHICKEN VEGETABLE STIR-FRY

CLASSIC CHICKEN PICCATA

SLOW-COOKER ROOT BEER BARBEQUED CHICKEN

MARLENE'S FAVORITE GO-TO ITALIAN CHICKEN

GREENS AND BEANS BALSAMIC CHICKEN

MARTHA'S SUNDAY BEST ARTICHOKE HEART CHICKEN

CREAMY CHICKEN ENCHILADAS

HOME-STYLE TURKEY POTPIE

ONE-POT TURKEY SAUSAGE DINNER

SALSA MEATLOAF

TURKEY SCALOPPINI AND CREAMY MUSHROOM SAUCE

TERIYAKI TURKEY CUTLETS

Popular entrées made with chicken or turkey are hard to beat because they are both terrific sources of satisfying protein, wonderfully versatile, and taste great! What's more, when served unadorned, skinless chicken breast meat averages just 130 calories per 4 ounces, with 2 grams of fat (and turkey breast meat has even less), while the same portion of skinless dark meat delivers a modest 160 calories and 8 grams of fat.

Up until World War II only the affluent could afford to eat chicken on a weekly basis, but today, chicken is an affordable and healthy dinner staple that appears regularly on most of our tables. Yet when it comes to combining the great taste of chicken with good nutrition, things often go astray. For example, more than half of all chicken entrées served in restaurants are fried. This is only compounded by the fact that rich or sugary sauces have also become the norm, rather than the exception. Unfortunately, at home, many traditional recipes for chicken fare no better. With creamy sauces and lots of oil, many of our favorite classic recipes are just as rich.

Like you, I frequently serve chicken, and the recipes in this chapter are, quite honestly, the everyday dishes that often grace our family table. No longer do I have to worry that the chicken curry from the local restaurant is swimming in fat or that the orange chicken my son Stephen craves is coated in sugar. Quick-fix techniques also abound, so classics such as Skillet Chicken Parmesan and No Bones Chicken Cacciatore can be prepared not only a better way, but in minutes. To round out the chapter, I've included several wonderful dishes that feature healthful, economical turkey. No longer just for Thanksgiving, turkey is also stellar when turned into a potpie, formed into a tasty Salsa Meatloaf, or served draped with a creamy mushroom sauce.

For the Love of Meat

There's no need to cut meat from your diet—if it's lean. Studies confirm that lean meat (as part of a healthy diet) is as healthy as lean chicken and fish with regard to its impact on cholesterol levels. Studies also show those who eat lean meats while dieting have an easier time sticking to their diet regimen. The USDA defines lean meat as having no more than 10 grams of fat, 4.5 grams of saturated fat, and 95 grams of cholesterol per 3-ounce cooked serving. Look for the words *loin* or *round* on the label when shopping for lean meats.

3-ounce cooked serving	Calories	Total Fat	Sat Fat	Cholesterol
CHICKEN				
Skinless chicken breast	130	2g	1g	75mg
Skinless chicken leg	150	7g	2g	80mg
Skinless chicken thigh	150	8g	2 g	80mg
LEAN CUTS OF PORK				
Pork tenderloin	120	3g	1g	60mg
Pork boneless top loin chop	170	5g	2g	60mg
Pork center loin chop	150	6g	2g	70mg
LEAN CUTS OF BEEF				
90% Lean ground beef	180	10g	5g	70mg
93% Lean ground beef	160	7g	3.5g	70mg
Top sirloin steak	155	5g	2g	75mg
Beef tenderloin	175	8g	3g	7mg
FISH				
Cod	100	1g	0g	50mg
Catfish*	130	5.5g	0g	50mg
Halibut	100	2g	0g	25mg
Salmon*	180	10g	2g	54mg
Scallops	75	1g	0g	30mg
Shrimp	85	1g	0g	165mg

*Average of wild and farm raised.

Best Oven-Fried Chicken

While there are lots of recipes for "oven-fried" chicken, the truth is most oven-fried chicken recipes don't look or taste anything like the Southern-fried specialty. Never one to give up in the search for the perfect recipe, I tested more batches of "fried" chicken than I, or my patient family, ever imagined we could eat. In the end it was the exact combination of spices (black pepper is key), breading (the winner is a blend of finely crushed cornflakes and breadcrumbs), and cooking method (using a wire rack), that produced oven-fried chicken finally good enough to be called the "best."

MAKES 4 SERVINGS

2 large egg whites

½ teaspoon garlic powder

½ teaspoon onion powder

¼ teaspoon cayenne pepper

½ teaspoon ground sage

¼ teaspoon dried thyme

1¼ cups cornflake cereal

¼ cup plain breadcrumbs

½ teaspoon black pepper

½ teaspoon salt

2 tablespoons all-purpose flour

1½ pounds skinned chicken pieces (such as 2 legs, 2 thighs, and 1 large breast cut in half)

1. Preheat the oven to 400°F. Place a wire rack on top of a baking sheet and spray with cooking spray.

2. In a shallow bowl, whisk together the egg whites with the garlic powder, onion powder, cayenne pepper, sage, and thyme.

3. Place the cereal in a plastic bag and crush thoroughly with a rolling pin. Place in a shallow bowl and mix together with the breadcrumbs, pepper, and salt.

4. Place the flour in a third shallow bowl.

5. To bread the chicken pieces, first dredge the chicken in the flour to coat. Next, dip each piece of chicken into the egg white mixture, followed by the crumb mixture, making sure to cover all surfaces. Repeat until all the chicken is coated.

6. Place the chicken pieces on the prepared rack and bake for 45 minutes, or until the chicken is golden brown and registers 180°F when tested with a meat thermometer in the thickest part.

> **DARE to COMPARE** ····································
> One extra crispy chicken breast at the Colonel's weighs in at 460 calories, 28 grams of fat, and 16 grams of carbohydrate.

NUTRITION INFORMATION PER SERVING (AVERAGE OF PIECES) ····································
Calories 255 | Carbohydrate 13g (Sugars 1g) | Total Fat 8g (Sat Fat 2g) | Protein 32g | Fiber 0g | Cholesterol 65mg | Sodium 325mg | Food Exchanges: 4 Lean Meat, 1 Starch | Carbohydrate Choices: 1 | Weight Watcher Smart Point Comparison: 6

Skillet Chicken Parmesan

Although my boys love to order chicken Parmesan when we dine out, the health content is always a concern—especially since it usually arrives thickly breaded, deeply fried, smothered in cheese, and served on a mountain of spaghetti! In an effort to satisfy their love of this dish I have come up with a terrific easy stove-top recipe that's filled with all of the same great flavors but none of the excess fat and carbs. To keep the calories and carbs under control, serve each portion with two-thirds to one cup of cooked multigrain pasta and a mountain of steamed vegetables.

MAKES 4 SERVINGS

⅓ cup breadcrumbs

⅓ cup grated Parmesan cheese

½ teaspoon dried oregano

¼ teaspoon garlic salt

1 large egg

4 boneless, skinless chicken breasts (about 1 pound)

1 tablespoon olive oil

¾ cup marinara sauce

¾ cup shredded part-skim mozzarella cheese

1. In a shallow bowl, mix together the breadcrumbs, Parmesan cheese, oregano, and garlic salt. In another shallow bowl, beat the egg until frothy.

2. Wrap the chicken breasts in plastic wrap and place on a cutting board. Gently pound each breast with a mallet to an even thickness (about ½ inch). Dip each chicken breast into the beaten egg to coat, and then roll in the breadcrumb mixture.

3. Heat the oil in a large nonstick skillet over medium-high heat. Add the chicken and cook for 4 to 5 minutes on each side, or until the chicken is well browned and just cooked through.

4. Spoon the marinara sauce evenly on top of the chicken, and sprinkle the mozzarella on top. Cover the pan, reduce heat to low, and cook for 3 more minutes, or until the cheese melts.

> **DARE to COMPARE**
> The Primo Chicken Parmesan dinner plate (or should I say platter) at Romano's Macaroni Grill® piles on 2220 calories, 148 grams of fat (52 of them saturated), 90 grams of protein, 126 grams of carbohydrate, and 4440 mg of sodium. Mama Mia!

NUTRITION INFORMATION PER SERVING (1 CHICKEN BREAST)
Calories 295 | Carbohydrate 13g (Sugars 1g) | Total Fat 11g (Sat Fat 4g) | Protein 39g | Fiber 0g | Cholesterol 135mg | Sodium 840mg | Food Exchanges: 4 Lean Meat, 1 Medium-Fat Meat, 2 Vegetable, 1 Fat, ½ Starch | Carbohydrate Choices: 1 | Weight Watcher Smart Point Comparison: 7

Garlic-Lime Chicken

This recipe is a wonderful example of how flavorful ingredients can meld to create a taste much greater than the sum of their parts. Pungent garlic, piquant lime juice, and sweet honey are all flavorful in their own right, but when combined in this recipe, they make a simply irresistible sauce.

MAKES 4 SERVINGS

⅛ teaspoon cayenne pepper

½ teaspoon onion powder

½ teaspoon dried thyme

¼ teaspoon paprika

⅛ teaspoon black pepper

½ teaspoon salt

4 boneless, skinless chicken breasts (about 1¼ pounds)

2 teaspoons canola oil, divided

½ teaspoon minced garlic

Juice of 1 lime (2 tablespoons juice)

⅓ cup reduced-sodium chicken broth

2 teaspoons honey

1½ tablespoons butter or margarine

1. In a small bowl, mix together the spices (cayenne through salt).

2. Wrap the chicken breasts in plastic wrap and place on a cutting board. Gently pound each breast with a mallet to an even thickness (about ½-inch). Coat them on both sides with the spice mixture.

3. Heat 1 teaspoon of the oil in a large nonstick skillet over medium-high heat. Add the chicken and cook for 5 minutes on each side, until well browned and cooked through. Transfer the chicken to a plate and keep warm.

4. Reduce the heat to low. Add the additional teaspoon of oil and the garlic to pan and cook for 30 seconds. Whisk in the lime juice, chicken broth, and honey, scraping up any browned bits. Continue stirring with a whisk and cook for 1 minute. Add the butter to the pan and whisk into the sauce until it is melted.

5. Return the chicken to pan and heat briefly while coating with the sauce.

NUTRITION INFORMATION PER SERVING (1 CHICKEN BREAST)
Calories 215 | Carbohydrate 4g (Sugars 3g) | Total Fat 7g (Sat Fat 2g) | Protein 32g | Fiber 0g | Cholesterol 75mg | Sodium 410mg | Food Exchanges: 4¼ Lean Meat, 1 Fat | Carbohydrate Choices: 0 | Weight Watcher Smart Point Comparison: 4

Chicken Curry in a Hurry

A common ingredient in many Thai or Asian chicken curries is coconut milk. The usual healthier substitute is light coconut milk, but one night when out of coconut milk, in desperation I added a splash of coconut extract to nonfat half-and-half for my chicken curry. Much to my surprise the substitution worked so well that I now use it whenever coconut milk is called for! My family adores this frequently made recipe just as it is, but shrimp or lean strips of beef are also excellent.

MAKES 4 SERVINGS

1 teaspoon canola oil

1 teaspoon minced garlic (2 cloves)

1 teaspoon minced ginger (fresh or jarred), or ½ teaspoon ground

1 medium onion, sliced or chopped

1 medium green bell pepper, chopped into medium cubes

1 pound boneless, skinless chicken breasts, cut into strips

½ cup nonfat half-and-half

¼ teaspoon coconut extract

2 teaspoons cornstarch

1 cup reduced-sodium chicken broth

1 tablespoon curry powder

2 teaspoons brown sugar

Dash of red pepper flakes

½ teaspoon salt

1 tablespoon peanut butter

1. Heat the oil in a large nonstick skillet over medium-high heat. Add the garlic and ginger (if using ground, wait and add it with the broth) and cook for 30 seconds. Add the onion and the bell pepper and cook for 3 to 4 minutes, or until slightly softened. Add the chicken and cook for 3 to 4 minutes, stirring occasionally, until lightly browned.

2. While the chicken is cooking, whisk together the half-and-half, coconut extract, and cornstarch in a small bowl. Set aside.

3. Add the chicken broth, curry powder, brown sugar, red pepper flakes, salt, and peanut butter directly into the skillet with the chicken and stir until combined.

4. Bring to a simmer and pour in the half-and-half mixture. Stir again and let simmer for an additional 1 to 2 minutes, or until the sauce thickens.

Marlene Says: If you like your chicken curry served over rice, be sure to start the rice ahead of time, as this dish cooks quickly. Instant brown rice is another great option. It's fluffy with a lighter taste than traditional brown rice, and cooks in just 10 minutes.

NUTRITION INFORMATION PER SERVING (1 CUP WITHOUT THE RICE)
Calories 200 | Carbohydrate 11g (Sugars 4g) | Total Fat 6g (Sat Fat 1g) | Protein 25g | Fiber 2g | Cholesterol 65mg | Sodium 230mg | Food Exchanges: 4 Lean Meat, 1 Vegetable, ¼ Carbohydrate | Carbohydrate Choices: 1 | Weight Watcher Smart Point Comparison: 3

No Bones Chicken Cacciatore

Chicken Cacciatore has always been one of my favorite dishes, but with a customary cooking time of over an hour it's hard to fit into a busy family schedule. A simple switch to quickly seared boneless chicken breasts rather than whole chicken parts has turned this Italian classic into a fast and easy weeknight staple.

MAKES 4 SERVINGS

4 boneless, skinless chicken breasts (about 1 pound)

2 tablespoons all-purpose flour

½ teaspoon garlic salt

1 tablespoon olive oil

1 small white onion, sliced

1 medium green bell pepper, cut into thin strips

3 garlic cloves, minced

1 (14-ounce) can diced tomatoes in juice

8 large white mushrooms, quartered

¼ cup reduced-sodium chicken broth

½ cup red wine

1 teaspoon dried oregano

1. Wrap the chicken breasts in plastic wrap and place on a cutting board. Gently pound each breast with a mallet to an even thickness (about ½ inch), and coat them with the flour and garlic salt.

2. Heat the olive oil in a large nonstick skillet over medium-high heat. Add the chicken breasts and cook for 3 to 4 minutes on each side, or until browned (chicken will cook through when returned to sauce). Transfer the chicken to a plate and keep warm.

3. Add the onion, bell pepper, and garlic to the skillet and cook for 3 to 4 minutes, or until the vegetables are slightly softened.

4. Add the tomatoes, mushrooms, chicken broth, red wine, and oregano to the pan and cook for 8 to 10 minutes, or until the juices have thickened slightly.

5. Return the chicken to the skillet and spoon the tomato mixture on top of breasts. Cover the skillet and simmer on low for an additional 5 minutes, or until the chicken is cooked through.

NUTRITION INFORMATION PER SERVING (1 CHICKEN BREAST)
Calories 220 | Carbohydrate 10g (Sugars 5g) | Total Fat 5g (Sat Fat 1g) | Protein 29g | Fiber 2g | Cholesterol 65mg | Sodium 510mg | Food Exchanges: 4 Lean Meat, 1½ Vegetable, ½ Fat | Carbohydrate Choices: ½ | Weight Watcher Smart Point Comparison: 3

20-Minute Perfect Poached Chicken

Twenty minutes to perfection! *After trying various methods of poaching, I can say that this is the easiest—and the best—way to poach chicken breasts. Poaching methods that keep the chicken simmering cannot match the moist tender breast meat that this recipe produces. Your yield will be about three cups cooked chopped breast meat that may be used in my Chicken Caesar Salad (page 195), Creamy Chicken Enchiladas (page 313), or any recipe that calls for cooked chicken.*

MAKES 4 SERVINGS

4 boneless, skinless chicken breasts (about 1 pound)

1. Place the chicken in a single layer in a large sauté pan and cover with water. Place over medium-high heat and bring to a boil.

2. Cover the pan, turn off the heat, and allow the chicken to sit for 20 minutes (keep lid closed). Remove the cover and transfer the chicken to a plate. Serve shredded or chopped as desired.

Or try this: Substitute chicken broth for water and add herbs for flavor to serve this as a light, flavorful dinner.

NUTRITION INFORMATION PER SERVING (¾ CUP CHOPPED)
Calories 130 | Carbohydrate 0g (Sugars 0g) | Total Fat 1.5g (Sat Fat 1g) | Protein 28 | Fiber 0g | Cholesterol 95mg | Sodium 160mg | Food Exchanges: 4 Lean Meat | Carbohydrate Choices: 0 | Weight Watcher Smart Point Comparison: 1

Jammin' Chicken

Reduced-sugar jam adds a sweetness to this dish that makes it a kid favorite. I prefer it when made with apricot jam, but my boys prefer orange marmalade. From fridge to table in 30 minutes or less, this recipe is also a fantastic choice when you are in a hurry or "jammin" to get dinner on the table.

MAKES 4 SERVINGS

4 boneless, skinless chicken breasts (about 1¼ pounds)

1 tablespoon vegetable oil, divided

¼ cup finely chopped white onion

½ cup reduced-sodium chicken broth

6 tablespoons reduced-sugar or sugar-free jam (apricot, orange marmalade, or raspberry)

1 tablespoon natural rice wine vinegar

1½ teaspoons reduced-sodium soy sauce

1. Wrap the chicken breasts in plastic wrap and place on a cutting board. Gently pound each breast with a mallet to an even thickness (about ½ inch thick).

2. Heat 2 teaspoons of the oil in a large nonstick skillet over medium-high heat. Add the chicken and cook for 4 to 5 minutes on each side until well browned and cooked through. Transfer the chicken to a plate and cover.

3. Add the remaining teaspoon of the oil to the pan, add the onion and cook for 2 to 3 minutes, or until softened. Pour in the broth, jam, vinegar, and soy sauce and whisk until smooth. Cook for 1 minute, or until slightly thickened.

4. Return the chicken to pan and heat briefly while coating with the sauce.

NUTRITION INFORMATION PER SERVING (1 CHICKEN BREAST) ·····························
Calories 210 | Carbohydrate 9g (Sugars 1g) | Total Fat 6g (Sat Fat .5g) | Protein 32g | Fiber 0g | Cholesterol 65mg | Sodium 200mg | Food Exchanges: 4½ Lean Meat, ½ Carbohydrate | Carbohydrate Choices: ½ | Weight Watcher Smart Point Comparison: 4

Honey Mustard–Glazed Chicken

Moist chicken thighs make for an economical and speedy weeknight supper when paired with a large salad and some whole-grain crusty bread. This honey mustard sauce is also delicious poured over chicken breasts, fish, or pork chops.

MAKES 4 SERVINGS

¼ cup low-sugar apricot preserves

1 tablespoon honey

1 tablespoon vegetable oil

2 tablespoons prepared mustard

8 skinless chicken thighs (about 2½ pounds)

1. Preheat the broiler.

2. In a small bowl, mix together the apricot preserves, honey, oil, and mustard.

3. Place the chicken thighs on a baking sheet coated with cooking spray. Broil for 20 minutes, turning halfway through cooking.

4. Remove the chicken from the broiler and cover with the honey mustard sauce. Place the chicken back under the broiler and cook for 2 to 3 more minutes, or until the honey mustard sauce is hot and has "glazed" the chicken.

Marlene Says: Yes, dark meat can be a healthful part of your diet. Chicken thighs are a better source of iron and zinc than chicken breast, and with the skin removed, contain less fat than most cuts of beef, pork, or lamb.

NUTRITION INFORMATION PER SERVING (2 THIGHS)
Calories 225 | Carbohydrate 9g (Sugars 8g) | Total Fat 9g (Sat Fat 2.5g) | Protein 27g | Fiber 0g | Cholesterol 110mg | Sodium 165mg | Food Exchanges: 4 Lean Meat, ½ Carbohydrate | Carbohydrate Choices: ½ | Weight Watcher Smart Point Comparison: 6

Quicker-Than-Take-Out Orange Chicken

Forget the modesty, I am just going to say that this recipe is one of my proudest makeovers. My son Stephen loves the Orange Chicken from Panda Express®, but watching him eat the heavily battered fried pieces of chicken in sugary sauce sent me on a mission to make it healthy. I started with a recipe that called for a cup of brown sugar and two to four cups of oil, and I triumphantly ended up with an incredible orange-flavored chicken knock-off that uses only two tablespoons each of brown sugar and oil.

MAKES 4 SERVINGS

SAUCE

½ cup water

⅓ cup light orange juice

½ cup granulated no-calorie sweetener*

2 tablespoons brown sugar

3 tablespoons rice vinegar

2 tablespoons reduced-sodium soy sauce

3 tablespoons lemon juice

¼ teaspoon ground ginger

⅛ teaspoon red pepper flakes

2 tablespoons cornstarch

CHICKEN

1¼ pounds boneless, skinless chicken breast, chopped

1 large egg, beaten

¼ cup all-purpose flour

2 tablespoons canola oil

1 small red pepper, chopped

1 small onion, chopped

1. To make the sauce, in a medium saucepan, whisk together the first nine ingredients (water through pepper flakes). Place over medium-high heat and bring to a low simmer.

2. In a small bowl, mix together 2 tablespoons of water and the cornstarch to create a slurry and whisk into the sauce. Bring the sauce to a low boil and cook for 1 minute, or until the sauce thickens and clears. Reduce the heat to low and allow to simmer.

3. Roll the chicken pieces in the egg and toss with flour to coat.

4. Heat 1 tablespoon of the oil in a large nonstick skillet over medium-high heat. Add half of the chicken and cook 4 to 5 minutes, or until well browned on all sides and chicken is cooked through. Transfer the chicken to a bowl and cover. Heat the remaining oil and cook the remaining chicken pieces. Add the chicken to the bowl and set aside.

5. Add the red pepper and onion to pan and cook for 4 to 5 minutes, or until slightly softened. Add the chicken to the pan and then the orange sauce. Stir to coat and serve.

* See page 382 for sweetener options

NUTRITION INFORMATION PER SERVING (1 CUP)
Calories 290 | Carbohydrate 18g (Sugars 8g) | Total Fat 9g (Sat Fat 1g) | Protein 32g | Fiber 0g | Cholesterol 100mg | Sodium 360mg | Food Exchanges: 4 Lean Meat, 1 Starch, ½ Carbohydrate | Carbohydrate Choices: 1 ½ | Weight Watcher Smart Point Comparison: 7

Orange Chicken Vegetable Stir-Fry

The addition of more fresh crisp vegetables is an even healthier way to enjoy the great taste of orange chicken. Here I have added a combination of a few colorful stir-fry favorites, but a prepackaged stir-fry mix would easily do.

MAKES 6 SERVINGS

2 tablespoons canola oil, divided

1 pound boneless, skinless, chicken breast cut into ¾-inch pieces

1 large carrot, sliced

1 small onion, cut into ¾-inch squares

2 large red bell peppers, cut into ¾-inch squares

2 cups broccoli florets

1 recipe orange chicken sauce (see previous page)

1. Heat 1 tablespoon of the oil in wok over medium-high heat.

2. Add the chicken and cook for 4 to 5 minutes, or until well browned on all sides and the chicken is barely cooked through. Transfer the chicken to a bowl and cover.

3. Add the remaining tablespoon of oil to the wok. Add the carrots and stir-fry for 3 minutes. Add the onion and peppers and stir-fry for 3 to 4 more minutes. Add the broccoli and cook for 1 minute.

4. Add the orange sauce and chicken to the wok, cover, and cook for 2 to 3 more minutes, or until the broccoli is crisp tender and chicken is thoroughly cooked.

NUTRITION INFORMATION PER SERVING (1½ CUPS)··
Calories 230 | Carbohydrate 16g (Sugars 6g) | Total Fat 6g (Sat Fat 1g) | Protein 28g | Fiber 1g | Cholesterol 100mg | Sodium 260mg | Food Exchanges: 2½ Lean Meat, 1 Vegetable, ½ Carbohydrate | Carbohydrate Choices: 1 | Weight Watcher Smart Point Comparison: 6

Classic Chicken Piccata

This Chicken Piccata recipe shows how a few simple pantry staples can be combined quickly and easily into a delightful dish. Pounding a chicken breast until it is quite thin (scaloppini) is the trick for creating fork-tender meat that cooks in minutes. A pan sauce of lemon juice, white wine, and a touch of butter provides a delicious splash of flavor. Adding the briny capers is traditional, but I have left them optional.

MAKES 4 SERVINGS

4 boneless, skinless chicken breasts (about 1¼ pounds)

¼ cup all-purpose flour

1 tablespoon olive oil

¼ cup white wine

¼ cup lemon juice (1 large lemon)

½ cup reduced-sodium chicken broth

1½ tablespoons capers (optional)

1 tablespoon butter or margarine

¼ teaspoon fresh chopped Italian parsley

1. Wrap the chicken breasts in plastic wrap and place on a cutting board. Gently pound each breast with a mallet to ⅛- to ¼-inch thickness. Dredge the chicken with the flour.

2. Heat the oil in a large nonstick skillet over medium-high heat. Add the chicken and cook for 2 to 3 minutes on each side, until well browned and barely cooked through. Transfer the chicken to a plate and cover.

3. Pour the white wine, lemon juice, and chicken broth into the skillet, whisking the browned bits from the bottom of the pan. Add the capers, if using. Whisk the sauce until slightly thickened.

4. Add the chicken back to the pan and cook for an additional 2 to 3 minutes, or until cooked through. Remove the chicken and place on plates or a serving dish.

5. Swirl the butter into the remaining sauce. Pour the sauce over the chicken and top with the parsley.

Perfect Pairing: Roasted Asparagus with Parmesan (page 257) is a terrific accompaniment for this dish.

NUTRITION INFORMATION PER SERVING (1 CHICKEN BREAST)
Calories 250 | Carbohydrate 8g (Sugars 1g) | Total Fat 9g (Sat Fat 2g) | Protein 32g | Fiber <1g | Cholesterol 75mg | Sodium 270mg | Food Exchanges: 4½ Lean Meat, ½ Starch | Carbohydrate Choices: ½ | Weight Watcher Smart Point Comparison: 5

Slow-Cooker Root Beer Barbequed Chicken

If you love the great taste of sweet, tangy barbeque sauce slathered on chicken (or anything else) you'll love this amazing recipe, which offers all of the traditional barbeque flavor with 75 percent less sugar and a fraction of the sodium of commercially prepared brands that can easily derail an otherwise healthy meal.

MAKES 6 SERVINGS

SAUCE

1 cup sugar-free root beer*

1 cup reduced-sugar ketchup

2 tablespoons apple cider vinegar

2 tablespoons molasses

2 tablespoons Worcestershire sauce

1½ teaspoons liquid smoke

½ teaspoon onion powder

½ teaspoon garlic powder

⅛ teaspoon paprika

2½ to 3 pounds skinless chicken breasts and thighs

* Sweetened with sucralose

1. To make the sauce, whisk together all the sauce ingredients (through the paprika) in a medium saucepan. Bring to a simmer and cook for 10 minutes.

2. Place the chicken in a slow cooker and pour ¾ cup of the barbecue sauce on top. Cover and cook for 3 to 4 hours on high, or 7 to 8 hours on low. Heat the remaining barbeque sauce for 10 to 15 more minutes, or until thick enough to coat the back of a spoon. Serve with cooked chicken.

Or try this: For *Oven Root Beer Barbecued Chicken*, brown the chicken pieces in a large skillet coated with cooking spray over medium-high heat. Transfer the chicken to a baking dish and coat with ¾ cup of the barbeque sauce. Bake for 45 to 55 minutes at 350°F, or until the chicken is completely cooked through. While the chicken is cooking, simmer the remaining sauce for 10 to 15 minutes, or until thick enough to coat the back of a spoon. Baste chicken with sauce before serving.

Marlene Says: Most barbecue sauces average 12 to 16 grams of carbohydrate (with 9 to 12 of them coming from sugar) per typical 2-tablespoon serving. To reduce the amount of sugar, make your own, or look for a reduced-sugar brand like KC Masterpiece Classic Blend.

NUTRITION INFORMATION PER SERVING (⅙ RECIPE)
Calories 210 | Carbohydrate 6g (Sugars 3g) | Total Fat 7g (Sat Fat 2g) | Protein 29g | Fiber 1g | Cholesterol 90mg | Sodium 420mg | Food Exchanges: 4 Lean Meat | Carbohydrate Choices: ½ | Weight Watcher Smart Point Comparison: 5

Marlene's Favorite Go-To Italian Chicken

This is one of my favorite go-to recipes. With just chicken breasts and a few seasonings on hand, I have an entrée that my family loves, served in minutes. As in my Classic Chicken Piccata recipe, pounding the breasts thin is the key to quick fork-tender meat. This is a great recipe for indoor or outdoor grilling, but you can also prepare this chicken dish in your favorite sauté pan.

MAKES 2 SERVINGS

2 boneless, skinless chicken breasts (about ⅔ pound)

¾ teaspoon garlic salt

½ teaspoon dried oregano

¼ teaspoon dried basil

1. Wrap the chicken breasts in plastic wrap and place on a cutting board. Gently pound each breast until thin with a mallet (about ¼ inch thick).

2. In a small bowl, combine the salt, oregano, and basil. Sprinkle the seasoning over the chicken breasts, coating both sides.

3. Grill over high heat for 2 to 3 minutes on each side, or until well browned and cooked through. Alternately, coat a non-stick grill or sauté pan with cooking spray and heat over medium-high heat. Add the chicken to the hot pan and cook for 2 to 3 minutes, or until well browned and cooked through.

Or try this: For *In-a-Flash Southwestern Chicken,* mix together ¾ teaspoon of each granulated sugar and chili powder, ½ teaspoon cumin, and ¼ teaspoon of each salt and paprika. Sprinkle on the chicken breasts and cook as directed.

NUTRITION INFORMATION PER SERVING (1 CHICKEN BREAST) ·
Calories 150 | Carbohydrate 1g (Sugars 0g) | Total Fat 1.5g (Sat Fat 0g) | Protein 30g | Fiber 0g | Cholesterol 65mg | Sodium 360mg | Food Exchanges: 4 Lean Meat | Carbohydrate Choices: 0 | Weight Watcher Smart Point Comparison: 2

Greens and Beans Balsamic Chicken

This dish, fashioned after one from a popular Italian restaurant, uses a combination of lightly wilted spinach and garbanzo beans bathed in sweet balsamic vinegar and topped with chicken to make a fantastic meal. As you read the ingredients note that several of them are used twice, first for the chicken and then again for the bed of spinach and garbanzo beans.

MAKES 4 SERVINGS

4 boneless, skinless chicken breasts (about 1 pound)

½ teaspoon minced fresh rosemary

Salt and pepper to taste

1 tablespoon plus 2 teaspoons olive oil

3 garlic cloves, minced and divided

½ cup plus 1 tablespoon reduced-sodium chicken broth

¼ cup plus 1 tablespoon balsamic vinegar

1 (15-ounce) can garbanzo beans, drained and rinsed

1 tablespoon lemon juice

½ tablespoon lemon zest (half a lemon)

8 to 10 cups fresh spinach leaves (1 large bag)

¼ cup freshly grated Parmesan cheese

1. Wrap the chicken breasts in plastic wrap and place on a cutting board. Gently pound the chicken breasts to an even ¼-inch thickness. Combine the rosemary, salt, and pepper and sprinkle over the chicken.

2. Heat 2 teaspoons of the olive oil in a large nonstick skillet over medium-high heat. Add ⅓ of the minced garlic and cook for 30 seconds. Add the chicken breasts and cook for 4 to 5 minutes on each side, or until golden brown.

3. Turn off the heat and immediately add 1 tablespoon of chicken broth and 1 tablespoon of the balsamic vinegar to the skillet. Turn the chicken in the vinegar mix to coat. Transfer the chicken to a plate, and drizzle with any remaining pan juices. Cover and set aside.

4. Add 1 tablespoon olive oil to the pan and turn the heat to medium. Sauté the remaining garlic for 30 seconds. Add the ½ cup chicken broth, balsamic vinegar, garbanzo beans, lemon juice, and lemon zest to the pan. Cook for 3 to 4 minutes, or until the liquid mixture is reduced by half. Season with salt and pepper.

5. Add the spinach to the pan in large handfuls, quickly rolling it in the sauce using tongs until it wilts just slightly. Transfer the spinach and the beans mixture to a serving platter and top with the chicken. Sprinkle with Parmesan and serve.

NUTRITION INFORMATION PER SERVING (¼ RECIPE)
Calories 320 | Carbohydrate 25g (Sugars 4g) | Total Fat 9g (Sat Fat 1.5g) | Protein 34g | Fiber 7g | Cholesterol 65mg | Sodium 200mg | Food Exchanges: 4½ Lean Meat, 1 Starch, 1 Vegetable, 1 Fat | Carbohydrate Choices: 1½ | Weight Watcher Smart Point Comparison: 8

Martha's Sunday Best Artichoke Heart Chicken

The "Martha" who inspired this recipe is my mother, and one of her special traditions is the ritual of Sunday dinner. In our house it always includes extra people, extra wine, and extraordinary food. This dish is an updated version of a longtime family favorite. It's easy but looks and tastes special enough for company. Noodles and a big green salad are good accompaniments.

MAKES 6 SERVINGS

2 tablespoons margarine or butter

2 tablespoons all-purpose flour

½ teaspoon salt

⅛ teaspoon white pepper

3 tablespoons brandy

2 teaspoons lemon juice

1½ cups reduced-sodium chicken broth

1 cup light sour cream

1 tablespoon olive oil

3 large bone-in chicken breasts, skinned and cut in half (about 2½ pounds)

2 (8-ounce) packages frozen artichoke hearts, thawed

1. Preheat the oven to 350°F.

2. In a small saucepan over medium heat, melt the butter. Stir the flour, salt, and pepper into the butter and cook for 1 minute. Whisk in the brandy, lemon juice, and broth. Continue whisking and cook for 3 to 4 minutes, or until sauce thickens slightly. Remove from the heat, add the sour cream, and whisk until smooth. Set aside.

3. Heat the olive oil in a large nonstick skillet over medium-high heat. Add the chicken and cook for 2 to 3 minutes on each side until well browned. Transfer the chicken to a 13 x 9-inch baking dish.

4. Pour the brandy sauce over the chicken, cover with foil, and bake for 45 minutes.

5. Remove the chicken from the oven and add the artichoke hearts by pressing them into the sauce. Bake for an additional 15 minutes, or until the artichokes are hot.

6. Transfer the chicken to a large platter and smother with the artichoke hearts and sauce.

NUTRITION INFORMATION PER SERVING (1 CHICKEN BREAST HALF)
Calories 300 | Carbohydrate 11g (Sugars 3g) | Total Fat 11g (Sat Fat 5g) | Protein 33g | Fiber 4g | Cholesterol 100mg | Sodium 450mg | Food Exchanges: 4 Lean Meat, 1 Vegetable, 1 Fat | Carbohydrate Choices: ½ | Weight Watcher Smart Point Comparison: 7

Creamy Chicken Enchiladas

This is an updated version of another simple but crowd-pleasing recipe I grew up with. If you think you might be tempted to make these enchiladas with full-fat ingredients and regular tortillas, first check out the Dare to Compare section, which will prove to you the great difference using a few healthier ingredients can make. My Shredded Spinach, Lettuce, and Fresh Orange Salad (page 178) is the perfect accompaniment for this dish.

MAKES 8 SERVINGS

1 (10-ounce) can reduced-fat, reduced-sodium cream of chicken soup

1 cup light sour cream

1 (4-ounce) can diced green chilies

8 (8-inch) reduced-carbohydrate, high-fiber tortillas

2 cups chopped or shredded cooked chicken

½ cup plus 2 tablespoons shredded reduced-fat cheddar cheese (or Mexican Blend)

2 tablespoons low-fat milk

½ cup diced green onions

1. Preheat the oven to 350°F. Spray a 13 x 9-inch baking pan with cooking spray.

2. In a medium bowl, mix together the soup, sour cream, and green chilies.

3. Warm the tortillas by wrapping them in a towel and placing them in the microwave at 50 percent power for 2 minutes.

4. Place 1 tortilla on a flat surface (keeping others covered), and spread 2 tablespoons of the soup mixture down the center of the tortilla. Spread ¼ cup of the chicken over the soup mixture and sprinkle with 1 tablespoon of the cheese. Roll the tortilla around the filling (enchilada style) and place into the baking pan, seam side down. Repeat with the rest of the tortillas.

5. Add the milk to the remaining soup mixture and spread over the enchiladas. Sprinkle the remaining 2 tablespoons of the cheese and the green onions over the top. Cover and bake for 30 minutes.

DARE to COMPARE
These better-for-you creamy chicken enchiladas have ⅓ less calories, carbohydrates, and sodium, ½ of the fat, and only ⅓ of the saturated fat of the original recipe. They have also had an increase in fiber from 2 to 12 grams per serving!

NUTRITION INFORMATION PER SERVING (1 ENCHILADA)
Calories 250 | Carbohydrate 24g (Sugars 3g) | Total Fat 9g (Sat Fat 4g) | Protein 21g | Fiber 12g | Cholesterol 45mg | Sodium 590mg | Food Exchanges: 2 Lean Meat, 1 Medium-Fat Meat, 1 Carbohydrate, 1 Fat Carbohydrate Choices: 1 | Weight Watcher Smart Point Comparison: 6

Home-Style Turkey Potpie

Nothing is as comforting as a creamy potpie. Unfortunately, in most recipes for potpie, that comfort comes from a rich gravy and an even heavier fat-laden crust. I was so stunned when I analyzed a potpie recipe featured on the Food Network (with over 100 grams each of fat and carbohydrates per serving) that I came up with my own! This family-pleasing version has all the traditional comfort intact, including a rich-tasting, creamy filling and tender pastry crust. I have chosen to make a large family-style potpie with turkey, but you can substitute chicken or create four individual pies if you wish.

MAKES 4 SERVINGS

CRUST

1 cup plus 1 tablespoon all-purpose flour

¾ teaspoon baking powder

¼ teaspoon baking soda

⅛ teaspoon salt

¼ cup low-fat milk

2 tablespoons margarine or butter, melted

FILLING

2 teaspoons olive oil

½ teaspoon minced garlic

3 large carrots, diced (about 1 cup)

3 celery ribs, diced (about 1 cup)

½ cup chopped onion

½ teaspoon dried thyme

1 (15-ounce) can reduced-sodium chicken broth

⅓ cup nonfat half-and-half or

1. Preheat the oven to 400°F.

2. To prepare the crust, combine 1 cup of the flour, baking powder, baking soda, and salt in a medium bowl. Add the milk and butter and mix with a spoon just until dough comes to together. Gently knead 3 to 4 times until it is soft and uniform. Dust the top and bottom with 1 tablespoon of the flour and roll or pat the dough to cover a 2-quart round casserole dish.

3. To make the filling, heat the oil in a large saucepan over medium-high heat. Add the garlic, carrots, celery, and onions, and cook for 5 to 6 minutes, or until slightly tender. Crush the thyme with your fingers and stir into the sauce. Pour the chicken broth into the pan and bring to a simmer.

4. In a small bowl, whisk together the evaporated milk and cornstarch until smooth. Add to the broth mixture to thicken. Add the peas and green beans to the pot, stir, and cook for 3 to 4 minutes. Stir in the turkey and remove from heat. Season with salt and pepper.

5. Pour the mixture into the casserole dish. Cover with the crust and crimp the edges. Brush the top with the beaten egg white.

low-fat evaporated milk

3 tablespoons cornstarch

½ cup frozen peas

1 cup frozen green beans

2 cups cooked turkey breast, cubed

Salt and pepper to taste

1 large egg white, beaten

1 large egg white, beaten with 2 teaspoons water

6. Bake for 20 to 25 minutes, or until crust is golden brown. Allow to set for 10 minutes before serving.

DARE to COMPARE··
When shopping the freezer case, beware: A single 10-ounce Marie Callendar®'s potpie has 670 calories. It also has 41 grams of fat (14 of them saturated), 55 grams of carbohydrate, and 1,000 mg of sodium. It does have less of something: it contains about one-half the protein.

NUTRITION INFORMATION PER SERVING (¼ PIE) ·····················
Calories 370 | Carbohydrate 40g (Sugars 7g) | Total Fat 10g (Sat Fat 4g) | Protein 32g | Fiber 4g | Cholesterol 45mg | Sodium 510mg | Food Exchanges: 4 Lean Meat, 2 Starch, 1 Vegetable, 1 Fat | Carbohydrate Choices: 2½ | Weight Watcher Smart Point Comparison: 8

One-Pot Turkey Sausage Dinner

This one-pot wonder puts a hearty, delicious, home-cooked meal on the table in under thirty minutes. Leftovers, if you have any, are fantastic the next day when the flavors have had more time to mingle.

MAKES 4 SERVINGS

1 small onion, thickly sliced

1 cooked turkey kielbasa sausage link (1 pound package), sliced into 1-inch slices*

5 medium red potatoes (¾ pound), sliced thick

1 tablespoon brown mustard

1 cup light apple juice (or ½ cup apple juice with ½ cup water)

1 teaspoon caraway seeds

6 cups shredded cabbage

* For low-sodium diets, kielbasa may be reduced to 8 ounces.

1. Spray a large pot with nonstick cooking spray and place over medium heat. Add the onion and sauté for 2 minutes. Add the kielbasa and cook for 2 more minutes, or until kielbasa and onions are browned. Add the potatoes to the pot.

2. In a small bowl, whisk together the mustard and apple juice. Pour over the sausage mixture. Sprinkle with the caraway seeds and stir.

3. Pile the cabbage on top of the sausage, cover, and cook for 20 minutes, or until the cabbage is tender.

Marlene Says: Making the simple switch from regular kielbasa (made with pork and beef) to turkey kielbasa reduced the fat in this recipe by 24 grams and the saturated fat by 12 grams. It also eliminates 200 calories!

NUTRITION INFORMATION PER SERVING (¼ RECIPE) ·······················
Calories 265 | Carbohydrate 23g (Sugars 8g) | Total Fat 10g (Sat Fat 3g) | Protein 20g | Fiber 2g | Cholesterol 75mg | Sodium 1060mg | Food Exchanges: 4 Lean Meat, 1 Starch, 1 Vegetable | Carbohydrate Choices: 1½ | Weight Watcher Smart Point Comparison: 6

Salsa Meatloaf

I'm skeptical when healthy recipes veer too far from the tried-and-true versions of the classic recipes we all know and love. Despite my doubts, I was intrigued when I came across a meatloaf recipe that replaced the customary breadcrumbs with a crushed high-fiber cereal. I am delighted to tell you that the cereal does a great job of binding this zesty meatloaf as well as adding a nice complementary flavor of its own. The extra bonus is that this delicious south-of-the-border creation boasts a sneaky five grams of fiber into every bite.

MAKES 6 SERVINGS

1¼ pounds lean ground turkey

1 large egg

1 large egg white

1 cup finely crushed Fiber One cereal or ½ cup breadcrumbs

¾ cup salsa

¼ cup reduced-fat Mexican blend cheese

¾ teaspoon chili powder

½ teaspoon cumin

½ teaspoon garlic powder

1. Preheat the oven to 350°F.

2. In a large bowl, combine the turkey, egg, egg white, cereal, salsa, cheese, chili powder, cumin, and garlic powder and mix with your hands until just combined. Be careful not to overwork. Place into a 9-inch loaf pan and pat down to smooth the top.

3. Bake for 55 to 60 minutes, or until the center of the meat registers 165°F on a meat thermometer.

4. Drain the juices from the pan and allow to rest for 10 minutes before serving.

NUTRITION INFORMATION PER SERVING (1 SLICE) ····················
Calories 200 | Carbohydrate 10g (Sugars 0g) | Total Fat 9g (Sat Fat 3g) | Protein 24g | Fiber 5g | Cholesterol 105mg | Sodium 240mg | Food Exchanges: 4 Lean Meat, ½ Starch, ½ Fat | Carbohydrate Choices: ½ | Weight Watcher Smart Point Comparison: 5

Turkey Scaloppini and Creamy Mushroom Sauce

This semi-homemade recipe takes advantage of reduced-fat soup to produce a winning meal with minimal effort. Turkey cutlets make a nice change, but of course skinless, boneless chicken breasts would make a great alternative. I have also seen similar recipes made with canned mushrooms but find that using fresh ones makes a big difference in giving this dish its homemade quality.

MAKES 4 SERVINGS

1¼ pounds boneless turkey breast cutlets

1 tablespoon olive oil

1 teaspoon plus ½ teaspoon crushed dried thyme

1 garlic clove, minced

1 (8-ounce) package sliced mushrooms

¼ cup sherry

⅓ cup water

1 (15-ounce) can reduced-fat, reduced-sodium cream of mushroom soup

½ teaspoon Worcestershire sauce

1. Wrap the turkey breasts in plastic wrap and place on a cutting board. With a mallet gently pound each cutlet until thin (about ⅛-inch thick).

2. In a large skillet, heat the oil over medium-high heat. Sprinkle 1 teaspoon of the thyme over the turkey and place in the skillet. Cook for 3 to 4 minutes on each side, until browned and barely cooked through. Transfer the turkey to a plate and cover.

3. Add the garlic and mushrooms to the skillet and sauté for 1 minute. Add the sherry, water, soup, Worcestershire sauce, and remaining ½ teaspoon of the thyme to the skillet. Whisk together and simmer on low for 5 minutes, or until slightly thickened.

4. Return the turkey to the pan and coat with the sauce. Simmer the turkey in the sauce for 5 more minutes before serving.

NUTRITION INFORMATION PER SERVING (1 CUTLET) ···
Calories 220 | Carbohydrate 9g (Sugars 3g) | Total Fat 4g (Sat Fat 1g) | Protein 33g | Fiber 1g | Cholesterol 85mg | Sodium 410mg | Food Exchanges: 4½ Lean Meat, ½ Carbohydrate | Carbohydrate Choices: ½ | Weight Watcher Smart Point Comparison: 4

Teriyaki Turkey Cutlets

The combination of sweet and salty comes together beautifully in this delicious homemade teriyaki marinade that also doubles as a sauce. Turkey cutlets make for a nice change of pace, but skinless chicken breasts or fresh fish can easily be substituted.

MAKES 4 SERVINGS

¼ cup reduced-sodium soy sauce

2 tablespoons dry sherry

1 tablespoon natural rice wine vinegar

1½ tablespoons brown sugar

1 teaspoon sesame oil

½ teaspoon grated ginger

¼ teaspoon minced garlic

1½ pound turkey breast cutlets

1. In a medium bowl, whisk together the soy sauce, sherry, vinegar, brown sugar, oil, ginger, and garlic.

2. Place the turkey in a shallow baking dish, and pour the marinade on top. Marinate the turkey breasts in the teriyaki sauce for at least 15 minutes (and up to 2 hours).

3. Spray a large skillet with nonstick cooking spray and place over medium-high heat. Remove the turkey from the dish, reserving the marinade, and add the turkey to the skillet. Cook the turkey cutlets for 5 minutes on each side, or until well browned.

4. While the cutlets cook, add the reserved marinade to a small saucepan, and place over medium-high heat. Bring the sauce to a low boil, and simmer for 3 minutes.

5. Drizzle the sauce over the turkey and turn to coat.

NUTRITION INFORMATION PER SERVING (1 CUTLET)
Calories 170 | Carbohydrate 5g (Sugars 2g) | Total Fat 2g (Sat Fat 0g) | Protein 32g | Fiber 0g | Cholesterol 70mg | Sodium 730mg | Food Exchanges: 4 Lean Meat | Carbohydrate Choices: 0 | Weight Watcher Smart Point Comparison: 3

Lean Beef and Pork

ALL-AMERICAN MEATLOAF MINIS

EVERYDAY ITALIAN MEATBALLS

TEX MEX CHILI BAKE

SKILLET BEEF STROGANOFF

SZECHWAN BEEF AND BROCCOLI STIR-FRY

CHILI'S®-STYLE GRILLED BEEF FAJITAS

NOT EVERYDAY BEEF TENDERLOIN WITH GORGONZOLA SAUCE

SMOTHERED STEAK BURGERS WITH MUSHROOM GRAVY

20-MINUTE PORK MARSALA

PORK CHOP SUEY

PORK SATAY WITH PEANUT SAUCE

SKILLET PORK CHOPS WITH ROSEMARY MUSTARD CREAM SAUCE

SWEET AND TANGY APRICOT PORK CHOPS

PORK TENDERLOIN WITH CRANBERRY PAN SAUCE

While red meat often takes a bad rap (and sometimes deservedly so), I have plenty of great news for you if you are a meat lover. Lean cuts of red meats, like beef and pork, are actually powerhouses when it comes to good nutrition—if you know how to prepare them.

Both beef and pork are important sources of vitamins and minerals such as zinc, phosphorus, iron, and several essential B vitamins, including vitamin B12, a nutrient that cannot be obtained from eating only vegetables. Lean beef and pork dishes can also help you reach and maintain your desired weight because not only does protein have a great satiety value (meaning it's belly filling), studies show that low-fat diets that are higher in protein result in more weight loss with a higher percentage of the weight loss coming from fat, and less from precious muscle.

The key to creating healthy, yet delicious, meat entrées is to start with lean meat—which fortunately today is easier than ever to find as today's cows and pigs are bred to be leaner, and markets carry a broader range of cuts. These leaner cuts of beef and pork have helped me craft flavorful meat entrées that are sure to satisfy. I have been sure to include plenty of recipes for everyday meals, but you'll also find dishes perfect for the fanciest of occasions. Beginning with the most popular "cut" of beef, lean ground, you'll find easy-to-make marvelous mini-meatloaves and wonderful Everyday Italian Meatballs. Lean sirloin steak is perfect for creating a quick Skillet Beef Stroganoff and last but definitely not least beef tenderloin steps up to the plate for the fabulous Not Everyday Beef Tenderloin with Gorgonzola Sauce. Beyond beef, tender pork also gets to shine. Pork tenderloin, the "other white meat," produces an amazing 20-Minute Pork Marsala and company-worthy Pork Tenderloin with Cranberry Pan Sauce, while lean boneless loin chops star in the scrumptious Sweet and Tangy Apricot Pork Chops.

All-American Meatloaf Minis

When it comes to comfort food, meatloaf is one of the great American classics. Unfortunately, when you need to get dinner on the table in a hurry, its usual baking time can easily take it off the menu. All it takes is one simple switch, however, to bring it back; baking the meatloaf in muffin tins turns long-cooking meatloaf into a fast-fix meal with homey appeal. My boys love that they each get their own meatloaf, and I love the fact they are perfectly portioned. A neat trick to prevent messy hands and speed clean-up is to place all of the ingredients in one very large resealable plastic bag, then zip it up and knead it together through the bag. Either scoop out the mixture or snip off one corner of the bag and squeeze the meat into the muffin cups. Top with the glaze as directed.

MAKES 6 SERVINGS

½ pound lean ground beef

½ pound lean ground turkey

⅔ cup rolled quick-cooking oats

½ cup finely chopped onion

1 large egg

2 tablespoons low-fat milk

½ teaspoon garlic powder

¼ teaspoon salt

¼ teaspoon black pepper

3 tablespoons ketchup or reduced-sugar ketchup*

1 teaspoon mustard

1 teaspoon molasses

* Subtract 2 grams of carbohydrate and sugar if reduced sugar ketchup is substituted.

1. Preheat the oven to 425°F. Spray 6 muffin-cups with non-stick cooking spray.

2. In a large bowl, use your hands to knead together the beef, turkey, oats, onion, egg, milk, garlic powder, salt, and pepper until evenly combined. Divide the meatloaf mixture into 6 balls and place in each muffin cup. Press and arrange ball to form to muffin cup but do not pack. Create a smooth rounded top.

3. In a small bowl, whisk together the ketchup, mustard, and molasses to make a glaze. Spoon the glaze on top of each mini meatloaf.

4. Bake uncovered for 20 to 25 minutes, or until well browned and cooked through. Let stand for 5 minutes before serving.

NUTRITION INFORMATION PER SERVING (1 MINI MEATLOAF)
Calories 175 | Carbohydrate 10g (Sugars 2g) | Total Fat 7g (Sat Fat 2.5g) | Protein 17g | Fiber 1g | Cholesterol 90mg | Sodium 250mg | Food Exchanges: 2 Lean Meat, ½ Starch | Carbohydrate Choices: ½ | Weight Watcher Smart Point Comparison: 4

Everyday Italian Meatballs

What makes these tasty meatballs "everyday" is not only how easy they are to make—no chopping is required—but how versatile they are. Whip 'em up and simmer them in marinara sauce to go with spaghetti, plop them into soup, stuff them into a sub sandwich, or serve them as an appetizer during the big game!

MAKES 18 MEATBALLS

½ pound lean ground beef

½ pound lean ground turkey

⅓ cup dry breadcrumbs

¼ cup grated Parmesan cheese

3 tablespoons dried minced onion

1 tablespoon dried parsley

1 large egg

2 tablespoons low-fat milk

1 teaspoon minced jarred garlic

1 teaspoon dried oregano

½ teaspoon salt

¼ teaspoon fresh ground pepper

1. Preheat the oven to 400°F.

2. In a large bowl, with a spoon or with your hands, gently mix together all of the ingredients until combined.

3. With wet hands, form into 1¼-inch balls. Place the meatballs onto an ungreased baking sheet and bake for 12 to 14 minutes, or until tops are browned and the meat is cooked through.

Or try this: Everyone loves meatballs! To create *Party Meatballs*, shape meat mixture into twenty-four 1-inch meatballs. Heat 2 cups jarred marinara and pour into a shallow 2-quart baking dish. Place meatballs on top of sauce and sprinkle with ¼ cup Parmesan cheese. (Approximately 55 calories, 5 grams protein, 5 grams carbohydrate, and 2 grams fat per meatball and sauce.)

NUTRITION INFORMATION PER SERVING (1 MEATBALL)
Calories 55 | Carbohydrate 2g (Sugars 0g) | Total Fat 2.5g (Sat Fat 1g) | Protein 6g | Fiber 0g | Cholesterol 15mg | Sodium 125mg | Food Exchanges: 1 Lean Meat | Carbohydrate Choices: 0 | Weight Watcher Smart Point Comparison: 1

Tex Mex Chili Bake

This easy, Mexican-style dish is a delicious alternative to the usual routine. It combines the great taste of Texas chili with corn tortillas and shredded cheese. It's low in fat but high in flavor and, as an extra bonus, it's an excellent source of fiber.

MAKES 4 SERVINGS

2 teaspoons extra-virgin olive oil

¾ cup chopped onion

1 garlic clove, minced

½ pound lean beef

1½ teaspoons cumin

½ teaspoon chili powder

1 (4-ounce) can diced green chilies

1 (15-ounce) can pinto beans, rinsed and drained

1 (14-ounce) can tomatoes, drained

1 tablespoon tomato paste

3 (8-inch) corn tortillas

⅔ cup reduced-fat shredded Mexican cheese blend

2 tablespoons chopped cilantro (optional for garnish)

1. Preheat the oven to 350°F.

2. Heat the oil in a large skillet over medium-high heat. Add the onion and cook for 3 minutes, or until translucent. Add the garlic, stir, and cook for 30 seconds. Add the beef, cumin, and chili powder and cook for 5 minutes, or until the beef is no longer pink.

3. Stir in the chilies, beans, tomatoes, and tomato paste. Break up the tomatoes, stir, and simmer for 5 minutes.

4. Spray a 9-inch pie plate with cooking spray. Lay 1 tortilla on the bottom of the pie plate. Spoon half of the beef mixture on top. Place the second tortilla on top followed by the rest of the beef mixture. Place the remaining tortilla on top, and sprinkle with the cheese. Sprinkle the cilantro around the edges, if using.

5. Place in the oven and bake for 15 minutes, or until hot and the cheese is melted. Cut into four wedges.

NUTRITION INFORMATION PER SERVING (¼ RECIPE) ·················
Calories 310 | Carbohydrate 38g (Sugars 6g) | Total Fat 6g (Sat Fat 2g) | Protein 26g | Fiber 10g | Cholesterol 25mg | Sodium 330mg | Food Exchanges: 2½ Lean Meat, 2 Starch | Carbohydrate Choices: 2 | Weight Watcher Smart Point Comparison: 7

Skillet Beef Stroganoff

Traditional stroganoff recipes are neither quick nor healthy. I don't know where my mother got her stroganoff recipe, but I do know it took all afternoon to cook and it included an entire quart of sour cream. She was thrilled when I found a way to make this classic favorite healthy and bring it to the table in only thirty minutes. A fast searing of the meat keeps it tender and light sour cream slashes the fat. You can also substitute lean ground beef for the sirloin to make a fast and fit Hamburger Stroganoff. Traditionally served over noodles, a three-quarter cup bed of cooked wide noodles will add 105 calories, 21 grams of carbohydrate, 4 grams of protein, and 1 gram of fiber to each serving.

MAKES 4 SERVINGS

1 pound lean boneless sirloin

2 teaspoons olive or canola oil

1 large onion, thinly sliced

1 teaspoon minced garlic

1 pound sliced mushrooms

½ teaspoon dried thyme

2 tablespoons all-purpose flour

½ cup reduced-sodium beef broth

2 teaspoons Worcestershire sauce

1 cup reduced-fat sour cream

¼ teaspoon salt (optional)

Pepper to taste

3 cups cooked wide noodles (optional)

1. Slice the meat across the grain into very thin slices, ⅛ inch thick (partially freezing the meat makes slicing easier). Heat 1 teaspoon of the oil in a very large nonstick skillet over medium-high heat and add half of the beef. Quickly stir-fry just until browned. Do not overcook. Remove the meat from the skillet, and set aside. Repeat with remaining meat.

2. Add the onion to the hot pan and cook for 3 minutes. Add the garlic and sauté for 30 seconds. Add the mushrooms and crush the thyme in with your fingers. Stir and cook for 3 to 4 more minutes, or until the onion and mushrooms are soft. Sprinkle the flour over the onion mixture, and stir.

3. Add the beef broth and Worcestershire. Stir and cook until the mixture bubbles and thickens. Reduce the heat and add the beef. Stir in the sour cream and salt, if using. Cook briefly until slightly thickened and hot.

DARE *to* COMPARE
Classic beef stroganoff delivers over 600 calories a serving with 40 grams of fat and 20 grams—more than a day's worth, of artery-clogging saturated fat.

NUTRITION INFORMATION PER SERVING (¼ RECIPE)
Calories 325 | Carbohydrate 16 (Sugars 2g) | Total Fat 14g (Sat Fat 7g) | Protein 31g | Fiber 2g | Cholesterol 115mg | Sodium 500mg | Food Exchanges: 4 Lean Meat, 1 Vegetable, ½ Carbohydrate, 2 Fat | Carbohydrate Choices: 1 | Weight Watcher Smart Point Comparison: 7

Szechwan Beef and Broccoli Stir-Fry

Like all Szechwan dishes this comes with a bit of heat. I have kept this recipe on the mild side (by Szechwan standards), but feel free to adjust the peppers to your own taste. A fresh and healthy twist is that the beef here is not fried, but simply marinated and seared ever-so-tender before being tossed with freshly steamed broccoli and flavorful Szechwan sauce. Your waistline will thank you.

MAKES 4 SERVINGS

1 pound lean sirloin or flank steak

1 tablespoon sherry

2 tablespoons reduced-sodium soy sauce, divided

1 teaspoon fresh minced ginger

2 teaspoons cornstarch

2 tablespoons plus ⅓ cup water, divided

1 pound broccoli florets

4 teaspoons canola oil, divided

1 teaspoon minced garlic

¼ reduced-sodium beef broth

2 teaspoons hoisin sauce or sugar

½ teaspoon black pepper

⅛ teaspoon (or more) red pepper flakes

1. Slice the meat across the grain into very thin slices (partially freezing the meat makes slicing easier).

2. Place the meat in a bowl and add the sherry, soy sauce, and ginger. Toss until well coated. Set aside. In another small bowl, whisk the cornstarch with 2 tablespoons water. Set aside.

3. Heat a wok or very large nonstick skillet on high. Add the broccoli and ⅓ cup water, cover and steam for 3 to 4 minutes, or until crisp-tender. Remove from the wok and set aside.

4. Heat 1 teaspoon of the oil in the wok or very large nonstick skillet over medium-high heat. Add the garlic and cook for 1 minute. Add half of the beef. Quickly stir-fry just until no longer pink. Do not overcook. Remove the meat from the skillet, and set aside. Repeat with remaining meat.

5. Add the beef broth, hoisin, black pepper, and desired amount of red pepper, to the empty wok. Add the cornstarch mixture and cook over medium heat until the sauce starts to thicken. Immediately add the meat and broccoli to the wok and toss to coat.

NUTRITION INFORMATION PER SERVING (¼ RECIPE) ···
Calories 255 | Carbohydrate 8g (Sugars 3g) | Total Fat 10g (Sat Fat 2.5g) | Protein 30g | Fiber 3g | Cholesterol 75mg | Sodium 420mg | Food Exchanges: 3½ Lean Meat, 1 Vegetable | Carbohydrate Choices: ½ | Weight Watcher Smart Point Comparison: 6

Chili's®-Style Grilled Beef Fajitas

I love going out for Mexican food and like many of you I figured that fajitas, with it's grilled meat and vegetables, would be one of the healthiest things on the menu. Wrong. A single beef fajita skillet at Chili's® has 790 calories, 49 grams of fat, 20 grams of carbohydrates, and 3,240 milligrams of sodium—without the extras! I say adios.

MAKES 6 SERVINGS

¼ cup lime juice

1 tablespoon plus 2 teaspoons olive oil, divided

3 garlic cloves, minced and divided

2 teaspoons reduced-sodium soy sauce

½ teaspoon liquid smoke

½ teaspoon cumin

½ teaspoon cayenne pepper

¼ teaspoon chili powder

1½ pounds flank steak or skirt steak

1 large onion, sliced

3 medium green or assorted bell peppers, cut into ½-inch slices

2 tablespoons sweet vermouth (optional)

¼ teaspoon salt

¾ cup salsa

Warm tortillas

1. Whisk together the lime juice, 2 tablespoons water, 1 tablespoon of the olive oil, 2 minced garlic cloves, soy sauce, liquid smoke, cumin, cayenne, and chili powder. Place the steak in a large bowl pour the marinade on top, and cover. Place in the refrigerator for at least 30 minutes, or up to overnight.

2. Heat the grill to medium high. Grill the steak for 4 to 5 minutes on each side, or until cooked through (or 150°F with a meat thermometer).

3. While the steak is cooking heat the remaining 2 teaspoons olive oil in a large sauté pan over medium high. Add the remaining garlic and sauté for 1 to 2 minutes, until slightly softened. Add the onion and peppers and continue cooking for 6 to 8 minutes, or until crisp tender.

4. Add 2 tablespoons water, the sweet vermouth, if desired, and salt. Continue cooking until the onions and peppers are soft and slightly carmelized.

5. Tuck meat into tortillas with onions and peppers, and serve with salsa.

NUTRITION INFORMATION PER SERVING (WITHOUT TORTILLAS)
Calories 230 | Carbohydrate 8g (Sugars 4g) | Total Fat 9g (Sat Fat 4.5g) | Protein 26g | Fiber 2g | Cholesterol 75mg | Sodium 380mg | Food Exchanges: 3½ Lean Meat, 1 Vegetable | Carbohydrate Choices: ½ | Weight Watcher Smart Point Comparison: 5

Not Everyday Beef Tenderloin with Gorgonzola Sauce

Beef tenderloin is the most luxurious cut of beef you can buy. So it may be a surprise to hear that tenderloin is also a lean cut of beef, with less fat per ounce than dark meat chicken. Cut from the loin and sold either whole or as filet mignon steaks, tenderloin is pricey and usually savored at special occasions. This recipe is for those occasions; birthdays, holidays, or any special meal for that matter. The creamy gorgonzola sauce is the crowning touch that renders a trip to the local steakhouse, with its high-fat fare and even higher prices, obsolete. Seared, Steamed, and Glazed Green Beans (page 252) and Parmesan Garlic Smashed Potatoes (page 277) are perfect accompaniments.

MAKES 4 SERVINGS

4 (6-ounce) filets mignon (1½ to 2 inches thick)

Salt and pepper to taste

1 tablespoons butter

1 garlic clove, minced

¼ teaspoon finely minced fresh rosemary

1 tablespoons flour

⅓ cup low-fat milk

⅓ cup nonfat half-and-half

2 tablespoons crumbled Gorgonzola cheese

Freshly cracked black pepper (optional) to taste

1. Preheat the broiler or grill to hot.

2. Pat the filets dry and season with the salt and pepper. Grill or broil each side for 6 minutes for medium rare. Add 1 to 2 minutes per side to cook to medium (or 145°F for medium rare and 155°F for medium). Set filets aside to rest for 5 minutes.

3. Melt the butter in a small saucepan over low heat. Add the garlic and rosemary and cook for 1 minute. Sprinkle in the flour and stir to make a paste. Whisk in the milk and half-and-half. Stir and cook for 3 to 4 minutes, or until thick. Add the Gorgonzola and stir until smooth. Season with pepper if desired.

4. To serve, drizzle the steak with 3 tablespoons of sauce.

DARE to COMPARE
An 8-ounce restaurant cut filet-mignon (the smallest steak many restaurants serve), topped with 3-ounces of blue cheese is 75% fat with 800 calories and 33 grams of artery-clogging fat.

NUTRITION INFORMATION PER SERVING (1 FILET)
Calories 340 | Carbohydrate 5g (Sugars 2g) | Total Fat 15g (Sat Fat 7g) | Protein 38g | Fiber 0g | Cholesterol 115mg | Sodium 190mg | Food Exchanges: 5 Lean Meat, 2 Fat | Carbohydrate Choices: 0 | Weight Watcher Smart Point Comparison: 8

Smothered Steak Burgers with Mushroom Gravy

The original Salisbury steak was named after a popular late-nineteenth-century diet doctor who recommended his patients eat plenty of beef. With their rich gravy those steaks would never be recommended by a nutritionist today. Here's a much more modern version made much healthier with lean ground beef and reduced-fat gravy. Only the taste is the same.

MAKES 4 SERVINGS

1 pound lean ground beef

1 large egg

⅛ teaspoon black pepper

¼ cup breadcrumbs

¼ cup minced onion

1 tablespoon Worcestershire sauce

2 garlic cloves, minced, divided

1 (8-ounce) package, or 2 cups, sliced mushrooms

1 cup thinly sliced onion

¾ teaspoon dried thyme

2 tablespoons all-purpose flour

1 tablespoon sherry

1 cup reduced-sodium beef broth

Salt and pepper to taste

1. In a medium bowl, mix together the beef, egg, pepper, breadcrumbs, minced onion, Worcestershire sauce, and 1 garlic clove. Shape into 3½-inch thick patties.

2. Spray a large nonstick skillet with cooking spray and place over medium heat. Add the patties, and cook for 4 minutes on each side, until cooked through. Remove the burgers, cover, and set aside.

3. Increase heat to medium high. Add the mushrooms and sliced onions. Crush the thyme in with your fingers and cook for 3 minutes. Sprinkle with the flour and stir. Add the sherry and broth and cook for 1 minute. Season with salt and pepper, and return the burgers to the skillet. Cook for 2 minutes, until thoroughly heated through.

NUTRITION INFORMATION PER SERVING (¼ RECIPE)
Calories 270 | Carbohydrate 16g (Sugars 1g) | Total Fat10g (Sat Fat 3g) | Protein 28g | Fiber 2g | Cholesterol 120mg | Sodium 250mg | Food Exchanges: 3½ Lean Meat, 1 Vegetable, 1 Fat, ½ Starch | Carbohydrate Choices: 1 | Weight Watcher Smart Point Comparison: 5

20-Minute Pork Marsala

This recipe comes by way of health columnist and cookbook author Jane Brody, once dubbed the "high priestess of health" by Time magazine. Over the years I have made just a couple of minor substitutions in adapting her incredibly simple and delicious Marsala recipe. One way I stay true to the original recipe is by using both red wine and Marsala, but you may choose to use beef broth to make it a bit more universally family friendly. Both the original and my adaptation use lean, far less expensive, and far easier to find pork tenderloin. It works so well my husband thinks it's veal.

MAKES 4 SERVINGS

1 pound pork tenderloin, well trimmed

2 teaspoons olive oil

3 garlic cloves, minced

1 tablespoon tomato paste

1 teaspoons flour

½ cup dry Marsala

½ cup red wine or reduced-sodium beef broth

8 ounces or 2 cups sliced mushrooms

1 teaspoon butter

1 tablespoon chopped fresh parsley

1. Cut the tenderloin into ¾-inch thick slices and pound to a ⅛-inch thickness.

2. Spray a nonstick skillet with cooking spray and place over medium-high heat. Add the cutlets. Brown for about 1 minute on each side, transfer to a plate, and cover to keep warm.

3. Heat the oil in the same skillet over medium heat. Add the garlic and cook for 1 minute. In a small bowl, whisk together the tomato paste, flour, Marsala, and red wine or beef broth, and mushrooms and pour into the pan. Simmer for 3 to 5 minutes, or until the mushrooms are tender. Add butter and stir.

4. Return the cutlets to the pan, turn in the sauce, and heat until warm. Garnish with parsley.

DARE *to* COMPARE
Veal Marsala at Romano's Macaroni Grill® comes served on a bed of capellini pasta and clocks in at 1,090 calories, 47 grams of fat, 2,680 milligrams of sodium, and 119 grams of carbohydrate. A bed of one cup cooked capellini will add approximately 200 calories and 42 grams carbohydrate per portion.

NUTRITION INFORMATION PER SERVING (¼ RECIPE)
Calories 245 | Carbohydrate 9g (Sugars 5g) | Total Fat 6g (Sat Fat 2g) | Protein 26g | Fiber 2g | Cholesterol 70mg | Sodium 95mg | Food Exchanges: 3½ Lean Meat, 1 Vegetable | Carbohydrate Choices: ½ | Weight Watcher Smart Point Comparison: 5

Pork Chop Suey

Make sure you use a good-size wok or a very large skillet for this one! The recipe yields about 12 cups of amazing chop suey that is chock-full of lean pork and crunchy vegetables. A bit of chopping is required but, unlike the traditional recipe, you do not need to cook each vegetable separately. Just add all the veggies in sequence as I have streamlined the cooking process by adjusting for their various cooking times. This super-slim yet filling dish also makes terrific leftovers.

MAKES 6 SERVINGS

½ teaspoon minced garlic

1 tablespoon oyster sauce

¼ teaspoon salt

2 teaspoons cornstarch, divided

1 pound pork tenderloin, cut cross width into ⅛-inch thick strips

2 teaspoons vegetable oil, divided

2 celery ribs, cut diagonally into ¼-inch thick slices

1 medium onion, halved lengthwise and cut into ¼-inch strips

1 green bell pepper, cut into ¼-inch thick strips and halved crosswise

½ pound bok choy, leaves and ribs sliced separately into ¼-inch thick slices

1 tablespoon water

6 ounces snow peas, cut diagonally into ¼-inch thick slices

1. In a small bowl, whisk together the garlic, oyster sauce, salt, and 1 teaspoon of the cornstarch. Add the pork and allow it to marinate for 15 minutes while chopping the vegetables.

2. Heat 1 teaspoon of the oil in a wok or large skillet over medium-high heat. Cook the pork for 2 to 3 minutes or until just no longer pink. Remove from the pan and cover to keep warm.

3. Turn the heat to high and drizzle remaining 1 teaspoon of the oil around the side of the wok. Stir-fry the celery for about 2 minutes, until crisp tender. Add the onion and pepper and stir-fry for 2 more minutes. Add the bok choy ribs and cook for 1 minute; then add the leaves and water and stir-fry 2 more minutes. Lastly, add in the pea pods, mushrooms, sprouts, and water chestnuts and cook for 2 minutes.

4. Add the pork back in with the vegetables. In a small bowl, whisk together the chicken broth, soy sauce, the remaining 1 teaspoon cornstarch, and the ginger. Make a well in the center of the stir-fry, and pour in the broth mixture. Without stirring, bring the sauce to a boil. As soon as it is no longer cloudy stir it into the pork and vegetables. Season with additional salt and pepper to taste.

¼ pound mushrooms, cut into ¼-inch slices

¼ pound mung bean sprouts

1 (6-ounce) can sliced water chestnuts, drained

¼ cup reduced-sodium chicken broth

2 teaspoons reduced-sodium soy sauce

½ teaspoon minced ginger

Salt and pepper to taste

Marlene Says: While Asian restaurants do have some healthful choices, the truth is most of our favorite Americanized Asian dishes are anything but healthy. Loaded with oil, carbs, and sodium, a single dish can easily deliver more fat than a Big Mac, sugar than a quart of Coke, or sodium than a plate of pickles! Check out some of my other better-for-you Asian favorites, including 5-Minute Egg Drop Soup, Stephen's Stir-Fry Rice, Lazy Pork Lo Mein, Sweet and Sour Shrimp Stir-Fry, Quicker-Than-Take-Out Orange Chicken, and Express Beef Lettuce Wraps.

NUTRITION INFORMATION PER SERVING (2 CUPS)
Calories 170 | Carbohydrate 13g (Sugars 5g) | Total Fat 5g (Sat Fat 1.5g) | Protein 19g | Fiber 4g | Cholesterol 50mg | Sodium 310mg | Food Exchanges: 2½ Lean Meat, 2 Vegetables | Carbohydrate Choices: 1 | Weight Watcher Smart Point Comparison: 2

Pork Satay with Peanut Sauce

Commonly found throughout Asia, satay, or sate, is meat, fish, or fowl that is marinated and then threaded on skewers like well-loved kabobs. Pork tenderloin makes terrific satay because while lean, it cooks up tender and juicy. These are served with a peanut sauce, making them a huge hit with kids (and their peanut-loving parents).

MAKES 4 SERVINGS

1½ pounds pork tenderloin, well trimmed and cut into 1 to 1½-inch cubes

1 teaspoon sesame oil

1 garlic clove, crushed

½ teaspoon salt

¼ teaspoon black pepper

1 tablespoon reduced-sodium soy sauce

1 tablespoon seasoned rice vinegar

3 tablespoons very hot water

2 tablespoons peanut butter

1 tablespoon hoisin sauce

¼ teaspoon grated fresh ginger

2 teaspoons brown sugar

Pinch of red pepper flakes (optional)

1. Soak eight wooden skewers in water for at least 30 minutes prior to grilling. Preheat the grill on medium high.

2. In a small bowl, whisk together the sesame oil, garlic, salt, and pepper with one teaspoon water and toss with the pork.

3. Place the skewers on the grill and cook for 5 to 6 minutes, turning once, or until well browned and cooked through.

4. While the pork is grilling, vigorously whisk together the remaining ingredients in a small bowl. Drizzle the satay sticks with peanut sauce and serve.

Fit Tip: With only 3 grams of fat in a cooked 3-ounce portion, pork tenderloin is the leanest cut of pork you can buy. Comparable in fat to that of boneless skinless chicken breast, it truly is the other white meat.

NUTRITION INFORMATION PER SERVING (¼ RECIPE) ·······················
Calories 255 | Carbohydrate 5g (Sugars 3g) | Total Fat 10g (Sat Fat 2.5g) | Protein 32g | Fiber 0g | Cholesterol 75mg | Sodium 550mg | Food Exchanges: 4½ Lean Meat, ½ High-Fat Meat, ½ Carbohydrate | Carbohydrate Choices: ½ | Weight Watcher Smart Point Comparison: 6

Skillet Pork Chops with Rosemary Mustard Cream Sauce

Elegant and oh-so-easy to prepare, these pork chops draped in cream sauce are a delicious indulgence. They are also great for both simple entertaining or adding a touch of class to an everyday dinner. Any leftover rosemary sprigs make a lovely garnish.

MAKES 4 SERVINGS

2 teaspoons canola oil

4 (6-ounce) pork chops

½ teaspoon finely chopped fresh rosemary

¼ cup chopped green onion

½ teaspoon minced garlic

½ cup reduced-sodium chicken broth

2 tablespoons light cream cheese, softened to room temperature

1½ tablespoons Dijon mustard

1. Heat the oil in a large nonstick skillet over high heat. Add the pork chops, brown for one minute and then turn to brown other side. Reduce the heat to medium and sprinkle the chops with the rosemary and green onion. Cover and cook for 4 minutes. Turn the chops over, cover, and cook for 4 minutes more (or until 145°F). Transfer the chops to a plate, brushing onions back into the pan, and cover to keep warm.

2. Add the garlic to the pan. Pour in the broth and use a whisk to scrape browned bits from the bottom of the pan. Add the cream cheese and whisk until sauce is well mixed. Add mustard and whisk until smooth. Pour the sauce over pork chops.

NUTRITION INFORMATION PER SERVING (1 PORK CHOP)
Calories 250 | Carbohydrate 2g (Sugars 1g) | Total Fat 11g (Sat Fat 3g) | Protein 32g | Fiber 0g | Cholesterol 80mg | Sodium 460mg | Food Exchanges: 4 Lean Meat, 1 Fat | Carbohydrate Choices: 0 | Weight Watcher Smart Point Comparison: 5

Sweet and Tangy Apricot Pork Chops

The combination of sweet jam, salty soy sauce, and tangy vinegar is a tasty way to dress up pork or chicken. I prefer the full fruit taste of reduced-sugar jam instead of the sugar-free variety, but both work equally well and both contain less than half the sugar of regular jams and "all-fruit" spreads. Apricot jam is my favorite, but orange marmalade and raspberry are also delicious in this dish.

MAKES 4 SERVINGS

½ cup reduced-sugar apricot jam

1½ teaspoons reduced-sodium soy sauce

1 tablespoon seasoned rice wine vinegar

½ teaspoon ginger

1 tablespoon water

Black pepper to taste

2 teaspoons canola oil

1¼ pounds ½-inch-thick boneless pork loin chops

¼ cup chopped green onion

1. In a small bowl, whisk together the jam, soy sauce, vinegar, ginger, water, and pepper.

2. Heat the oil in a large sauté pan over medium-high heat. Add the pork chops and sear for 3 to 4 minutes on each side, or until brown (middle will be pink). Transfer the chops to a plate and cover to keep warm.

3. Reduce heat to medium. Add the sauce and cook for 1 minute. Return the chops to the pan and cook in the sauce for an additional 5 minutes, or until middle is no longer pink. Sprinkle with the green onions.

Fit Tip: When purchasing meat, remember that "loin" = lean. Top or center loin chops are the leanest of chops. Select those that are well trimmed.

NUTRITION INFORMATION PER SERVING (¼ RECIPE)
Calories 200 | Carbohydrate 7g (Sugars 2g) | Total Fat 7g (Sat Fat 2g) | Protein 25g | Fiber 1g | Cholesterol 65mg | Sodium 125mg | Food Exchanges: 3½ Lean Meat, ½ Fruit | Carbohydrate Choices: ½ | Weight Watcher Smart Point Comparison: 5

Pork Tenderloin with Cranberry Pan Sauce

This is another lovely entrée that's easy enough for every day and yet wonderful to serve when entertaining. I have demonstrated it many times in cooking classes and while it is terrific any time of year, I find it works particularly well with fall and holiday menus when you need an entrée that's elegant and fuss-free and fits every diet. Dried cranberries create the beautiful ruby red pan sauce, and because it's such a light dish, there are plenty of calories left over for dessert.

MAKES 4 SERVINGS

¼ cup port wine or chicken broth

¼ cup dried cranberries

½ teaspoon ground ginger

½ teaspoon dry mustard

1¼ pounds pork tenderloin

Salt and pepper to taste

1 teaspoon canola or olive oil

2 garlic cloves, minced

⅓ cup reduced-sodium chicken broth

¼ cup orange juice

1 tablespoon balsamic vinegar

1 tablespoon reduced-sugar raspberry jelly

1 tablespoon butter

1. Preheat the oven to 400°F.

2. In a small bowl, whisk together the port, cranberries, ginger, and mustard. Set aside. Season the pork with the salt and pepper.

3. Heat the oil in a large nonstick skillet over medium high. Add the tenderloins and brown well on all sides. Remove the meat and transfer to a baking sheet. Roast in the oven for 20 minutes, or until a meat thermometer reads 145°F. Remove from the oven, cover, and let rest for 5 to 10 minutes.

4. While the meat roasts, make the pan sauce. Add the garlic to the skillet and sauté for 1 minute. Add the port mixture, broth, orange juice, and vinegar, and cook over low heat for 5 to 8 minutes, until the mixture reduces slightly and the cranberries are plump and softened. Increase the heat to medium and stir in the jelly until it melts. Swirl the butter into the sauce just before serving. Season with salt and pepper if desired.

5. To serve, slice the meat and lay it onto plates. Spoon sauce over each serving.

NUTRITION INFORMATION PER SERVING (¼ RECIPE)
Calories 270 | Carbohydrate 9g (Sugars 8g) | Total Fat 9g (Sat Fat 3g) | Protein 33g | Fiber 1g | Cholesterol 100mg | Sodium 200mg | Food Exchanges: 4 Lean Meat, ½ Fruit, 1 Fat | Carbohydrate Choices: ½ | Weight Watcher Smart Point Comparison: 7

Fabulous Fish and Seafood

CRISPY PARMESAN FISH

CRUNCHY CHEDDAR FISH STRIPS

CORNMEAL-CRUSTED "FRIED" CATFISH
WITH HOMEMADE TARTAR SAUCE

SOUTH OF THE BORDER SNAPPER VERA CRUZ

EASY BAKED COD WITH LEMON BUTTER DILL SAUCE

FABULOUS 15-MINUTE HALIBUT

PERFECT PAN-SEARED SCALLOPS

CRAB CAKES WITH MUSTARD DILL SAUCE

HONEY DIJON GRILLED SHRIMP SKEWERS

SPICY KUNG PAO SHRIMP

SOUTHERN-STYLE SHRIMP CREOLE

SWEET-AND-SOUR SHRIMP STIR-FRY

SALMON PACKETS WITH FRESH TOMATO BASIL RELISH

ORANGE-GINGER GLAZED SALMON

Seafood (which includes both fish and shellfish) is fantastic for anyone watching their health. Fresh seafood is low in calories, saturated fat, and sodium, while high in B vitamins and minerals, such as iodine, phosphorus, and zinc. Moreover, "fatty" fish, such as salmon, halibut, and tuna, are excellent sources of omega-3 fatty acids, which are heralded for their role in minimizing the development of degenerative diseases and protecting your heart. The Dietary Guidelines go so far as to state that Americans should consume more fish to live "longer, healthier, and more active lives." The bottom line is that people who love to eat foods from the sea are healthier than those who don't.

Of course like with any other food, seafood is only as healthy as its preparation. And for seafood that often spells trouble. While we all know that steamed or broiled fish is best, a quick glance at any restaurant menu is all that is required to see that it's the crispy, crunchy, flavor-filled seafood dishes, served with creamy or buttery sauces, that we crave. (And who would ever guess that something as innocent sounding as a crab cake appetizer could deliver over 500 calories and 30 grams of fat?) In this chapter you'll learn how to make tempting seafood dishes that will satisfy every craving, while still minding your health. With over a dozen easy-to-prepare, remarkable recipes—from Crispy Parmesan Fish and Cornmeal-Crusted "Fried" Catfish with Homemade Tartar Sauce to Easy Baked Cod with Lemon Butter Dill Sauce and my boys' all-time favorite, Sweet-and-Sour Shrimp, I think you will agree that these dishes bring out the best seafood has to offer.

(Don't forget to check the index for other incredible fish entrees that appear in other chapters, such as the Baja Fish Tacos in the Food in Hand chapter, the "Cup of Red" Clam Chowder in Quick-Fix Soups and Chilis chapter, or the Creamy Seafood Linguine in Great Pasta-bilities.)

Crispy Parmesan Fish

Panko, or Japanese breadcumbs, are the secret to creating this simple yet utterly delicious Parmesan fish. Panko have jagged edges, a more flaky consistency, and a coarser texture than regular breadcrumbs, resulting in a lighter and far crisper coating (making them perfect for oven "frying"). Once available only at Asian and specialty markets, they are now easy to find at most grocery stores. Look for them on the breadcrumb aisle.

MAKES 4 SERVINGS

½ cup panko breadcrumbs

¼ cup grated Parmesan cheese

½ teaspoon garlic salt

⅛ teaspoon pepper

2 teaspoons butter, melted

1¼ pounds white fish (like cod, halibut, or tilapia)

1. Preheat the oven to 400°F. Spray a baking sheet with cooking spray.

2. In a shallow bowl, combine the panko, Parmesan, garlic salt, and pepper. Add the melted butter and mix well.

3. Lightly coat the fish with cooking spray and roll in the crumb mixture, pressing to coat. Place the fish on a baking sheet and cook for 12 to 14 minutes, turning once halfway through, or until fish is golden brown and flakes easily when tested with a fork.

Perfect Pairing: Try serving this with the Stewed Italian Zucchini Parmesan on page 261.

NUTRITION INFORMATION PER SERVING (¼ RECIPE)
Calories 190 | Carbohydrate 6g (Sugars 0g) | Total Fat 5g (Sat Fat 2g) | Protein 29g | Fiber 0g | Cholesterol 20mg | Sodium 420mg | Food Exchanges: 4 Lean Meat, ½ Starch | Carbohydrate Choices: ½ | Weight Watcher Smart Point Comparison: 3

Crunchy Cheddar Fish Strips

This kid-friendly recipe with a sophisticated twist is adapted from Gourmet *magazine. Crushed cheddar cheese crackers give a satisfying crunch and rich cheese flavor to update ordinary fish sticks. It took only one bite for my kids to declare these strips "the best." These could easily become a new family favorite.*

MAKES 4 SERVINGS

2 teaspoons canola oil

1½ cups reduced-fat cheddar cheese crackers

¼ teaspoon black pepper

⅓ cup Dijonnaise or Dijon mustard

1¼ pound white fish fillets, cut into 8 1½-inch wide strips

1. Set cooking rack in lower third of the oven and preheat to 475°F. Coat a large baking pan well with cooking spray.

2. Place the crackers in a resealable plastic bag and finely crush with a rolling pin or mallet. Transfer to a shallow flat bowl and add the pepper.

3. In a large bowl, coat the fish with the Dijonnaise. Roll the fish in the cracker crumbs until evenly coated. Place on baking sheet. Bake for 7 minutes, then spray strips lightly with cooking spray, turn and bake for 7 more minutes, or until golden brown.

Or try this: For *Cheddar Chicken Tenders*, replace the fish with uncooked, uncoated chicken tenders. Coat and bake as directed. (Add 20 calories, 1 gram of fat and 3 grams of protein per serving.)

NUTRITION INFORMATION PER SERVING (¼ RECIPE) ·······················
Calories 245 | Carbohydrate 18g (Sugars 0g) | Total Fat 5g (Sat Fat 1g) | Protein 31g | Fiber 2g | Cholesterol 70mg | Sodium 510mg | Food Exchanges: 4 Lean Meat, 1 Starch, 1 Fat | Carbohydrate Choices: 1 | Weight Watcher Smart Point Comparison: 5

Cornmeal-Crusted "Fried" Catfish with Homemade Tartar Sauce

Here's another oven-fried fish recipe for those of us, or y'all, who love fish that's crunchy and golden on the outside and tender and moist inside. Catfish and cornmeal star in this delectable down-home Southern specialty served up with a dollop of creamy homemade tartar sauce.

MAKES 4 SERVINGS

CORNMEAL-CRUSTED FISH:

6 tablespoons cornmeal

3 tablespoons all-purpose flour

¾ teaspoon Old Bay seasoning

¼ teaspoon dried thyme

⅛ teaspoon red pepper flakes

¼ cup low-fat milk

1¼ pounds catfish fillets, cut into 4 pieces

HOMEMADE TARTAR SAUCE:

3 tablespoons light mayonnaise

3 tablespoons nonfat plain yogurt

1 tablespoon finely minced onion

1 teaspoon sweet or dill pickle relish

1 teaspoon granulated sugar

1. Preheat the oven to 450°F. Spray a baking sheet with cooking spray.

2. In a shallow flat bowl, combine the cornmeal, flour, Old Bay, thyme, and red pepper flakes.

3. Dip the fish pieces in the milk and roll in the crumb mixture, pressing to coat. Place the fish on a baking sheet and cook for 12 to 14 minutes, turning once halfway through, or until fish is golden brown and flakes easily when tested with a fork.

4. While the fish is cooking, combine the mayonnaise, yogurt, onion, pickle relish, and sugar. Serve fish with tartar sauce.

DARE to COMPARE ································

The average restaurant serving of cornmeal-crusted fried catfish served with tartar sauce can have as many as 800 calories, 50 grams of fat, 40 grams of carbohydrate (or more), and 2,000 milligrams of sodium (and that's without the sides).

NUTRITION INFORMATION PER SERVING (¼ RECIPE) ································
Calories 255 | Carbohydrate 18g (Sugars 4g) | Total Fat 8g (Sat Fat 2g) | Protein 26g | Fiber 2g | Cholesterol 75mg | Sodium 320mg | Food Exchanges: 4 Lean Meat, 1 Starch, 1 Fat | Carbohydrate Choices: 1 | Weight Watcher Smart Point Comparison: 6

South of the Border Snapper Vera Cruz

This easy stovetop dish is crafted after one of the most famous dishes from Veracruz, a seaside town on the Caribbean coast of Mexico. Rich in flavor but low in calories, its flavors are influenced by both Spain and Mexico. I have designated the green olives as optional because even though they are a traditional ingredient in this dish I prefer to leave them out. Corn tortillas are a nice complement for mopping up the rich tomato and vegetable-laced topping.

MAKES 4 SERVINGS

1 tablespoon canola oil

1 medium onion, sliced

1 teaspoon minced garlic

1 green bell pepper, julienned

1¼ pounds red snapper or other white fish

1 (15-ounce) can stewed tomatoes

½ teaspoon cumin

1 teaspoon dried oregano

¼ cup chopped green olives (optional)

¼ cup chopped cilantro

1. Heat the oil in a large nonstick skillet over medium-high heat. Add the onion and garlic and cook for 3 minutes. Add the bell pepper and continue to cook for 3 to 4 more minutes, or until softened. Remove from the pan and set aside.

2. Add the fish to the pan and brown on both sides. Top with the onions and pepper. Add the tomatoes, and sprinkle with the cumin, oregano, and olives, if desired. Top with the cilantro and cover.

3. Cook for 10 minutes, or until fish is cooked through. Remove the lid and simmer for 3 to 4 minutes more to thicken sauce.

NUTRITION INFORMATION PER SERVING (¼ RECIPE)
Calories 215 | Carbohydrate 12g (Sugars 7g) | Total Fat 5g (Sat Fat 1g) | Protein 31g | Fiber 2g | Cholesterol 50mg | Sodium 320mg | Food Exchanges: 4 Lean Meat, 2 Vegetables, 1 Fat | Carbohydrate Choices: 1 | Weight Watcher Smart Point Comparison: 3

Easy Baked Cod with Lemon Butter Dill Sauce

With its incredibly mild flavor and dense white flaky flesh, cod is both popular and versatile. I like to buy it fresh when I can, but frozen fish is also a terrific option. Keeping a bag of frozen fish fillets in your freezer is an easy and economical way to keep fish on your weekly menu. The best way to thaw fish is in the refrigerator overnight in its original packaging. For a faster thaw, place the packaged fish in very cold water for two to three hours. It doesn't matter if your fish is fresh or frozen, this effortless recipe always turns out delicious.

MAKES 4 SERVINGS

1¼ pounds fresh or thawed cod, cut into 4 pieces

1½ tablespoons butter, melted

1½ tablespoons minced fresh dill (or 1½ teaspoons dried)

1 tablespoon fresh lemon juice

¼ teaspoon garlic powder

Pinch of salt

Fresh pepper to taste

1. Preheat the oven to 400°F.

2. Spray a baking dish with cooking spray. Pat the fish dry and arrange in a single layer in the baking dish.

3. In a small bowl combine the butter, dill, lemon juice, garlic powder, salt, and pepper to taste. Drizzle over the fish. Bake for 15 minutes, or until fish flakes easily when tested with a fork.

Perfect Pairing: Pair this with fresh steamed broccoli, Classic Creamy Coleslaw (page 183), and whole grain rolls for a wholesome meal in minutes.

NUTRITION INFORMATION PER SERVING (¼ RECIPE)
Calories 170 | Carbohydrate 0g (Sugars 0g) | Total Fat 5g (Sat Fat 3g) | Protein 28g | Fiber 0g | Cholesterol 80mg | Sodium 150mg | Food Exchanges: 4 Lean Meat, 1 Fat | Carbohydrate Choices: 0 | Weight Watcher Smart Point Comparison: 3

Fabulous 15-Minute Halibut

Simply fabulous is all I have to say about this dish. Did I also mention that it's fast, too? And that the luscious creamy topping will make a fish lover out of anyone? Oh yes, it's also healthy. Simple, fast, luscious, healthy halibut. Fabulous!

MAKES 4 SERVINGS

2 teaspoons canola oil

1¼ pounds halibut, cut into 4 pieces

¼ cup light mayonnaise

2 tablespoons lemon juice

2 tablespoons grated Parmesan cheese

1 garlic clove, minced

½ teaspoon Dijon mustard

⅛ teaspoon Tabasco sauce

2 to 3 tablespoons chopped green onion for garnish

1. Preheat the oven to 400°F. Heat the oil in a large nonstick skillet over medium-high heat. Add the halibut and brown on both sides.

2. Remove the fish from the skillet and place in baking dish. Immediately transfer dish to the oven and cook for 7 to 8 minutes, or until fish flakes easily when tested with a fork.

3. While the fish is cooking, mix together all remaining ingredients except the green onion. Spoon the mayonnaise mixture over the fish, turn oven to broil and broil fish and topping for 1 minute. Garnish with the green onions.

NUTRITION INFORMATION PER SERVING (¼ RECIPE)····························
Calories 225 | Carbohydrate 1g (Sugars0g) | Total Fat 10g (Sat Fat 2g) | Protein 31g | Fiber 0g | Cholesterol 50mg | Sodium 260mg | Food Exchanges: 4 Lean Meat, 1 Fat | Carbohydrate Choices: 0 | Weight Watcher Smart Point Comparison: 4

Perfect Pan-Seared Scallops

I really enjoy scallops but for the longest time the ones I made at home never stood up to those I ordered in a restaurant. Then I learned that the key to creating the lovely brown color found in restaurant-quality scallops is to make sure the scallops are thoroughly dry and have enough space between them while they sear in a hot skillet. Scallops release moisture when they cook, and if they are crowded in a pan, they braise rather than sear and brown. Follow this recipe and you will be enjoying perfectly cooked scallops too. The Homemade Tartar Sauce served with the Cornmeal-Crusted "Fried" Catfish on page 345 makes a great accompaniment.

MAKES 4 SERVINGS

16 sea scallops, about 1¼ pounds

Salt and pepper to taste

4 teaspoons canola oil

1. Place the scallops on a paper towel-lined plate and pat dry. Season with salt and pepper.

2. Heat 2 teaspoons of the oil in a very large nonstick skillet over high heat. When oil is very hot (just prior to smoking), place half of the scallops in the skillet, at least ½ inch apart from each other. Cook for about 2 minutes, or until underside is evenly browned. Turn the scallops and cook the second side for 1 to 2 minutes, or until the scallops have become firm on the sides but the center third is still lightly opaque. Place scallops on plate.

3. Wipe out the skillet with paper towels. Add the remaining oil and turn heat to high. When oil and pan are very hot again, add the remaining dried scallops and cook for 1 to 2 minutes, or until the underside is browned. Turn the scallops and cook second side 1 to 2 minutes or until the scallop have become firm on the sides but the center third is slightly opaque.

4. Place all of the scallops back in the pan and cook for 30 to 45 seconds, or until just cooked through.

NUTRITION INFORMATION PER SERVING (¼ RECIPE) ······················
Calories 140 | Carbohydrate 3.5g (Sugars 0g) | Total Fat .5g (Sat Fat 0g) | Protein 24g | Fiber 0g | Cholesterol 45mg | Sodium 230mg | Food Exchanges: 3½ Lean Meat | Carbohydrate Choices: 0 | Weight Watcher Smart Point Comparison: 2

Crab Cakes with Mustard Dill Sauce

Crab cakes are always a special treat. Unfortunately, when dining out it is hard to tell what you'll get, lots of crab, or lots of filler. The best thing about making crab cakes at home is that crab cakes are easy—and you determine what goes in them. Delicious crabmeat should take center stage, with only real lump meat crab and just enough breadcrumbs and mayo to hold the patties together. A single dollop of mustard dill sauce makes the perfect embellishment for these scrumptious cakes.

MAKES ABOUT 4 SERVINGS

CRAB CAKES:

1 pound lump crabmeat
(1-pound cans can be found
in the seafood department)

¾ cup dry breadcrumbs,
divided

2 egg whites, lightly beaten

3 tablespoons light mayonnaise

2 tablespoons chopped fresh
parsley

2 teaspoons Worcestershire
sauce

½ teaspoon Old Bay seasoning

Black pepper to taste

MUSTARD DILL SAUCE:

¼ cup plain low-fat yogurt

2 tablespoons light mayonnaise

¾ teaspoon prepared yellow
mustard

1½ teaspoons fresh minced dill
(or ½ teaspoon dried)

Pinch of sugar

1. Place the crabmeat in a large bowl. Add the remaining crab cake ingredients, using ½ cup of the breadcrumbs, and gently mix together with a large spoon, taking care to keep as many large crab pieces as possible. Mix all sauce ingredients in a small bowl and set aside.

2. Use your hands to shape the crabmeat mixture into 6 patties (using about ⅓ cup of mixture for each crab cake). Coat a large nonstick sauté pan with cooking spray and place over medium heat. Lightly dust both sides of the crab cakes with the remaining breadcrumbs.

3. Add the crab cakes to the pan. Cook the crab cakes about 5 minutes on each side, or until lightly browned and warmed through. Repeat as necessary to cook all the crab cakes, using additional cooking spray if needed. Serve the crab cakes with mustard dill sauce.

DARE *to* COMPARE ··
The nutritional content of crab cakes varies greatly depending on how they are made. Some recipes use lots of breadcrumbs to keep them "light" while others simply pack in the fat, like Ruby Tuesday's®, whose crab cakes have 32 grams of fat per serving *before* the tartar sauce.

NUTRITION INFORMATION PER CRAB CAKE ···
Calories 175 | Carbohydrate 11g (Sugars 0g) | Total Fat 4g (Sat Fat ½g) | Protein 20g | Fiber 2g | Cholesterol 70mg | Sodium 480mg | Food Exchanges: 3 Lean Meat, 1 Starch, 1 Fat | Carbohydrate Choices: 1 | Weight Watcher Smart Point Comparison: 3

Honey Dijon Grilled Shrimp Skewers

Succulent sweet shrimp is America's favorite seafood. There are plenty of ways to prepare it, but serving it grilled and basted with honey and mustard has got to be one of the most popular taste combinations ever to grace a casual restaurant. I never argue with success (although I have added some cherry tomatoes for better health). You may substitute yellow mustard for the Dijon and agave nectar for the honey, if you prefer.

MAKES 4 SERVINGS

1 pound large to extra-large raw shrimp (21 to 25 count), peeled and deveined

1 pint cherry tomatoes

1 tablespoon butter, melted

3 tablespoons Dijon mustard

1 tablespoon honey

2 tablespoons water

1. Presoak 8 bamboo or wooden skewers in cold water for at least 20 minutes to prevent burning.

2. Thread the shrimp and tomatoes alternately onto skewers, starting and ending with tomatoes. In a small bowl, mix together the butter, Dijon, honey, and water. Set aside.

3. Heat a grill until hot. Coat grill with cooking spray and heat on medium high. Lay the shrimp skewers onto the grill. Cook for 1 to 2 minutes, or until the underside of the shrimp turns pink. Turn skewers over and brush cooked side of shrimp with sauce. Cook for 1 to 2 additional minutes, or until underside turns pink and shrimp is cooked through. Brush remaining sauce onto freshly cooked side of shrimp and serve.

NUTRITION INFORMATION PER SERVING (2 SKEWERS OR ¼ RECIPE)
Calories 160 | Carbohydrate 10g (Sugars 6g) | Total Fat 5g (Sat Fat 2g) | Protein 25g | Fiber 1g | Cholesterol 160mg | Sodium 460mg | Food Exchanges: 3 Lean Meat, ½ Vegetable, 1 Fat | Carbohydrate Choices: ½ | Weight Watcher Smart Point Comparison: 3

Spicy Kung Pao Shrimp

My husband loves Asian Kung Pao dishes, but ordering them out isn't good for his wallet—or his waistline. Restaurant-made Kung Pao dishes have an excessive amount of oil and are overloaded with nuts, making them one of the most caloric dishes on any stir-fry menu. This recipe solves the Kung Pao dilemma. Serve over rice with an accompanying bowl of Egg Drop Soup (page 153).

MAKES 4 SERVINGS

⅓ cup peanuts

3 tablespoons reduced-sodium soy sauce

2 tablespoons rice vinegar

2 tablespoons cooking sherry

1 tablespoon hoisin sauce

1 tablespoon granulated no-calorie sweetener

2 teaspoons chili garlic sauce

2 teaspoons cornstarch

1 tablespoon water

2 teaspoons canola oil, divided

1 red bell pepper, cut into ¾-inch cubes

1½ teaspoons minced ginger

2 tablespoons minced garlic

16 ounces shrimp, peeled and deveined

8 ounces sliced water chestnuts, chopped

4 green onions, sliced diagonally

1. Preheat the oven to 325°F. Place the peanuts on an ungreased baking sheet and bake for 5 to 8 minutes or until slightly browned and toasted.

2. In a small bowl, whisk together the soy sauce, vinegar, sherry, hoisin, sweetener, and chili garlic sauce. Set aside. In a separate cup combine the cornstarch and the water.

3. Heat 1 teaspoon of the oil in a large wok or sauté pan over medium-high heat. Add the bell pepper and cook for 3 to 4 minutes, or until slightly softened. Remove the pepper and set aside. Add the remaining oil, ginger and garlic and stir until fragrant. Add the shrimp and cook about 3 minutes, or just until pink. Add the water chestnuts and return the bell pepper to the pan.

4. Move the shrimp and vegetables to the edges of the pan. Pour the sauce into the pan and bring to a low simmer. Add the cornstarch mix and cook for 2 to 3 minutes, until sauce thickens and clears. Add the green onions and peanuts and stir-fry all for 1 minute. Serve.

DARE to COMPARE ·······························
An order of Kung Pao shrimp at PF Chang's® contains 775 calories, 36 grams of fat, 48 grams of carbohydrate and 2,500 milligrams of sodium.

NUTRITION INFORMATION PER SERVING (¼ RECIPE) ··························
Calories 220 | Carbohydrate 15g (Sugars 6g) | Total Fat 9g (Sat Fat 1g) | Protein 22g | Fiber 4g | Cholesterol 160mg | Sodium 490mg | Food Exchanges: 3 Lean Meat, ½ ½ Vegetable, Starch, 2 Fat | Carbohydrate Choices:1 | Weight Watcher Smart Point Comparison: 5

Southern-Style Shrimp Creole

Like all great Creole recipes this one includes the holy trinity of onion, celery, and green pepper. Add aromatic spices, diced tomatoes, hot sauce, and shrimp and you have one Southern delight. What it doesn't have is an unhealthy butter and flour roux as its base or the all-day cooking common to many Creole dishes. I made sure to give this recipe a proper Louisiana "bite," but add as much hot sauce as you like. My Dad eats this dish with the hot sauce bottle close by.

MAKES 4 SERVINGS

1 tablespoon vegetable oil

1 medium onion, chopped

1 red bell pepper, chopped

1 green bell pepper, chopped

2 celery ribs, chopped

1 teaspoon minced garlic

1½ teaspoons dried thyme

1½ tablespoons Wondra or all-purpose flour

1 (14-ounce) can diced tomatoes

1 cup reduced-sodium chicken broth

1 tablespoon Worcestershire sauce

½ teaspoon hot sauce

1 pound medium shrimp, peeled and deveined

Black pepper to taste

1. Heat the oil in a large saucepan over medium heat. Add the onion, bell peppers and celery. Cover and cook for 7 to 8 minutes, stirring occasionally until the vegetables are softened. Add the garlic and thyme, and sauté for 1 minute.

2. Sprinkle the flour over vegetables and stir. Add the tomatoes, broth, Worcestershire and hot sauce. Cover and simmer for 5 minutes.

3. Remove the lid and add the shrimp. Stirring often, cook the shrimp for 4 to 5 minutes, or until shrimp is pink and fully cooked. Add the black pepper to taste.

NUTRITION INFORMATION PER SERVING (¼ RECIPE)
Calories 145 | Carbohydrate 13g (Sugars 5g) | Total Fat 3.5g (Sat Fat 0g) | Protein 15g | Fiber 3g | Cholesterol 110mg | Sodium 420mg | Food Exchanges: 2 Lean Meat, 2 Vegetables, ½ Fat | Carbohydrate Choices: 1 | Weight Watcher Smart Point Comparison: 2

Sweet-and-Sour Shrimp Stir-Fry

Whether it's shrimp, pork, or chicken, sweet-and-sour dishes are the most popular on any Asian menu. Classic "sweet-and-sour" dishes originated in ancient China and they rely on sweet, such as sugar, to counterbalance sour, such as vinegar. With the help of a modern-day sugar substitute, I have duplicated the addictive taste of the take-out favorite with just a fraction of the sugar. The saved calories and carbs can be spent much more wisely on a small bed of brown rice.

MAKES 4 SERVINGS

¾ cup coarsely chopped carrots

¾ cup chopped green bell pepper

½ cup plus ¼ cup water

½ cup pineapple chunks (optional)

6 tablespoons granulated no-calorie sweetener*

3 tablespoons ketchup

1 tablespoon reduced-sodium soy sauce

⅓ cup rice vinegar

2 teaspoons cornstarch

2 teaspoons olive oil

1 teaspoon minced ginger

1 pound large shrimp (21 to 25 count), peeled and deveined

1. Place the carrots, bell pepper, and ½ cup water in a medium saucepan. Bring to a boil and cook for 1 minute. Drain the vegetables and rinse thoroughly with cold water. If using, add the pineapple, and set aside.

2. Return the empty saucepan to the heat. Add the sweetener, ketchup, soy sauce, and vinegar. Whisk together and bring to a low simmer.

3. Dissolve the cornstarch into the remaining ¼ cup of water. Add to the pan and cook for 2 to 3 minutes, stirring until thickened and clear. Stir in the vegetables and pineapple. Cover and turn off heat.

4. Heat the oil in a large sauté pan over medium heat. Add the ginger and shrimp to the pan and cook shrimp 2 to 3 minutes on each side, until opaque. Pour the sauce over shrimp and toss to coat and heat through.

> **DARE to COMPARE** ·············
> An average 1-cup serving of take-out sweet-and-sour shrimp contains 400 calories, 21 grams of fat, 42 grams of carbohydrate, 30 grams of sugar, and just 12 grams of protein.

* See page 382 for sweetener options.

NUTRITION INFORMATION PER SERVING (¼ RECIPE) ·············
Calories 140 | Carbohydrate 14g (Sugars 5g) | Total Fat 1g (Sat Fat 0g) | Protein 18g | Fiber 2g | Cholesterol 150mg | Sodium 520mg | Food Exchanges: 2 Lean Meat, 1 Vegetable, ½ Carbohydrate | Carbohydrate Choices: 1 | Weight Watcher Smart Point Comparison: 2

Salmon Packets with Fresh Tomato Basil Relish

This is one of my favorite cooking school recipes. The elegance, ease, and versatility of salmon combined with an intoxicating topping make this meal extra special. Use foil packets to seal in the flavor and to make clean-up a snap. Though the dish comes together quickly, the packets can be made ahead of time and kept in the fridge for several hours before baking. If your special evening includes more than two, the recipe can easily be doubled or tripled.

MAKES 2 SERVINGS

- 2 large Roma tomatoes, seeded and diced
- 1 tablespoon sweet vermouth or white wine
- 2 tablespoons fresh julienned basil
- 1 medium shallot, finely chopped
- 2 teaspoons minced garlic
- 2 teaspoons extra-virgin olive oil
- 1 teaspoon lemon juice
- Dash red pepper flakes
- Salt and pepper to taste
- 8 to 10 spinach leaves
- 2 (5-ounce) skinned salmon fillets

1. Preheat the oven to 375°F.

2. In a small bowl, mix together the tomatoes, vermouth, basil, shallot, garlic, olive oil, lemon juice, and red pepper. Season with salt and pepper to taste, and set aside. Take 2 large pieces of foil and spray with cooking spray. Divide the spinach between the two sheets of foil.

3. Place fillets on top of the spinach. Top each fillet with the tomato mixture. Bring up the sides of the foil, fold over, and seal to create a "packet."

4. Place sealed packets onto a baking sheet and bake for 20 minutes.

NUTRITION INFORMATION PER SERVING (½ RECIPE)
Calories 350 | Carbohydrate 6g (Sugars 6g) | Total Fat 15g (Sat Fat 4g) | Protein 35g | Fiber 2g | Cholesterol 90mg | Sodium 100mg | Food Exchanges: 4 Medium-Fat Meat, 1 Vegetable, 1 Fat | Carbohydrate Choices: ½ | Weight Watcher Smart Point Comparison: 8

Orange-Ginger Glazed Salmon

Salmon is truly one of the world's healthiest foods. High in omega-3 fatty acids, selenium, vitamins D and B12, and protein, it's an absolute powerhouse of good nutrition. Best of all, it tastes great. The orange citrus glaze and delightful mix of sweet and tangy with just a bit of heat makes this dish special. If you prefer to grill the salmon, cook it about 5 minutes per side.

MAKES 4 SERVINGS

¼ cup lime juice (about 2 large limes)

¼ cup light orange juice

¼ cup low-sugar orange marmalade

2 teaspoons freshly grated ginger (or 1 teaspoon powdered)

½ teaspoon dried mustard

Pinch of salt

Dash of hot pepper flakes

2 teaspoons butter

4 (5-ounce) salmon fillets, rinsed and dried

1. Combine the lime juice, orange juice, orange marmalade, ginger, mustard, salt, and pepper flakes in a small saucepan and bring to a boil. Reduce the heat and simmer on low heat for 5 minutes, until reduced to almost one-half. Remove from heat; swirl in the butter. Set aside.

2. While sauce is cooking, spray a skillet with nonstick cooking spray and place over medium-high heat. Add the salmon and cook for 3 to 4 minutes per side, or until well browned on both sides.

3. Spread sauce across salmon and serve.

Family Focus: It's never too early to start taking care of your heart. Research at the Cleveland Heart Center has shown that 17% of teens (age 12 to 19), already have some evidence of plaque formation. The addition of foods rich in omega-3 fatty acids, such as salmon, walnuts, flaxseeds, cauliflower, and broccoli, make for delicious heart-healthy choices for everyone in the family—no matter what their age.

NUTRITION INFORMATION PER SERVING
Calories 310 | Carbohydrate 9g (Sugars 6g) | Total Fat 18g (Sat Fat 4.5g) | Protein 29g | Fiber 0g | Cholesterol 90mg | Sodium 155mg | Food Exchanges: 4 Medium-Fat Meat, ½ Carbohydrate, 1 Fat | Carbohydrate Choices: ½ | Weight Watcher Smart Point Comparison: 9

Pies and Fruit Desserts

APPLE CRUMBLE PIE

OLD-FASHIONED PUMPKIN PIE

NO-BAKE CREAMSICLE PIE

TRIPLE CHOCOLATE CHEESECAKE PIE

BERRIES IN A CLOUD

MIXED BERRIES WITH ORANGE CUSTARD SAUCE

EASY, ELEGANT BALSAMIC STRAWBERRIES

STRAWBERRY CHEESECAKE CRÊPES

CHERRY BERRY PIE CUPS

FAST, FRESH FRUIT TART

STRAWBERRY BANANA KABOBS

HOT APPLE STIR-FRY

5-MINUTE BLACKBERRY CRISP

WARM CINNAMON APPLE CRISP

When it comes to foods that we can't live without, it doesn't get any more basic than pumpkin and apple pie. Pies are known for their home-style goodness and nothing quite welcomes like a pie. Of course, there are many delicious recipes for each of these pies, but my versions of these pies are extra special. Why? Because my pumpkin and apple pies are better for you, but they don't taste it!

I felt the need to improve on these two classics because of my own family. My father and my stepdaughter both have type 2 diabetes, and they both love pie! The problem for anyone watching carbs or calories is that a simple piece of apple pie (depending on the type) can use all of the carbohydrates and most of the calories for an entire meal. (An average piece of apple pie can easily have 500 calories, and 60 grams of carbohydrate, or more.) Because it's hard to give up all of your carbs on one food—and pretty unrealistic, especially at a holiday meal like Thanksgiving, where there are lots of carbs to choose from—I am truly proud that I have created recipes for delectable pies that can easily fit into any diet.

Beyond the wonderful pies in this chapter you will find an assortment of sweet desserts with the natural goodness of fruit. These good-for-you desserts are simple to make, beautiful to serve, and perfectly complement any meal. The tricky thing with most fruit desserts is that because we know fruit is good for us, we tend to overlook the fact that they can have just as many calories, and often an even higher sugar content, as many of the desserts we tend to avoid. Rest assured that you will not find that to be the case with these desserts because I have kept the added sugars (and the added fats) to a minimum, allowing the luscious fruit to take center stage. The Warm Apple Crisp is as sweet as ever, the Fast, Fresh Fruit Tart as light as it is fresh, and the luscious Strawberry Cheesecake Crêpes are hard to resist. Mother Nature would be proud.

For the Love of Fruit

Naturally low in fat and calories, and high in fiber, vitamins, minerals, and antioxidants, fruit is indisputably one of Mother Nature's finest foods. Health organizations recommend everyone, no matter what their diet (including those with diabetes), eat between two and four servings, or two cups of fruit per day. But like all good things, more is not always better. Fruit is not an all-you-can-eat food, especially for those moderating their sugar or carbohydrate intake, or limiting calories.

While all fruit, with the exception of coconut and avocado, is predominately carbohydrate, the density of calories, carbs, sugar, and fiber among fruits varies greatly. This chart is designed to help you get the most bang for your fruit buck when it comes to adding satisfying portions of fruit to your diet (or your recipes). Fruit at the top can be enjoyed in larger portions while those at the bottom are better minimized.

Fruit	Serving	Fiber
Strawberries	1¼ cups whole	4g
Watermelon	1¼ cups cubed	1g
Raspberries	1 cup fresh	8g
Melon (honeydew, cantaloupe)	1 cup diced	1.5g
Grapes	1 cup/15 each	1g
Apple with skin	1 small	3g
Papaya	1 cup	2.5g
Fresh Peach	1 large	2.5g
Blackberries	¾ cup	6g
Blueberries	¾ cup	2.5g
Fresh Cherries	12	2g
Fresh Orange	Medium	3g
Pineapple	¾ cup chunks	1.5g
Grapefruit	½ whole	2g
Applesauce	½ cup	2g
Banana	½ large	2g
Apple/Grapefruit/Orange Juice	½ cup	0g
Prune/Grape/Cherry Juice	⅓ cup	0g
Dried Plums/Prunes	3	2g
Dried Raisins/Cranberries	2 tablespoons	1g

Each serving size on this chart contains approximately 60 calories and 15 grams of carbohydrate, equal to one carbohydrate choice or one fruit exchange. Fruits that contain more fiber are better at controlling and stabilizing blood sugar. (One-half of the fiber may be subtracted from the 15 grams of carbohydrate for carbohydrate counting.)

Apple Crumble Pie

"No-sugar-added" apple pies may seem to be a better choice, but more often than not, they have just as much sugar and carbohydrates as regular apple pie. Most no-sugar-added pies simply add concentrated sources of fruit, such as concentrated apple juice, to replace the granulated sugar. And these simple fruit sugars are no better for us than sugar! On the other hand, this delicious apple pie really does have half the calories and carbohydrates, and a fraction of the sugar of a traditional apple pie, making it a healthier choice for everyone. If that weren't enough, it's topped with sweet streusel "crumble" topping that will have everyone clamoring for more. Enjoy.

MAKES 8 SERVINGS

6 tablespoons rolled oats

⅓ cup plus 6 tablespoons granulated no-calorie sweetener, divided*

¼ cup graham cracker crumbs

2 tablespoons packed dark brown sugar

¼ cup plus 1 tablespoon all-purpose flour, divided

1½ teaspoons cinnamon, divided

3 tablespoons cold butter, cut into ½-inch cubes

6 cups peeled apple slices (about 2½ pounds)

1 tablespoon lemon juice

1 prepared single piecrust (refrigerated or frozen)

1. Preheat the oven to 425°F

2. In a medium bowl, mix the rolled oats, ⅓ cup of the sweetener, graham cracker crumbs, brown sugar, ¼ cup of the flour, and 1 teaspoon of the cinnamon. Cut in the butter using a pastry blender or by hand, until the mixture resembles coarse meal.

3. In a large bowl, toss the apples with the remaining 6 tablespoons sweetener, 1 tablespoon flour, ½ teaspoon cinnamon, and the lemon juice. Pour the apple mixture into the piecrust and bake for 15 minutes.

4. Remove the pie from the oven and sprinkle the topping on the top. Lower temperature to 375°F and bake for an additional 20 to 25 minutes, or until the crumble is crisp and golden brown and the apples are tender.

> **DARE to COMPARE**
> Bob Evans® includes a No-Sugar Apple Pie Ala Mode on the menu but it *still* contains a dazzling 642 calories, 36 grams of fat, and 71 grams of carbohydrate.

* See page 382 for sweetener options.

NUTRITION INFORMATION PER SERVING
Calories 230 | Carbohydrate 34g (Sugars 17g) | Total Fat 10g (Sat Fat 3g) | Protein 2g | Fiber 3g | Cholesterol 15mg | Sodium 125mg | Food Exchanges: 1 Fruit, 1 Carbohydrate | Carbohydrate Choices: 2 | Weight Watcher Smart Point Comparison: 4

Old-Fashioned Pumpkin Pie

It just wouldn't be Thanksgiving without pumpkin pie. Using a technique from Cook's Illustrated, this slimmed down version involves heating the pumpkin filling before it's placed in the crust and baked. After baking dozens of pumpkin pies they found this technique resulted in a richer pumpkin flavor and a crispier crust. The touch of molasses brings additional depth and color, which are often lost when sugar substitutes are used.

MAKES 8 SERVINGS

1 (15-ounce) can pumpkin purée (not pumpkin pie filling)

1½ teaspoons ground cinnamon

½ teaspoon ground ginger

¼ teaspoon ground nutmeg

¼ teaspoon ground cloves

1 tablespoon molasses

¾ cup granulated no-calorie sweetener *

1 (12-ounce) can low-fat evaporated milk

2 teaspoons cornstarch

1 teaspoon vanilla extract

2 large eggs

2 large egg whites

1 deep-dish unbaked single piecrust (refrigerated or frozen)

1. Preheat the oven to 425°F.

2. Place the pumpkin purée, spices, molasses, and sweetener in a medium pot over medium heat. Bring to a sputtering simmer and cook for 3 to 4 minutes, stirring constantly. Remove from the heat.

3. In a medium bowl whisk together the milk, cornstarch, vanilla extract, eggs and egg whites. Pour the mixture into the pumpkin and whisk until smooth. Pour the filling into the prepared piecrust.

4. Bake for 10 minutes. Reduce the heat to 350°F and bake for an additional 30 to 35 minutes, or until the center is just set. Cool the pie to room temperature and then store in refrigerator.

* See page 382 for sweetener options.

NUTRITION INFORMATION PER SERVING ··
Calories 210 | Carbohydrate 26g (Sugars 8g) | Total Fat 9g (Sat Fat 4.5g) | Protein 6g | Fiber 2g | Cholesterol 65mg | Sodium 220mg | Food Exchanges:1½ Carbohydrate, 2 Fat | Carbohydrate Choices: 1½ | Weight Watcher Smart Point Comparison: 7

No-Bake Creamsicle Pie

Low in calories and carbohydrates, this cool and creamy pie is the perfect summer treat. The sugar-free gelatin sweetens without adding sugar and imparts the same lovely color and flavor of an orange creamsicle.

MAKES 8 SERVINGS

½ cup graham cracker crumbs

1 tablespoon margarine or butter, melted

2 tablespoons egg white

⅔ cup boiling water

1 package (4 servings) sugar-free orange gelatin

1 cup low-fat cottage cheese

1 cup light cream cheese

2 cups light whipped topping, thawed

1. Preheat the oven to 350°F.

2. Mix together the graham cracker crumbs, margarine, and egg white until well mixed. Press into the bottom only of a 9-inch pie plate. Bake for 8 to 9 minutes, or until the crust is crisp. Set aside to cool.

3. Place the water in a glass bowl and microwave on high for 3 minutes until boiling. Pour the gelatin into the water and whisk until thoroughly dissolved. Set aside to cool.

4. Place the cottage cheese into the bowl of a food processor and pulse until smooth. Add cream cheese and continue processing until smooth. Pour in the sugar-free gelatin. Scrape down the sides and continue mixing until all ingredients are combined. Transfer the mixture to a large bowl.

5. Gently fold in whipped topping. Pour mixture into crust and refrigerate until set about 4 hours or overnight.

Or try this: Feel free to use different gelatin flavors. I find that both lemon and lime work equally well. Adding a bit of fresh citrus zest with the gelatin boosts the flavor.

NUTRITION INFORMATION PER SERVING ⋯⋯⋯⋯⋯⋯⋯⋯⋯
Calories 160 | Carbohydrate 9g (Sugars 6g) | Total Fat 9g (Sat Fat 7g) | Protein 7g | Fiber 0g | Cholesterol 25mg | Sodium 290mg | Food Exchanges: ½ Carbohydrate, 2 Fat | Carbohydrate Choices: ½ | Weight Watcher Smart Point Comparison: 7

Triple Chocolate Cheesecake Pie

Triple chocolate cheesecake—it's enough to make you swoon. Rich with the flavors of chocolate and cream cheese, this no-bake mousse-like pie tastes downright decadent. I was inspired by a recipe I found on-line (see Dare to Compare); it makes chocolate lovers cheer!

MAKES 10 SERVINGS

1 cup chocolate graham cracker crumbs

⅓ cup plus 1 tablespoon cocoa powder, divided

¾ cup granulated no-calorie sweetener, divided *

1 tablespoon margarine or butter, melted

1 tablespoon canola oil

2 tablespoons egg white*

2 ounces semisweet baking chocolate, chopped (or ⅓ cup semisweet chocolate chips)

8 ounces light tub-style cream cheese, at room temperature

4 ounces nonfat cream cheese, at room temperature

1 (8-ounce) tub light whipped topping, thawed

3 tablespoons sugar-free fudge topping

2 ounces sugar-free chocolate, for garnish

1. Preheat the oven to 350°F. Lightly coat a 9-inch pie pan with cooking spray.

2. In a medium bowl, combine the graham cracker crumbs, 1 tablespoon of the cocoa powder, ¼ cup of the sweetener, the margarine, and oil. Add the egg white and stir well. Press the crumb mixture into the sides and bottom of the pie plate. Bake for 8 to 10 minutes, and set aside to cool.

3. Place the chocolate in a small microwave-safe bowl and heat for 1 to 1½ minutes, or until it appears shiny and looks partially melted. Remove and stir. Set aside.

4. Using an electric mixer, beat together the cream cheeses in a medium bowl for 2 minutes, or until creamy. Beat in the melted chocolate, and the remaining ½ cup sweetener and ⅓ cup cocoa powder. Gently beat in the whipped topping.

5. Spoon the filling into the cooled crust and smooth the top. Refrigerate at least 2 hours or until set. Before serving, slightly warm the fudge sauce. Stir well and drizzle over the pie.

DARE to COMPARE ·······················

The original recipe for this pie had 420 calories, 32 grams of fat, 20 grams of saturated fat, 35 grams of carbohydrate, and 25 grams of sugar.

* See page 382 for sweetener options.

NUTRITION INFORMATION PER SERVING ·································

Calories 225 | Carbohydrate 25g (Sugars 12g) | Total Fat 10g (Sat Fat 6g) | Protein 7g | Fiber 2g | Cholesterol 10mg | Sodium 260mg | Food Exchanges: 1½ Starch, 1 Lean Meat, 2 Fat | Carbohydrate Choices: 1½ | Weight Watcher Smart Point Comparison: 9

Berries in a Cloud

This dessert is as light as a cloud. Every time I make it I think of Katie, a dietetic intern who was working with me when we tested it. She was so thrilled with the results that she ran home and made it for her roommates who promptly called her "an angel." Any type of fresh berries or fruit can be used and, in a pinch, you can use thoroughly thawed frozen berries.

MAKES 4 SERVINGS

½ cup fat-free sour cream

4 ounces light tub-style cream cheese

4 tablespoons granulated no-calorie sweetener, divided*

1 cup light whipped topping

1 cup fresh blueberries, rinsed and drained

1 cup fresh raspberries, rinsed and drained

2 tablespoons low-sugar or sugar-free berry-flavored jam

1 tablespoon water

1. In a medium bowl using an electric mixer, beat the sour cream, cream cheese, and 3 tablespoons (4 packets) sweetener until creamy. Using a spoon or spatula, fold in the whipped topping until blended.

2. Mix the berries together in a small bowl.

3. Create "clouds" by spooning ½ cup of the creamy mixture into each of the four glass bowls. Use the back of a spoon to spread the mixture along the sides and create a well in the center of each bowl. Fill each well with ½ cup of the berries.

4. Combine the remaining tablespoon (or 1 packet) of sweetener with the jam and water. Microwave on high for 30 to 60 seconds, until melted.

5. Using a teaspoon, drizzle the melted jam mixture across the top of each bowl.

* See page 382 for sweetener options.

NUTRITION INFORMATION PER SERVING
Calories 190 | Carbohydrate 23g (Sugars 13g) | Total Fat 7g (Sat Fat 6g) | Protein 6g | Fiber 3g | Cholesterol 15mg | Sodium 180mg | Food Exchanges: 1 Carbohydrate, ½ Fruit, 1 Fat | Carbohydrate Choices: 1½ | Weight Watcher Smart Point Comparison: 6

Mixed Berries with Orange Custard Sauce

The creamy orange custard sauce may be poured over berries while it's still warm or after it is chilled. If serving chilled, pour the custard sauce into a small bowl and place plastic directly on top of the sauce. Refrigerate for at least an hour, or overnight. Before serving, whisk the sauce lightly before pouring over the berries.

MAKES 4 SERVINGS

2½ cups fresh mixed berries

¾ cup low-fat milk

½ cup nonfat half-and-half

2 large egg yolks, beaten

3 tablespoons granulated no-calorie sweetener*

2 teaspoons cornstarch

¾ teaspoon vanilla extract

½ teaspoon orange zest

Fresh mint, for garnish

1. Evenly distribute the berries among 4 serving dishes. Place in the refrigerator to chill until serving.

2. In a small saucepan over medium heat, whisk together the remaining ingredients. Whisking constantly, cook for 5 to 6 minutes, or until custard is thick enough to coat a spoon.

3. Pour ¼ cup of the custard sauce over each serving of berries, garnish with mint, if desired, and serve.

Fit Tip: Berries are among the lowest in sugar of all fruits. Berries, including raspberries, blackberries, blueberries, and strawberries, are not only low in fat, carbs, and calories but are high in fiber, minerals, and antioxidants, making them a fabulous addition to any diet.

* See page 382 for sweetener options.

NUTRITION INFORMATION PER SERVING
Calories 120 | Carbohydrate 18g (Sugars 10g) | Total Fat 3.5g (Sat Fat 1g) | Protein 5g | Fiber 4g | Cholesterol 110mg | Sodium 60mg | Food Exchanges: ½ Carbohydrate, ½ Fruit | Carbohydrate Choices: 1 | Weight Watcher Smart Point Comparison: 3

Easy, Elegant Balsamic Strawberries

Balsamic vinegar is wonderful for bringing out the flavor of fresh strawberries. If you have never tried a ruby red strawberry with a splash of sweetened balsamic vinegar (especially with a pinch of pepper), you are in for a scrumptious surprise. If you prefer to use the agave nectar instead of the sweetener, add 15 calories and 4 grams of carbohydrate for each serving.

MAKES 4 SERVINGS

2 tablespoons balsamic vinegar

1 tablespoon plus 1 teaspoon granulated no-calorie sweetener*

Pinch of black pepper (optional)

16 ounces (3 cups) halved fresh strawberries

¼ cup light sour cream

1. In a medium bowl, mix together the vinegar, 1 tablespoon sweetener, and pepper. Add the strawberries and stir.

2. In a small bowl, mix together the sour cream and 1 teaspoon sweetener. (If necessary, add a couple drops of water to thin.)

3. Divide the strawberries among four bowls. Garnish the strawberries with the sour cream mixture.

Chef's Tip: True aged balsamic vinegar is made from white grape juice that is reduced and aged in wooden barrels for a minimum of 12 years. Its distinct dark color and natural sweetness do not come from added sugar, but from the aging process.

* See page 382 for sweetener options.

NUTRITION INFORMATION PER SERVING
Calories 60 | Carbohydrate 10g (Sugars 7g) | Total Fat 1g (Sat Fat 0g) | Protein 2g | Fiber 2g | Cholesterol 5mg | Sodium 15mg | Food Exchanges: ½ Fruit | Carbohydrate Choices: ½ | Weight Watcher Smart Point Comparison: 1

Strawberry Cheesecake Crêpes

Ready-to-use crêpes make this recipe a snap to put together. I particularly like Melissa's brand crêpes as they are low in calories and taste as good as homemade. Look for them in the produce section of your local market.

MAKES 8 SERVINGS

2½ cups sliced strawberries

2 tablespoons granulated no-calorie sweetener (or 3 packets)

½ cup low-fat cottage cheese

¼ cup light tub-style cream cheese

1½ tablespoons granulated no-calorie sweetener*

¾ cup light whipped topping

8 (9-inch) crêpes

Powdered sugar, for garnish

1. Reserve about 8 strawberry slices to use later for garnish. In a small bowl, mix together the remaining strawberries and 2 tablespoons of sweetener.

2. Place the cottage cheese in the bowl of a food processor or blender and process until smooth.

3. In a medium bowl, beat the cream cheese and remaining sweetener. Add the cottage cheese and mix well. Gently fold in the whipped topping.

4. To assemble the crêpes, place 2 tablespoons of the cream cheese mixture into the center of each crêpe. Top with ¼ cup strawberries. Fold in half. Sprinkle the tops with the powdered sugar and a strawberry slice or two for garnish.

> **DARE to COMPARE**
> Swap out the usual Strawberry Shortcake for crêpes and save your diet. *Good Housekeeping* estimates a serving of Classic Strawberry Shortcake has over 400 calories, 20 grams of fat, and 50 grams of carbohydrate.

* See page 382 for sweetener options.

NUTRITION INFORMATION PER SERVING
Calories 110 | Carbohydrate 15g (Sugars 6g) | Total Fat 3.5g (Sat Fat 2.5g) | Protein 4g | Fiber 1g | Cholesterol 10mg | Sodium 190mg | Food Exchanges: ½ Fruit, ½ Carbohydrate | Carbohydrate Choices: 1 | Weight Watcher Smart Point Comparison: 3

Cherry Berry Pie Cups

Nobody will believe you created these perfect cherry "pies" in under 30 minutes (and of course you don't have to tell). Fresh raspberries complement the cherry pie filling perfectly and add a fresh homemade quality while refrigerated piecrust makes them as easy as, well, pie!

MAKES 12 SERVINGS

1 package refrigerated piecrust

1 (20-ounce) can no-sugar-added cherry pie filling

¼ cup granulated no-calorie sweetener*

1 pint fresh raspberries

Light whipped topping, for garnish

1. Preheat the oven to 425°F. Place one piecrust on a cutting board or flat surface and roll out lightly to an 11-inch diameter. Using a 4-inch round cutter, cut out six rounds. Set scraps aside. Repeat with the second piecrust.

2. Lightly press the pastry rounds into 12 muffin cups, pressing into the bottom and up the sides. Set aside.

3. In a medium bowl, mix together the cherry pie filling and the sweetener. Gently fold in the raspberries. Spoon about 3 tablespoons of the filling into each crust-lined cup.

4. Bake for 19 to 22 minutes, or until the edges are golden brown and the filling is bubbly.

5. Let cool slightly and serve warm or cool. Garnish each pie cup with a dollop of whipped topping.

   Marlene Says: Look in the refrigerated section of your supermarket for pre-made, ready-to-use piecrusts or dough, not ready-to-fill piecrusts, for this recipe.

   * See page 382 for sweetener options.

········ **NUTRITION INFORMATION PER SERVING** ···
Calories 135 | Carbohydrate 18g (Sugars 12g) | Total Fat 7g (Sat Fat 2.5g) | Protein 1g | Fiber 1g | Cholesterol 5mg | Sodium 150mg | Food Exchanges: 1 Starch, 1 Fat, ½ Fruit | Carbohydrate Choices: 1 | Weight Watcher Smart Point Comparison: 5

Fast, Fresh Fruit Tart

When the weather is warm and fresh berries are abundant, there is no food more beautiful on a table than a lovely fruit tart. To make this fast and fresh, I start with a store-bought piecrust and fill it with an incredible no-bake foolproof pastry cream. For the topping I like to use a mixture of berries, including strawberries, blueberries and raspberries, but sliced fresh peaches, apricots, and kiwi all work grand. A tart pan is an option, but not required.

MAKES 8 SERVINGS

½ package refrigerated piecrust

4 ounces light tub-style cream cheese

1 (3.5-ounce) package sugar-free vanilla pudding mix

1 cup low-fat milk

½ teaspoon vanilla extract

1½ cups light whipped topping

3 cups assorted fresh berries

2 tablespoons low-sugar jam (optional)

1. Preheat the oven to 350°F.

2. On a lightly floured surface roll the crust into a large 12-inch circle. Place dough onto a cookie sheet. (Alternatively, place dough into a 10-inch tart pan pressing dough onto bottom and up sides and trim.) Roll about ¾ inch of the outside of the dough, all the way around, inward and crimp to create an edge. Prick crust liberally with a fork. Bake for 15 minutes, or until golden brown. Remove from the oven and cool completely.

3. In a medium bowl using an electric mixer, beat the cream cheese for 1 minute, or until creamy. Beat in the pudding mix and milk for 2 minutes, or until thick. On low speed, beat in the vanilla and half of the whipped topping until smooth. Use a spatula to fold in the remaining whipped topping. (If the crust is still warm, cover the filling and refrigerate until the crust is completely cooled.)

4. Spread the filling onto the crust. Decorate the top with the berries. To "gloss" fruit if desired, place jam in a microwave-safe dish and cook for 1 minute. Brush melted jam on top of the fruit.

DARE to COMPARE ·······························
Martha Stewart's Classic Fruit Tart has almost twice the calories, double the fat and saturated fat, and four times the sugar as my Fast, Fresh Fruit Tart.

NUTRITION INFORMATION PER SERVING ·······························
Calories 215 | Carbohydrate 25g (Sugars 6g) | Total Fat 11g (Sat Fat 6g) | Protein 3g | Fiber 2g | Cholesterol 15mg | Sodium 380mg | Food Exchanges:1 Carbohydrate, ½ Fruit, 2 Fat | Carbohydrate Choices: 1½ | Weight Watcher Smart Point Comparison: 7

Strawberry Banana Kabobs

Many people believe that those with diabetes or those who are watching their sugar intake can't eat sugar, but they can easily make room for a nice big bowl of fruit for dessert. Both of these assertions are incorrect. Yes, fruit is healthy, but like all foods high in sugar (or carbohydrates), eating it in moderation, especially when you need to control your blood sugar, is key. What I like about this fruit kabob combo is that besides making it easy to control portion size, it smartly mingles a higher sugar fruit (bananas) with the great taste and added nutrition of a naturally lower sugar one (strawberries), to help to keep the carbs in check. Light vanilla or lemon yogurt or sweetened light sour cream makes a great dip.

MAKES 4 SERVINGS

2 bananas (about ½ pound)
8 large strawberries

1. Cut each banana into six 1-inch thick slices. Trim the strawberries, and cut in half.

2. Thread the strawberries and bananas onto four long wooden skewers, starting and ending with strawberry halves.

Family Focus: Get the kids in the kitchen for this recipe! Have them pick some of their favorite fruits for the kabobs. Berries, melon, and watermelon are all lower sugar fruits.

NUTRITION INFORMATION PER SERVING
Calories 70 | Carbohydrate 17g (Sugars 15g) | Total Fat 0g (Sat Fat 0g) | Protein 0g | Fiber 4g | Cholesterol 0mg | Sodium 0mg | Food Exchanges: 1 Fruit | Carbohydrate Choices: 1 | Weight Watcher Smart Point Comparison: 0

Hot Apple Stir-Fry

While I was scanning a wok cookbook I came across something rather intriguing—a chapter on sautéed and "stir-fried" desserts! The recipe that caught my attention was for an apple stir-fry with maple syrup used as the stir-fry sauce. I lightened that original recipe by using sugar-free maple flavored syrup and a touch of butter. These apples are delicious served right out of the wok, but they are also delightful as a topping for light vanilla ice cream.

MAKES 6 SERVINGS

1 tablespoon butter

3 medium apples (about 1 pound), peeled and sliced (about 4 cups)

¾ teaspoon ground cinnamon

½ cup sugar-free maple-flavored syrup

¼ cup water

¾ teaspoon vanilla extract

1. Melt the butter in a medium saucepan over medium-high heat. Add the apples and cinnamon and sauté for 6 to 8 minutes, or until lightly brown and just tender.

2. Mix together the syrup, water, and vanilla, and stir into the apples. Cook for 1 to 2 minutes, or until the mixture bubbles.

Perfect Pairing: Serve with a scoop of light no-sugar-added ice cream for a delicious contrast of hot and cold.

NUTRITION INFORMATION PER SERVING (½ CUP) ·················
Calories 100 | Carbohydrate 19g (Sugars 14g) | Total Fat 3g (Sat Fat 2g) | Protein 0g | Fiber 2g | Cholesterol 10mg | Sodium 55mg | Food Exchanges: ½ Fruit, ½ Carbohydrate | Carbohydrate Choices: 1 | Weight Watcher Smart Point Comparison: 2

5-Minute Blackberry Crisp

There's quick. And then there's really *quick. This fantastic crisp takes five minutes from start to finish—and that's if you dawdle. The kitchen magic use of a crushed granola bar to imitate a crunchy oven-baked topping is courtesy of my assistant, Sophia. You can even eat this guilt-free for breakfast (like I sometimes do).*

MAKES 1 SERVING

¾ cup frozen blackberries

1 tablespoon granulated
   no-calorie sweetener*

½ teaspoon cornstarch

1 bar (½ package) Nature
   Valley Oats 'n' Honey
   Granola Bar, crushed

Light whipped topping for
   garnish (optional)

1. In a small microwavable bowl, mix together the berries, sweetener, and cornstarch. Microwave for 1 minute.

2. Remove and top with the granola pieces. Serve with the whipped topping.

Chef's Tip: While fresh is best most of the time, that is not the case here. Frozen berries exude more liquid when they cook, which creates the sauce with this berry crisp. Assorted frozen berries also work great.

* See page 382 for sweetener options.

NUTRITION INFORMATION PER SERVING ·····················
Calories 155 | Carbohydrate 28g (Sugars 9g) | Total Fat 3.5g (Sat Fat 0g) | Protein 4g | Fiber 4g | Cholesterol 0mg | Sodium. 70mg | Food Exchanges: 1 Carbohydrate, ½ Fruit | Carbohydrate Choices: 1½ | Weight Watcher Smart Point Comparison: 3

Warm Cinnamon Apple Crisp

In order to get a nice golden brown topping most apple crisp recipes use lots of brown sugar. I found that using graham cracker crumbs in place of some of the flour gives the illusion of more brown sugar as it creates a satisfyingly sweet crunchy topping—everyone's favorite part of an apple crisp. This recipe reduces the amount of sugar per serving by over two tablespoons per serving, leaving this dessert simply full of apples.

MAKES 6 SERVINGS

5 cups peeled apple slices (about 2 pounds)

¾ cup granulated no-calorie sweetener, divided *

½ teaspoon plus ¾ teaspoon cinnamon, divided

1 tablespoon plus ¼ cup all-purpose flour, divided

6 tablespoons old-fashioned rolled oats

¼ cup graham cracker crumbs

¼ cup walnuts (optional)

1 tablespoon brown sugar

3 tablespoons cold margarine or butter, cut into ½-inch pieces

1. Preheat the oven to 375°F. Coat an 8-inch baking dish with cooking spray.

2. In a large bowl, mix the apples, ¼ cup of the sweetener, ½ teaspoon of the cinnamon, and 1 tablespoon of the flour.

3. In a medium bowl combine the remaining ½ cup sweetener, ¾ teaspoon cinnamon, and ¼ cup flour with the oats, graham cracker crumbs, walnuts, and brown sugar. Cut in the margarine using a pastry blender or by hand, until the mixture resembles coarse meal and butter is the size of peas.

4. Pour the apples into the prepared pan. Top with the crumble mixture.

5. Bake for 30 minutes, until the top is crisp and apples are fork tender.

> **DARE to COMPARE** ·······················
> An order of Warm Apple Crisp at the Cheesecake Factory® has 1305 calories, 28 grams of saturated fat and 193 grams of carbohydrate! The classic recipe in the *Joy of Cooking* serves up 400 calories, 16 grams of fat, and 50 grams of sugar).

* See page 382 for sweetener options.

NUTRITION INFORMATION PER SERVING (¾ CUP) ·······························
Calories 175 | Carbohydrate 29g (Sugars 15g) | Total Fat 6g (Sat Fat 2g) | Protein 3g | Fiber 3g | Cholesterol 15mg | Sodium 70mg | Food Exchanges: 1 Fruit, 1 Carbohydrate | Carbohydrate Choices: 2 | Weight Watcher Smart Point Comparison: 4

Classic Cookies and Cakes

AMAZING PEANUT BUTTER COOKIES

BETTER-FOR-YOU CHOCOLATE CHIP COOKIES

OATMEAL RAISIN COOKIES

SIMPLE MERINGUE COOKIES

CHOCOLATE ALMOND MERINGUE COOKIES

LEMON TEA CAKES

NO-BAKE PEANUT BUTTER OAT BITES

CHOCOLATE CHERRY BARS

BLUEBERRY CHEESECAKE BARS

SOFT-BATCH CHOCOLATE CHIP BAR COOKIES

QUICK 'N' HEALTHY CARROT CUPCAKES

PERFECT WHITE CUPCAKES

BLACK-AND-WHITE TWO-BITE CUPCAKES

GINGERBREAD GEMS

ONE-BOWL DARK CHOCOLATE SNACK CAKE

FRESH BANANA CAKE

PUMPKIN PECAN CAKE WITH WHIPPED CREAM CHEESE FROSTING

UNBELIEVABLE CHOCOLATE CAKE

WHIPPED CREAM CHEESE FROSTING

CHOCOLATE WHIPPED CREAM FROSTING

LEMON BUNDT CAKE

Before I became a dietitian, I was a baker. Not as a professional but just someone who loved to bake—a lot. So when I tell you that I believe everyone deserves to eat cake (and cookies and other sweet treats), I mean it. I can't even imagine a birthday celebration without a cake or Christmas without cookies. It's no surprise that my first book was a dessert book, but what is surprising (and something I would have never imagined) is that that book would focus on desserts that are low in sugar, fat, and calories. Back in my early baking days, like for most bakers, copious amounts of fat and sugar were a given.

As I advanced in my career and starting teaching classes in "light" cooking, I spent a lot of time testing the ways to reduce the fat in baked goods—without affecting the taste or texture. But when I was asked to teach a class in low-sugar desserts, it created a whole new challenge. Fortunately for me, and for the hundreds of thousands of others who have now enjoyed my books, a new sugar substitute (Splenda granulated sweetener) arrived on the market that could stand up to my taste and quality demands, and the rest, as they say, is history.

Since then I have developed hundreds of recipes—for healthy desserts low in sugar—including lots of cookies and lots of cakes. Quite honestly, I still find each new recipe a challenge, as fat and sugar perform numerous functions when baking (see Reduced-Sugar Baking Tips on page 382). Moreover, I am not satisfied until each recipe tastes just as good as the sweet treats we all know and love—which means lots of testing (and even more tasting!). As a baker at heart, I am truly thrilled to share with you the rewards of my labor. You will find cookies in this chapter for every occasion, and every taste, from cookie jar cookies like Amazing Peanut Butter Cookies (that simply couldn't be easier) and classic Oatmeal Raisin Cookies, to delectable easy-to-tote bar cookies like my Blueberry Cheesecake Bars. My moist-and-easy cakes are designed to impress, and they include Fresh Banana, Lemon Bundt, and one of my holiday favorites—Pumpkin Pecan Cake with Whipped Cream Cheese Frosting. I also urge you to try the two cake classics I am particularly proud of—the perfectly perfected Perfect White Cupcakes and my Unbelievable Chocolate Cake—the namesake recipe that launched my first cookbook.

For the Love of Sugar

Cooking—and especially baking—with less sugar can be challenging.
That's why I'm happy to say that today there are more reduced-calorie sweetening options than ever, including those that are all-natural. *Every recipe that calls for a "sweetener" was tested with each of the sweeteners below. Please use the information provided to select the sweetening choice that suits you and yours best.*

Sucralose: Recipes were tested and analyzed with generic, no-calorie, sucralose-based sweeteners. Granulated sucralose measures 1:1 for sugar. It is the measurable sweetener that delivers the best tasting-results with the least calories and carbohydrates. Generic store brands are identical to better-known brands. I buy the least expensive.

All-Natural Stevia: There are many types and brands of all-natural stevia-based sweeteners; they differ greatly, however, in sweetness, taste, and safeness. All recipes were tested with Truvia Baking Blend, made with 25% real sugar. It has 75% fewer calories and carbs when compared to sugar, and no aftertaste (as is common with stevia). The blend is twice as sweet as sugar, so you simply use half the amount of sweetener called for in any recipe. Baking time may need to be extended slightly. In the recipes in this book, the caloric difference averages less than 10 additional calories per serving when compared to using a no-calorie sweetener.

Granulated Sugar. Even when made with sugar, my reduced-fat recipes are healthier than their higher-calorie counterparts. When using regular sugar in baked goods, omit 1/4 teaspoon of baking soda per cup of sweetener and expect to increase baking time by as much as 7 to 10 minutes for cakes, 5 minutes for muffins, and 3 to 5 minutes for cookies. Check all baked goods according to the recipe's test for doneness. (Tip: The normal substitution for sugar is 1:1 for granulated no-calorie sweetener. However, you can cut one-fourth of the sugar called for in most baked goods with the only effect being slightly reduced sweetness.

	Granulated Sucralose (Any Brand)	Stevia/Sugar Baking Blend (Truvia Baking Blend)	Sugar
Equivalent Measure	1 cup	½ cup	1 cup
Calories	96	190	784
Carbohydrates	24	47	190
Recipe Adjustments	None	May need a few more minutes baking time	See "Granulated Sugar" above

Amazing Peanut Butter Cookies

Made with only a handful of ingredients—and no flour—these peanut butter cookies are almost too good to be true. The foolproof batter comes together quickly using only a large spoon and one bowl, yet the taste and texture are as good as any cookie recipe requiring far more ingredients and effort. The elimination of the flour and reduction of sugar make it easy to fit these into any carbohydrate-conscious diet.

MAKES 24 COOKIES

1 cup peanut butter

¾ cup granulated no-calorie sweetener *

¼ cup packed dark brown sugar

½ teaspoon baking soda

1 teaspoon vanilla extract

1 large egg*

* Use of a large egg, not medium or extra large, is critical for this recipe

1. Preheat the oven to 350°F.

2. Combine the peanut butter, sweetener, brown sugar, baking soda, and vanilla in a medium bowl and stir until well mixed. Add the egg and stir until dough is formed.

3. Shape the dough, by level tablespoons, into 1-inch balls. Place onto an ungreased baking sheet and flatten balls with a fork, forming a crisscross pattern on top of each cookie.

4. Bake for 9 to 11 minutes, or until cookies are golden brown on the bottom but still slightly soft in the center. Remove from the oven and let cool on the baking sheet for 5 minutes. Remove to wire racks to finish cooling.

> **DARE to COMPARE** ················
> One peanut butter cookie at Subway® contains 220 calories, including 26 grams of carbohydrate, 16 grams of sugar, and 12 grams of fat, but pales in comparison to Starbuck's version, which packs 400 calories, 19 grams of fat, 54 grams of carbohydrate, and 30 grams (a full day's worth) of added sugar in each cookie.

* See page 382 for sweetener options.

NUTRITION INFORMATION PER SERVING (1 COOKIE) ··············
Calories 80 | Carbohydrate 6g (Sugars 4g) | Total Fat 5g (Sat Fat 1g) | Protein 4g | Fiber 1g | Cholesterol 10mg
Sodium 120mg | Food Exchanges: ½ Carbohydrate, 1 Fat | Carbohydrate Choices: ½ | Weight Watcher Smart Point Comparison:3

Better-For-You Chocolate Chip Cookies

What's life without homemade chocolate chip cookies? This recipe was first featured in my book Marlene Koch's 375 Sensational Recipes, and is simply too good not to share. Made with classic ingredients—real butter, sugar, chocolate chips, and even nuts—these chocolate chippers are better for you and taste far better than store-bought!

MAKES 30 COOKIES

1 cup all-purpose flour

½ cup white whole wheat or whole wheat pastry flour

¾ teaspoon baking soda

½ cup butter, softened

¼ cup packed dark brown sugar

¼ cup granulated sugar

¼ cup granulated no-calorie sweetener*

1½ teaspoons vanilla extract

1 large egg

½ cup mini chocolate chips

¼ cup chopped pecans or walnuts

1. Preheat the oven to 375°F. Spray a cookie sheet with non-stick cooking spray.

2. In a small bowl, combine the all-purpose flour, white whole wheat flour, and baking soda.

3. In a large bowl, with an electric mixer, beat the butter, sugars, and sweetener until very light and creamy. Beat in the vanilla and egg. Add the flour mixture and beat just until blended. Stir in the chocolate chips and nuts.

4. Drop the dough by level tablespoons onto a baking sheet 2 inches apart. Flatten the cookies by pressing down on the dough with a spatula or the bottom of a glass.

5. Bake for 7 to 9 minutes, or until lightly browned and set. Cool on the baking sheet until firm. Remove to wire racks to finish cooling.

* See page 382 for sweetener options.

NUTRITION INFORMATION PER SERVING (1 COOKIE)
Calories 80 | Carbohydrate 10g (Sugars 4g) | Total Fat 4.5g (Sat Fat1g) | Protein 1g | Fiber 1g | Cholesterol 20mg | Sodium 75mg | Food Exchanges: ½ Carbohydrate, 1 Fat | Carbohydrate Choices: ½ | Weight Watcher Smart Point Comparison: 3

Oatmeal Raisin Cookies

There's nothing better than coming home to the sweet scent of cinnamon wafting from freshly baked oatmeal cookies. I guarantee that even the most discerning sweet tooth will not detect that I have made this cookie-jar favorite more wholesome with the addition of white whole wheat flour and applesauce.

MAKES 20 COOKIES

½ cup white whole wheat flour

¼ cup all-purpose flour

1½ cups old-fashioned rolled oats

⅓ cup raisins, roughly chopped

½ teaspoon baking soda

1 teaspoon ground cinnamon

¼ teaspoon ground nutmeg

⅓ cup margarine or butter, softened

6 tablespoons packed dark brown sugar

2 large egg whites

2 tablespoons unsweetened applesauce

½ teaspoon vanilla extract

6 tablespoons granulated no-calorie sweetener*

1. Preheat the oven to 350°F. Spray a baking sheet with cooking spray.

2. In a small bowl, combine the flour, oats, raisins, baking soda, cinnamon, and nutmeg and stir until well mixed.

3. In a large bowl, with an electric mixer, beat the butter and brown sugar until light and creamy. Beat in the egg whites, applesauce, vanilla, and sweetener. (The mixture will not get creamy.) Stir in the flour mixture.

4. Drop the dough by level tablespoons onto a baking sheet, 2 inches apart. Flatten the cookies by pressing down on the dough with a spatula or the bottom of a glass.

5. Bake for 7 to 9 minutes, or until light brown on top. Transfer the cookies to a wire rack to cool.

Or try this: For *Cranberry Orange Oatmeal Cookies*, substitute ⅓ cup chopped dried cranberries for the raisins and add 1 teaspoon orange zest to the batter. For Oatmeal Chocolate Chip Cookies, eliminate the nutmeg and substitute ⅓ cup mini chocolate chips for the raisins (adds ½ gram of fat and 5 calories per cookie).

* See page 382 for sweetener options.

NUTRITION INFORMATION PER SERVING (1 COOKIE)
Calories 75 | Carbohydrate 12g (Sugars 4g) | Total Fat 2g (Sat Fat 0g) | Protein 2g | Fiber 1g | Cholesterol 0mg
Sodium 65mg | Food Exchanges: 1 Starch | Carbohydrate Choices: 1 | Weight Watcher Smart Point Comparison: 3

Simple Meringue Cookies

Meringue cookies are terrific! Requiring just a few ingredients, and no flour, meringue cookies are among the lowest calorie and carbohydrate cookies you can make. They are also one of the most versatile as they can be flavored many ways. The vanilla can be replaced with extracts such as peppermint, orange, or lemon—extracts or flavorings that contain no oil are best—or a few tablespoons of crushed sugar-free peppermint can be added for a fun-filled holiday cookie.

MAKES 24 COOKIES

4 large egg whites
¼ teaspoon cream of tartar
¾ cup granulated sugar
½ teaspoon vanilla extract

1. Preheat the oven to 225°F. Line 2 baking sheets with parchment paper or silicone baking mats.

2. Place egg whites, cream of tartar, and sugar in a metal mixing bowl and place over simmering water. Heat for 2 to 3 minutes or until the sugar dissolves.

3. Remove the bowl from the heat and beat the egg whites with an electric mixer on high for 5 minutes or until stiff peaks form. Stir in the vanilla.

4. Using a tablespoon, spoon the batter onto cookie sheets, mounding meringue high in the center and forming a peaked "kiss" top. Bake for 45 minutes, or until meringues feel firm to the touch and can gently be lifted from parchment.

5. Turn off the oven and allow the meringues to dry in oven for 1 additional hour. Store in an airtight container.

Marlene Says: To ensure the egg whites reach maximum volume, keep them at room temperature and make sure the mixing bowl and beaters are clean and free of grease. It is easier to separate eggs when they are cold, but once you do that, cover the egg whites and let them come to room temperature before using (about 30 minutes).

NUTRITION INFORMATION PER SERVING (2 COOKIES)
Calories 50 | Carbohydrate 12g (Sugars 6g) | Total Fat 0g (Sat Fat 0g) | Protein .5g | Fiber 0g | Cholesterol 0mg | Sodium 20mg | Food Exchanges: ½ Carbohydrate | Carbohydrate Choices: ½ | Weight Watcher Smart Point Comparison: 2

Chocolate Almond Meringue Cookies

The winning combination of almond and chocolate dresses up these delectable meringues. Because they are made with a touch less sugar, these meringues will flatten while they bake, creating a more traditional cookie appearance. Once they are cool, be sure to store in an airtight container to keep them crisp.

MAKES 24 COOKIES

4 large egg whites

¼ teaspoon cream of tartar

½ cup granulated sugar

¼ teaspoon almond extract

2 ounces semisweet chocolate, finely chopped

1. Preheat the oven to 225°F. Line 2 baking sheets with parchment paper or silicone baking mats.

2. Place egg whites, cream of tartar, and sugar in a metal mixing bowl and place over simmering water. Heat for 2 to 3 minutes or until the sugar dissolves.

3. Remove the bowl from the heat and beat the egg whites with an electric mixer on high for 5 minutes or until stiff peaks form. Using a spatula, gently fold in the almond extract and chocolate.

4. Using a tablespoon, spoon the batter onto the baking sheet. Gently smooth the tops to form flat discs (about 2 inches in diameter). Bake for 1 hour, or until the meringues feel firm to the touch and can gently be lifted from the parchment.

5. Turn off the oven and allow meringues to dry in oven for 1 additional hour. Store in an airtight container.

NUTRITION INFORMATION PER SERVING (2 COOKIES)
Calories 60 | Carbohydrate 12g (Sugars 12g) | Total Fat 1g (Sat Fat 0g) | Protein 2g | Fiber 0g | Cholesterol 0mg | Sodium 20mg | Food Exchanges: 1 Carbohydrate | Carbohydrate Choices: 1 | Weight Watcher Smart Point Comparison: 3

Lemon Tea Cakes

These are a lemon lover's delight. The secret to these delicately flavored, tender cake-like cookies is the addition of lemon extract, which imparts a lovely, but never sour, lemon flavor. I guarantee that your guests will be impressed because these light-as-air cookies truly taste and look like they belong on a tea cart in an elegant restaurant.

MAKES 24 COOKIES

1½ cups cake flour

1½ teaspoons baking powder

½ cup granulated no-calorie sweetener *

¼ cup margarine or butter, softened

¼ cup light tub-style cream cheese

¼ cup powdered sugar

1 large egg

1 tablespoon lemon juice

1 teaspoon lemon extract

1 tablespoon lemon zest (from 1 large lemon)

1 tablespoon powdered sugar

1. Preheat the oven to 350°F. Coat a cookie sheet with non-stick baking spray.

2. In a medium bowl, stir together the cake flour, baking powder, and sweetener.

3. In a separate large bowl, with an electric mixer, beat the margarine, cream cheese, and ¼ cup powdered sugar until light and fluffy. Add the egg, lemon juice, extract, and zest and beat until fully incorporated. Add the flour mixture and beat just until combined.

4. Roll the dough, by level tablespoons, into 1-inch balls and place on the prepared cookie sheet. Flatten the cookies by pressing down on the dough with a spatula or the bottom of a glass.

5. Bake for 6 to 7 minutes, or until bottoms of cookies are lightly browned. Transfer to a wire rack to cool.

6. Just prior to serving, dust the cookies with powdered sugar.

Marlene Says: A very small strainer or sieve works well for dusting cookies, muffins, and cakes with powdered sugar.

* See page 382 for sweetener options.

NUTRITION INFORMATION PER SERVING (1 COOKIE) ·······················
Calories 65 | Carbohydrate 9g (Sugars 1.5g) | Total Fat 2.5g (Sat Fat 1.5g) | Protein 1g | Fiber 0g | Cholesterol 15mg | Sodium 15mg | Food Exchanges: ½ Carbohydrate | Carbohydrate Choices: ½ | Weight Watcher Smart Point Comparison: 2

No-Bake Peanut Butter Oat Bites

These candy-like no-bake peanut butter cookies are perfect when you want to make a sweet treat—quickly! Wholesome rolled oats pair with peanut butter to produce a creamy, fudgelike nibbler that is ready in minutes. They also make a nice gift when set into individual candy wrappers and placed in a fancy box.

MAKES 22 BITES

3 tablespoons packed light brown sugar

½ cup granulated no-calorie sweetener*

2 tablespoons butter or margarine

¼ cup low-fat milk

⅓ cup peanut butter

½ teaspoon vanilla extract

1¾ cups rolled quick oats

1. In a small saucepan over medium-high heat, whisk together the brown sugar, sweetener, butter, milk, and peanut butter. Boil the mixture for 1 minute.

2. Remove the mixture from the heat and stir in the vanilla and oats until thoroughly coated.

3. Drop dough using one tablespoon per cookie onto a baking sheet lined with parchment paper. Refrigerate for at least 20 minutes, or until firm.

* See page 382 for sweetener options.

NUTRITION INFORMATION PER SERVING (1 COOKIE)
Calories 70 | Carbohydrate 9g (Sugars 4g) | Total Fat 3g (Sat Fat 1g) | Protein 2g | Fiber 1g | Cholesterol 5mg | Sodium 0mg | Food Exchanges: ½ Starch, ½ Fat | Carbohydrate Choices: ½ | Weight Watcher Smart Point Comparison: 3

Chocolate Cherry Bars

Looking for a holiday cookie that's easy, delicious, and yet guilt-free? These cakelike dark rich chocolate bars draped with a beautiful cherry topping will fill the bill. To cut them neatly, wait until the bars are fully cooled and use a sharp knife that has been dipped in water. Use a flat spatula to remove them from the pan. These bars are also terrific served with a dollop of light whipped topping.

MAKES 12 BARS

¼ cup margarine or butter

¼ cup prune purée (or small jar baby food prunes)

¼ cup packed dark brown sugar

¾ cup granulated no-calorie sweetener*

1 large egg, beaten

1½ teaspoons vanilla extract

⅔ cup all-purpose flour

⅓ cup tablespoons cocoa powder

½ teaspoon baking powder

¼ teaspoon baking soda

1 cup light cherry pie filling

1. Preheat the oven to 325°F. Coat an 8 x 8-inch pan with non-stick baking spray.

2. In a medium glass bowl, heat the butter in the microwave for 30 seconds, or until melted.

3. Add the prune purée, brown sugar, sweetener, egg, and vanilla and stir until smooth.

4. Sift in the flour, cocoa powder, baking powder, and baking soda. Mix just until combined. Do not overmix. Spoon the batter into the prepared pan and smooth.

5. Bake for 18 to 20 minutes, or until a toothpick inserted into the center comes out clean. Pour cherry pie filling over chocolate bars and cool.

Marlene Says: Cherries have been named a "super-food." Tart cherries are among the fruits with the highest levels of disease-fighting antioxidants. Researchers have also linked cherries to lowering weight and reducing the risk for heart disease and diabetes.

* See page 382 for sweetener options.

NUTRITION INFORMATION PER SERVING (1 BAR)
Calories 80 | Carbohydrate 11g (Sugars 4g) | Total Fat 4g (Sat Fat 2g) | Protein 1g | Fiber 1g | Cholesterol 20mg | Sodium 45mg | Food Exchanges: 1 Starch | Carbohydrate Choices: 1 | Weight Watcher Smart Point Comparison: 3

Blueberry Cheesecake Bars

Store-bought piecrusts are usually packed with extra calories and fat that fail to deliver anything extra when it comes to taste. By comparison, this buttery-tasting, better-for-you crust is delicious and versatile and can be used in any recipe requiring either a shortbread or graham cracker crust. Here I've topped it with luscious cheesecake studded with fresh blueberries. Yum!

MAKES 15 BARS

CRUST

½ cup all-purpose flour

½ cup crushed graham cracker crumbs

3 tablespoons granulated no-calorie sweetener*

3 tablespoons butter or margarine

FILLING

8 ounces tub-style light cream cheese

½ cup (4 ounces) nonfat cream cheese, at room temperature

⅔ cup granulated no-calorie sweetener*

1 large egg

1 large egg white

¾ teaspoon vanilla extract

¼ teaspoon almond extract

1 cup fresh blueberries

1. Preheat the oven to 325°F. Coat an 8 x 8-inch square pan with cooking spray.

2. To make the crust, mix the flour, graham cracker crumbs, and sweetener together in a medium bowl.

3. Cut in the butter with a pastry blender or by hand until the mixture resembles fine crumbs. Pour the crust mixture onto the bottom of the prepared pan and press into an even layer. Bake the crust for 5 minutes, and then set aside.

4. While the crust is baking, make the filling. Beat the cream cheeses and sweetener together in a medium bowl with an electric mixer. Beat in the egg, egg white, and extracts until mixture is just smooth. Do not overmix. Gently fold in the blueberries.

5. Pour the filling onto the crust and spread evenly. Bake for 23 to 25 minutes, or until the edges are firm and the center is set but still slightly soft.

6. Cool at room temperature for 20 minutes, then refrigerate for at least 2 hours before cutting into bars.

* See page 382 for sweetener options.

NUTRITION INFORMATION PER SERVING (1 BAR) ···
Calories 100 | Carbohydrate 8g (Sugars 2g) | Total Fat 5g (Sat Fat 3g) | Protein 4g | Fiber 0g | Cholesterol 25mg | Sodium 130mg | Food Exchanges: ½ Starch, 1 Fat | Carbohydrate Choices: ½ | Weight Watcher Smart Point Comparison: 4

Soft-Batch Chocolate Chip Bar Cookies

Bar cookies, a cross between a cookie and a cake, are enjoyed by everyone. I make them when I'm looking to save time (no dropping, rolling, or shaping) or when I need a dessert I can easily tote. I knew this recipe was a winner when my son Stephen came back for seconds, thirds, and more until they were all gone. Butterscotch or peanut butter chips can also be substituted and taste just as good.

MAKES 24 COOKIES

6 tablespoons margarine or butter, softened

⅓ cup dark brown sugar

1 large egg

½ cup granulated no-calorie sweetener*

¼ cup prune purée (or 2-ounce jar baby food prunes)

1½ teaspoons vanilla extract

1½ cups all-purpose flour

1 teaspoon baking soda

⅔ cup miniature semisweet chocolate chips

1. Preheat the oven to 350°F. Coat a 13 x 9-inch baking pan with nonstick baking spray.

2. In a large bowl, with an electric mixer, beat the butter and brown sugar together until light and fluffy. Add the egg, sweetener, prune, and vanilla and beat until smooth.

3. In a separate medium bowl, whisk together the flour and baking soda. Add the flour mixture to the wet ingredients and stir together by hand until combined. Stir in the chocolate chips.

4. Spread the mixture into the prepared baking pan. Bake for 12 to 13 minutes, or until light brown and center feels firm to the touch.

Marlene Says: These better-for-you bars have one-half the fat and sugar of the original recipe. To make them even more wholesome, substitute one-half the all-purpose flour with white whole wheat flour.

* See page 382 for sweetener options.

NUTRITION INFORMATION PER SERVING (1 BAR)
Calories 100 | Carbohydrate 12g (Sugars 6g) | Total Fat 4.5g (Sat Fat 2.5g) | Protein 2g | Fiber 0g | Cholesterol 20mg | Sodium 60mg | Food Exchanges: 1 Carbohydrate, 1 Fat | Carbohydrate Choices: 1 | Weight Watcher Smart Point Comparison: 4

Quick 'n' Healthy Carrot Cupcakes

While anything with carrots in its name may sound healthy, carrot cakes are notoriously high in sugar, fat, and calories. My carrot cupcakes have all the flavor of traditional carrot cake, but with less than half the calories and a fraction of the added sugar; they fit easily into any diet. Don't let the long list of ingredients put you off; these cupcakes can be made in minutes. Serve dusted with powdered sugar, or to make them truly special, top with the Whipped Cream Cheese Frosting on page 406.

MAKES 12 CUPCAKES

1½ cups white whole wheat flour

1 teaspoon baking soda

1 teaspoon baking powder

1½ teaspoons ground cinnamon

½ teaspoon ground nutmeg

¼ cup chopped walnuts

1¼ cups finely shredded carrots

1 large egg

1 large egg white

¼ cup canola oil

¼ cup prune purée (or 2½-ounce jar baby food prunes)

1 teaspoon vanilla extract

⅔ cup buttermilk

¼ cup packed brown sugar

⅔ cup granulated no-calorie sweetener*

1 tablespoon powdered sugar (optional)

1. Preheat the oven to 350°F. Lightly spray a 12-muffin tin with nonstick baking spray (paper or foil liners may be added before spraying).

2. In a large bowl, combine the flour, baking soda, baking powder, cinnamon, nutmeg, walnuts, and carrots.

3. In a medium bowl, whisk together the egg, egg white, oil, prune purée, vanilla, buttermilk, brown sugar, and sweetener. Pour the oil mixture into the flour mixture and stir until combined. Spoon the batter into muffin tins, filling each cup two-thirds full.

4. Bake for 16 to 18 minutes, or until the center of the cupcake springs back when lightly touched. Remove from the oven. If desired, dust the muffins with powdered sugar just prior to serving.

> **DARE to COMPARE** ·····················
> A piece of Carrot Cake at Denny's® will set you back 799 calories. It's packed not only with carrots but with 45 grams of fat (with 13 grams of them saturated) and 99 grams of carbohydrate, (including the equivalent of 19 teaspoons of sugar).

* See page 382 for sweetener options.

NUTRITION INFORMATION PER SERVING (1 CUPCAKE) ·······················
Calories 150 | Carbohydrate 20g (Sugars 6g) | Total Fat 7g (Sat Fat .5g) | Protein 3g | Fiber 2g | Cholesterol 20mg | Sodium 160mg | Food Exchanges: 1 Carbohydrate, 1 Fat | Carbohydrate Choices: 1 | Weight Watcher Smart Point Comparison: 5

Perfect White Cupcakes

I don't often refer to a recipe as "perfect," but there is no other way to describe this cupcake. The versatility of a classic white cupcake is timeless, and this perfectly white little cake is exceptional. I usually serve them simply dusted with a touch of powdered sugar while they are still warm, but the possibilities are endless. Topping them with the Whipped Cream Cheese Frosting (page 406) makes them heavenly, light cherry pie filling makes them beautiful, and a dollop of light whipped topping crowned with a fresh strawberry slice is pure perfection. If you are a chocolate lover, try the Black-and-White Two-Bite Cupcakes (page 398), or top these cupcakes with the same Dark Fudge Frosting.

MAKES 12 CUPCAKES

1¾ cups cake flour

2 teaspoons baking powder

½ teaspoon baking soda

⅓ cup butter or margarine

⅓ cup granulated sugar

⅓ cup granulated no-calorie sweetener* (or 8 packets)

3 large egg whites

1 teaspoon vanilla extract

½ teaspoon almond extract

⅔ cup low-fat milk

1. Preheat the oven to 325°F. Lightly spray a 12- muffin tin with nonstick baking spray (paper or foil liners may be added before spraying).

2. In a medium bowl, sift together the flour, baking powder, and baking soda. Set aside.

3. In a large bowl, with an electric mixer, cream the butter and sugar until fluffy. Add the sweetener, egg whites, and extracts, and continue mixing until all ingredients are incorporated.

4. Stir in one-third of the flour mixture into the wet mixture. Stir in one-third of the milk. Repeat until all ingredients are combined. *Do not overmix.*

5. Scoop the batter into the muffin cups (about ¼ cup each). Bake for 15 to 17 minutes, until the center springs back when touched or a toothpick comes out clean.

* See page 382 for sweetener options.

NUTRITION INFORMATION PER SERVING (1 CUPCAKE)
Calories 130 | Carbohydrate 18g (Sugars 7g) | Total Fat 4g (Sat Fat 3.5g) | Protein 3g | Fiber 0g | Cholesterol 15mg | Sodium 160mg | Food Exchanges: 1 Carbohydrate, 1 Fat | Carbohydrate Choices: 1 | Weight Watcher Smart Point Comparison: 5

Black-and-White Two-Bite Cupcakes

A great way to satisfy your sweet tooth while keeping your diet in check is to enjoy dessert in smaller portions. These black and white mini-cupcakes are the perfect size to satisfy any sugar craving. Topped with a smear of dark fudge frosting, these are a real treat at a cost of only 115 calories.

MAKES 24 CUPCAKES

1 recipe Perfect White Cupcake batter (page 397)

DARK FUDGE FROSTING

1½ ounces unsweetened baking chocolate

1 tablespoon butter

½ cup cocoa powder, preferably Dutch process

⅔ cup granulated no-calorie sweetener*

1 cup powdered sugar

⅓ cup light sour cream

¼ teaspoon vanilla

2 to 3 teaspoons low-fat milk

1. Preheat the oven to 350°F. Lightly spray a 24 mini-muffin tin with nonstick baking spray.

2. Spoon approximately 2 tablespoons of the cake batter into each muffin cup, filling two-thirds full.

3. Bake for 8 to 10 minutes, or until the center of the cupcake springs back when touched. Remove from the oven and set on a baking rack to cool.

4. While the cupcakes are cooling, make the frosting. Place the baking chocolate and butter in a medium microwavable bowl and microwave for 1 minute. Remove from the microwave and stir. (Add additional time if needed to completely melt the chocolate.)

5. Let cool slightly; then add the cocoa powder and sweetener and beat with an electric mixer until smooth. Add the powdered sugar, sour cream, and vanilla and continue to beat for one minute or until thick and smooth. Add 1 teaspoon of milk at a time if needed for desired consistency.

6. Coat each cooled cupcake with 1 tablespoon frosting.

* See page 382 for sweetener options.

NUTRITION INFORMATION PER SERVING (1 CUPCAKE)
Calories 115 | Carbohydrate17g (Sugars 8g) | Total Fat 4g (Sat Fat 2.5g) | Protein 2g | Fiber 0g | Cholesterol 25mg | Sodium 80mg | Food Exchanges: 1 Carbohydrate, 1 Fat | Carbohydrate Choices: 1 | Weight Watcher Smart Point Comparison: 5

Gingerbread Gems

These wholesome gingerbread gems are made extra special with minced crystallized ginger. Packed with spices and the richness of molasses, they make great eating all year long. Serve with a cold glass of low-fat milk for a perfect combination.

MAKES 18 GEMS

¾ cup all-purpose flour

¾ cup white whole wheat flour

½ cup granulated no-calorie sweetener*

1 teaspoon baking powder

¾ teaspoon baking soda

¾ teaspoon ground cinnamon

¾ teaspoon ground ginger

¼ teaspoon ground cloves

1 large egg

½ cup low-fat milk

¼ cup unsweetened apple-sauce

3 tablespoons molasses

2 tablespoons vegetable oil

3 tablespoons minced crystal-lized ginger

1. Preheat the oven to 350°F. Coat an 18 mini-muffin tin with nonstick baking spray.

2. In a medium bowl, mix together flours, sweetener, baking powder, baking soda, cinnamon, ginger, and cloves.

3. In a large bowl, beat the egg. Add the milk, applesauce, molasses, oil, and crystallized ginger.

4. Add the dry ingredients to the wet mixture and stir just until combined. *Do not overmix.* Portion rounded tablespoon-fuls of batter into the cups.

5. Bake 15 minutes. Gems are done when center springs back when touched, or a toothpick comes out clean.

Marlene Says: Unlike most refined sweeteners that contain only empty calories, molasses is a good source of iron, potassium, copper, and calcium. Blackstrap molasses is the least refined variety and boasts the deepest flavor and the most nutrients.

* See page 382 for sweetener options.

NUTRITION INFORMATION PER SERVING (1 GEM)
Calories 70 | Carbohydrate 12g (Sugars 3g) | Total Fat 2g (Sat Fat 0g) | Protein 2g | Fiber 1g | Cholesterol 10mg | Sodium 90mg | Food Exchanges: 1 Starch | Carbohydrate Choices: 1 | Weight Watcher Smart Point Comparison: 2

One-Bowl Dark Chocolate Snack Cake

Who can live without chocolate cake? Not me. And this recipe proves that you don't have to either. This is one sweet afternoon snack you can actually feel good about eating. One bowl and ten minutes is all it takes to get this chocolaty snack cake into the oven. It's nice and moist, but sturdy enough to be eaten out of hand.

MAKES 9 SERVINGS

3 tablespoons canola oil

½ cup prune purée (or 4-ounce jar baby food prunes)

1½ teaspoons vanilla extract

3 tablespoons packed dark brown sugar

¾ cup granulated no-calorie sweetener *

1 cup plus 2 tablespoons buttermilk

1 cup all-purpose flour

½ cup cocoa powder

1½ teaspoons baking powder

1 teaspoon baking soda

2 teaspoons powdered sugar (optional)

1. Preheat the oven to 325°F. Spray an 8 x 8-inch baking pan with nonstick baking spray.

2. In a large bowl, whisk together the oil, prune purée, vanilla, brown sugar, sweetener, and buttermilk.

3. Sift the flour, cocoa powder, baking powder, and baking soda into the wet ingredients. Whisk until smooth.

4. Pour the batter into the prepared cake pan and smooth the top. Bake for 18 to 20 minutes, until the center springs back when touched, or a toothpick inserted in the center comes out clean.

5. Before serving, dust with powdered sugar, if desired.

Family Focus: Get the kids into the kitchen! Learning cooking skills to create healthy meals teaches kids how to be fit for the rest of their lives. Starting with chocolate cake makes it extra fun.

NUTRITION INFORMATION PER SERVING (1 PIECE)
Calories 190 | Carbohydrate 27g (Sugars 7g) | Total Fat 6g (Sat Fat 1.5g) | Protein 6g | Fiber 3g | Cholesterol 0mg | Sodium 210mg | Food Exchanges: 1½ Carbohydrate, 1 Fat | Carbohydrate Choices: 1½ | Weight Watcher Smart Point Comparison: 6

Fresh Banana Cake

Overripe bananas impart the best flavor to this wonderfully moist cake. You can always keep a supply on hand by mashing overripe bananas and freezing them in a sealed container or freezer bag where they will keep for up to two months. Thaw before using.

MAKES 9 SERVINGS

½ cup cake flour

½ cup white whole wheat flour

6 tablespoons granulated no-calorie sweetener*

¾ teaspoon baking powder

½ teaspoon baking soda

⅔ cup mashed banana

3 tablespoons vegetable oil

⅓ cup buttermilk

1 large egg

1½ teaspoons vanilla extract

1. Preheat the oven to 350°F. Coat an 8 x 8-inch baking pan with nonstick baking spray.

2. In a medium bowl, sift together the flours, sweetener, baking powder, and baking soda.

3. In a large bowl, whisk together the mashed banana, oil, buttermilk, egg, and vanilla.

4. Pour the dry ingredients into the wet ingredients and stir until just combined. *Do not overmix.*

5. Pour the batter into the prepared baking pan and smooth. Bake for 18 to 20 minutes, until the center of the cake springs back when touched, or a toothpick inserted into the center comes out clean. Set the cake on a wire rack to cool.

* See page 382 for sweetener options.

NUTRITION INFORMATION PER SERVING (1 PIECE)
Calories 120 | Carbohydrate 15g (Sugars 4g) | Total Fat 5g (Sat Fat .5g) | Protein 2g | Fiber 1g | Cholesterol 25mg | Sodium 190mg | Food Exchanges: 1 Carbohydrate, 1 Fat | Carbohydrate Choices: 1 | Weight Watcher Smart Point Comparison: 4

Pumpkin Pecan Cake with Whipped Cream Cheese Frosting

This is a guaranteed crowd pleaser. Tender and light and adorned with fluffy cream cheese frosting, this spicy cake also packs two grams of fiber and a nice dose of vitamin A. No one will ever guess that something this good is so healthy.

MAKES 16 SERVINGS

2 large eggs

2 large egg whites

⅓ cup packed dark brown sugar

1 cup granulated no-calorie sweetener*

1 (15-ounce) can pumpkin purée

½ cup canola oil

¼ cup unsweetened applesauce

1 cup all-purpose flour

1 cup white whole wheat flour

½ cup chopped pecans

1½ teaspoons baking soda

1½ teaspoons baking powder

2 teaspoons ground cinnamon

1 teaspoon ground ginger

½ teaspoon ground nutmeg

¼ teaspoon ground cloves

1 recipe Whipped Cream Cheese Frosting (page 406)

1. Preheat the oven to 350°F. Coat a 13 x 9-inch baking pan with nonstick baking spray.

2. In a large mixing bowl, with an electric mixer, beat together the eggs, egg whites, brown sugar, and sweetener for 3 to 4 minutes, or until tripled in volume. With a large wooden spoon, mix in the pumpkin, oil, and applesauce.

3. Sift the flours, pecans, baking soda, baking powder, and spices into the bowl. Stir to combine but *do not overmix*. Spoon the batter into the prepared baking pan and smooth.

4. Bake for 20 to 25 minutes, or until the center of the cake springs back when lightly touched, or a toothpick inserted into the center comes out clean.

5. When fully cooled, spread the frosting on top.

Marlene Says: Toasting pecans keeps them crunchy and enhances their flavor. To toast, place pecans in a pie pan or on an ungreased baking sheet and bake at 325°F for 5 to 8 minutes, or until lightly browned and fragrant.

* See page 382 for sweetener options.

NUTRITION INFORMATION PER SERVING (1 PIECE)
Calories 245 | Carbohydrate 27g (Sugars 10g) | Total Fat 12g (Sat Fat 2g) | Protein 6g | Fiber 2g | Cholesterol 25mg | Sodium 270mg | Food Exchanges: 2 Carbohydrates | Carbohydrate Choices: 2 | Weight Watcher Smart Point Comparison:8

Unbelievable Chocolate Cake

I believe everyone deserves chocolate cake. This signature recipe comes from my very first cookbook, and to this day it is still one of my most beloved recipes. Why? Because in only 10 minutes, using a single bowl and a whisk, I can whip up a light and tender dark chocolate cake that everyone can enjoy no matter what their diet! This recipe can be doubled and baked as a 13 x 9-inch sheet cake (bake for 28 to 30 minutes) or as two 9-inch rounds (bake for 18 to 20 minutes) to create a layer cake. Fill and frost with Chocolate Whipped Cream Frosting (page 407).

MAKES 9 SERVINGS

¼ cup canola oil

1 large egg

1 teaspoon vanilla extract

¼ cup packed dark brown sugar

1 cup granulated no-calorie sweetener*

1 cup buttermilk

1¼ cups cake flour

1 teaspoon baking powder

1 teaspoon baking soda

¼ cup cocoa powder, preferably Dutch processed

¼ cup hot water

1. Preheat the oven to 350°F. Coat an 8 x 8-inch baking pan with nonstick baking spray.

2. In a large bowl, whisk together the oil and egg until the mixture is frothy and thick.

3. Add the vanilla, brown sugar, and sweetener. Beat with a whisk for 2 more minutes until the mixture is thick and smooth. Add the buttermilk and whisk until smooth.

4. Sift the flour, baking powder, baking soda, and cocoa powder and stir into the wet ingredients. Whisk vigorously for 1 to 2 minutes, or until the batter is smooth. Pour the hot water into the batter and whisk one more time until the batter is again nice and smooth. The batter will be thin.

5. Pour the batter into the prepared pan and tap the pan on the counter to level the surface and to help remove any bubbles.

6. Bake for 18 to 20 minutes, until the center springs back when touched or a toothpick inserted into the center comes out clean. Do not overbake. Cool the cake on a wire rack.

* See page 382 for sweetener options.

NUTRITION INFORMATION PER SERVING (1 PIECE) ·······················
Calories 160 | Carbohydrate 22g (Sugars 8g) | Total Fat 7g (Sat Fat 1g) | Protein 3g | Fiber 1g | Cholesterol 25mg | Sodium 180mg | Food Exchanges: 1½ Carbohydrate, 1 Fat | Carbohydrate Choices: 1½ | Weight Watcher Smart Point Comparison: 6

Whipped Cream Cheese Frosting

Because frostings are comprised of essentially two ingredients—sugar and fat—it's almost impossible to find one that's not high in one or the other. This light and fluffy frosting is a rare exception. One of my most prized recipes; it manages to keep the sugar, fat, and calories in check and still tastes absolutely delicious.

MAKES 2¼ CUPS

8 ounces tub-style light cream cheese

4 ounces nonfat cream cheese

¼ cup granulated no-calorie sweetener*

1 cup light whipped topping

1. In a small mixing bowl, beat the cream cheeses with an electric mixer until smooth. Add the sweetener and beat for 1 minute longer.

2. On slow speed, beat in the whipped topping and beat briefly, just until combined and fluffy.

* See page 382 for sweetener options.

NUTRITION INFORMATION PER SERVING (2 TABLESPOONS)
Calories 40 | Carbohydrate 3g (Sugar 1g) | Total Fat 2g (Sat Fat 1.5g) | Protein 2g | Fiber 0g | Cholesterol 0mg | Sodium 80mg | Food Exchange: 1 Fat | Carbohydrate Choice: 0 | Weight Watcher Smart Point Comparison: 1

Chocolate Whipped Cream Frosting

This frosting is for chocolate lovers. With a bit less cream cheese and a bit more whipped topping than my Whipped Cream Cheese Frosting, it's incredibly light and creamy, but tastes just as decadent. It's a fantastic topper for any of the cakes, but my assistant swears it's best right out of the bowl!

MAKES 2 CUPS

4 ounces tub-style light cream cheese

¼ cup cocoa powder

⅓ cup granulated no-calorie sweetener*

2 cups light whipped topping, divided

1. In a small mixing bowl, beat the cream cheese, cocoa powder, and sweetener with an electric mixer until well blended.

2. On slow speed, beat in 1 cup of the whipped topping to incorporate. Add the remaining 1 cup and beat on low very briefly until combined and fluffy.

> **DARE to COMPARE**
> Two tablespoons of Pillsbury ready-to-use reduced-sugar frosting has 100 calories, 17 grams of carbohydrate, and 9 grams of sugar.

* See page 382 for sweetener options.

NUTRITION INFORMATION PER SERVING (2 TABLESPOONS)
Calories 45 | Carbohydrate 4g (Sugar 1g) | Total Fat 2g (Sat Fat 1.5g) | Protein 2g | Fiber 0g | Cholesterol 0mg | Sodium 80mg | Food Exchange: 1 Fat | Carbohydrate Choice: 0 | Weight Watcher Smart Point Comparison: 1

Lemon Bundt Cake

Poor Bundt cakes. For too long, rich, dense Bundt cakes have been literally off the table for anyone counting calories (or fat, carbohydrates, or sugar), but this luscious lemon Bundt cake changes all that. While preserving the rich taste of a traditional lemon Bundt cake, this lighter version has only a fraction of the fat and calories and sugar. Make this anytime you feel the need to splurge or for any special occasion. It only tastes like it's bad for you!

MAKES 12 SERVINGS

2¼ cups cake flour

1 teaspoon baking powder

¾ teaspoon baking soda

⅛ teaspoon salt

¾ cup granulated no-calorie sweetener

6 tablespoons butter or margarine

½ cup granulated sugar

2 large eggs

2 large egg whites

½ teaspoon lemon extract

1 cup plain nonfat Greek yogurt or sour cream

1 tablespoon powdered sugar (optional)

1. Preheat the oven to 350°F. Coat a 12-cup Bundt pan with nonstick baking spray.

2. In a medium bowl, stir together the flour, baking powder, baking soda, salt, and sweetener.

3. In a large bowl, with an electric mixer, beat the butter and sugar until very light and fluffy (about 4 minutes). Add the eggs and egg whites one at a time and beat until creamy.

4. Stir in ½ of the flour mixture by hand into the creamed mixture and then ½ of the yogurt. Repeat, gently mixing each time just to incorporate the flour and yogurt mixtures.

5. Bake for 30 minutes. Cake is done when the center springs back when touched, or a toothpick comes out clean. Dust with powdered sugar before serving if desired.

DARE to COMPARE.....................................

One piece of traditional Glazed Lemon Bundt cake has over 400 calories, 20 grams of fat, and 60 grams of carbohydrate per piece (with 30 grams of sugar!).

NUTRITION INFORMATION PER SERVING (1 PIECE)
Calories 210 | Carbohydrate 32g (Sugars 10g) | Total Fat 7g (Sat Fat 4g) | Protein 5g | Fiber 0g | Cholesterol 50mg | Sodium 190mg | Food Exchanges: 2 Starch, 1 Fat | Carbohydrate Choices: 2 | Weight Watcher Smart Point Comparison: 8

Delectable Creamy Desserts

CREAMY OLD-FASHIONED VANILLA PUDDING

WARM MICROWAVE CHOCOLATE PUDDING

ALL-PURPOSE NO-BAKE VANILLA CHEESECAKE

EVERYDAY CHEESECAKE

KEY LIME CHEESECAKE "CUPCAKES"

FROZEN ALMOND MINI CHEESECAKES

DELECTABLE COCONUT CUSTARD

GUILT-FREE BANANA CREAM PIE IN A BOWL

CREAMY INSTANT PUMPKIN MOUSSE

PEANUT BUTTER MOUSSE

EASY ULTRA-RICH CHOCOLATE MOUSSE

10-MINUTE SOFT FROZEN STRAWBERRY YOGURT

FROZEN LEMONADE SQUARES

QUICK, CREAMY FUDGE PUDDING POPS

No dessert spells luxury in quite the same way as creamy desserts. These luscious desserts are characterized by their sweet taste and smooth silky texture and nothing soothes, comforts, or satisfies quite like something creamy. Creamy puddings, I find, are the most comforting, while decadent cheesecakes and mousses pacify the sweet tooth when we have the desire to indulge.

Creamy desserts are composed primarily of dairy products such as milk, cream, eggs, and cream cheese—which gives them a lush mouthfeel. Unfortunately, the problem is that full-fat dairy products also lend an extraordinary amount of fat—much of it saturated—to recipes. When you couple that fact with the amount of added sugar necessary to make the creamy indulgences we all love, like cheesecake and mousse, the caloric cost is often as astonishing as their taste. But like all of the recipes in this book, the great news is that I have crafted over a dozen guilt-free recipes for everyone who enjoys delectable creamy desserts.

Let me tempt you by recommending the creamy and oh-so-chocolaty Warm Microwave Chocolate Pudding. This sweet and satisfying dessert delivers a serving of homemade satisfaction in just minutes. If you are in search of old-fashioned goodness, the Delectable Coconut Custard will fill the bill, and if you're in the mood for something cool and creamy, the Guilt-Free Banana Cream Pie in a Bowl is guaranteed to please. But for indulgence, look no further than the two cheesecake recipes that I find indispensable for special occasions, as they are so easy to dress up. Fresh strawberries and store-bought, no-added-sugar cherry topping are two of my favorite toppers. Last, because there is nothing quite as decadent as mousse, I've supplied you with not one, but a trio of marvelous rich and creamy mousses that will add a luxurious finale to any meal. (P.S.: If the words "creamy and chocolaty" speak to you, then you must not ignore the Easy Ultra-Rich Chocolate Mousse).

Creamy Old-Fashioned Vanilla Pudding

With the proliferation of packaged puddings it's easy to forget that homemade vanilla pudding is a delectable dessert staple that can be made quickly and easily with ingredients kept on hand. The classic recipe calls for whole milk to keep it rich and creamy, but here a bit of nonfat half-and-half lends creaminess while a single egg adds both color and richness. Because much of its flavor comes from vanilla extract, for best results use "pure" vanilla and not imitation flavoring.

MAKES 4 SERVINGS

3 tablespoons cornstarch

½ cup granulated no-calorie sweetener*

½ cup nonfat half-and-half

1 large egg, slightly beaten

1½ cups low-fat milk

1 teaspoon vanilla extract

1. In a medium saucepan, whisk together the cornstarch, sweetener, half-and-half, and beaten egg. Whisk until smooth, then whisk in the milk.

2. Place saucepan over medium heat. Cook, continually stirring, until the pudding is thick and bubbly. Cook for 1 minute more. Remove from heat. Stir in the vanilla.

3. Pour into a medium bowl, or divide among four dessert dishes. Cover with plastic wrap. Cool and refrigerate until ready to serve.

Chef's Tip: Thoroughly beating the egg into the milk mixture before it is heated eliminates the need for tempering the egg with hot milk before its addition. Be sure to stir the pudding continually as the mixture heats up.

* See page 382 for sweetener options.

NUTRITION INFORMATION PER SERVING (½ CUP)
Calories 110 | Carbohydrate 15g (Sugars 5g) | Total Fat 2g (Sat Fat 1g) | Protein 6g | Fiber 0g | Cholesterol 50mg | Sodium 90mg | Food Exchanges: ½ Low-Fat Milk, ½ Carbohydrate | Carbohydrate Choices: 1 Weight Watcher Smart Point Comparison: 4

Warm Microwave Chocolate Pudding

This deep dark chocolate pudding delivers the convenience of a sugar-free mix with the great taste of homemade. It's also a good source of protein, calcium, fiber, and antioxidants, making it a dessert you can feel really good about eating. Be sure to make this in a medium-size bowl, as the pudding mixture expands considerably during cooking.

MAKES 2 SERVINGS

1 tablespoon cornstarch

3 tablespoons cocoa powder, preferably Dutch-process

1 tablespoon powdered nondairy coffee creamer

¼ cup granulated no-calorie sweetener*

1 cup low-fat milk, divided

1. In a medium microwave-safe bowl, stir together the cornstarch, cocoa, creamer, and sweetener. Add ⅓ cup of the milk to the bowl and whisk thoroughly until smooth. Whisk in the remaining milk until thoroughly mixed.

2. Microwave on high for 1½ minutes. Remove and stir. Continue cooking for 1½ to 2 minutes, or until pudding bubbles up and appears thickened.

3. Remove and stir. Divide into two cups and let stand at room temperature for 5 minutes to cool slightly. Serve warm. (To chill, cover the surface with plastic wrap and place in refrigerator.)

* See page 382 for sweetener options.

NUTRITION INFORMATION PER SERVING (½ CUP) ·············
Calories 110 | Carbohydrate 18g (Sugars 6g) | Total Fat 3g (Sat Fat 2g) | Protein 6g | Fiber 3g | Cholesterol 5mg | Sodium 65mg | Food Exchanges: 1 Low-Fat Milk | Carbohydrate Choices: 1 | Weight Watcher Smart Point Comparison: 4

All-Purpose No-Bake Vanilla Cheesecake

A wonderful no-bake cheesecake recipe is one that every baker (or cheesecake lover) should own. The best of these recipes uses the same ingredients you'd find in a traditional baked cheesecake with one exception: gelatin is used instead of eggs to bind the ingredients. Initially I thought it would be simple to create a luscious, healthy no-bake cheesecake, but this recipe took me over a dozen attempts. The result is a no-bake cheesecake recipe I am proud for you to own. Fresh berries make a fabulous topping.

MAKES 12 SERVINGS

¾ cup crushed vanilla wafer cookies (about 21 cookies)

1½ tablespoons margarine or butter, melted

1 packet unflavored gelatin

1 cup low-fat milk

8 ounces light tub-style cream cheese, room temperature

8 ounces nonfat cream cheese, room temperature

¾ cup granulated no-calorie sweetener*

1 teaspoon vanilla extract

½ teaspoon lemon zest

⅛ teaspoon almond extract (optional)

½ cup light sour cream

1 cup light whipped topping

1. In a medium bowl, mix together the crushed wafer cookies and margarine. Lightly coat a 9-inch springform pan with cooking spray, and press the mixture onto the bottom of the pan. Place in the freezer until ready for the filling.

2. In a medium microwave-safe bowl, sprinkle the gelatin over the milk, and allow it to set for at least 2 minutes. Place in the microwave and heat for 1 minute, or until the gelatin dissolves. Let cool while beating the cream cheese mixture.

3. In a large bowl using an electric mixer, beat the cream cheeses together. Add the sweetener, vanilla, lemon zest, and almond extract, if using. Add cooked milk mixture and beat until smooth. Slowly and with a large spoon, gently fold in the sour cream, and then the whipped topping.

4. Pour the cheesecake into the crust and chill in the refrigerator 4 hours or overnight, until set.

* See page 382 for sweetener options.

NUTRITION INFORMATION PER SERVING (1 PIECE) ·····················
Calories 130 | Carbohydrate 12g (Sugars 6g) | Total Fat 6g (Sat Fat 3g) | Protein 7g | Fiber 0g | Cholesterol 15mg | Sodium 220mg | Food Exchanges: 1 Carbohydrate, ½ Lean Meat, ½ Fat | Carbohydrate Choices: 1 Weight Watcher Smart Point Comparison: 5

Everyday Cheesecake

If it's cheesecake you crave, I guarantee this creamy cheesecake will curb even your worst craving. If you have never made a cheesecake or do not own a springform pan, don't worry. Cheesecake batter is simple to make and an ordinary cake pan is all you really need. Baking it in a water bath will ensure the cheesecake bakes up nice and creamy all the way through.

MAKES 12 SERVINGS

1 tablespoon margarine or butter, melted

½ cup graham cracker crumbs

1 cup plus 2 tablespoons granulated no-calorie sweetener, divided*

12 ounces light tub-style cream cheese, room temperature

12 ounces nonfat cream cheese (block or tub-style), room temperature

2 tablespoons cornstarch

1 teaspoon vanilla extract

¼ teaspoon almond extract

2 large eggs

2 large egg whites

1 cup light sour cream

1. Preheat the oven to 325°F. Coat an 8-inch round cake pan with nonstick cooking spray. (If you use an 8-inch springform pan, it will need to be tightly wrapped with a sheet of heavy-duty foil to make it waterproof.)

2. Place the melted margarine or butter in the cake pan. Toss in the graham-cracker crumbs and 2 tablespoons of the sweetener. Using your hands, mix and pat crumbs onto bottom of pan. Bake the crust for 10 minutes. Remove from oven and place the cake pan inside a 13 x 9-inch or larger baking pan with 2- to 3-inch sides.

3. Beat the cream cheeses together until smooth with an electric mixer. Add the remaining 1 cup of sweetener, the cornstarch, and extracts. Beat on low until smooth. Add the eggs and then egg whites, beating briefly after each addition to incorporate. Stir in the sour cream with a large spoon.

4. Carefully pour the cheesecake mixture into the cake pan. Place the baking pan in the oven and pour hot water into it until it reaches halfway up the sides of the outside of the cake pan. Bake for 50 to 55 minutes or until sides of cake appear firm but center still jiggles slightly. Remove from oven and water bath and cool to room temperature. Place in the refrigerator and chill at least 4 hours before serving.

* See page 382 for sweetener options.

NUTRITION INFORMATION PER SERVING (1 PIECE) ·················
Calories 175 | Carbohydrate 13g | Sugars 5g | Total Fat 8g (Sat Fat 4.5g) | Protein 10g | Fiber 0g | Cholesterol 35mg | Sodium 320mg | Food exchange: 1½ Lean Meat, 1 Carbohydrate | Carbohydrate Choices: 1 | Weight Watcher Smart Point Comparison: 6

Key Lime Cheesecake "Cupcakes"

If you love Key lime pie, you are certain to love these creamy cakes in a cup. Aromatic Key limes are easiest to find in peak season from June through August, but bottled Key lime juice and the zest of a "regular" Persian lime work just fine. These luscious "cupcakes" are perfect for entertaining.

MAKES 12 SERVINGS

¾ cup graham cracker crumbs

2 tablespoons margarine or butter, melted

2 tablespoons plus ¾ cup granulated no-calorie sweetener, divided *

1½ cups low-fat cottage cheese

8 ounces light tub-style cream cheese

3 tablespoons cornstarch

2 tablespoons Key lime juice (3 to 4 Key limes)

Zest of 2 Key limes or 1 Persian lime

1 teaspoon vanilla extract

1 large egg

1 large egg white

1. Preheat the oven to 325°F. Coat a 12-cup muffin tin with nonstick baking spray.

2. In a medium bowl, mix together the graham cracker crumbs, margarine, and 2 tablespoons of the sweetener until well combined.

3. Sprinkle a heaping tablespoon of crust mixture into each muffin cup. Press gently to form a crust on the bottom of each cup. Set aside.

4. Using a food processor, blend the cottage cheese until very smooth and creamy. Spoon the cottage cheese into a large bowl. Add the cream cheese, the remaining ¾ cup sweetener, the cornstarch, lime juice, zest, and vanilla and beat with an electric mixer until creamy. Add the egg and the egg white and beat until just blended.

5. Spoon ¼ cup of cheesecake filling into each muffin cup. Bake for 18 to 20 minutes, or until the cheesecakes are set but centers jiggle slightly. Cool to room temperature. Chill in the refrigerator until firm, at least 2 hours.

* See page 382 for sweetener options.

NUTRITION INFORMATION PER SERVING (1 CUPCAKE) ···
Calories 140 | Carbohydrate 12g (Sugars 6g) | Total Fat 7g (Sat Fat 4g) | Protein 7g | Fiber 0g | Cholesterol | 35mg | Sodium 270mg | Food Exchanges: 1 Lean Meat, 1 Carbohydrate, ½ Fat | Carbohydrate Choices: 1 | Weight Watcher Smart Point Comparison: 5

Frozen Almond Mini Cheesecakes

Sophisticated and cool, the almond crust really makes these reduced-carb mini cheesecakes exceptional. Look for ground almonds or almond meal near the nuts in your supermarket. If you prefer to grind the nuts yourself, see my tip in Marlene Says. For an extra touch of class and color, garnish each cheesecake with a fresh stemmed cherry.

MAKES 12 SERVINGS

½ cup ground almonds

¼ cup all-purpose flour

1 tablespoon margarine or butter, melted

2 tablespoons granulated no-calorie sweetener*

1 cup light cream cheese

½ cup nonfat cream cheese

½ cup light sour cream

½ cup granulated no-calorie sweetener*

¼ cup low-fat milk

¼ teaspoon almond extract

1. Line a 12-cup muffin tin with muffin cups and spray lightly with cooking spray.

2. In a medium bowl, mix together the almonds, flour, margarine, and sweetener until well combined. Press an even layer into the bottoms of each muffin cup.

3. In a large bowl, beat together the cream cheeses until slightly softened. Add all remaining ingredients and beat until smooth. Pour into muffin cups to evenly fill each cup. Place tins into freezer for at least 4 hours, or overnight.

4. To remove cheesecakes, dip the bottom of the tin into warm water or rub a warm towel over the bottom and edge to remove cakes. Remove muffin wrapper while frozen. Set out at least 10 minutes before serving.

Marlene Says: To grind almonds, place whole almonds (about 6 tablespoons for this recipe) in a clean coffee grinder or food processor. Pulse until nuts resemble a coarse meal. Do not overprocess or the nuts will turn into a paste. Adding one tablespoon of flour while grinding reduces the chance of overprocessing the nuts.

* See page 382 for sweetener options.

NUTRITION INFORMATION PER SERVING (1 CAKE)
Calories 130 | Carbohydrate 8g (Sugars 3g) | Total Fat 8g (Sat Fat 4g) | Protein 6g | Fiber 1g | Cholesterol 15mg | Sodium 170mg | Food Exchanges: 1 Low-Fat Meat, ½ Carbohydrate, 1 Fat | Carbohydrate Choices: ½ | Weight Watcher Smart Point Comparison: 5

Delectable Coconut Custard

Packed with protein and calcium and low in fat, old-fashioned custard is a wonderfully wholesome dessert that can be enjoyed any time of day (even for breakfast). Moreover, because this recipe is baked in individual ramekins, portion control is never a problem. For traditional egg custard simply omit the shredded coconut and coconut extract and increase the vanilla extract to 1½ teaspoons. Store these covered in the refrigerator and they will keep for several days.

MAKES 6 SERVINGS

2 large eggs

2 large egg whites

⅔ cup granulated no-calorie sweetener*

1 teaspoon vanilla extract

½ teaspoon coconut extract

1 (12-ounce) can low-fat evaporated milk

1½ cups low-fat milk

¼ cup toasted shredded coconut (reserve 2 tablespoons for garnish)

1. Preheat the oven to 325°F.

2. In a medium bowl, whisk together the eggs, egg whites, sweetener, vanilla and coconut extracts. Set aside.

3. In a small saucepan, bring the milks to a low simmer. Whisk a small amount of the hot milk into egg mixture to temper the eggs. Whisk in the remaining milk. Pour the mixture into a large measuring cup with a pour spout.

4. Sprinkle 1 teaspoon of the shredded coconut into each 6-ounce custard cup or ramekin. Pour the custard mixture into the cups on top of shredded coconut. Set the cups in a large baking dish and place in oven. Pour very hot water into the baking dish until the water reaches halfway up the sides of the custard cups.

5. Bake the custard for 45 to 55 minutes, or until edges are set and centers jiggle slightly when shaken. Cool and refrigerate to set. Top each cup with 1 teaspoon of toasted coconut before serving.

* See page 382 for sweetener options.

NUTRITION INFORMATION PER SERVING (1 CUSTARD) ······················
Calories 145 | Carbohydrate 15g (Sugars 12g) | Total Fat 5g (Sat Fat 3g) | Protein 10g | Fiber 0g | Cholesterol 80mg | Sodium 150mg | Food Exchanges: ½ Low-Fat Milk, ½ Medium-Fat Meat, ½ Starch | Carbohydrate Choices: 1 | Weight Watcher Smart Point Comparison: 6

Guilt-Free Banana Cream Pie in a Bowl

It's hard to believe that only five ingredients and five minutes result in a homemade dessert that tastes as incredible and is as satisfying as this one. Inspired by Southern-style pudding—the sweet blend of creamy pudding, vanilla wafers, and sliced bananas—this is a little bowl of heaven.

MAKES 4 SERVINGS

1½ cups low-fat milk

1 (4-serving size) package sugar-free banana instant pudding mix

1½ cups light whipped topping

1 medium banana, thinly sliced

8 vanilla wafers

4 coarsely crushed vanilla wafers, for garnish (optional)*

* Optional cookie garnish adds 18 calories, ½ gram of fat, and 3 grams of carbohydrate.

1. In a medium bowl, whisk together the milk and pudding until smooth. Chill 10 minutes in refrigerator, or until set. Gently fold in 1 cup of whipped topping.

2. Place 2 wafers in the bottom of each bowl. Top each with ¼ cup of the banana cream filling. Evenly distribute banana slices among bowls, reserving 4 slices for garnish. Top with another ¼ cup of the filling. Garnish "pies" with 2 tablespoons light whipped topping, a banana slice, and an additional vanilla wafer if desired.

DARE to COMPARE••••••••••••••••••••••••••••••••••••••
When it comes to the richest desserts I have ever seen, Emeril Lagasse deserves a prize. A single slice (1/10 of a 9-inch pie) of his signature banana cream pie serves up over 1,100 calories, 70 grams of fat (that's two *days'* worth of saturated fat), 125 grams of carbohydrate, and 100 grams of sugar (more than ½ cup per piece!).

NUTRITION INFORMATION PER SERVING (1 BOWL)••••••••••••••••••••••••••••••••••
Calories 180 | Carbohydrate 28g (Sugars 15g) | Total Fat 5g (Sat Fat 3g) | Protein 5g | Fiber 1g | Cholesterol 5mg | Sodium 360mg | Food Exchanges: 1 Carbohydrate, ½ Low-Fat Milk, ½ Fruit, ½ Fat | Carbohydrate Choices: 2 | Weight Watcher Smart Point Comparison: 6

Creamy Instant Pumpkin Mousse

Not just for Thanksgiving, pumpkin is a superfood rich in potassium, vitamin A, beta carotene, and a surprising amount of fiber that should be enjoyed all year long. This instant mousse recipe tastes similar to pumpkin pie, but is far more luscious. I like to garnish it with a gingersnap.

MAKES 8 SERVINGS

1 (4-serving size) package fat-free sugar-free instant butterscotch pudding mix

¾ cup low-fat milk

1 (15-ounce) can pumpkin purée

1 teaspoon ground cinnamon

¼ teaspoon ground ginger

⅛ teaspoon ground cloves

1. In a large bowl, beat together the pudding mix and milk until slightly thickened. Add the pumpkin, cinnamon, ginger, and cloves, and mix until well combined.

2. Gently fold in the whipped topping in three additions.

3. Pour ½ cup of the mousse into each of the eight serving dishes. Chill for 30 minutes before serving.

Marlene Says: Although vanilla-flavored pudding can be substituted, the rich flavor of butterscotch enhances the flavor of the pumpkin magnificently. For an even richer mousse, beat ½ cup light tub-style cream cheese into pudding mix before adding milk. (Adds 30 calories and 2 grams fat per serving).

NUTRITION INFORMATION PER SERVING (½ CUP)
Calories 100 | Carbohydrate 14g (Sugars 6g) | Total Fat 3.5g (Sat Fat 3g) | Protein 1g | Fiber 2g | Cholesterol 0mg | Sodium 150mg | Food Exchanges: ½ Carbohydrate, 1 Vegetable, ½ Fat | Carbohydrate Choices: 1 Weight Watcher Smart Point Comparison: 4

Peanut Butter Mousse

This is sooo good. *The comforting taste of peanut butter and smooth cream cheese blend together to make a rich-tasting peanut butter mousse that only pretends to be decadent. I recommend you portion it quickly or you'll be tempted to eat the entire bowl.*

MAKES 8 SERVINGS

½ cup low-fat smooth peanut butter

4 ounces light tub-style cream cheese, at room temperature

4 ounces fat-free cream cheese, at room temperature

½ cup granulated no-calorie sweetener*

¼ cup low-fat milk

½ teaspoon vanilla extract

1 8-ounce tub light whipped topping, thawed

1. In a large bowl using an electric mixer, beat the peanut butter and cream cheeses. Add the sweetener, milk, and vanilla. Beat until smooth.

2. Gently fold in the whipped topping in three additions.

3. Portion into eight serving dishes. Chill for at least 30 minutes, or until ready to serve.

Or try this: This is extra decadent when topped with a drizzle of reduced-sugar chocolate syrup and/or a single chocolate wafer cookie.

* See page 382 for sweetener options.

NUTRITION INFORMATION PER SERVING (½ CUP)
Calories 190 | Carbohydrate 15g (Sugars 6g) | Total Fat 10g (Sat Fat 5g) | Protein 8g | Fiber 1g | Cholesterol 5mg | Sodium 210mg | Food Exchanges: 1 Carbohydrate, 2 Fat | Carbohydrate Choices: 1 | Weight Watcher Smart Point Comparison: 7

Easy Ultra-Rich Chocolate Mousse

There's nothing I like better than taking a great recipe and making it even better. A couple of tips: the chocolate used does makes a difference. Bittersweet chocolate chips and Dutch process cocoa powder will give you the richest, darkest chocolate flavor. I love the touch of orange zest, but if you prefer, half a teaspoon of instant coffee powder can be used in its place. Last, making the chocolate mixture for this is really quick and easy, but be careful not to forget about it as it chills. A quick stir every ten minutes or so while it cools will keep the gelatin from clumping as it cools.

MAKES 4 SERVINGS

¼ cup cold water

1 envelope unflavored gelatin

¾ cup low-fat evaporated milk

⅓ cup bittersweet or semi-sweet chocolate chips

⅓ cup unsweetened cocoa powder

½ cup granulated no-calorie sweetener*

1 large egg yolk

1 tablespoon granulated sugar

1 teaspoon vanilla extract

½ teaspoon orange zest, optional

¾ cup light whipped topping, thawed

1. Place the water in a 1 or 2 cup capacity glass measuring cup. Sprinkle gelatin over water. Let set for 3 minutes to allow gelatin to soften. Add the milk to the measuring cup (filling cup up to the one-cup mark). Stir briefly. Microwave on high for 1½ minutes.

2. While milk is heating place chocolate chips, cocoa powder, sweetener, sugar, extract and zest, if desired, into a blender. Add hot milk and blend for 15 seconds, add yolk, and blend until smooth. Pour chocolate mixture into a medium bowl and let cool slightly. Refrigerate for 30 to 45 minutes, stirring occasionally, until it is cold and begins to thicken.

3. Fold the whipped topping into chocolate mixture with a spatula and refrigerate for at least one hour or until ready to serve.

DARE to COMPARE......................................
Melted chocolate chips and cream are often used in easy-to-make rich chocolate mousse recipes. It's hard to conceive, but I calculated that one of the most popular brands delivers a whopping 820 calories including an entire day's worth of fat and added sugars, and a full meal's worth of carbs, in a single one-half cup serving!

* See page 382 for sweetener options.

NUTRITION INFORMATION PER SERVING (½ CUP) ·····················
Calories 195 | Carbohydrate 24g (Sugars 11g) | Total Fat 8g (Sat Fat 3.5g) | Protein 8g | Fiber 3g | Cholesterol 0mg | Sodium 120mg | Food Exchanges: 1½ Carbohydrate, 1 Lean Meat, 1 Fat | Carbohydrate Choices: 1½ | Weight Watcher Smart Point Comparison: 6

10-Minute Soft Frozen Strawberry Yogurt

When it comes to selecting a "better-for-you" frozen dessert, frozen yogurt often tops the list. Unfortunately, many frozen yogurts are loaded with sugar (not to mention artificial colorings and preservatives). Conversely, this easy recipe which falls between a creamy ice cream and a fresh fruity sorbet, which is packed only with the goodness of real strawberries and calcium rich yogurt.

MAKES 6 SERVINGS

1 (16-ounce) package frozen, unsweetened strawberries, slightly thawed

6 tablespoons granulated no-calorie sweetener*

1 cup low-fat plain yogurt

½ teaspoon almond extract

1. Place one-third of the strawberries into a food processor. Process until the fruit is chopped into small pieces. Transfer contents into a large bowl and set aside. Continue processing one-third of the next two batches until all the strawberries are chopped. Return all of the berries to the processor.

2. Add the sweetener, yogurt, and extract to the food processor. Process until smooth, scraping down the sides.

3. Serve immediately for soft-serve, or cover and freeze to firm up for 30 to 45 minutes. (For extra creamy yogurt place the mixture into either an ice cream maker and process according to directions or a shallow pan to freeze. Break it up and process again in the food processor before serving.)

Marlene Says: This recipe is even more delicious when made with Greek yogurt. Greek yogurt is strained longer, resulting in a thicker, creamier texture with more protein. Always select a nonfat or low-fat variety.

* See page 382 for sweetener options.

NUTRITION INFORMATION PER SERVING (½ CUP)
Calories 100 | Carbohydrate 18g (Sugars 16g) | Total Fat 1g (Sat Fat .5g) | Protein 4g | Fiber 3g | Cholesterol 5mg | Sodium 45mg | Food Exchanges: 1 Fruit | Carbohydrate Choices: 1 | Weight Watcher Smart Point Comparison:3

Frozen Lemonade Squares

A lemon lover's dream! *Adapted from a contest-winning recipe held by the makers of Splenda brand sweeteners, these creamy and refreshing bars are the perfect cool-down treat for a hot summer day. To make serving a snap, run a sharp knife under hot water before slicing.*

MAKES 9 SERVINGS

1 cup graham cracker crumbs

1¾ cups granulated no-calorie sweetener, divided*

2 tablespoons margarine or butter

2 cups plain nonfat yogurt

⅓ cup lemon juice (about 1 to 1½ lemons)

Zest of 1 lemon

½ teaspoon lemon extract

1 cup light whipped topping

1. Spray an 8-inch square baking pan with cooking spray. Set aside.

2. In a medium bowl, mix together the graham cracker crumbs, ¼ cup of the sweetener, and the margarine until crumbly. Press the mixture evenly into the bottom of the prepared pan.

3. In a large bowl, whisk together the yogurt, the remaining sweetener, the lemon juice, lemon zest, and lemon extract. Gently fold in the whipped topping. Pour into the crust and smooth the top.

4. Cover the pan and place in freezer for at least 4 hours.

5. Before serving, allow to stand at room temperature for 10 minutes. Cut into 9 portions using a heated sharp knife.

> **DARE to COMPARE**
> By using a sugar substitute in this recipe I eliminated 160 calories and 40 grams of sugar per serving—that's the equivalent of 13 teaspoons of sugar in each bar!

* See page 382 for sweetener options.

NUTRITION INFORMATION PER SERVING (1 BAR)
Calories 115 | Carbohydrate 15g (Sugars 6g) | Total Fat 4.5g (Sat Fat 3g) | Protein 3g | Fiber 0g | Cholesterol 10mg | Sodium 70mg | Food Exchanges: 1 Carbohydrate | Carbohydrate Choices: 1 | Weight Watcher Smart Point Comparison: 5

Quick, Creamy Fudge Pudding Pops

Instant sugar-free chocolate pudding mix makes preparing your own sugar-free frozen fudge popsicles a snap. Foolproof, these are perfect for kids to help with. The hardest part will be their waiting for the chocolaty pops to freeze. You will need some popsicle molds and sticks for making this.

MAKES 6 SERVINGS

1 package (4-serving size) sugar-free, fat-free instant chocolate pudding mix

2 cups cold water

1 cup light whipped topping

1 tablespoon cocoa powder

2 tablespoons granulated no-calorie sweetener*

1. In a medium bowl, whisk together the pudding mix and water until smooth. Set in the refrigerator for 5 minutes.

2. Gently whisk the remaining ingredients into the pudding mix. Spoon rounded ⅓ cup of the mixture into each popsicle mold or small paper cup. Insert a popsicle stick into the center. Freeze for 4 hours or overnight, until solid.

3. To remove the pops, dip bottoms of molds into warm water for 10 seconds or run the bottom of the cups under warm water until pops release.

Marlene Says: To keep the popsicle sticks upright in paper cups, cover the top of each filled cup tightly with foil. Make a small slit in the center of the foil and insert stick.

* See page 382 for sweetener options.

NUTRITION INFORMATION PER SERVING (1 POP) ·······················
Calories 50 | Carbohydrate 8g (Sugars 1g) | Total Fat 1.5g (Sat Fat 1.5g) | Protein 1g | Fiber <1g | Cholesterol 0mg | Sodium 180mg | Food Exchanges: ½ Carbohydrate | Carbohydrate Choices: ½ | Weight Watcher Smart Point Comparison: 2

Eat What You Love... and Lose!

If eating pasta, pizza, and pancakes, or cookies, cake and luscious creamy treats—and still losing weight—sounds like a dream, you're in luck. Countless readers have shared that they not only lost weight when cooking with this book, but also lowered their blood sugar (and blood pressure) and even had more energy. And they did it all without ever counting a single calorie, carb, or "point."

As a dietitian I also know the importance of planning and structure when it comes to helping people reach their dietary and health goals. As such, I included a variety of tools for meal planning, including the simple plate method, in the Meal Planning section when I wrote the original version of this book. Now, in this updated edition, I am delighted to provide you with even more! Here you will find fourteen days' worth of delectable calorie/carb-controlled menus along with tips on using them to jump-start your way to better health. What you won't find is the feeling of deprivation that accompanies most "diets." With crispy cinnamon French toast for breakfast and creamy Chicken Salad for lunch, or Chili's restaurant-style Beef Fajitas for dinner, and, yes, even Unbelievable Chocolate Cake.

For the Love of Better Health

On the following pages you will find two full weeks worth of delicious healthy calorie/carb controlled menus that have been designed to help promote weight loss (or maintenance), blood sugar management, and overall good health. Enjoy!

EVERY MENU:

- Includes three delicious meals and three snacks to keep your energy high, your blood sugar under control, and your belly and taste buds satisfied from morning till night.
- Includes the powerful one-two punch of protein and fiber to keep hunger at bay while helping you melt away fat, not muscle.
- Features a 1,200 and 1,600 calorie level. To determine the one that's best for you, simply go to *www.marlenekoch.com* and click on the Personal Calorie Calculator found under the Nutrition Tools tab**.
- Includes Smart Point Comparisons (averaging just 28 points for the 1200-calorie menus!)
- Meets American Heart Association guidelines. They are all low in saturated fat and added sugars, average 2300 mg of sodium or less, and contain between 25 and 35 grams of fiber.

MENU AND SHOPPING TIPS:

- Take a few minutes to go over the menus; then use the recipes to create a shopping list. The pantry list on page 23 will help keep you stocked up with the ingredients used most often in this book. With a few fresh add-ons, your meal will be complete.
- Feel free to make substitutions or mix-and-match menus, as long as calories (or points) are kept in check. To assist you, the total calories and points for meals are provided. A journal can help you track calories or points consumed daily – and keep you on track!
- For blood sugar control the 1200-calorie menus average 30 grams of carbohydrates per meal and range up to 15 grams of carbs per snack. The 1600-calorie menus average 45 grams of carbohydrates per meal with a maximum of 22 grams per snack. If you have diabetes, be mindful of carbs when combining meals and snacks or making swaps.

**If you have a medical condition or take medications, it's always best to check with your doctor or registered dietitian before making major dietary changes.

Eat What You Love—And Lose!

Monday Day 1

	1200 Calories	**1600 Calories**
Breakfast	**Breakfast BLT (p. 103)** ½ cup light orange juice Calories 285 I SP 9	**Breakfast BLT (p. 103)** ¾ cup light orange juice ½ medium apple Calories 365 I SP 10
Snack	1 medium apple	1 medium apple 12 almonds (½ oz)
Lunch	**Quick Pita Pizza (p. 218)** Topped with choice of vegetables and 5 slices turkey pepperoni 1½ cups green salad with 2 tbsp low-fat dressing Calories 325 I SP 9	**Quick Pita Pizza (p. 218)** Topped with choice of vegetables and 5 slices turkey pepperoni 1½ cups green salad with 2 tbsp low-fat dressing Calories 325 I SP 9
Snack	**Skinny Dip & Chips (p.123)**	**Skinny Dip & Chips (p.123)**
Dinner	**20 Minute Pork Marsala (p. 333)** ½ cup pasta (whole wheat blend suggested) **Seared, Steamed, and Glazed Green Beans (p. 252)** Calories 395 I SP 8	**20 Minute Pork Marsala (p. 333)** ¾ cup pasta (whole wheat blend suggested) **Seared, Steamed, and Glazed Green Beans (p. 252)** Calories 445 I SP 13
Snack	Reduced calorie/sugar hot chocolate (packet)	**Rich and Creamy Hot Chocolate (p. 47)** ½ medium banana
Total (meals and snacks)	Calories: 1180 Smart Point Comparison: 29 Carbohydrate: 132 g I Fiber 30 g Protein 75 g I Fat: 40 g	Calories: 1575 Smart Point Comparison: 35 Carb: 182 g I Fiber: 33 g Protein: 88 g I Fat: 48 g

Tuesday Day 2

	1200 Calories	1600 Calories
Breakfast	**Cinnamon Roll Oatmeal (p. 99)** with 2 tbsp low-fat milk and 2 tbsp chopped nuts Calories 250	SP 7	**Cinnamon Roll Oatmeal (p.99)** with 2 tbsp low-fat milk and 2 tbsp chopped nuts 1 hard boiled egg Calories 320	SP 9
Snack	½ cup blueberries	1 cup blueberries ½ cup low-fat cottage cheese or light Greek yogurt
Lunch	**Dilly of A Tuna Sandwich (p. 204)** **5 Minute Skinny Slaw (p. 180)** Calories 300	SP 7	**Dilly of A Tuna Sandwich (p.204)** **5 Minute Skinny Slaw (p. 180)** Calories 300	SP 7
Snack	Medium orange 1 slice reduced fat cheese	Medium orange 1 slice reduced fat cheese
Dinner	**Jammin' Chicken (p. 302)** ½ cup prepared instant brown rice 1 ½ cups steamed broccoli with 1 tsp margarine Calories 390	SP 8	**Jammin' Chicken (p. 302)** 1 cup prepared instant brown rice 1 ½ cups steamed broccoli with 1 tsp margarine Calories 500	SP 13
Snack/ Dessert	**Warm Microwave Chocolate Pudding (p. 412)**	**Warm Microwave Chocolate Pudding (p.412)** with ½ cup sliced strawberries and 2 tbsp light whipped topping
	Calories: 1175 Smart Point Comparison: 28 Carbohydrate: 132 g	Fiber: 25 g Protein: 79 g	Fat: 36 g	Calories: 1550 Smart Point Comparison: 34 Carbohydrate: 176 g	Fiber: 38 g Protein: 103 g	Fat: 46 g

Wednesday Day 3

	1200 Calories	1600 Calories
Breakfast	**Breakfast in a Glass Smoothie (p. 57)** 1 slice light wheat toast 2 tsp low-sugar jam Calories 200	SP 5	**Breakfast in a Glass Smoothie (p. 57)** 1 slice light wheat toast 2 tsp low-sugar jam Calories 200	SP 5
Snack	½ grapefruit ½ tsp low-calorie sweetener or sugar	1 whole grapefruit 1 tsp low-calorie sweetener or sugar ⅓ cup pistachios (in shells)
Lunch	**Chicken Caesar Wrap (p. 211)** ½ cup reduced sodium V8 Calories 380	SP 9	**Chicken Caesar Wrap (p. 211)** ¾ cup reduced sodium V8 Calories 400	SP 10
Snack	1½ cups carrot and celery sticks	1 cup carrot and celery sticks ½ cup low-fat cottage cheese
Dinner	**Speedy Black Bean Soup with Jalapeno Cream (p. 154)** with 2 tbsp reduced-fat Mexican blend cheese **Shredded Spinach Lettuce and Fresh Orange Salad (p.178)** Calories 380	SP 9	**Speedy Black Bean Soup with Jalapeno Cream (p. 154)** with 2 tbsp reduced-fat Mexican blend cheese and ¼ avocado, sliced **Shredded Spinach Lettuce and Fresh Orange Salad (p.178)** Calories 460	SP 11
Snack	**1 Amazing Peanut Butter Cookie (p. 383)** or 2 tsp peanut butter on ½ medium apple Calories: 1170 Smart Point Comparison: 26 Carbohydrate: 130 g	Fiber: 33 g Protein: 84 g	Fat: 34 g	**1 Amazing Peanut Butter Cookie (p. 383)** or 2 tsp peanut butter on ½ medium apple ½ cup low-fat milk Calories: 1540 Smart Point Comparison 35 Carbohydrate: 160 g	Fiber: 38 g Protein: 104 g	Fat: 52 g

Thursday Day 4

	1200 Calories	**1600 Calories**
Breakfast	**South of the Border Wrap (p. 101)** ½ cup low-fat milk Calories 295	SP 7	**South of the Border Wrap (p. 101)** 1 cup low-fat milk Calories 350	SP 9
Snack	1 medium orange	1 medium orange
Lunch	**Italian Sausage and Escarole Soup (p. 158)** 8 wheat crackers or 1 small wheat roll **Mixed Greens with Italian Vinaigrette (p.173)** Calories 350	SP 9	**Italian Sausage and Escarole Soup (p. 158)** 8 wheat crackers or 1 small wheat roll **Mixed Greens with Italian Vinaigrette (p.173)** ½ cup sliced canned peaches Calories 410	SP 9
Snack	1 stick light string cheese	2 sticks light string cheese
Dinner	**Corkscrew Chicken Broccoli Alfredo (p. 232)** with 1 tbsp grated Parmesan cheese Sliced tomatoes with 1 tbsp low-fat Italian dressing Calories 395	SP 10	**Corkscrew Chicken Broccoli Alfredo (p. 232)** with 1 tbsp grated Parmesan cheese	Sliced tomatoes with 1 tbsp low-fat Italian dressing 1 small wheat roll with 1 tsp margarine or butter Calories 500	SP 13
Snack	1 cup grapes (about 15)	1 cup grapes (about 15) 12 almonds (½ ounce)

1200 Calories	1600 Calories
Calories: 1210 Smart Point Comparison: 27 Carbohydrate: 138 g	Fiber: 30g Protein: 83 g	Fat: 37 g	Calories: 1580 Smart Point Comparison: 34 Carbohydrate: 179 g	Fiber: 34 g Protein: 103 g	Fat: 48 g

Friday Day 5

	1200 Calories	**1600 Calories**
Breakfast	**Fruit and Yogurt Breakfast Sundaes (p. 120)** 1 slice light wheat toast with 2 tsp peanut butter Calories 235 | SP 6	**Fruit and Yogurt Breakfast Sundaes (p. 120)** 1 slice light wheat toast with 1 tbsp peanut butter Calories 265 | SP 7
Snack	½ medium banana	1 medium banana
Lunch	**Deli-Style Roast Beef Sandwich (p. 209) 5-Minute Skinny Slaw (p. 180)** Calories 370 | SP 9	**Deli-Style Roast Beef Sandwich (p. 209) 5-Minute Skinny Slaw (p. 180)** ¾ cup low-fat milk Calories 445 | SP 12
Snack	2 deviled egg halves or 1 boiled egg and 2 tsps light mayonnaise	½ cup low-fat cottage cheese topped with cinnamon, low-calorie sweetener and 2 tbsps sliced almonds
Dinner	**Southern-Style Shrimp Creole (p. 355)** with ½ cup prepared instant brown rice 1 ½ cups spinach salad with 2 tbsp low-fat dressing Calories 300 | SP 7	**Southern-Style Shrimp Creole (p. 355)** ¾ cup prepared instant brown rice 1½ cups spinach with 2 tbsp low-fat dressing Calories 500 | SP 8
Snack	**5-Minute Blackberry Crisp (p. 377)**	**5-Minute Blackberry Crisp (p. 377)**

1200 Calories:
Calories: 1175
Smart Point Comparison: 26
Carbohydrate: 141 g | Fiber: 24 g
Protein: 69 g | Fat: 37 g

1600 Calories:
Calories: 1540
Smart Point Comparison: 35
Carbohydrate: 181 g | Fiber: 28
Protein: 96 g | Fat: 45 g

Saturday Day 6

	1200 Calories	1600 Calories
Breakfast	**Everyday Cinnamon French Toast (p. 220)** with 2 tbsp sugar-free syrup ½ cup (or 6-ounce container) light Greek yogurt ½ cup fresh or frozen thawed raspberries Calories 330	SP 8	**Everyday Cinnamon French Toast (p. 220)** with 2 tbsp sugar-free syrup ½ cup (or 6-ounce container) light Greek yogurt, ½ cup fresh or frozen thawed raspberries Calories 330	SP 8
Snack	1 medium apple	1 medium apple
Lunch	**1 ½ cups or two servings, "Spaghetti-ed" Spaghetti Squash (p. 265)** 1 cup steamed broccoli drizzled with 1 tsp each olive oil and lemon juice Calories 310	SP 5	**1 ½ cups or two servings, "Spaghetti-ed" Spaghetti Squash (p. 265)** with 2 tbsp grated Parmesan cheese 1 cup steamed broccoli drizzled with 1 tsp each olive oil and lemon juice Calories 360	SP 7
Snack	2 stalks celery with 2 tsps peanut butter	1 slice light bread with 1 tbsp peanut butter and 2 tsps reduced sugar jam 2 stalks celery
Dinner	**Chili's-Style Grilled Beef Fajitas (p. 329)** 1 low-carb high fiber tortilla (80 – 100 calories) 1 cup shredded lettuce and chopped tomatoes Calories 335	SP 7	**Chili's-Style Grilled Beef Fajitas (p. 329)** 2 low-carb high fiber tortillas (80 – 100 calories) ¼ avocado, sliced 1 cup shredded lettuce and chopped tomatoes Calories 495	SP 11
Snack	**Creamy Old-Fashioned Vanilla Pudding (p. 411)**	**Creamy Old-Fashioned Vanilla Pudding (p. 411)** ½ medium banana, sliced
	Calories: 1210 Smart Point Comparison: 26 Carbohydrate: 142 g	Fiber: 31 g Protein: 81 g	Fat: 35 g	Calories: 1595 Smart Point Comparison: 35 Carbohydrate: 180 g	Fiber: 46 g Protein: 96 g	Fat: 54 g

Sunday Day 7

	1200 Calories	1600 Calories
Breakfast	**Greek Frittata or Classic Italian Frittata (p. 110 or 108)** 1 slice light wheat toast with 1 tsp margarine or butter Orange wedges (½ medium orange) Calories 295 | SP 7	**Greek or Classic Italian Frittata (p. 110 or 108)** 2 slices light wheat toast with 2 tsp margarine or butter Orange wedges (1 medium orange) Calories 400 | SP 9
Snack	1 cup grapes	1 cup grapes
Lunch	**Spinach, Tuna, and White Bean Salad (p. 199)** Calories 330 | SP 7	**Spinach, Tuna, and White Bean Salad (p. 199)** 8 whole wheat crackers or saltines Calories 410 | SP 9
Snack	1 cup baby carrots	1 cup baby carrots 3 tbsp **Healthy Hummus** (p. 125 or store-bought)
Dinner	**Skillet Chicken Parmesan (p. 297)** ½ cup cooked pasta 1 cup steamed or sautéed green beans with 1 tsp olive oil Calories 440 | SP 10	**Skillet Chicken Parmesan (p. 297)** ¾ cup cooked pasta 1 cup steamed or sautéed green beans with 1 tsp olive oil Calories 500 | SP 11
Snack	3 cups light popcorn (~80 calories)	4 cups light popcorn (~105 calories)
	Calories: 1240 Smart Point Comparison: 28 Carbohydrate: 130 g | Fiber: 27 g Protein: 91g | Fat: 40 g	Calories: 1600 Smart Point Comparison: 36 Carbohydrate: 180 g | Fiber: 34 g Protein: 101 g | Fat: 53 g

Monday
Day 8

	1200 Calories	**1600 Calories**

Breakfast

1200 Calories:
Pumped Up Peanut Butter Smoothie (p. 66)
Calories 320 | SP 9

1600 Calories:
Pumped Up Peanut Butter Smoothie (p. 66) ½ medium banana
Calories 375 | SP 9

Snack

1200 Calories:
1 slice light wheat toast
1 tablespoon reduced-sugar jam

1600 Calories:
1 slice light wheat toast
1 tablespoon reduced-sugar jam

Lunch

1200 Calories:
1 ½ cups Creamy Broccoli Cheddar Soup (p. 150)
Wedge Salad with Buttermilk Ranch Dressing (p. 174)
Calories 265 | SP 8

1600 Calories:
1 ½ cups Creamy Broccoli Cheddar Soup (p. 150)
Wedge Salad with Buttermilk Ranch Dressing (p. 174)
Calories 265 | SP 8

Snack

1200 Calories:
½ cup fresh or canned peach slices (in juice, drained)

1600 Calories:
½ cup fresh or canned peach slices (in juice, drained)
⅓ cup low-fat cottage cheese

Dinner

1200 Calories:
Pasta Primavera (p. 227)
topped with 1 tbsp
Parmesan Cheese
1½ cups salad greens with ⅓ cup garbanzo beans and 2 tbsp reduced-fat dressing
Calories 400 | SP 9

1600 Calories:
Pasta Primavera (p. 227)
topped with 1½ tbsp
Parmesan Cheese
1½ cups salad greens with ½ cup garbanzo beans and 2 tbsp reduced-fat dressing
1 whole wheat roll with 1 tsp margarine

Snack

1200 Calories:
5-oz. cup Light Greek Yogurt

1600 Calories:
5-oz. cup Light Greek Yogurt
2 tbsp sliced almonds

1200 Calories:
Calories: 1195
Smart Point Comparison: 30
Carbohydrate: 140 g | Fiber: 25 g
Protein: 82 g | Fat: 37 g

1600 Calories:
Calories: 1580
Smart Point Comparison: 37
Carbohydrate: 179 g | Fiber: 29 g
Protein: 99 g | Fat: 51 g

**Tuesday
Day 9**

	1200 Calories	1600 Calories
Breakfast	**Quick Overnight Oatmeal (p.100)** (made with steel cut or old fashioned oats) 2 tbsp low-fat milk ½ cup blueberries Calories 200	SP 5	**Quick Overnight Oatmeal (p.100)** (made with steel cut or old fashioned oats) 1 cup low-fat milk ½ cup blueberries Calories 280	SP 7
Snack	1 hardboiled or soft cooked egg	1 hardboiled or soft cooked egg
Lunch	**Chicken Salad Sandwich (p. 205)** ¾ cup fresh cooked or canned green beans Calories 315	SP 6	**Chicken Salad Sandwich (p. 205)** ¾ cup fresh cooked or canned green beans Calories 315	SP 6
Snack	1 cup Chocolate Milk (1 cup low-fat milk with 1 tablespoon lite chocolate syrup)	1 cup Chocolate Milk (1 cup low-fat milk with 1 tablespoon lite chocolate syrup)
Dinner	**Baja Fish Tacos (p.222) ⅓ cup Simple Southwest Black Beans (p. 288)** 1 cup chopped lettuce and tomatoes avocado slices (⅛ of an avocado) Calories 410	SP 10	**Baja Fish Tacos (p.222) ⅔ cup Simple Southwest Black Beans (p. 288)** 1 cup chopped lettuce and tomatoes avocado slices (¼ of an avocado) Calories 500	SP 13
Snack	Medium orange	Medium orange ¼ cup mixed nuts
	Calories: 1210 Smart Point Comparison: 27 Carbohydrate: 142 g	Fiber: 28 g Protein: 84 g	Fat: 32 g	Calories: 1585 Smart Point Comparison: 37 Carbohydrate: 184 g	Fiber: 33 g Protein: 102 g	Fat: 47 g

Wednesday Day 10

	1200 Calories	1600 Calories
Breakfast	**Ham and Egg Panini (p.104)** 1 cup light orange juice Calories 300 I SP 8	**Ham and Egg Panini (p.104)** 1 cup light orange juice Calories 300 I SP 8
Snack	½ cup applesauce sprinkled with cinnamon	¾ cup applesauce sprinkled with cinnamon or 1 medium apple
Lunch	**Very Veggie Wrap (p. 210)** Iced tea with lemon Calories 270 I SP 6	**Very Veggie Wrap (p. 210)** ¾ cup low-fat milk Calories 350 I SP 9
Snack	2 stalks of celery with 2 tsps peanut butter	2 stalks of celery with 2 tsps peanut butter 1 cup grapes (~15)
Dinner	**Marlene's Favorite Go-To Italian Chicken (p. 310)** **Parmesan Garlic Smashed Potatoes (p. 277)** Steamed broccolini topped with 1 tsp olive oil and 1 tsp Parmesan Calories 375 I SP 8	**Marlene's Favorite Go-To Italian Chicken (p. 310)** **Parmesan Garlic Smashed Potatoes (p. 277)** Steamed broccolini topped with 1 tsp olive oil and 1 tsp Parmesan 1 wheat roll with 1 tsp margarine Calories I SP
Snack	**Creamy old-Fashioned Vanilla Pudding (p.411)**	**Creamy old-Fashioned Vanilla Pudding (p.411)** Topped with 2 tbsp sliced almonds
	Calories: 1180 Smart Point Comparison: 28 Carbohydrate: 133 g I Fiber: 24 g Protein: 83 g I Fat: 35 g	Calories: 1560 Smart Point Comparison: 35 Carbohydrate: 180 g I Fiber: 28 g Protein: 95 g I Fat: 50 g

Thursday Day 11

	1200 Calories	1600 Calories
Breakfast	**1 Breakfast Oatmeal Square (p.84)** ½ cup plain Greek yogurt with 1 tbsp reduced-sugar jam ½ cup fresh or frozen thawed sliced strawberries Calories 200 l SP 6	**2 Breakfast Oatmeal Squares (p.84)** ½ cup plain Greek yogurt with 1 tbsp reduced-sugar jam ½ cup fresh or frozen thawed sliced strawberries Calories 280 l SP 9
Snack	Medium orange	Medium orange 7 walnut halves
Lunch	**Fajita Beef Salad (p. 198)** 1 reduced-carb high-fiber tortilla Avocado slices (¼ avocado) Calories 350 l SP 9	**Fajita Beef Salad (p. 198)** 1 reduced-carb high-fiber tortilla Avocado slices (¼ avocado) 3 tbsp reduced fat Mexican cheese Calories 420 l SP 10
Snack	¾ cup reduced-fat milk with 2 tsps lite chocolate syrup	¾ cup reduced fat milk with 2 tsp lite chocolate syrup
Dinner	**Orange Chicken Stir-Fry (p. 306)** ⅔ cup cooked instant brown rice Calories 345 l SP 9	**Orange Chicken Stir-Fry (p. 306)** ⅔ cup cooked instant brown rice Calories 355 l SP 9
Snack	¾ cup fresh or canned drained pineapple chunks	½ cup fresh or canned drained pineapple chunks ½ cup no-sugar added vanilla ice cream
	Calories: 1160 Smart Point Comparison: 27 Carbohydrate: 140 g l Fiber: 24 g Protein: 80 g l Fat: 31 g	Calories: 1560 Smart Point Comparison: 38 Carbohydrate: 172 g l Fiber: 31 g Protein: 96 g l Fat: 52 g

Friday
Day 12

	1200 Calories	1600 Calories
Breakfast	**1 Turkey Breakfast Sausage (p. 280)** 1 large egg (scrambled or over easy) 1 Light Multigrain English Muffin 1 tsp margarine or butter Calories 280	SP 8	**1 Turkey Breakfast Sausage (p. 280)** 2 large eggs (scrambled or over easy) 1 Light Multigrain English Muffin 1 tsp margarine or butter Calories 350	SP 10
Snack	1 cup fresh raspberries	1 cup fresh raspberries
Lunch	**Rotisserie Chicken Noodle Soup (p. 250)** 1½ cups salad greens with 2 tbsp low-fat dressing Calories 250	SP 5	**Rotisserie Chicken Noodle Soup (p. 250)** 1½ cups salad greens with 2 tbsp low-fat dressing 8 wheat thin crackers (or 5 wheat saltines) Calories 315	SP 7
Snack	8 wheat thin crackers (or 5 wheat saltines)	1 medium banana with 2 tsps peanut butter
Dinner	**Crispy Parmesan Fish (p. 343)** ½ of 10-oz. baked potato with 1 tbsp light sour cream 1 cup cooked wilted spinach with 1 tsp olive oil Calories 375	SP 8	**Crispy Parmesan Fish (p. 343)** ½ of 10-oz. baked potato with 1 tbsp light sour cream 1 cup cooked wilted spinach with 1 tsp olive oil 1 slice bread toasted with 1 tsp each margarine and Parmesan Calories 510	SP 12
Snack	**1 Oatmeal Square (p. 84)** ½ cup low-fat milk Calories: 1190 Smart Point Comparison: 28 Carbohydrate: 131 g	Fiber: 24 g Protein: 92 g	Fat: 31 g	**1 Oatmeal Square (p. 84)** 1 cup low-fat milk Calories: 1590 Smart Point Comparison: 37 Carbohydrate: 178 g	Fiber: 30 g Protein: 108 g	Fat: 49 g

Saturday Day 13

	1200 Calories	1600 Calories
Breakfast	**Wholesome Blueberry Pancakes (p. 119)** topped with ¼ cup blueberries and 2 tablespoons sugar-free maple pancake syrup Calories 210	SP 6	**Wholesome Blueberry Pancakes (p. 119)** topped with ¼ cup blueberries and 2 tbsp sugar-free maple pancake syrup 1 cup low-fat milk Calories 320	SP 10
Snack	12 almonds (½-oz.)	12 almonds (½-oz.) 1 5-ounce cup light Greek yogurt (or ½ cup)
Lunch	**Way Better for You Tuna Melt (p. 213)** 1½ cups celery sticks and cherry tomatoes Calories 360	SP 7	**Way Better for You Tuna Melt (p. 213)** 1½ cups celery sticks and cherry tomatoes, 1 cup light orange juice Calories	SP 8
Snack	½ cup sliced carrots and ½ cup sugar snap peas with 2 tbsp low-fat ranch dressing	½ cup sliced carrots and ½ cup sugar snap peas with ¼ cup guacamole
Dinner	**Smothered Steak Burgers with Mushroom Gravy (p. 332)** ½ cup cooked noodles ¾ cup cooked green beans with 1 tsp margarine or butter Calories 405	SP 9	**Smothered Steak Burgers with Mushroom Gravy (p. 332)** ½ cup cooked noodles ¾ cup cooked green beans with 1 tsp margarine or butter Calories 405	SP 9
Snack	1 serving fruit (page 362)	1 serving fruit (page 362) 1 stick light string cheese
	Calories: 1195 Smart Point Comparison: 26 Carbohydrate: 142 g	Fiber: 21 g Protein: 77 g	Fat: 35 g	Calories: 1585 Smart Point Comparison: 37 Carbohydrate: 178 g	Fiber: 24 g Protein: 105 g	Fat: 48 g

Sunday
Day 14

	1200 Calories	1600 Calories
Breakfast	**1 Turkey Breakfast Sausage patty (p. 107)** Egg scramble - 1 large egg and 1 egg white cooked with ½ cup sautéed non-starchy vegetables 1 slice light wheat toast with 1 tsp margarine or butter Calories 265	SP 7	**1 Turkey Breakfast Sausage patty (p. 107)** Egg scramble - 1 large egg and 1 egg white cooked with cooking spray and ½ cup sautéed non-starchy vegetables 2 slices light wheat toast with 2 tsp margarine or butter Calories 340	SP 9
Snack	½ large grapefruit with 1 teaspoon sweetener	
Lunch	**Turkey Joe (p. 220)** 1 ½ cups spinach salad with 2 tbsp low-fat dressing Calories 270	SP 7	**Turkey Joe (p. 220)** 1 ½ cups spinach salad with 2 tbsp low-fat dressing 1 cup low-fat milk Calories 380	SP 11
Snack	1 medium apple	1 medium apple 1 slice reduced-fat cheese
Dinner	**No Bones Chicken Cacciatore (p. 300)** ½ cup prepared pasta ¾ cup sautéed zucchini with 1 tsp olive oil Calories 385	SP 7	**No Bones Chicken Cacciatore (p. 300)** ¾ cup prepared pasta ¾ cup sautéed zucchini with 1 tsp olive oil Calories 430	SP 8
Snack	1 piece Unbelievable Chocolate Cake with 2 tbsp light whipped topping	1 piece Unbelievable Chocolate Cake topped with ½ cup sliced strawberries and 2 tbsp light whipped topping
	Calories: 1210 Smart Point Comparison 28 Carbohydrate: 135 g	Fiber: 25 g Protein: 85 g	Fat: 39 g	Calories: 1610 Smart Point Comparison 36 Carbohydrate: 177 g	Fiber: 30 g Protein: 104 g	Fat: 54 g

Acknowledgments

Each time I embark on writing a new cookbook I am hopeful that it will get easier, quicker, or somehow less work than the last. But with each new book a familiar routine unfolds: long days in the kitchen, countless recipe revisions (and far too much tasting), and even longer nights on the computer. But fueled by my family and readers (who have been gracious enough to share their stories of how my recipes help them and their families live healthier, more delicious lives), I continue to be encouraged and inspired. Of course, this tremendous support cannot go unacknowledged, so first and foremost, I thank my two boys, Stephen and James, for their love, support, patience, and never-ending appetites. (There is no tougher critic for healthy recipes than a fast-food loving teenager!) For her inspiration, I thank my stepdaughter, Colleen, who reminds me every day that everyoneshould be able to guiltlessly enjoy the foods they love. And, of course, loving thanks go to my husband Chuck, who lived among the chaos (and the endless loads of dishes) with unwavering love and support. Over the course of the project I was fortunateto have many dedicated assistants. Thank you, Katie Boswell, for kicking off the project with me. Your enthusiasm really helped to get the ballrolling. An enormous thank you goes to SophiaOrtiz, who not only became part of the project,but part of our family. I am sure you came todread the words "just once more," but you nevershowed it. My sincere appreciation also goes to Megan Gillespie, and especially to Miss Molly Zapp. Your dependability, calm demeanor, andediting prowess were invaluable. For years of supportive collaboration, conversations, editing, support, and friendship, I thank PJ Dempsey. I can't imagine a better lifeline. At Running Press I thank Jennifer Kasius, my editor, for taking the time and energy required to share my vision, and Amanda Richmond for her beautiful art direction and dedicated work on the book. For the photographs kudos once again to my team of Steve Legato and Carole Haffey, who, with kind support and effortless skill, manage to make every dish look as mouthwatering on the page as they do on the table. Last, but never least, I am indebted to my family and friends. Without your encouragement and assistance, such a project would not be possible.

Index

Boldfaced page numbers indicate a photograph.

Notes

Notes

Notes

Also Available from Marlene's
EAT *what you* LOVE
COOKBOOK SERIES!

More from Marlene....

Visit Marlene online at www.marlenekoch.com today for:

Marlene's Free Monthly Newsletter Featuring
Sensational Recipes and Fun Giveaways.
Featured Seasonal Recipes
Personalized nutrition tools to help you feel your best!

Connect with Marlene:

Facebook: www.facebook.com/kochmarlene
(Join the fun and like, share and comment or ask....)
Twitter: @marlenekoch
Questions? Comments? Connect or click on:
"Ask Marlene" at www.marlenekoch.com where
Good Health is always delivered with Great Taste!